Developmental Psychology for Family Law Professionals

Theory, Application, and the Best Interests of the Child

Benjamin D. Garber, PhD, is a New Hampshire-licensed psychologist, state-certified guardian ad litem, practicing parenting coordinator, and expert consultant to courts across the country. He is a nationally acclaimed speaker, an award-winning popular press writer, and the author of numerous peer-reviewed professional publications in child development, mental health practice, and the law. He is also is the author of *Keeping Kids Out of the Middle: Child-Centered Parenting in the Midst of Conflict, Separation, and Divorce* (2008).

Across all of these professional roles and in writing this book, Dr. Garber pursues the singular goal of helping families, communities, schools, and the courts to better understand and respond to the developmental and systemic needs of children. Learn more at www.healthyparent.com.

Developmental Psychology for Family Law Professionals

Theory, Application, and the Best Interests of the Child

BENJAMIN D. GARBER, PhD

SPRINGER PUBLISHING COMPANY

New York

Springer Publishing Company, LLC
11 West 42nd Street
New York, NY 10036
www.springerpub.com

Acquisitions Editor: Jennifer Perillo
Production Editor: Pamela Lankas
Cover Design: Steve Pisano
Composition: International Graphic Ser

Ebook ISBN: 978-0-8261-0526-4

10 11 12 13 / 5 4 3 2 1

The author and the publisher of this ' to be reliable to provide information generally accepted at the time of public ing, our knowledge base continues to expand. Therefore, as new information becomes available, changes in procedures become necessary. We recommend that the reader always consult current research and specific institutional policies before performing any clinical procedure. The author and publisher shall not be liable for any special, consequential, or exemplary damages resulting, in whole or in part, from the readers' use of, or reliance on, the information contained in this book. The publisher has no responsibility for the persistence or accuracy of URLs for external or third-party Internet Web sites referred to in this publication and does not guarantee that any content on such Web sites is, or will remain, accurate or appropriate.

Readers are advised that no published work or generic source should ever be mistaken as sufficient for understanding, diagnosing, or adjudicating a specific matter. This book only offers general guidelines with which to understand certain areas of child and family development and the means with which to apply these principles to certain family law matters. Proper understanding of a specific individual's needs calls for the careful administration of direct, reliable, and valid assessment tools.

Library of Congress Cataloging-in-Publication Data

Garber, Benjamin D. (Benjamin David), 1959-
    Developmental psychology for family law professionals : theory, application, and the best interests of the child / Benjamin D. Garber.
      p. cm.
    Includes bibliographical references and index.
    ISBN 978-0-8261-0525-7 (alk. paper)
    1. Developmental psychology. 2. Families—Psychological aspects. 3. Parent and child. 4. Domestic relations. I. Title.
  BF713.G365 2009
  155.02'4346015—dc22   2009030047

Printed in the United States of America by The Hamilton Printing Company.

This volume is dedicated to you, the family court professional, who wades patiently and skillfully through the raging tides of caregiver conflicts, who faces the damage done by ignorant and ill and substance-abusing parents, who endures the bottomless pit of paperwork and delay and who risks sanity, no less than life and limb, confident that our children's health and happiness are worth all of this and more. May the blessing of even one child's smile carry you through many rough seas.

This book is dedicated, as well, to my three muses, Zoe, Mollie, and Laura, not only for their insight, perspective, and feedback, but for sharing in the profound and incomparable adventure of growing up together.

Contents

Preface   *ix*

Acknowledgment   *xv*

PART I: ONE SIZE CAN NEVER FIT ALL   **1**

1   Why a Perspective on Child and Family Development?   5

2   Caveat Lector: On the Limitations and Relevance of   19
        Developmental Theory, Statistics, and Methods

PART II: DEVELOPMENTAL THEORY IN OVERVIEW   **41**

3   Cognitive Development   43

4   Language Development   55

5   Social and Emotional Development   69

6   The Child's Defense Mechanisms: Regression, Stress, and   95
        Impediments to Developmental Capacity

7   Developmental Asynchrony and Décalage   105

PART III: IN THE BEST DEVELOPMENTAL INTERESTS OF THE CHILD:
TOPICS IN SEPARATION, VISITATION, AND REUNIFICATION   **141**

8   A Child's Understanding of Time, Separation, and Loss   143

9   Custodial Schedules and Infant Overnights   153

10 On Visitation Resistance and Refusal   165

11 Growing Up Apart: Child–Parent Separation   179

12   Development and Parent–Child Reunification   201

13   Development and the Termination of Parental Rights   215

**PART IV: ADVANCED APPLICATIONS OF DEVELOPMENTAL
THEORY TO FAMILY LAW PRACTICE**   **227**

14   What Is a "Mature Minor"?   229

15   Psychological Assessment and Diagnosis in Family Law   247

16   Alienation, Estrangement, and Alignment: The Tools and   263
Weapons of Affiliation

17   Development in the Mirror: On Becoming (and Remaining)   279
a Family Law Professional

APPENDICES
Appendix I: Learn More Now: Agencies, Organizations, and Experts   295

Appendix II: Preserving Families, Serving Children's Needs, and   309
Building Our Shared Future: A Proposal for a National Program of
Continuing Parent Education

Appendix III: Select Resources for Involuntary Separation: 311
Incarcerated, Enlisted, or Hospitalized Parents

Appendix IV: Mentoring Youth: Anchoring Kids Cast Adrift   319

Appendix V: On Compassion Fatigue, Burnout, and   321
Vicarious Traumatization

References   **325**

Index   **381**

Preface

Developmental Psychology for Family Law Professionals: Theory, Application, and the Best Interests of the Child is a practical application of developmental theory to the practice of family law. It intends to help you to ask questions that are developmentally informed and to better understand the breadth of experience, reams of reports and depth of emotion that must be digested in the course of seeking to understand each child's unique needs. It will provide you with new tools with which you might better understand the developmental needs, synchronies, and trajectories of children and—perhaps most critically—it will urge you to see each child in terms of fit and growth. Ultimately, this book seeks to guide you to recommend outcomes that anticipate changing developmental needs.

Succeeding in these combined goals is intended first and foremost to improve family court outcomes in the best interests of each child, but may simultaneously improve the validity of your work and thereby solidify your footing in deposition, as well as under direct and cross-examination. To the extent that *Developmental Psychology for Family Law Professionals: Theory, Application, and the Best Interests of the Child* makes your work more scientifically based and your conclusions more reliable and valid, you may be in better standing the next time an injured and acrimonious parent brings you before a licensing board, a malpractice hearing, or an appeals court (see chapter 17).

Succeeding in these goals may further benefit the courts and the communities they serve by decreasing recidivist traffic. Developmentally informed family court outcomes seek not only to fit children's present needs, but to implement outcomes that anticipate and account for continuing growth. This may mean that revolving door litigants have fewer reasons to return to court, can invest critical resources in their children rather than their attorneys, and our courts' tremendous backlog and burden might thereby diminish.

But *Developmental Psychology for Family Law Professionals: Theory, Application, and the Best Interests of the Child* must not be misunderstood to be a recipe book that can ever replace your own insights, intuitions, compassion, and skill. In the best of circumstances, this book will serve as reliable metric but, like the shoemaker's tape measure, it remains up to you when and where and how to apply it.

A WORD ABOUT WORDS

I've taken certain liberties in writing this book in the interests of making an already complex subject a bit more readable and succinct, even if perhaps a bit less politically correct. Here I would like to point out certain choices in word usage, particularly as regards references to age and developmental stage, gender (and family roles, both in case examples and in distinctions between developmental research and theory.

Age and Stage References

Some aspects of development are continuous over time (e.g., height). Others are marked by qualitative shifts that are commonly referred to as stages, as in "the terrible twos." Many developmental theorists discussed in the pages to follow speak in terms of successive stages like so many steps in a flight of stairs.

In the case of discontinuous growth, it is useful to refer to the onset of a stage in terms of an associated landmark skill or capacity. Thus, the stage of physical growth known as puberty is commonly marked by specific physical "landmarks" (as measured by Tanner Stages, e.g., Sun et al., 2005). The same is true of stages of cognitive, social, and emotional development, even if the landmark features are not as readily apparent.

When stages of development are commonly associated with specific chronological ages, those ages are stated. However, all such ages must be understood to be approximations only: "Individuals differ considerably in the timing of the development of psychosocial maturity, making it difficult to define a chronological boundary between immaturity and maturity" (Cauffman & Steinberg, 2000a, p. 758). Research demonstrates time and again that the specific age at which a specific developmental milestone appears can vary dramatically by individual, culture, language, opportunity, diet, and a host of other environmental variables. Thus, "[even] for Piaget, the key element was the sequence, not the age of cognitive transformations" (Lourenco & Machado, 1996, p.147). The most valid and meaningful aspect of any such discussion will always be the sequence of steps.

Even as approximations, references to specific developmental milestones must further be understood to assume a full-term gestation of 40 weeks in utero. For example, a reference to the typical child beginning to walk unassisted at twelve months in fact refers to twenty-one months postconception. This is important in the case of the child born two months prematurely whose first birthday actually occurs at nineteen months post-conception and who, therefore, might look quite different from his peers on their first birthdays.

Gender References

In telling the story of development and its application to family law practice, references are made to boys and girls and caregivers of both genders for ease of expression without implying anything specific to either gender. For example, a child's ability to tolerate separation from a primary caregiver might begin with the phrase, "Her capacity to maintain a secure internal image of the missing parent..." rather than writing out the awkward "his/her" and "s/he." However, there are a number of sex-specific developmental differences. In these instances, the distinction will be made explicitly, as in the statement, "Boys' early gross motor development typically precedes that of female age mates."

Family Role References

Again, for ease of reference, the hypothetical families who populate this book are framed in the terms of a conventional, heterosexual, married, "Leave it to Beaver" family structure. Thus, children are discussed in relationship to one mother and one father, paternal relatives and maternal relatives. In fact, the research literature upon which this book is based is more or less explicitly limited to exactly this population. Nevertheless, this book intends no such bias. To the fullest extent possible, the family law matters discussed here are intended to apply to children and their caregivers regardless of race, religion, culture, gender, age, generation, sexual orientation, and/or the legal status of the adult relationship or of the caregiver–child relationship.

This means that, unless specifically noted to the contrary, a discussion of a child's attachment to his mother can reasonably be generalized to apply to the quality of the relationship between a little girl and her foster or adoptive father. By the same token, a discussion about the quality of communication between coparents will most commonly refer to a heterosexual married—or previously married—couple, but is reasonably generalized to apply to any pair of adults who share the primary responsibility for a child. These generalizations are expected and encouraged, with the caveat that they probably go beyond the research data that informs them.

I also note that I write at a time of transition in family law. Where terms like "custody" and "visitation" were ubiquitous 10 years ago, they are slowly being replaced by more awkward but politically correct terms such as "parenting rights and responsibilities" and "parenting time," respectively. In the interests of readability and space, I intermix these terms as I see fit, never intending to connote ownership as might be inferred from the word "custody" or irrelevance and disinterest as might be associated with "visitation."

Specifically, in the text that follows, the "custodial parent" and the "residential parent" are interchangeable references to the adult who is vested by court order (or by happenstance) with day-to-day decision-making responsibility for a child. The "parent on duty" (or POD) is the adult who has the immediate responsibility for the child's care. Finally, in the context of transition between two caregivers, as commonly occurs between separated and divorced parents or between a foster and a birth parent, the "sending parent" is the adult who is giving up POD responsibility and the "receiving parent" is the adult who is accepting POD status.

Case Examples

When it seems useful, I have taken the liberty of illustrating the application of developmental principles with hypothetical and fictitious case examples, derived from my experience and that of collaborating colleagues. In every instance, relevant details have been changed to protect confidentiality and privilege, except when case law is cited. Even in these latter, precedent-setting instances, we must agree that the real children's lives, must never be unduly exploited or publicized.

REFERENCES, CITATIONS, AND RESOURCES IN THIS BOOK

Developmental Psychology for Family Law Professionals: Theory, Application, and the Best Interests of the Child provides you, the front-line family law professional, with the relevant and up-to-date data with which to make developmentally informed, systemically oriented, and therapeutic recommendations in the best interests of the child. However, it is impossible for any single text, or compendium of texts, to discuss all that is known about child development, let alone apply this data to a field as diverse and provocative as family law. In this regard, *Developmental Psychology for Family Law Professionals* must not stand on its own. This book simply cannot adequately do the job that it intends between two covers.

Professional ethics, relevant procedural guidelines and particular court preferences commonly mandate that our work be grounded in relevant, peer-reviewed, empirical research (e.g., Gould & Martindale, 2008). In service of this goal, *Developmental Psychology for Family Law Professionals* is peppered with a tremendous number and great breadth of links to further information. Citations to up-to-date literature are provided wherever possible. Separate bibliographies of relevant resources are devoted to several topics deserving of attention far greater than what I can provide. Direction to relevant associations, agencies, and Web sites appear throughout the text and are summarized in Appendix I. Copious footnotes elaborate and provide alternate interpretations and competing ideas. At the potential risk of interrupting the flow of the text, these links intend to empower you to go far beyond this text, to learn more about the particular issues that arise in a particular case, and thereby to better understand and fulfill the needs of each unique child.

Children are not well served if social policy is based on lawyers' opinions and judges' instincts or the views of advocacy groups, rather thanon the sound foundation of knowledge actually available.

—*Leslie Shear et al., Amici curiae* brief, In re Marriage of LaMusga

[B]y what manifesto was the family law bench imbued with greater wisdom and knowledge about the children than that possessed by the consenting parents themselves?

—*Tom Altobelli, Federal Magistrate, Sydney, Australia*

Acknowledgments

I am indebted beyond words to Zoe, Mollie, and Laura for the emotional support, encouragement, and patience that allows me not only to work as a family law professional myself, but to carve out the time to write about the experience. If there is any gratitude due for the lessons this book seeks to impart, it is due to these three amazing women.

To Janice Pieroni of Story Arts Management (Boston, Massachusetts): My undying gratitude for insight, skill, resourcefulness, support, and the often necessary kick-in-the-pants, above and beyond the call of duty.

Any errors contained within this book are entirely my own. However, any benefits that might accrue from this book are entirely to the credit of the generous souls who have shared their hopes and dreams, pain and joy in the best interests of their children.

> Eeyore was saying to himself,
> "This writing business.
> Pencils and what-not.
> Over-rated, if you ask me.
> Silly stuff. Nothing in it."
> —*Winnie the Pooh*

One Size Can Never Fit All

Mothers of more than one child will tell you that no two children can be brought up alike. Everybody knows that this is true. Yet when our children reach school age, for the sake of convenience we assume that their mental natures can be brought up exactly alike, and we turn them over to school with a cheerful carelessness that, when one stops to consider, is just a little difficult to explain.

—Alice Grant

A presumption which applies a "one size fits all" approach does a disservice to the legitimate needs of children to be heard and to experience high quality post-separation parenting.

—Family Law Council of Australia

It is a failing of our professional training and our family courts alike that the tremendous breadth and depth of developmental research has no necessary and organized place in child-centered forensic decisions. The pages that follow seek to repair this schism by addressing a succession of familiar child-centered legal questions from a developmental perspective.

But perhaps the gap between research and courtroom, like the mythical river Styx, is a necessary and intentional boundary. Perhaps this schism is planned and functional, keeping empiricists and jurists, theorists and attorneys on opposite shores. If so, then what I have construed here as a systemic weakness may, in fact, be a useful division which, were it bridged, would somehow contaminate or undermine the work of those on one or both sides of the divide.

It is true that our legal system depends heavily on judicial discretion and case law precedent (Bradbrook, 1971; Emery, 1999). But is it, therefore, also true that the introduction of an empirically based structure with which to guide legal outcomes risks compromising judges' authority and litigants' due process rights? To this I respond respectfully that the best interests of the child must trump all else. To operate our family courts intentionally ignorant of relevant and reliable data is to fail not only to meet a "best interests" threshold, but to fail to serve our future, as well. Thus, I recommend the incorporation of empirically sound research into child-centered forensic outcomes. In taking this stand, I am by no means alone. Glendon (1986, p. 59), for example, voices a similar position quite clearly: "[I]n divorce law, the traditional stronghold of judicial discretion, the judge's discretionary power should be brought within a framework of clear, ordered and consistent principles."

By grounding family law processes in developmental theory and research, one may ask, aren't we taking the first, fatal first step down the slippery slope toward automating judicial outcomes? Doesn't this discussion ultimately ignore the individual child, curtail judicial discretion, and necessarily lead to heuristic-driven, generic decisions akin to custody under the laws of chattel?

No. Having learned to value the child as an individual—not as property—we can never, in good conscience, turn back. For better or worse, our jobs are secure. The need is simply too great, the permutations on each motion too many and the research far from complete. The applications of developmental theory and research that follow will provide you, the family law professional, with firmer ground to stand upon as you seek to understand and respond to each child's unique needs, but must not be misconstrued as prescribing generic answers by age.

Among the the issues addressed in Part I:

- Why not all developmental research is created equal
- The importance of context: How does developmental research apply to the child sitting in front of you?
- Does developmental research meet *Daubert* standards?

The chapters that follow can only inform forensic investigation and judicial discretion, never supplant them. The simple breath-taking reality underlying all of our work is that each child is an individual unlike all others, growing up in a unique constellation of relationships and resources, opportunities and crises, strengths and weaknesses—that, in fact, one size will never fit all.

Why a Perspective on Child and Family Development?

[L]aw guardians and guardians ad litem ought to be well trained in family law and have some meaningful education in child development, rather than a course consisting of a lecture of a few hours with no measure of comprehension or capacity.

—*Patricia Ann Grant and Steven Klee*

Family law professionals and shoemakers have at least two things in common. First and foremost, both are concerned with "fit." The shoemaker measures the tangible dimensions of the foot with tools that are readily available. Tape measure. A black and silver mechanism known as a Brannock Device. With a steady hand, a little training, and a lot of experience, the shoemaker can reliably fit any individual's unique need for footwear.

Across guilds and training and jurisdictions, family law professionals share an interest in doing something quite similar. As family law attorneys, mediators, guardians ad litem, parenting coordinators, child protection workers and jurists, we are working to tailor family circumstances to fit a child's unique needs. We are tasked to cobble together parenting resources, caregiving environments, social supports, educational opportunities, and therapies to serve the child's best interests.

Unlike the shoemaker, we don't have a uniform set of reliable and meaningful tools with which to do our work. As a result, we individually gravitate toward whatever collection of instruments and processes and impressions our training and experience and the practical limits inherent in our work setting provide us. Unfortunately, these tools tend to be borrowed from other endeavors and can be all-too blunt. Few have an empirically established relationship to the questions we are seeking to answer or even the consensual validation of our peers.

Worse, we're seldom certain what to measure (Tippins & Wittman, 2005). Although the shoemaker can identify the dimensions from heel to toe, around the arch and across the width of the foot, we speak blithely about "needs" and "best interests," concepts that are at least as ill-defined as they are overused. True, some relevant defining criteria have been legislated,[1] even if they've never actually been empirically tested. But even these efforts to make our measurements more specific leave us to juggle a handful of competing ideas and opinions, uncertain what they mean and how they are weighted.

Shoemakers and family law professionals share a second common interest in growth. No one is ever surprised when a child's foot grows, yet we have never created a shoe that will adjust accordingly. Instead, the ritual of shoe-shopping is for some as frequent and expectable as the change of the seasons. Shoemakers, of course, thrive in this way. Their business depends in large part upon refitting children over and over again across time.

In the same way that the shoemaker might anticipate foot growth, we are generally able to anticipate the pace and trajectory of a child's social and emotional growth. We have the means to foresee the child's faltering movement toward autonomy, his or her burgeoning capacity for cognitive abstraction, and ever-expanding social investments. We know a great deal about the environments that are most likely to foster these healthy changes and those which are likely to impede them. But, like the shoemaker, we seldom craft outcomes that adequately anticipate this growth.

This failing is not an entrepreneurial strategy intended to keep our calendars busy and our bank accounts full. The tragic reality of our times is that if every family law professional could magically dispense with each case in a single day, our days would still be full. Nationally, the demand for services that span the spectrum of family law is endless. Divorce runs rampant. Custody matters can seem never-ending. The horror of child abuse and neglect and the litigation associated with foster care, termination of parental rights, and adoption is a business unto itself. Our courtrooms are bursting at the seams. Tragically, a 5-year-old caught up in family litigation will spend no less than 20% of her young life being dragged through the courts.[2]

In fact, the family court system's failure to craft developmentally informed decisions is the result of precisely the sort of conflict that it exists to resolve. As in so many troubled families, the academic "parent" and the judicial "parent" never really learned to communicate. Each ignores the other at a cost to both, but none so much as their "child," namely, the litigating family.

Those of us who see the harm done by a court system that decides matters of parenting rights and custodial responsibilities with no clear and consistent understanding of fit and growth, those of us who see the damage done to children whose caregivers are stuck in revolving-door litigation, and those of us who seek to better understand what is truly in each child's best interests must now discover developmental psychology and its application to family law matters.

This chapter collapses the first seven or eight lectures from a college-level developmental psychology course into a few pages. This is essential reading for those who have never taken the opportunity to consider why development is important, how change unfolds over time, and how the growing child must be understood as one part of a growing, changing, and—in the cases of immediate concern—conflicted family system. This is the foundation on which we can begin to ask the questions that inform this book and, most immediately, the conflict that can arise when a child's needs and those of his or her family are at odds.

THE PURPOSE OF DEVELOPMENTAL PSYCHOLOGY

If psychiatry is the offspring of Freud and the stepchild of today's drug companies, psychology might best be considered its half brother. Born of William James and Hermann Ebbinghaus, fostered by Pavlov and Binet, by Watson and Skinner, psychology's roots are far more deeply embedded in measurement and research than in clinics and hospitals. In fact, at least half of all doctoral level psychologists' full-time employment is not in a direct service environment.[3] Psychology's longest standing and most significant contribution rests in its accumulated empirical understanding of human growth, behavior, thinking, and feeling.

Put aside your preconceptions of Freudian analysts and their couches. The psychologist-*cum*-researcher is a scientist who defines a narrow question of interest, gathers a selection of people who are believed to fairly represent the larger population at issue, administers standardized measures, and then interprets the collected data in an effort to make generalizations that add incrementally to an accumulating understanding of the species.

Developmental psychology research asks questions about change over time and the contexts that foster or inhibit it; about the unfolding, up-and-down, back-and-forth progression of maturation from conception through adulthood that defines the growth of thinking, feeling, behavior and relationships. Such as:

- How do children learn language?
- Are there gender differences in the development of self-recognition among infants?
- Do the elderly lose cognitive abilities or perform more slowly?

The accumulated result of tens of thousands of such endeavors spanning the last century has created a vast (but far from complete) body of knowledge accounting for the direction, landmarks, and vicissitudes of human growth from conception onward. This book seeks to apply this invaluable data to the questions that come before family courts.

THE VALUE OF THE INDIVIDUAL

It is both a blessing and a burden that twenty-first century Western society values the individual apart from the group. The blessing is heard in countless stories celebrating individuals whose perseverance and commitment and skills allowed them to stand out among their peers. Think Rosa Parks, Helen Keller, Stephen Hawking, or Sandy Kofax. It is highlighted in countless moral dilemmas posed to thoughtful students of philosophy in which the value of an individual is weighed against that of a larger group.[4] We explicitly nurture the ethic that anyone can succeed and that everyone deserves a fair chance, no matter the situation. We mandate that "no child be left behind." We pass laws and enact legislation that level the playing field (e.g., the Individuals with Disabilities in Education Act) and that raise the needs of the individual above those of the group in some situations (e.g., Health Insurance Portability and Accountability Act), even while the needs of the group clearly trump those of the individual in others (e.g., the PATRIOT Act).

Of course, the burden associated with a legal system that values the individual is its cost. It will always be cheaper to fit people into stereotyped molds based on age or gender or height or IQ or skin color. In fact, Western culture abhors and frequently prohibits such generalizations under the banner of prejudice—racism, sexism, ethnocentrism, and ageism, for example—but we take this high road at a tremendous practical cost. Our commitment to the individual requires a constant and incalculable flow of finite resources—time, effort, and money—devoted to understanding and responding to the individual's needs, wishes, and abilities. This may be nowhere as obvious and expensive as it is in the family court system.

Family law matters have only come to emphasize the child's individual needs in the last 50 years. Prior to that time, broad rules-of-thumb determined children's welfare without the need for expensive and time-consuming investigations, assessments, legal counsel, depositions, experts, hearings, and trials. In the days of chattel (Mason, 1994), for example, a delinquent or runaway child was simply and exclusively considered his or her father's property very much like his ox and plow. More recently, the Tender Years Doctrine (Artis, 2004) made a child's postseparation or postdivorce placement no less a foregone conclusion, albeit in favor of the mother whose nurturance was legally determined to be both necessary and irreplaceable. Under these standards (and several other similarly black-and-white models), there was little or no need for court involvement or for the many and varied professionals who now fill them. By sacrificing individuality, child welfare questions were answered simply and immediately.

The court's involvement in family matters may be as old as the idea of *parens patriae*, the ancient ethic that allowed the government to trump parental decisions in the interest of child welfare.[5] In contemporary Western society, the court exercises its authority under the banner of the best interests of the child (BIC) standard. The BIC standard stands today as the single overarching ethic guiding child- and family-related mandates across legal, educational, political, and institutional arenas.[6] For all of its broad endorsement, however, the BIC standard lacks explicit definition and the means to reliably measure its parameters (Garber, 2009).

By analogy, if the American Medical Association (AMA) were to mandate that pediatricians are to serve the best interests of their child-patients without further definition, there would likely be as many different "best practices" as there are physicians. The same tummy ache would be ignored in one office, medicated in a second, and referred for surgery by a third. Recognizing the harm that would result from such chaos, the AMA and its allied licensing and oversight bodies has integrated a wealth of empirical pediatric data into a best practices model.[7]

Mental health professionals have begun to do the same. Psychiatry[8] and, to some lesser degree, psychology (Goodheart, Kazdin, & Sternberg, 2006), has begun to adopt standards of care intended to integrate a wealth of research data into clinical practice in the interest of improving individual outcomes.

As family law professionals, we can do no less (e.g., Gould & Martindale, 2008). To continue to work in an idiosyncratic and empirically uninformed manner risks harm to the children whose best interests we are committed to serve. Child-centered legal decisions that are developmentally untenable, ill suited to the family system, and "antitherapeutic" (Wexler, 1999) add harm due to a dysfunctional court system to the harm being done by a dysfunctional family system.

The phrase *child-centered* appears often throughout this book and motivates my practice across a wide variety of professional endeavors. The phrase intends to convey the idea that understanding and seeking to fulfill children's needs is a priority—in fact, is often the first and most important priority. Unfortunately, some have mistaken this phrase to mean a process that gives the child control. In fact, it is often the case that giving the child control or allowing the child's wishes to trump his or her needs is the opposite of child-centeredness. I firmly maintain that our goal as healthy adults is to help our children be healthy, not happy. A healthy child can make his or her own happiness.

THE VALUE OF THE COMMUNITY: DEVELOPMENT AND CHILD-SPECIFIC NORMS

As a child grows and accumulates experience, the definition of "age-appropriate" widens. Thus, normal and healthy behavior is quite easy to define at birth but increasingly difficult as the years go on. This variability is not only due, in part, to differences associated with the broad variables of culture, climate, language, and religion, but is at least equally attributable to the norms specific to a community, a school district, or a neighborhood.

With this in mind, the responsible family law professional couches a comprehensive understanding of a child's behavior, feelings, and needs not only in an understanding of abstract developmental norms such as those presented here, but in an understanding of how those norms vary in ways that are specific to each child's world.

Fortunately, this mandate is much easier to fulfill than it may sound. Observing a child at play among his or her friends or neighbors, on the playground, or in a classroom at school and eliciting impressions from teachers, coaches, religious school educators, clergypersons, and tutors will all help to inform this context. Collecting standardized and/or quantitative norm-based impressions can augment this process (e.g., Achenbach, 1979; Conners, Sitarenios, Parker, & Epstein, 1998; Kovacs, 1992[9]; March, 1997; Moos, 1993). Mental health professionals conducting custody evaluations are ethically bound to consider this breadth of perspective (e.g., Kirkland, McMillan, & Kirkland, 2005), but the practice has much broader applications when developmental issues are at stake.

"CHILDREN ARE SIMPLY SMALL ADULTS": IS THERE A HOMUNCULUS AMONG US?

Early literature, myth, and religion variously characterize the child as a full-grown adult in miniature, a concept sometimes identified as a *homunculus*. Perhaps because children's physical attributes appear to differ from those of adults only in size, it is easy to imagine that children's thinking and feelings and relationships duplicate comparable adult processes in miniature. To proceed in this manner, however, is to ignore decades of developmental science, to forget one's own experience of childhood and—most tragically—to do harm to the children whom we hope to serve.

If a metaphor is necessary, better to think of the successive stages of thinking and feeling and relating from infancy into adulthood as a stepwise series of caterpillar–butterfly transformations. Child development is a sequence of qualitative changes, each new stage as different from its predecessor as the Monarch is from its prechrysalis self, except that somehow the caterpillar remains underneath the surface. This means that as child-centered professionals we must take care not to fall into the trap of expecting that children can think adult thoughts, only slower, or cope with adult feelings, only more briefly.

It is because human development is a process of qualitative change that this book is necessary. It is only when we genuinely understand how thinking and feeling and relating differ at each successive stage along the path toward maturity that we can begin to craft genuinely child-centered and developmentally informed forensic remedies.

A DEVELOPMENTAL/SYSTEMIC APPROACH

By no means is this book the first publication to marry developmental theory and research to child-centered legal process (e.g., Cauffman & Steinberg, 2000a; Greenberg, Gould, Schnider, Gould-Saltman, & Martindale, 2003; Hartson & Payne, 2007; Hodges, 1991; Johnston & Roseby, 1997). Neither is this the first book to suggest that legal process, rules, and roles must be understood from a family systems perspective (Wexler, 1999), a credit that belongs to the emerging field of therapeutic jurisprudence (Babb, 1997; Hora & Schma, 1998; Winick, 1997; Winick & Wexler, 2003).[10] This movement propounds the idea that, "courts [must] take into consideration the whole family, broadly defined, in making decisions about a child. It also requires a court to respect the child's attachments to family members and other intimate relationships, attempt to maintain family ties wherever possible, and focus on family strengths rather than deficits" (Brooks & Roberts, 2002, p. 455).

This book is, however, the first to break down the artificial wall that otherwise separates the study of child development and the study of family systems so as to advise family law professionals about kids' needs. The distinction between these two fields of study is an artifact grown out of politics and personalities akin, for example, to the division that medicine makes between cardiology and pulmonology. Like the heart and the lungs, child development and family systems can each be studied as distinct fields, but always with the understanding that each is constantly influencing the other and that the two together are part of a much larger dynamic system.

In like manner, child development can only be understood as it occurs in the context of family, and family, in turn, must be understood as it accommodates the inexorable processes of its members' development. Understanding (not to mention writing about) this dynamic interaction is difficult because our thinking is better suited to linear explanations. It is far easier to understand simple *if > then* domino-like contingencies than complex, interactive affects. For this reason, the history of psychology (and perhaps the history of any field of thought) is riddled with oversimplified, linear solutions. Once upon a time, for example, psychology believed in the concept of the schizophrenogenic mother (Fromm-Reichman, 1948). Today, we find that we must give up the appealing simplicity of such explanations in favor of trying to understand the many interactive feedback loops within and between child and family. We must understand that "individuals co-create their own development and environment while being simultaneously affected by the environment and the interactions in which they participate" (Ambert, 2001, p. 13). Or perhaps more exactly, "parenting is directly influenced by forces emanating from within the individual parent (personality), within the individual child (child characteristics of individuality), and from the broader social context in which the parent–child relationship is embedded. Specifically, marital relations, social networks, and jobs influence individual personality and the general psychological well-being of parents and, thereby, parental functioning and, in turn, child development" (Belsky, 1984, p.84).

WHEN THE INTERESTS OF THE CHILD AND THE INTERESTS OF THE FAMILY ARE AT ODDS

I take as necessary foundation for all that follows the central proposition that the healthy family exists to serve the needs of the child(ren) regardless of its members' gender, genetics, generation, geography, longevity, legal status, or number. This idea, drawn from ethology and contemporary sociobiology and consistent with the court's expectation that, "natural bonds of affection lead parents to act in the best interests of their children,"[11] mandates that, by definition, the interests of the child cannot conflict with the interests of the healthy family.[12,13]

This is not to say that conflict cannot erupt within the healthy family system. In fact, such conflicts are the necessary and natural growing pains that facilitate the group's continuing identity. Thus, parents and children will argue, coparents will disagree, and siblings will bicker without creating meaningful fault lines within the group unless and until the unifying motive of serving the child's best interests is compromised.

By the same token, conflicts commonly erupt between the healthy family and other families, and between the healthy family and the community in which it exists. Like intrafamilial conflicts, these tensions need not compromise the family's integrity so long as a focus on the children's needs is maintained. The disputes that erupt between families, and those that emerge between one family and its encompassing towns or cities, the schools which they attend, the religious, athletic, and social institutions to which they belong, may be more the fodder of civil law than family law and more the bailiwick of sociology than of psychology, but they all serve the same purpose. They reinforce the healthy family's shared identity and its coherence around their children's needs.

The dysfunctional or unhealthy family, then, is a group that never established—or has lost or distorted—its child-centered purpose. When this occurs, it is likely to take one of four forms, presented here from the most common and least destructive to the least common and most destructive dynamics:

1. The caregivers share a primary interest in meeting the child(ren)'s needs but interpret and implement this goal differently.
2. The caregivers are divided by two or more children's competing needs.
3. One caregiver is genuinely committed to fulfilling the child(ren)'s needs but the other is not.
4. Neither caregiver is committed to meeting the child(ren)'s needs.

A spectrum of remedies may be available to respond to each of these unhealthy dynamics, from coparents' spontaneous negotiation and reference to media resources through self-selected educational and clinical interventions to mediation, arbitration, and court-mandated outcomes, including the (re)allocation of parenting authority (Garber, 2006). These, in turn, set the stage for discussion of the court's presumption in entering the family under the aegis of *parens patraie* [14] and the conditions under which the child's voice might be heard, as is allowed in some jurisdictions under the mature minor concept.

SUMMARY

Odd as it may sound, we must approach these life-altering family law matters thinking of the children whom we serve in the same way that shoemakers think about feet. Our work product must first and foremost consider fit and anticipate growth. It is only from this perspective that we can genuinely begin to understand the best interests of the child.

NOTES

1. Criteria seeking to define the "Best Interests of the Child Standard" (BICS) have been set forth in The British Children's Act (1989), The Uniform Marriage and Divorce Act (National Conference, 1970) and the Michigan Custody Guidelines (2001), for example.
2. The duration of the divorce process varies by jurisdiction, in part due to varied legal requirements and in part due to the courts' case backlogs. See http://www.divorcesource.com/
3. See http://research.apa.org/des99t3.pdf accessed 10/17/08.
4. For example: "A fat man leading a group of people out of a cave on a coast is stuck in the mouth of that cave. In a short time high tide will be upon them, and unless he is unstuck, they will all be drowned except the fat man, whose head is out of the cave. But, fortunately, or unfortunately, someone has with him a stick of dynamite. There seems no way to get the fat man loose without using that dynamite which will inevitably kill him, but if they do not use it everyone will drown. What should they do?" (Ross, 2008, adapted from *Moral Reasoning*, by Victor Grassian, Prentice Hall, 1981, 1992).
5. *Parens patriae* is the 16th-century British ruling that allows the Court to extend its authority into the family to protect a child, as when a parent is abusive or neglectful. It is the legal foundation, as further example, of

compulsory education for minors in the United States and thereby sets the stage for one of the chief discussions of the mature minor concept in *Wisconsin v. Yoder* (United States Supreme Court, 406 U.S. 205 [1972]).

6. The best-interests standard pervades our contemporary institutions, from the United Nations' 1959 Declaration for the Rights of Children (United Nations, 1959), to the Charter of Fundamental Rights of the European Union (European Union, 2005). It is explicitly referenced by organizations as diverse as theAmerican Academy of Pediatrics (Diekema, 2005), the American Academy of Pediatric Dentistry (2003), the American School Counselor Association (2004), the National Association of Social Workers (1996), the American Academy of Child and Adolescent Psychiatry (1999), and the American Psychological Association (APA; 2002) and is no less popular among legal professional groups, throughout local, state, and federal legislation and court rulings on all levels. By 2005, "every state…indicates that custody decisions are to be made according to [the] 'best-interests of the child' standard" (Emery, Otto, & O'Donohue, 2005, p. 5). In one recent review (Garber, 2007b), over 90 references to serving the "best interests of the child" (or a variant of the phrase) were identified in the Wisconsin statutes regarding, "Actions Affecting the Family" as in the direction that, "the Guardian ad litem shall be an advocate for the best-interests of the minor child."

7. In fact, the AMA has addressed the best interest standard as it applies to pediatrics quite explicitly: "Medical decision-making for pediatric patients should be based on the child's best interest, which is determined by weighing many factors, including effectiveness of appropriate medical therapies, the patient's psychological and emotional welfare, and the family situation. When there is legitimate inability to reach consensus about what is in the best interest of the child, the wishes of the parents should generally receive preference" (Levine, 2008).

8. The American Psychiatric Association discusses evidence-based practice standards for adults at http://www.psych.org/MainMenu/PsychiatricPractice/PracticeGuidelines_1.aspx. Comparable standards for the care of children are discussed by the American Academy of Child and Adolescent Psychiatry at http://www.aacap.org/cs/root/member_information/practice_information/practice_parameters/practice_parameters

9. A sample interpretation of Kovac's (1992) Child Depression Inventory–Teacher Report form is available from the author at http://www.psychassessments.com.au/products/22/prod22_report2.pdf

10. The reader is directed to the International Network on Therapeutic Jurisprudence and the associated Web site available at http://www.law.arizona.edu/depts/upr-intj/. The Web site includes a searchable database of relevant literature and resources.

11. The original reference to United States Supreme Court Chief Justice Warren Burger's majority opinion in *Parham v. J.R.* (442 U. S. 584, 602 [1979]) is given even greater meaning by the Court's opinion in *Hodgson v. Minnesota* (497 U.S. 417 [1989]): "The law's concept of the family rests on a presumption that parents possess what a child lacks in maturity, experience, and capacity for judgment required for making life's difficult decisions. More importantly, historically, it has recognized that natural bonds of affection lead parents to act in the best interests of their children.... As with so many other legal presumptions, experience and reality may rebut what the law accepts as a starting point; the incidence of child neglect and abuse cases attest to this. That some parents may at times be acting against the best interests of their children...creates a basis for caution, but is hardly a reason to discard wholesale those pages of human experience that teach that parents generally do act in the child's best interests."

12. Perhaps more concretely, this definition of the healthy family is drawn from the lessons learned from Sherif et al.'s (1961) "Robber's Cave" experiments (see chapter 16). Readers unfamiliar with this seminal work are advised to read at least a summary, as is available online at http://psychclassics.yorku.ca/Sherif/. In short, Sherif and colleagues demonstrate how shared goals within and competition between groups creates coherent groups, dynamics that are referred to later in the present book as alignment and alienation.

13. This definition restricts the use of the term "family" to adults with children without any connotation or value judgment about those constellations of individuals who choose not to have or are incapable of having children. Intimate adult partnerships regardless of sex, age, or legal endorsement create a mutual identity often referred to as "family" around some other shared motive(s)—one or both member's well-being, the maintenance of a home, dedication to a pet, a common occupational, political or religious commitment, for example.

14. See supra, note number 6.

2 Caveat Lector: On the Limitations and Relevance of Developmental Theory, Statistics, and Methods

Practical limitations have caused psychologists to study various paths or types of development as if they were distinct from one another. As a result, it is far too easy to focus on children's cognitive or linguistic, social or emotional development (to name just a few among many) to the exclusion of the others. This puts the student of ontogeny at risk of becoming like one of the fabled blind men who encounters an elephant for the first time: Grabbing hold of only one piece, he mistakes it for the whole. Indeed, in the same way that the blind men argue over the nature of the unfamiliar beast, developmentalists have argued over which narrow area of study is more important or has primacy (Lazarus, 1984; Zajonc, 1984).

In fact, none of the specialized threads of development differentiated by areas of training or licensure, publications, or professional association can exist or grow independent of the others. The individual must be understood to develop as a whole being—thinking and feeling and communicating and relating (and in terms of spirituality and creativity and...)—each climbing the scaffolding created by the others, each bootstrapping its way upward toward an imperfect patchwork of emerging maturity.

As if this weren't enough, I would argue that the individual's growth and development can be reasonably understood only within the framework of family relationships and that the family, in turn, must be understood within the context of the community, and so on, in a potentially infinite fractal progression.[1]

As a case in point, consider the prototypical 10-year-old boy who appears distracted and disruptive in class. At the level of the individual, the child might meet the diagnostic criteria for attention-deficit disorder and require medication. At the level of the family, we might discover that his home is in chaos because his parents are divorcing and, on this basis, recommend family therapy (Garber, 2001). At the level of the community, we might then realize that the child has been socialized in a media-intensive environment, which implicitly teaches that attention should be paid in brief bursts while one multitasks, and, on this basis, recommend changes to the classroom and the teaching method (Sax, 2007).

Recognizing these concentric circles of complexity, I must ask the reader to understand development as a larger fabric—a patchwork of interdependent skills—even as I proceed to discuss individual areas of development and their relevance to family law process. This chapter will examine some of the limitations of developmental theory and the research that has been done to support it.

THE LIMITATIONS OF DEVELOPMENTAL THEORY AS APPLIED TO FAMILY LAW

As important as it is to build a bridge between developmental psychology and child-centered forensic process, we must do so with tremendous caution. We must never allow research data or the scientific method to undermine due process, to replace a careful assessment of each child's strengths and weaknesses, or to supplant a thorough evaluation of the context within which that child must grow. We must take developmental theory as a starting place, never an ending place, always careful to see each child as a unique human being deserving of our best efforts, our greatest wisdom, and our full compassion.

This book provides a broad overview of child development. In doing so, I hope to provide you with a foundation on which you can conduct evaluations, guide negotiations, direct settlements and build child-centered remedies. But this book must not be mistaken as providing remedies. To determine that the child standing before you can or cannot think, feel, behave, or relate in a specific manner exclusively on the basis of developmental research is to misinterpret my purpose, to miscarry justice, and—most critically—to risk harming the child.

Not only must the ideas and the data presented in this book be taken as nothing more than a foil against which a specific child can be highlighted, the developmental theory itself must be understood to be dynamic in its own right. As novel data-gathering and statistical analysis processes are explored, as innovative methods and mechanisms are put to work, as larger and more diverse populations are understood, our knowledge changes.

Case in point: While Jean Piaget's ideas about the sequence and landmarks of cognitive development have withstood more than 50 years of empirical scrutiny (see chapter 3), the ages that he attributed to specific developments have gradually eroded over the years. New methodologies reveal that cognitive abilities once believed to be absent until later in childhood are present much earlier on.

ON RELIABILITY, VALIDITY, AND ADMISSIBILITY

Any discussion of scientific principles relevant to legal process is necessarily prefaced by a review of both the empirical stability and the admissibility of those principles. In short, no matter how promising or provocative a theory, it will be of little value unless and until it is found to be scientifically sound and can be heard before the court.

Psychology has held its researchers (and less so, its clinicians) to the highest standards of science, arguably, partly in response to the field's longstanding sibling rivalry with psychiatry and its Oedipal conflicts with medicine. Developmental research, in general, works within the rigors of the scientific method, demands that data be reported in terms of statistical probabilities, and generally publishes within the constraints of blind peer review consistent with the standards established by the National Institutes of Health (Breckler, 2007).[2]

The informed consumer of developmental research reasonably asks a number of questions of any given study before endorsing it or introducing the associated data, methodology, or theory to the court. These include an assessment of its generalizability, reliability, validity, and whether it meets the standard of evidence.

GENERALIZABILITY: LEAPING THE
CHASM FROM RESEARCH TO LITIGATION

Because it is routinely impractical (if not simply impossible) to study all members of a population, developmental researchers generally publish one of two types of studies. Single case studies summarize observations of a particular individual. These appeared more frequently early in the twentieth century and among psychoanalytic (that is, Freudian) publications. Single case studies persist today either to provide an in-depth report on a unique phenomenon or to illustrate an interesting new process, application, or finding (e.g., Dyer, 2004).

More commonly, developmental research collects data from among a number of individuals who are assumed to represent a larger population. The members of the resulting pool of participants, referred to as a "*sample*," are typically limited by the researcher's demographic constraints (e.g., age, socioeconomic status, race, gender, family composition) and practical matters that can be much harder to define. The graduate student who solicits dissertation subjects through a local newspaper ad, for example, may inadvertently end up studying children whose parents subscribe to the particular newspaper in which he or she advertised, children whose parents are literate, or children whose parents are not both employed full time and who are therefore available to participate during business hours. Understanding both the explicit and implicit limitations of a sample will bear on the generalizability of the study's conclusions.

Generalizability (more technically referred to as *external validity*) asks the question: To what extent are observations about the particular sample studied likely to be true of the entire population and, therefore, relevant to a particular child who was not involved in the study but who is a member of that population? For example, if 100 left-handed, red-headed 10-year-old males all prove to be dyslexic, we must ask whether this means that all such boys are dyslexic and, therefore, whether Henry, the left-handed, red-headed 10-year-old standing before the court should be assumed to be dyslexic. Can we make arguments (or hand down decisions) based in part on the observations and measurements of researchers who may have worked thousands of miles away and years before?

Yes, but we must do so with great caution.

In general, published findings will be relevant to the child standing in front of you to the extent that the child is representative of the sample studied. At one extreme, were a child who had been the subject of a single case research study to then become involved in litigation, the conclusions of that study would be entirely true of the child, limited only by the reliability and validity of the methods used in the study. As far-fetched as this may seem, in fact this is precisely analogous to what occurs when a child has completed an evaluation (e.g., psychological assessment) pursuant to litigation. In neither instance is there a question of generalizability. The data are specifically about the child him- or herself.

At the other extreme, litigators and their hired experts commonly seek to stretch published data in an effort to draw generalizations that may be relevant to a more-or-less demographically dissimilar child. This is a very familiar and necessary practice, if only because the likelihood that research has been published involving subjects who exactly represent a particular court-involved child is extremely low. It is, however, a practice that risks stretching generalizability to the breaking point.

The informed consumer of psychological research will determine the generalizability of a particular study's conclusions on the basis of the degree of similarity between the demographics of the sample and the situation of the particular child in question. As a rule of thumb, a study's relevance to a particular child's situation will increase to the degree that the study can be shown to be consistent with the child's age; gender; cultural, ethnic, and religious characteristics; physical and mental health status; and family structure.

Is the child's age consistent with the age(s) of the children in the study?

This may appear to be an obvious consideration that is easily determined, but the question is more complex than it appears. Particularly when the questions at issue concern infants and toddlers, age must be understood relative to conception, not birth. This is referred to as *gestational age.* Thus, the differences between two children who celebrate the same birthday may, in part, be attributable to the fact that one was born prematurely. As a result, in such cases, differences that might otherwise be attributable to environment or gender or other distinguishing variables must be considered in light of the fact that the two children are not, in fact, age-mates.

Gestational age differences have been associated with physical, social, and behavioral developmental differences (Clark, Woodward, Horwood, & Moor, 2008). Preterm infants can be at very high risk for a wide range of health complications (American Academy of Pediatrics, 2000) and learning difficulties (van Baar, Ultee, Gunning, Soepatmi, & de Leeuw, 2006).

Are the conclusions relevant to children of the same gender?

Or, in the alternative, does the study conclude that the child's gender is irrelevant? Although a large portion of the literature in child development glosses over differences associated with gender or demonstrates that such differences are not statistically relevant, we must nevertheless take care not to generalize across gender without caution. For some variables, gender differences are associated with the relative age at which a milestone appears, as is the case with specifics of motor development (Junaid & Fellowes, 2006), social reasoning (Horn, 2003), and achievement (Mello, 2008). On the other hand, a child's gender can be strongly related to the form that the developmental milestone takes, as is obviously the case with puberty.

Is the child's cultural, ethnic, and religious environment comparable to that of the children in the study?

The meaning and acceptability of children's behaviors as well as the timing of many developmental occurrences have been shown to be culture-dependent (Shweder, 1991). Bornstein and colleagues (2008), for example, find important differences in parenting across cultures with direct bearing on child development.[3]

Is the child's health and/or history of illness, injury, and trauma comparable to that of the children in the study?

Developmental research seeks to qualify change across time either among healthy ("normal" or "typical") children or within a circumscribed group of atypical children. As examples, research has documented developmental differences characteristic of autism (Burack, Charman, Yirmiya, & Zelazo, 2001), diabetes (Yu, Kail, Hagen, & Wolters, 2000) and trauma (Tedeschi, Park, & Calhoun, 1998). Studies demonstrate developmental differences associated with early sexual abuse (Porter, 2006), parental conflict and divorce (Grych & Fincham, 2001), and loss (Thompson, Kaslow, Price, Williams, & Kingree, 1998).

Does the child reside in a family structure comparable to that of the children in the study?

Family composition and stability bear not only on general development (Wen, 2005), but also on academic achievement (Lillard & Gerner, 1999) and a host of adult outcome variables (Sroufe, Egeland, Carlson, & Collins, 2005). Unfortunately, many development studies fail to describe the family-composition demographics of the sample studied or to discuss family composition as a dependent variable.

When conducting an experiment, a *dependent variable* is that criterion that is observed as it may be affected by changes controlled by the experimenter. An *independent variable* is the factor that the experimenter manipulates. Among family law professionals, one might study career longevity (dependent variable) as a function of professional complaints (independent variable) to evaluate the hypothesis that as number of malpractice and licensing board complaints increases, tenure decreases. In developmental research, it would be reasonable to consider changes in the dependent variable of height as it varies with the independent variable of age. More immediately, one might study how the dependent variable of academic achievement varies as a function of duration of custody litigation (independent variable).

PSYCHOMETRIC PROPERTIES: RELIABILITY AND VALIDITY

When evaluating a research study, it is important to understand how robust are its conclusions. At issue is the statistical strength of a conclusion—the probability that a measurement or observation is not due to chance, is reproducible, and is meaningful.

To illustrate, consider once again the shoemaker. A particularly ambitious shoemaker tires of constantly measuring and cobbling together shoes fitted to each customer's unique needs and declares that he has created a one-size-fits-all shoe. To prove this remarkable claim, he demonstrates that his omnibus footwear indeed fits the next customer to walk in the door. On this basis he proclaims his success.

The charitable among us observe that the shoemaker may have simply gotten lucky. The cynics wonder whether the demonstration was rigged. Either way, we agree that one success cannot substantiate his claim. But how many would? Statistically, the strength of his claim increases (in part) with the number of confirmatory observations.

The same is true of all measurement in the social sciences. The larger the sample tested, the more statistically robust the conclusions may be. Thus, single case studies can provide a great deal of qualitative information, but can generate robust conclusions only about the particular child studied. Studies that examine one or more particular attributes among dozens or hundreds of children have the statistical power to generate more robust conclusions. Studies that statistically collapse data across many independent but comparable studies can be the most statistically powerful. The latter is known as *meta-analysis*.

For example, a number of researchers independently observed intelligence differences between children raised in foster care and those raised in orphanages. Because each of these studies included relatively few children, their respective observations were relatively weak. In response, van IJzendoorn, Luijk, and Juffer(2008) pooled the data gathered in 75 independent studies, including nearly 4,000 children from 19 countries. By examining such a large pool of data, these researchers were able to demonstrate that intelligence differences attributable to variables such as language, culture, IQ instrument, and age were together much weaker than intelligence differences attributable to type of caregiving environment. In this way, meta-analysis provided strong support for the conclusion that the intelligence of children raised in foster care is greater than the intelligence of children raised in orphanages, independent of country, language, IQ instrument, and a host of other potentially confounding variables.

Cause and Effect

Cause and effect is often suggested but can seldom be concluded in social science research. For example, the van IJzendoorn et al. (2008) meta-analysis described here might be misinterpreted to infer that care setting causes intelligence differences. In fact, all that can actually be concluded is that the dependent variable (intelligence) is strongly related to the independent variable (care setting). Although it may be true that care setting causes intelligence differences, it is equally plausible that intelligence could be responsible for care setting differences, as when, for example, foster parents prefer to take in more intelligent children, leaving less intelligent children to be placed in orphanages. In lieu of clear causality, such outcomes are referred to as *correlational*, that is, the two variables are known to be co-related.

Are the results reliable and valid?

The social science literature is riddled with discussion of these two concepts as they bear on the measurement and meaning of research data (Shadish, Cook, & Campbell, 2002). Although there are numerous specific types of reliability and validity, two specifics are relevant to the discussion of development that follows.

Reliability

Reliability refers to the repeatability of a measurement. Repeatability is important to assure that two or more measurements are comparable—that, in fact, apples are being compared to apples.

For example, in the late 1600s, carpenters commonly spoke of measurements in terms of number of thumb-lengths, a reference that we have inherited in the phrase "rule of thumb." Although an individual carpenter's repeated measurements using his own thumb might be relatively reliable, different carpenters measuring with their respective thumbs inevitably cut boards quite differently. By contrast, marking the chief carpenter's thumb length on sticks that are distributed to all carpenters as their new standard (hence, the ruler) increases reliability.

Reliability is of critical importance in social science research, where very few dependent variables are tangible and subject to physical measurement. Thus, a great deal of research, scores of publications, and volumes of subsequent analysis are devoted to the development of relevant measurement tools. Mental health professionals commonly devote long hours and even years of training to become proficient (that is, to establish and maintain interrater reliability) in the administration, scoring, and interpretation of particular measurement devices.

Standardization works in favor of reliability. Standardization refers to the establishment of precise conditions and procedures for an observation or measurement. For example, most of us understand that we will know whether a diet is working if we place the bathroom scale on a hard floor and wear the same clothes at each successive measurement. Thus, we are standardizing the measurement process. By contrast, placing the scale on the carpet and wearing fewer clothes at each successive measurement may make it appear that the diet is a huge success, but the absence of standardized measurement makes the results less than reliable (even if falsely reinforcing).

This problem haunts many well-intended and creative forensic applications of otherwise sound social science procedures. The relative absence of standardized forensic processes, combined with the vagaries of practical limitations of place, of persons present, and of timing imposed by the court, can hobble many assessments. I have elsewhere (Garber, 2009) detailed the hurdles that stand in the way of applying existing parent–child attachment measures to custody-related questions. In brief, for all of these instruments' impressive reliability, the absence of standardized forensic applications stretches the instruments' value to the breaking point.

Validity

Validity describes the meaningfulness or usefulness of a reliable measure. In short, a reliable measurement can be valid, but an unreliable measurement cannot offer reliability. We can speak, for example, of the predictive validity of weight loss for the risk of diabetes or cardiac illness only to the extent that the measure of weight loss is reliable. When the bathroom scale rests on three inches of deep-pile shag, weight loss data will be unreliable and have no meaningful relationship to anything.

The meaningfulness or validity of a reliable measure can be discussed in many ways:

- *Concurrent validity* refers to the strength of the relationship between two simultaneous and reliable measures. Questions of concurrent validity arise when two instruments purport to measure the same construct. For example, the Wechsler Intelligence Scale for Children and the Stanford Binet Intelligence Test are each well respected and reliable tools commonly used to measure children's cognitive strengths and weaknesses. By administering both instruments to a sample of children, one can speak to the agreement between the two measures or their concurrent validity. As one further example, developmental research concerned with the quality of parent–child relationships (with obvious potential value in family law matters) routinely relies on a highly reliable but unwieldy tool called The Strange Situation (Ainsworth & Wittig, 1969). Introduction of a more facile means of measuring the same variable, a tool called the attachment Q-set (van IJzendoorn, Vereijken, Bakermans-Kranenburg, & Riksen-Walraven, 2004) required careful demonstration of the tools' concurrent validity (Moss, Bureau, Cyr, & Dubois-Comtois, 2006).
- *Criterion validity* speaks to the relationship between a measure and a specific benchmark or criterion. For example, chapter 15 discusses the extent to which otherwise reliable and valid psychological assessment measures relate to caregiving quality.
- *Predictive validity* or *developmental coherence* (Main, 1991) refer to an association across time between an antecedent dependent measure and a subsequent independent measure. The tremendous potential value of developmental psychology's observations for forensic process resides largely in the potential to make valid predictions of child outcomes as related to each of several divergent choices. Thus, we ask, for example, whether infants who overnight with absent fathers have different developmental outcomes than those who do not (Solomon, 2005), if child abuse affects later academic achievement (Boden, Horwood, & Fergus-

son, 2007), and how the experience of parental alienation in childhood is related to functioning decades later (Baker, 2007).

Research Design: Measuring Change Across Time

Questions of predictive validity call for a careful understanding of how we measure change across time. Matters of development call for different research methods than the questions studied by many other social scientists, largely because age is the primary dependent variable. In seeking to answer questions of predictive validity, researchers generally employ one of three observational strategies or *research designs*.

- *Cross-sectional research* infers developmental differences by examining contemporaneous groups representing different ages. The shoemaker interested in understanding growth, for example, might measure the heel-to-toe dimension among a group of 3-year-olds, a group of 6-year-olds, and a group of 12-year-olds. On this basis, he might plot a typical growth curve and plan his inventory accordingly. Taylor (2004) used this same cross-sectional methodology to understand gender constancy within groups of children from 3 to 7 years old in order to draw conclusions about the development of this measure across this age span. Cross-sectional research tends to be the least time- and resource-intensive and is therefore quite common. By virtue of basing conclusions on inferences between individuals, however, cross-sectional research may be the weakest of the three methodologies.
- *Prospective* or *longitudinal research* measures change across time within individuals. Thus, a pediatrician might record children's height at every annual visit from birth through kindergarten in order to generalize about growth over time.

  Because of the time involved and the simple reality that researchers and their subjects age at the same rate, longitudinal studies can be very expensive. Furthermore, the tendency for research subjects to drop out (known as *attrition*) can complicate interpretation of the data collected. Nevertheless, the opportunity to record change within individuals across time eliminates the concern that differences recorded in a cross-sectional design might, in fact, be due primarily to the differences between subjects, making longitudinal research the preferred methodology of many researchers. Fortunately, there are a number of very large and impressive ongoing longitudinal studies of child development spanning decades. Among these, the 30-year Minnesota Study of Risk and Adaptation from Birth to Adulthood (Sroufe et al., 2005) and the Adverse Childhood Experiences (ACE) Study[4] are among the greatest sources of data informing developmental theory and this book.

■ *Retrospective research* begins by identifying individuals who meet a specific criterion (e.g., honor roll graduates, autism diagnoses, adults whose parents divorced) and looks backward through incidental historical data to infer developmental trends. Hill and Nathan (2008), for example, assessed a sample of incarcerated men in order to distinguish the predictive pathways associated with the childhood experiences of parental conflict and parental violence. Retrospective research has the advantage that attrition is irrelevant, but the reliability of incidental data (e.g., report cards, police reports, hospital records) and subjects' memories is always a concern.

Chief among the concerns associated with research that requires subjective report is the effect of suggestibility. *Suggestibility* describes the extent to which an interviewee will conform his or her responses to the perceived expectation of the interviewer (Hünefeldt, Lucidi, Furia, & Rossi-Arnaud, 2008), a matter of significant concern in the context of any child-centered forensic evaluation (Garber, 2007b).

RESEARCH AND STANDARDS OF EVIDENCE: *DAUBERT* AND *FRYE*

Does developmental research meet the standards of evidence?

The family law professional whose work depends, in part, on developmental theory and research may be challenged under a collection of precedent-setting cases sometimes referred to as the *Daubert* Trilogy (Berger, 2000).[5,6] These cases intend, in the first instance, to clarify the conditions under which the courts can allow expert testimony. At the level of the state and family courts, variations of *Daubert* and its predecessor, *Frye*, govern when and how scientific data can be introduced into litigation.

In broad overview, these criteria address the following questions:

Are the data relevant to the case?

Relevance speaks to the generalizability or external validity of data, a subject broached earlier in these pages. Given that the developmental research brought to bear addresses the needs and abilities of children who share as many demographic characteristics with the child at issue as possible, relevance might still be challenged on the basis of the specific child's court involvement. That is, the vast majority of what we know about child development is based on observations of typical, non–court-involved kids. With the exception of specific pockets of research studying the effects of, for example, divorce (Amato, 2001), sexual abuse (Fergusson, Boden, & Horwood, 2008), or parental incarceration (Hairston & Addams, 2001) on children, we don't generally know how the stress that brings children into the court system and the stress associated with the court system itself might affect development.

Relevance is further subject to challenge on the basis of criterion validity. That is, a reliable instrument can be valid for some applications, but not others. The thermometer outside your window is likely a very reliable guage of ambient air temperature and a valid means of predicting what to wear outdoors. However, the same instrument has no necessary value for assessing barometric pressure, wind chill, or which parent will serve a child's needs better. Thus, chapter 15 discusses the extent to which many familiar and reliable psychological assessment instruments may be valid for some purposes (e.g., diagnosis) but entirely lacking in established validity for other purposes (e.g., custody).

Are the data replicable?

Admissibility calls for a method or outcome to be replicable, that is, to have been demonstrated by more than one researcher, research facility, or in more than one independent publication. Baute (2008) takes the position, for example, that, "[e]ven the use of the American Psychiatric Association nosology [that is, categorization of illnesses], *DSM-III-R* (American Psychiatric Association, 1987, or its revisions) can now be questioned on the grounds of its lack of reliability and testability."

Are the data falsifiable?

Richardson and Ginsburg (1998) define this concept simply: "If any behaviors, including exactly opposite behaviors, can be said to support a theory, then the theory cannot be falsified. If a theory cannot be falsified,...[it] should not be admissible as scientific evidence."[7] Thus, if I call "heads" at the flip of a coin, the outcome is falsifiable. When the coin settles, I will be either right or wrong. If, however, the coin has two heads (that is, the game is rigged) or the outcome is otherwise ambiguous, then the coin toss ceases to be falsifiable. I can argue that I win no matter what occurs.

This two-headed coin-falsifiability dilemma is unfortunately common in the social sciences. The defense mechanisms of Freudian psychology, for example, are often invoked to explain why otherwise falsifying data (the absence of symptoms or the presence of contradictory symptoms) are, in fact, consistent with a particular diagnosis. For example, alcoholism is often diagnosed on the basis of clinical interviews and self-report questionnaires. A person who indicates that he/she drinks daily to the point of intoxication, has lost jobs due to drunkenness, and has a failing liver might be considered alcoholic. On the other hand, a person who refutes all such "evidence" might still be diagnosed as alcoholic and considered to be in denial.

What is the error rate?

In common usage, "*error rate*" refers to the probability that an event will be determined to have occurred when it did not (false positive), and the probability that an event will be determined to have *not* occurred when, in fact, it did (false negative). In the case of the coin toss, the error rate should be near zero. The fact of a heads-or-tails outcome should be marred only by those very few coins that land standing on edge.

In the case of mental health diagnosis, the error rate can be unknown and unknowable. As one primary example, consider clinical diagnosis in common practice. The frequency with which nondepressed individuals are diagnosed with major depression (false positive) and genuinely depressed people are not given this diagnosis (false negative) is unknown. Efforts to operationalize the nosology in the form of the *Diagnostic and Statistical Manual of Mental Disorders* (*DSM-IV*; American

Psychiatric Association, 1994) or the *International Statistical Classification of Diseases and Related Health Problems* (*ICD-10*; World Health Organization, 1992) serve to diminish this problem, but it remains a serious impediment both to clinical intervention and to the admissibility of some diagnoses more than others (e.g., Redding, Floyd, & Hawk, 2001).

Have the data undergone peer review and publication?

As a general rule, publication in one of the many journals concerned with developmental psychology requires rigorous peer review. That is not to say, however, that peer review guarantees the scientific accuracy r value of a study (Marsh, Jayasinghe, & Bond, 2008). Indeed, important changes of the peer-review process have been recommended (Hadjista-vropoulos & Bieling, 2000).

Have the data been generally accepted within the scientific community?

This is the substance of *Frye*, the standard that held sway prior to *Daubert* and which is still recognized in a number of states.[8] Regrettably, the definition of "general acceptance" has been vague from the start. The *Frye* court is often quoted as declaring that "[j]ust when a scientific principle or discovery crosses the line between the experimental and demonstrable stages is difficult to define. Somewhere in this twilight zone the evidential force of the principle must be recognized" (54 App. D.C., at 47, 293 F., at 1014).

It is thus quite difficult to determine whether a particular developmental theory would qualify as generally accepted and might therefore constitute a reasonable basis of family law process. However, if the United States Supreme Court's incorporation of developmental theory establishes a precedent for reference to such theory in other family law matters, then the precedent for much of the work that informs this book and which might begin to inform your work has been set. For example, in 1972, Justice William O. Douglas wrote in the dissenting opinion in *Wisconsin v. Yoder* (406 U.S. 205, 1972) that

> there is substantial agreement among child psychologists and sociologists that the moral and intellectual maturity of the 14-year-old approaches that of the adult.[9]

In a more recent instance, Justice Stevens wrote the majority opinion in *Thompson v. Oklahoma* (487 U.S. 815, 1988), with explicit reference to the developmental theories of Erikson and Kohlberg, among others, concluding that

> the Court has already endorsed the proposition that less culpability should attach to a crime committed by a juvenile than to a comparable crime committed by an adult. The basis for this conclusion is too obvious to require extended explanation. Inexperience, less education, and less intelligence make the teenager less able to evaluate the consequences of his or her conduct, while, at the same time, he or she is much more apt to be motivated by mere emotion or peer pressure than is an adult. The reasons why juveniles are not trusted with the privileges and responsibilities of an adult also explain why their irresponsible conduct is not as morally reprehensible as that of an adult.[10,11]

STIRRING THE POT: PARENTAL ALIENATION SYNDROME, RELIABILITY, VALIDITY, AND *DAUBERT*

As a case in point, consider the contemporary controversy associated with *parental alienation syndrome* (or PAS). At issue is whether evidence of a diagnosable "syndrome" should be admitted into the court under the *Frye* standard of general acceptance and/or the *Daubert* standards of falsifiability.

In medicine, a "syndrome" is a discrete and identifiable collection of signs and symptoms that appear together, which together are strongly or exclusively indicative of the presence of a specific illness, and which share a single cause. Down's syndrome (DS) is a familiar example. DS is a relatively familiar[12] genetic difference marked by a constellation of symptoms including mental retardation, characteristic facial features, and heart, vision, and hearing defects. Its underlying genetic causes have been empirically determined, making the diagnosis falsifiable. Its existence is universally acknowledged and relevant research is widely published in peer-reviewed journals. On these bases, DS is generally acknowledged to meet both *Frye* and *Daubert* standards of admissibility.

By contrast, any number of "syndromes" have been posited in the social sciences, but these are seldom consensually validated, achieve limited or no peer-reviewed publication, and are rarely falsifiable (Duncan, 1996).[13] Richardson and colleagues (Richardson, Ginsburg, Gatowski, & Dobbin, 1995; Richardson & Ginsburg, 1998), for example, illustrate the point by examining cult-related brainwashing and child sexual abuse accommodation syndrome. In each case, they find the purported syndrome to be empirically flawed, unfalsifiable, and therefore inadmissible under *Daubert*.

Repressed memory syndrome provides an excellent example. Claims that memory of traumatic events can be repressed and later recovered are not generally supported by science (Piper, Lillevik, & Kritzer, 2008; cf., Dalenberg, 2006). Of particular concern is the idea that a litigant's claim to have recovered a previously repressed memory cannot be differentiated from an implanted memory and therefore cannot be disproven.

PAS suffers from the same deficiencies. Coined by Gardner in 1992, PAS attributes some children's refusal to visit with or otherwise be in contact with a noncustodial parent (usually the father) to efforts by the custodial parent (usually the mother) to damage the relationship. PAS is described as "a disorder that arises primarily in the context of child-custody disputes. Its primary manifestation is the child's campaign of denigration against a parent, a campaign that has no justification. It results from the combination of a programming (brainwashing) parent's indoctrinations and the child's own contributions to the vilification of the target parent" (Gardner, 1998). Bone and Walsh (1999) elaborate, stating that, in their view, "Children do not naturally lose interest in and become distant from their nonresidential parent simply by virtue of the absence of that parent. Also, healthy and established parental relationships do not erode naturally of their own accord. They must be attacked. Therefore, any dramatic change in this area is virtually always an indicator of an alienation process that has had some success in the past."[14]

The circularity of this reasoning precludes falsifiability. By thinking backward from effect (the child refuses contact with Dad) to cause (therefore Mom is alienating), it becomes impossible for visitation refusal to result from any other cause, when, in fact, there are a great many competing explanations for such a child's behavior (Garber, 1996; Drozd & Olesen, 2004).

For this and related reasons, "PAS has been largely discredited by the scientific community. Testimony that a party to a custody case suffers from the syndrome should therefore be ruled inadmissible both under the standard established in *Daubert* and the stricter *Frye* standard" (National Council of Juvenile and Family Court Judges, 2006, p. 19). Wood (1994) provides an excellent and detailed analysis, summarizing that, "evidence of PAS [must] be excluded because of its causation problems, its unreliability under Daubert, and its lack of general acceptance under Frye...because admitting this evidence endangers children, PAS must first gain the acceptance of child advocates, psychologists, and child abuse evidentiary experts—not family law attorneys who have latched onto the theory hoping to use it as an effective custody battle weapon or a defense to child abuse allegations" (see also Hoult, 2006; see chapter 16 for further discussion).[15]

SUMMARY

Far too many ill-informed consumers of science see a conclusion in print associated with a name and an impressive title and take it as truth. In serving a child's best interests, we have an obligation to look far beyond these superficial signs of value and purported relevance. We must know enough to know what we don't know and be mature enough to ask for others' help in interpreting the data. This calls at least for an elementary understanding of research methods and their limitations, of reliability and validity, and of how these constructs bear on the admissibility of a theory, a method, or an expert's testimony. In the chapter to follow we apply these principles in the course of discussing cognitive development.

NOTES

1. In a similar vein, consider a contemporary variation on Haeckel's (1899) proposition: Ontogeny recapitulates phylogeny, which recapitulates cosmology.
2. The American Psychological Association (APA), which publishes a majority of contemporary English research in psychology, recognizes the National Institutes of Health (NIH) standards for peer review (see http://www.apa.org/ppo/issues/nihpeerstatement.html). The NIH standards are discussed at: http://www.csr.nih.gov/review/peerrev.htm
3. To illustrate: "Italian mothers were more sensitive and optimally structuring, and Italian children were more responsive and involving, than Argen-

tine and U.S. dyads. In terms of region, rural mothers were more intrusive than metropolitan mothers…" (Bornstein et al., 2008, p. 666).

4. For an overview, go to http://www.acestudy.org/

5. The *Daubert* Trilogy refers to three United States Supreme Court cases: *Daubert v. Merrill Dow Pharmaceuticals, Inc., General Electric Co. v. Joiner,* and *Kumho Tire v. Carmichael.* Of particular relevance to this presentation are the guidelines Justice Blackmun set forth in *Daubert.* For a thorough discussion of these decisions and their use in contemporary courtrooms, see Merlino, Murray, and Richardson (2008). For a comparison of *Daubert* standards and the alternate standards associated with *Frye v. United States* still in use in many jurisdictions, see Cheng and Yoon (2005). Finally, Zeedyk and Raitt (1998) offer a valuable discussion of these various admissibility criteria with regard to psychological data.

6. Noting that some would argue that social science research should be exempted from *Daubert* (see discussion in Richardson et al., 1998), I am taking the broader view that the standards of the *Daubert* Trilogy are relevant to all matters brought before the court.

7. Noting Kaye's (2005) reminder that the Supreme Court's dissenting opinion in *Daubert* posited that the idea of "falsifiability" was mysterious and ill-defined.

8. *Frye* remains the governing standard in Alabama, Arizona, California, Colorado, the District of Columbia, Florida, Illinois, Kansas, Maryland, Michigan, Minnesota, Mississippi, New Jersey, New York, Pennsylvania, and Washington (Bernstein, 2002).

9. The case involved the Amish custom (or necessity) of excusing their children from public school to assist during harvest time. Justice Douglas argued on the basis of developmental theory that the young teenagers involved had the maturity to make their own choices. The full text of this opinion was retreived April 4, 2008, and remains available at: http://supreme.justia.com/us/406/205/case.html

10. This landmark case reversed a lower court's decision that a 15-year-old found guilty of murder should be put to death: *Thompson v. Oklahoma,* 487 U.S. 815 (1988).

11. It is interesting, if incidental, to note how these two cases, *Yoder* and *Thompson,* while both couched in developmental theory, may be seen as reaching opposite conclusions. In *Yoder,* the Court determines that teens are comparable to adults and should therefore be granted comparable privileges. In *Thompson,* quite the opposite conclusion is asserted.

12. Downs syndrome affects approximately 1 in every 800 live births. Learn more from the National Downs Syndrome Society at http://www.ndss.org/ or 1.800.221.4602.

13. Battered woman's syndrome (BWS; aka "battered person syndrome") may be an important exception. Originally posited by Walker (1979), this syndrome has been incorporated into the *International Classification of Diseases, Ninth Edition (ICD9*; code 995.81) and has arguably received broad consensual support (see, for example, Rothenberg, 2002). Nonetheless: "BWS may indeed exist, but to date there is insufficient empirical evidence to show this syndrome meets the rigorous diagnostic criteria of psychology or the law. If BWS does exist, there is no reliable means to identify those who suffer from it from those who merely claim it as a legal defense" (Dixon, 2002). To date, the United State Supreme Court has refused to recognize the closely associated battered person syndrome. See *Moran v. Ohio* 469 US 948 (1984).

14. Bone and Walsh (1999) go to the extent of recommending that PAS can exist and must be acknowledged by the court even in the absence of a child's resistance to a parent. They refer to this as "attempted" PAS as in "when the criteria of PAS are present, but the child is not successfully alienated from the absent parent. This phenomenon is still quite harmful and the fact of children not being alienated should not be viewed as neutral by the court."

15. An APA 1996 Presidential Task Force on Violence and the Family noted the lack of data to support so-called "parental alienation syndrome" and raised concern about the term's use. However, we have no official position on the purported syndrome (American Psychological Association, 2005).

Developmental Theory in Overview

The sobering fact of family law is that to be in the business of orchestrating parent–child relationships is to be directly influential on a particular child's developmental path.

—*Mary Duryee et al., Amici curiae* brief in Montenegro v. Diaz

Too many people grow up. That's the real trouble with the world, too many people grow up. They forget. They don't remember what it's like to be 12 years old. They patronize, they treat children as inferiors. Well I won't do that.

—*Walt Disney*

It is the height of hubris to presume to evaluate another human being, much less an entire family system. However, having chosen to work in family law, we have agreed to do just that. Daily, we presume to make observations and recommendations and judgments, to write reports and render decisions that change the direction of others' lives. As a matter of respect no less than one of ethics or the law, we must therefore be scrupulously thorough, self-consciously unbiased, completely open-minded, and unflinchingly child-centered. We must know the laws that govern each jurisdiction, the ways in which ethnicity and religion and language bear on each family's choices, and the norms against which our observations can be understood.

Sadly, most family law professionals have never taken a course in child development or family dynamics. Even those with mental health backgrounds (e.g., social work, psychology) likely had one course as an undergraduate, at best. The chapters that follow cannot remedy this problem, but may offer a start. My purpose is to provide a foundation in cognitive, verbal, physical, social, and emotional development that we can then apply in Parts III and IV to specific issues in family law.

Cognitive Development

In evaluating the testimony of a child, you should consider...the age of the child and any evidence regarding the child's level of cognitive development....You should not discount or distrust the testimony of a child solely because he or she is a child.

—California Penal Code

When you are a Bear of Very Little Brain, and you Think of Things, you find sometimes that a Thing which seemed very Thingish inside you is quite different when it gets out into the open and has other people looking at it.

—A.A. Milne

The word "cognition" is derived from the Latin word *cognoscere*, meaning "to know." Today the word is used broadly to refer to thinking processes and to (artificially) distinguish thinking from emotions and behavior. A neurologist or neuropsychologist might say that cognition refers to "executive functions," meaning higher order, logical, and sequential processes such as planning, prioritizing, and selectively attending to information.

In this chapter, we explore the stepwise growth of cognitive processes, from the newborn's sensorimotor experience of the world through the young adult's emerging ability to consider abstract, global concepts. These are the structures with which children struggle to understand the changes imposed on them when families undergo conflict and change. They are similarly the structures within which a child's capacity to be interviewed must be understood. But these structures must never be understood as existing independent of the child's concurrent social, emotional, linguistic, and physical development, nor as developing independent of the larger context we call family.

COGNITIVE DEVELOPMENT VERSUS IQ

In developmental psychology, the study of cognitive development generally includes the growth of thinking processes and the understanding of the rules that govern the physical world in which we live. By contrast, *intelligence* is a theoretical construct within the superordinate concept of cognition that intends to capture the individual's innate capacity for learning. Instruments have been standardized and validated with which to assess intelligence in the form of an intelligence quotient, or IQ. The informed reader is careful to neither confuse IQ with the larger concept of cognition, nor to mistake IQ as necessarily fully and validly representing an individual's intelligence. As the prior chapters have illustrated, we must always be wary of the measurement instrument's reliability and validity, as well as person-specific variables such as the test-taker's motivation, fatigue, and rapport with the test administrator (Cronbach & Meehl, 1955).

The most commonly used childhood IQ measurement tool is the Wechsler Intelligence Scale for Children (WISC-IV; Wechsler, 2003). This instrument provides a single composite Full Scale IQ score and multiple subtest scores allowing discussion not only of a child's overall intelligence, but of the child's relative intellectual strengths and weaknesses.[1] The WISC-IV has established strong reliability and validity (Williams, Weiss, & Rolfhus, 2003).

Achievement must be differentiated from intelligence as one further aspect of cognition. Achievement refers to the individual's relative success in acquiring information, especially with regard to academic progress. A wide variety of individually administered and group-administered achievement tests are currently in use, some quite narrowly defined and others explicitly designed for financial, legal, and political purposes, as under the No Child Left Behind (2001; Public Law 107-110) legislation.

As a practical definition, if intelligence is a cup, IQ describes how big the cup is and achievement describes how full the cup is. Building on this analogy, underachievement and overachievement can be described in terms of how full a particular individual's cup is relative to its capacity. How and when the vessel of intelligence grows is the subject of the work of Jean Piaget.

PIAGET'S THEORY

Jean Piaget (1896–1980) was an *epistemologist*, a researcher concerned primarily with understanding the development of understanding. Although numerous theorists have attempted to explain how cognitive skills grow over time, Piaget's theory remains by far the most influential and widely studied (e.g., Piaget 1977, 1983).

Piaget's theory describes qualitative changes or stages in the growth of cognition from infancy through adolescence. These caterpillar–butterfly transitions were originally described as universal and later understood to emerge within the context of the individual's social experience (Piaget & Inhelder, 1966/1973) and cultural idiosyncracies (Bringuier, 1980). Furthermore, Piaget allows for *décalage*, the asynchronous achievement of higher order logical processes in some content domains but not in others (Tomlinson-Keasey, Eisert, Kahle, Hardy-Brown, & Keasey, 1979).

Piaget's stages of cognitive development are described in Table 3.1.

The Sensorimotor Period (0–2 Years)

Piaget observed that the infant experiences the world entirely through direct sensation and interaction, by way of the five senses and motor contact. Innate abilities and reflexes (e.g., sucking, grasping, looking, and listening) create an entirely me-here-now experience.

Learning occurs even during the infant's first months, in the form of what Piaget termed primary and secondary circular reactions, known more generally in psychology as *conditioning*. For example, an infant's spontaneous discovery that thumb-sucking yields tension relief will graudually lead to intentional repetitions of the behavior. This is the beginning of self-soothing and, on a larger scale, self-regulation.

Object permanence first appears early in the sensorimotor period, commonly by 6 to 8 months and perhaps as early as 3 months (Baillargeon, 1987). Object permanence describes the child's understanding that an object continues to exist when it leaves his or her immediate sensory experience, a critical conceptual milestone for many other aspects of development, particularly early social relationships.[2]

By the end of the first year, the infant begins to explore his or her environment visually, then tactilely, and still later motorically (that is, by rolling, crawling, and toddling). Imitation of facial expressions and vocal sounds becomes possible (Lacerda, von Hofsten, & Heimann, 2001) and serves as a cornerstone of the caregiver–child relationship.

By 18 months, the sensorimotor child begins to experiment with cause and effect, building associations between antecedent events (e.g., drop toy) and subsequent events (parent's attention). This sets the stage for early symbolic thought and language, the association between a sound and a concrete referent.

The Preoperational Period (2–7 Years)

The early preoperational child (2–4 years, sometimes recognized as the *Preconceptual Substage*) is yet to emerge from his or her egocentric universe. Experience is all about self. The concept known as *"theory of mind"* (Wellman, 1985)—that is, the ability to consider that others have different perspectives, feelings, and ideas—is only slowly emerging.

The preoperational child's thinking has become rich with symbolic representation. Events can be anticipated. Objects can be represented by other objects, by pictures, and by sounds. Language blossoms.

The preoperational period is often characterized by failures of conservation. In this context, "conservation" refers to the cognitive ability to simultaneously consider multiple features of an object or event. The preoperational child is typically unable to understand more than one attribute of an object or an event at a time.

In the classic Piagetian conservation task, child and experimenter each have an identical glass of milk in front of them on a table. The preoperational child correctly identifies that each has the same amount of milk. When the experimenter pours her milk into a short, squat glass, the child sees that one glass appears to have more milk in the vertical dimension and therefore believes that that glass now contains more milk. The child's limited perspective on the height of the two glasses without understanding of how the two dimensions work together to define volume determines this error.

The same idea can be captured in interview and without props. Ask a child, "Which weighs more, one pound of feathers or one pound of metal?" The question appears self-evident to you, but the preoperational child will insist that the metal weighs more.

Conservation failures have a direct bearing on interviews with young children. In the same manner that this child cannot integrate the height and width of the two drinking glasses to equate volume, he's unlikely to be able to consciously integrate his experience of a caregiver's sensitive caring and firm discipline. Thus, the 4-year-old scolded by an anxious parent immediately prior to meeting you is prone to relate that that parent is "mean," whereas the same child recently treated to an ice cream cone will describe the same parent in glowing terms.

Later in the Preoperational Stage (a period sometimes recognized as the *Intuitive Substage*), the child begins to demonstrate early logical problem solving. Show this child 10 apples and 3 oranges and he or she can tell you that there are more apples but cannot explain why. Ask the same child whether there are more apples or more fruit, and he or she will reply that there are more apples.

Concrete Operations (7–11 Years)

This stage marks the onset of genuine logical problem solving. The Concrete Operations child understands that objects can be arranged in a graduated continuum (e.g., from tallest to shortest), a skill known as *seriation*, and that objects can be classified according to different criteria. This latter skill allows for the emergence of conservation skills.

Perhaps most dramatically, the child who has achieved Concrete Operations can take others' perspectives, a skill known as *decentration*. This child understands that others have a different physical perspective on an event, as when an experimenter sits across a table and the two view objects between them from different angles. This is the foundation of the social skill of empathy.

Curiously, the pre-Concrete Operations child often holds divergent and contradictory feelings and beliefs without any inherent sense of the contradiction. It is only with the attainment of concrete thinking that the child can begin to spontaneously reconcile the two in an effort to build a coherent sense of the world (Bradmetz & Schneider, 1999).

The Concrete Operations child's cognitive leaps are largely restricted to immediate, here-and-now objects and events. Application of these and related skills to abstract, anticipated, or hypothetical events develops only later.

Formal Operations (11–13 Years and Older)

Achievement of Formal Operations is seldom documented prior to age 11 (e.g., Webb, 1974) and often coincides with the onset of puberty, although some suggest that as few as 50% of adults may ever actually demonstrate this level of cognitive functioning (Arlin, 1975).[3]

Formal Operations is marked by the ability to think abstractly, to consider hypothetical situations and their contingent outcomes, and to entertain all of those provocative "what-if" questions that some associate with the idealism of older teenagers and young adults. Formal Operations is known as the "problem solving" stage, in that individuals who attain this degree of cognitive sophistication are better able to consider problems and their potential remedies from a variety of angles and perspectives in order to come up with the most reasonable solutions.

Arlin (1982) has established a simple paper-and-pencil, self-administered test suitable for large group administration with which to assess respondents as having achieved concrete, high concrete, transitional, low formal, or high formal operational thinking.[4]

The abstract, cognitive skills inherent in Formal Operations are considered necessary (even if not sufficient) in many forensic venues, most particularly with regard to adjudication of minors as adults in criminal matters, with regard to informed consent decisions, and with regard to the identification of a "mature minor" in the context of custody matters and health care decisions (see chapter 14). For example, Grisso and Vierling (1978, p. 419) discuss cognitive developmental capacities as relevant to informed consent as follows:

> [A]lthough a child in the previous stage (Concrete Operations) can think logically, it is questionable whether prior to the formal operations stage

he/she can perform inductive and deductive operations (Piaget's "transformation") or hypothetical reasoning at a level of verbal abstraction that would be represented by many consent situations involving treatment alternatives and risks. Further, emergence of the formal operations stage allows a child to become sufficiently flexible in thinking (i.e., is less bound by Piaget's "centration") to attend to more than one aspect of a problem at once—for example, to entertain alternative treatments and risks simultaneously.

Post-Piagetian, Post–Formal Operations

Whereas Piaget posited that achievement of Formal Operations represents a final developmental equilibrium, many developmentalists have since proposed that cognitive growth continues throughout life and well beyond Formal Operations (Morra, Gobbo, Marini, & Sheese, 2008). In general, these theories refer to the development of wisdom or, "the ability that allows the individual to grasp human nature, which operates on the principles of contradiction, paradox and change" (Clayton, 1982).

Arlin (1975, 1989) conceptualizes Formal Operations as a stage of mature problem solving. By contrast, she identifies a post–Formal Operations stage as one of problem finding, characterized by "creative thought vis-a-vis 'discovered problems'; the formulation of generic problems; the raising of general questions from ill-defined problems; and the slow, cognitive growth represented in the development of significant scientific thought" (Arlin, 1975, p. 603; references excised).

The dramatic shift that characterizes the onset of Formal Operations can sometimes be inferred in a very simple way. Psychologists commonly ask children, "If you could have three magic wishes, what would you wish for?" Children who have yet to reach Formal Operations predictably wish for me-here-now things: the latest video game, a million dollars, and "my own horse," for example. Once Formal Operations are established and abstract thinking is available, wishes become broader and more global and begin to include abstractions like "an end to war," "housing for the homeless," or "a cure for AIDS."

Much as this simple tool can be useful, it also can be easily corrupted. Children can choose or be forced by circumstance to compromise their childhood far too often and too quickly when they are triangulated into adult conflict, as when they are adultified, parentified, and/or alienated (see chapter 16). The 8-year-old little girl who has been drawn into her parents' conflict might wish for a new doll, a pretty dress, and "my dad to have a new girlfriend" or "all my mommy's bills to be paid." This is not evidence that the Formal Operations stage has somehow been prematurely achieved so much as evidence of the extent to which the child has been triangulated into the adult conflict.

PIAGET, *FRYE*, AND *DAUBERT*

Piaget's work is among the most researched, most replicated, and most referenced in the child development literature. In one author's opinion, "assessing the impact of Piaget on developmental psychology is like assessing the impact of Shakespeare on English literature" (Lourenco &

Table 3.1

PIAGETIAN MILESTONES IN COGNITIVE DEVELOPMENT

APPROXIMATE AGE RANGE	STAGE	NOTABLE MILESTONES
Birth through first year	Sensorimotor Period	The world exists as it is directly experienced; object permanence slowly emerges
2 through 7 years	Preoperational Thought	Symbolic thinking develops but conservation fails; thinking is all me-here-now (immediate and concrete)
7 through 11 years	Concrete Operations	Conservation, seriation, and decentration develop as me-here-now thinking diminishes
11 years into adulthood	Formal Operations	Abstract and hypothetical thought, understanding that others have unique perspectives, and ability to decentrate
Adulthood	Post–Formal Operations (Post-Piagetian)	Acceptance of multiple causality, paradox, and contradiction

Machado, 1996, p. 143). This suggests that Piaget's work likely fulfills standards under both *Frye* (common acceptance) and the *Daubert* Trilogy (publication in peer-reviewed journals), which were introduced in chapter 2.

But is Piaget falsifiable? That is, can the assertion that a child has attained formal operations, for example, be disproven? Perhaps. Because Piaget's stages are defined as sequential and qualitatively different, the likelihood of false positives (that is, erroneously crediting a child with greater maturity than he or she has actually attained) is very low.[5] However, the problem with developmental assessment in any context is the likelihood of underestimating capacity due to limitations of the child's motivation, attention, compliance, language and/or anxiety, thereby yielding a false negative outcome.

This is, in fact, the case with many of Piaget's specific tasks. Although subsequent research has largely confirmed his stages and their sequence, the ages that he assigned have varied with various experimental procedures. McGarrigle and Donaldson (1975; see also Dockrell, Campbell, & Nielson, 1980), find that implicit experimenter expectations routinely create false negative findings, suggesting that conservation of number appears much earlier than Piaget had suggested. Other similar findings (Winer, Hemphill, & Craig, 1988; Miller & Baillargeon, 1990) suggest generally that the ages associated with Piaget's stages are less important than the conceptual milestones that he identifies and their sequence.

Despite this concern regarding falsifiability and its potential implications for admissibility under *Daubert*, Piagetian theory is often invoked in child-centered forensic process. Lamb and Kelly (2001) cite Piaget in support of arguments both for and against infant overnights with noncustodial caregivers (see chapter 9). Walker (2002) bases recommendations concerning children's participation in abuse evaluations on cognitive capacities as defined by Piaget.[6] The developmental capacity to lie as it bears on children's testimony is discussed in Piagetian terms by Ford (2008) and again, independently, in *The Commonwealth of Massachusetts v. Cheryl Amirault LeFave* (SJC-07529).

Piaget has been invoked, as well, in *amicus curaie* briefs heard before the United States Supreme Court with regard to adolescents' ability to make well-informed and independent political decisions (Professor David Moshman in the Supreme Court of the United States, *Federal Election Commission, et al. v. Senator Mitch McConnell, et al.*) and in favor of enrollment diversity in higher education institutions (American

Council on Education and 53 other higher education organizations in the Supreme Court of the United States, *Jennifer Gratz, et al. v. Lee Bollinger, et al.*). Finally, as mentioned above, Piaget is referenced as foundational by Supreme Court justices themselves in *Wisconsin v. Yoder* (406 U. S. 205, [1972]).

SUMMARY

The child's capacity to understand the world in which he or she lives emerges over time in a sequence of qualitative developments best defined by Piaget. The family law professional's familiarity with the nature of these successive stages is necessary, but not sufficient. A given child's cognitive capacities, including measures of his or her intelligence and achievement, may bear on if and how that child can be interviewed, provide testimony or an opinion in matters that may shape the rest of his or her life. But cognition is only one thread in the tapestry of the developing person. Thus, we move forward to consider the concurrent emergence of language, social, and emotional capacities.

NOTES

1. Discussion of IQ tests and their construction, administration, and interpretation is well beyond the scope of this text. Readers interested in further detail concerning the WISC-IV are directed to Weiss, Saklofske, Prifitera, and Holdnack (2006).
2. Researchers have debated whether object permanence (retention of the existence of an inanimate object) and person permanence (retention of the existence of a person) emerge at the same time (e.g., Bell, 1970). For many years person permanence was thought to appear much later in development, the assumption being that people are much more affectively stimulating and therefore harder to cognitively "capture." In fact, Jackson, Campos, and Fischer (1978) demonstrate that the two tasks are identical: "There is not a unitary ability called person permanence that develops simultaneously across all tasks involving people" (p. 9).
3. A case in point: Hosek, Harper, and Domanico (2005, p. 166), studying medication compliance among 16–24-year–olds, find that "69% of the sample had yet to begin the transition from concrete thinking to formal or abstract reasoning."

4. The Arlin Test of Formal Reasoning (ATFR) is available from Slosson Educational Publications (see http://www.slosson.com/onlinecatalog store_c51436.html).
5. Nevertheless, Lourenco and Machado (1996) point out that in seeking to demonstrate the appearance of Piagetian milestones earlier than Piaget posited, many post-Piagetian researchers are making false-positive errors. That is, by oversimplifying experimental tasks, they risk crediting children with developmental skills that have not actually been obtained.
6. See also Eisen, Quas, and Goodman (2002).

4 Language Development

Language permits an individual to express both a personal identity and membership in a community, and those who share a common language may interact in ways more intimate than those without this bond....Just as shared language can serve to foster community, language differences can be a source of division. Language elicits a response from others, ranging from admiration and respect, to distance and alienation, to ridicule and scorn.

—*United States Supreme Court,* Hernandez v. New York

"When I use a word," Humpty Dumpty said in rather a scornful tone, "it means just what I choose it to mean—neither more nor less."

—*Lewis Carroll*

We live in a world of words, a world in which one's ability to use words is routinely mistaken for intelligence or education, social status, sophistication, or maturity. We rely on words to determine a child's thoughts and feelings, wishes and goals, memories and experience far more than we rely upon other, possibly divergent but sometimes useful expressions, such as drawing and play (Ellis, 2000).[1] We are trained to interview using words, to keep careful records of a child's utterances, and to summarize our beliefs and recommendations in words. The law, in fact, more than any other field, is focused on the precise usage and meaning of words as the means of defining and delimiting our freedoms.

Anyone with any experience with children is aware that language does not spring fully developed from an infant's mouth at birth. Nevertheless, few family law professionals factor in the development of a child's ability with language—the ability to understand his/her verbal environment, the ability to comprehend questions, and the ability to express his/her own experience—into a forensic evaluation, unless the child evinces obvious or documented speech and language differences or difficulties.

We know the dangers of asking leading questions (Milchman, 2007), and may have adopted techniques for eliciting the full breadth of the child's experience (Garber, 2007b). We seldom, however, generally account for the child's normative limits of language expression and comprehension. This chapter discusses the development of these capacities as they bear on a child's participation in family law matters. Above and beyond understanding the typical course of language development, the family law professional must be acutely attuned to how a particular child's language skills might facilitate or impede a genuine understanding of his or her wishes, needs, and experience with regard to the family.

TYPICAL LANGUAGE DEVELOPMENT

Healthy children acquire language skills in a rather uniform progression across languages and cultures, from the neonate's primitive pairing of sound and experience (e.g., mother's voice = comfort) to the young adult's grasp of figurative language (e.g., idiom, proverbs, metaphor; Nippold, 2007; Yang, 2006). These steps are described in broad strokes in Table 4.1.[2] However, differences in early language exposure and/or medical complications of hearing or the physical mechanisms of speech can delay or derail the process (Bishop & Leonard, 2000).

Comprehension Versus Expression

Any discussion of language development necessarily distinguishes between verbal comprehension or understanding, on one hand, and verbal expression or production, on the other. Although one might expect that the two develop synchronously, in fact comprehension generally precedes production, sometimes by a tremendous amount (Smolensky, 1996). Case in point: it's more than likely that the breadth and depth

Table 4.1

MILESTONES IN THE TYPICAL DEVELOPMENT OF RECEPTIVE AND EXPRESSIVE LANGUAGE

APPROXIMATE AGE RANGE	RECEPTIVE LANGUAGE MILESTONES	EXPRESSIVE LANGUAGE MILESTONES[3]
At birth	Newborns respond to sound in their environment, notably by being startled by sudden, loud noises. Newborns can distinguish their own mother's voice from other female voices and their own mother's native language from other languages.	Newborns have a repertoire of expressive sounds that generally correspond to pleasure or pain.
Through 3 months	Child begins to orient his/her face toward speaker; may quiet down as if to attend to an unfamiliar voice.	Child begins to smile in recognition of familiar face; coos and babbles.
4 through 6 months	Child begins to understand simple, common words, such as "no."	Babbling begins to sound speech-like in intonation and prosody; child's speech sounds and gestures can communicate basic wishes.
7 through 12 months	Child orients to his/her name, turns to look toward speaker; enjoys "patty-cake"-type games and demonstrates recognition of common labels (e.g., "dog," "juice," "bed").	Word-initial consonant sounds occur (e.g., /b/ as in "bed" or /d/ as in "dog"); utterance of first real word (e.g., "Mama" or "Dada").
12 through 24 months	Child will look toward or point to named objects and can follow simple commands, such as "Touch your nose."	First two-word utterances (e.g., "Me go." or "Where car?") occur.
2 through 3 years	Child understands and complies with complex commands, such as "Put the bus on the shelf"; begins to contrast opposites (e.g., big/little, hot/cold).	Child uses many more labels for immediate and familiar objects and events; three-word utterances begin to use adjectives and adverbs (e.g., "Bus go fast!").

(continued)

Table 4.1 *(continued)*

APPROXIMATE AGE RANGE	RECEPTIVE LANGUAGE MILESTONES	EXPRESSIVE LANGUAGE MILESTONES[3]
3 through 4 years	Child successfully distinguishes between "who," "what," "where," and "when" questions.	Sentences can be four and five words long and begin to integrate nonimmediate (past or distant) experiences.
4 through 5 years	Story comprehension and recall skills appear. Adult conversation is easily understood, within limits of 1,500- to 2,000-word vocabulary.	Articulation is clear and understood by everyone. Long and complex utterances with subsidiary clauses (e.g., "The dog ate the cookie, the one that we got from Sally, and then he ate his dinner."). Child experiments with command language (which may sound "bossy") and with forbidden "potty" words (e.g., profanity overheard) for effect.
11 through 13 years	Child comprehends and uses abstract imagery (e.g., parable), analogy, and metaphor, concurrent with onset of Piagetian Formal Operations (Duthie, Nippold, Billow, & Mansfield, 2008).	

of your own language comprehension as an educated adult far exceeds that of your spoken or written usage.

The reality that verbal comprehension precedes verbal production underlies one of the most commonly encountered errors among parents of toddlers. Observing that 2-year-old Billy can only say a handful of words, for example, Mom and Dad assume that he understands only as much as he can say, and they therefore speak freely in his presence. When Mom and Dad are at odds, this means that the toddler is at high risk for triangulation into the adult conflict and alienation by one or both from the other. These parents will readily (and incorrectly) reassure the inquiring family law professional, "Don't worry. He doesn't understand what we're saying."

Language comprehension precedes expression, in part, because meaning is first derived preverbally through *prosody*, the contextual clues that accompany words (e.g., intonation, emotion, and behavior). When an infant experiences an utterance consistently paired with pleasure, for example, that utterance by itself begins to carry pleasurable meaning. This early and constant "paired-associate" method of learning amounts to what might be called emotional communication.

Much of early social and emotional development (discussed in chapter 5) is built on the quality of the emotional communication "fit" between parent and child.

Children read and respond to emotional expression long before words take on specific meaning (Tronick, 1989). The mother who holds her baby while yelling at her partner, for example, exposes the child not only to angry words (which themselves may have no meaning to the young child), but also to a host of incidental autonomic physical signals. She reflexively tightens her muscles. Her breathing becomes rapid and shallow. Her heart rate races. The child reads these cues and responds in kind, quickly building the association between verbal tone and emotion, if not between specific words and fear.[4] The result is a primitive sound–emotion comprehension that far precedes the development of actual language.

Given that a child's hardware for hearing (the inner ear mechanisms) and verbal understanding (Wernicke's region of the brain[5]) are age-appropriate and physically intact, language comprehension will develop on the scaffolding of cognitive, social, and emotional development. This means that a healthy, typically developing child's gradual acquisition of meaning will parallel quite closely his or her progression through Piaget's stages, from the concrete sensorimotor through the symbolic and toward the abstract (Homer & Hayward, 2008).

Given that the hardware associated with language expression (Broca's region[6]) and speech (lips, tongue, mouth) are age appropriate and physically sound, language expression will emerge differentially by gender and social experience.

Because unrecognized and undiagnosed childhood sensory deficits are so easily and so often mistaken for a wide variety of unrelated physical, psychological, and learning problems, it is always important to determine that a child has completed a thorough hearing and vision test. Be aware that public school–administered screenings may not prove sufficient and that referral to a qualified pediatric audiologist, ophthalmologist, and/or ear, nose, and throat physician may be appropriate when more subtle sensory differences are suspected.

Variations in Language Development

Girls tend to say more earlier and to talk about different things than boys (Bornstein, Leach & Haynes, 2004; Wehberg et al., 2008). Preterm and latter-born children say less than full-term and first-born children of the same age (Kern & Gayraud, 2007). Children with more direct verbal interaction with caregivers (especially with mothers) similarly tend to say more and earlier (Westerlund & Lagerberg, 2008). Finally, higher socioeconomic status (SES) families tend to raise children who say more at younger ages than lower SES families (Paul & Fountain, 1999). This means that our best child informants are likely to be first-born girls from wealthy families with attentive moms. Latter-born, impoverished boys rasied by single dads, by contrast, may have much less to say.

Say What You Mean and Mean What You Say: Recognizing Expressive Mimicry

Although the developmental linguist's research demonstrates that comprehension precedes expression, clinicians and family law professionals are aware that many children's expressive language skills appear to develop in advance of their language comprehension skills. How can this be? In its most benign and typical occurrence, this apparent developmental asynchrony is due to expressive language *mimicry*, the child's natural tendency to experiment with new words even before acquiring their meaning.

Among typically developing children, expressive language mimicry is a natural and normal mechanism of socialization (de Klerk, 2005). Kids expectably repeat the words that their peers use so as to fit in with others, even when their meanings are unclear or entirely idiosyncratic. This is how teenage slang proliferates. It's also the mechanism that motivates fashion trends and makes or breaks entertainment figures, video games, Internet sites, television shows, and cell phone choices.

Unfortunately, when families are in turmoil, something as simple as expressive language mimicry can become horribly destructive.

Consider, for example, the 5-year-old who arrives home from school and announces to his mother, "I want sex." Much as any parent's blood pressure would skyrocket in this situation, the strongest likelihood is that the kindergartener imitated this unfamiliar word overheard on the playground either because he saw that the child who used it received a great deal of very rewarding instant attention and/or he mistook the word as referring to a new toy or a yummy candy. With this healthy, child-centered understanding, the parent takes a deep breath and then plays dumb, asking in as neutral a tone as possible, "What's that?" Only a calm, neutral response that presumes nothing can elicit the truth: "I don't know" or "Sally got a pink one that sings!"

When these otherwise natural and expectable bombshells fall in the supercharged environments associated with family dysfunction and litigation, they can be deadly. The angry, depressed, and fearful divorcing mother, for example, is ready to assume the worst and might therefore respond, *"Did your daddy touch you?"* This unexpected red-alert reaction startles the little boy, who then becomes upset and confused, behavior that the adult easily mistakes as confirmation of trauma. Police are called. Attorneys are hired. What may have originally been entirely benign and meaningless quickly becomes distorted into a bitter, destructive, and resource-draining process.[7] Read more about this phenomenon in chapter 7, "Words Gone Awry."

Precocious Language

Evidence that a child is using language far in advance of his or her peer group can be evidence of advanced cognitive development, impressive intelligence and/or a sign of family dysfunction. In the case of the former, the gifted child will use his or her impressive vocabulary correctly in discussing a wide range of topics. For this child, genuine comprehension and sophisticated expression both outstrip a typical age-mate's skills.

In the case of the dysfunctional family, the child's impressive vocabulary is likely to be quite narrow, his or her usage rigid or stereotyped and given very limited meaning. This is not precocious language and cognitive sophistication so much as it is due to inappropriate exposure to adult matters, as when a child is artificially promoted by an immature, self-centered, and/or needy parent into an ally, a process known as *adultification*, or to become a caregiver to the parent him- or herself, a process known as *parentification* (Burton, 2007; Chase, 1999). In both of these dysfunctional but tragically common dynamics, the child is likely to experience the parent's neediness and associated attention as a compliment. In an effort to fit into the new and dysfunctional role, the child will adopt many of the adult's words. Thus, the adultified 10-year-old might talk about mortgages and taxes, might discuss her dad's dating behaviors or her mom's job search, all with very impressive language. But the meaning is shallow or nonexistent. Ask this child what a mortgage is and the answer will be empty of genuine understanding: "It's something that you pay" or "it has to do with the house." What first may appear to be linguistic sophistication may quickly prove to be a form of mimicry that reveals the family's dynamics.

Even more insidious is the effect of *alienation*, that abusive dynamic whereby one caregiver exposes a child to information about another caregiver, resulting in the child's otherwise unjustifiable loss of a sense of security in the targeted caregiver. Alienation (mentioned in chapter 2 and discussed at length in chapter 16) is commonly seen in a child's incorporation of the aligned parent's verbatim words and phrases about the targeted caregiver. When this occurs, the child's words are predictably rote, rigid, and repetitious. Eleven-year-old Billy might report that his dad "cheated on us" but be unable to define the concept or evidence the associated indignation. Asked to justify the expressed charge, the child may rely on one or a small handful of exaggerated or even fabricated incidents that may echo verbatim from Mom's independent report of the same matters. Push a little harder, and Billy will take the offensive, quickly accusing you of "being on Dad's side!"

Recognizing that children often use words and phrases that they don't genuinely understand is an excellent reason for the investigating family law professional to "play dumb." Rather than assume what a child means when using a critical word (e.g., "hit," "touch," "pee-pee," "friend," or even "Daddy" or "Mommy"), it is routinely worthwhile to raise a confused eyebrow, shrug your shoulders, and ask a curious, nonconfrontational, "What does that mean?" For example, many preschool and early elementary school children will report that their parents are "divorced." Rather than assume that you and the child share a common understanding of the term, stop to ask. The simple question can open the door to understanding the child's broader thinking, experience, and place in the family dynamics:

"Okay, you live with your mom. Do you have a dad?"
"Yeah but he doesn't live with us. They're 'vorced."
"...they're 'vorced...?"
"Yeah. Mommy told me."
"What's that mean?"
"You know, 'vorce means Daddy hit Mommy so the police kicked him out."

The need to inquire about meaning and definition is no less true of the teary-eyed and fragile middle-schooler, the swaggering, condescending teen, and the light-hearted, entertaining "What, me worry?" 10-year-old. One 15-year-old boy, pants hanging below his boxers, tongue ring and tattoos boldly in place, memorably informed the guardian ad litem investigating his parents' postdivorce, child-support case that he refused to spend time with his father because "he's a pedophile." Shocked, the guardian had the presence of mind to calmly ask what that word meant. The teen tried to duck the question, but finally admitted that he had no idea what the word meant; his mother had told him to say it.

NEGLECT, ABUSE, AND LANGUAGE EXPERIENCE

The typical and universal path of early-language development requires exposure to language models. The infant's experience of language rhythms, intonation patterns, and the unique set of sounds (*phonemes*) that compose a specific language help to organize developing brain structures in a manner that opens the door to continuing language development. In fact, the babbling 2- or 3-month-old's spontaneous repertoire will include the sounds common to all languages. By 12 to 18 months of age, however, the speech sounds that are absent in the child's auditory environment have dropped out of his or her sound vocabulary in favor of those sounds that constitute the ambient language and can be relatively difficult to master later as part of second-language learning (Midaeva & Lyubimova, 2008).

For this reason, contemporary developmental linguists refer to a *sensitive period* for language development.[8] In general, a sensitive period is a window of opportunity during which the brain may be particularly receptive to certain kinds of input and after which development is relatively difficult or imperfect, though usually not impossible (Shafer & Garrido-Nag, 2007).

Children who endure the extremes of abuse and neglect in their early years may, among many other developmental deficiencies, lack adequate early-language experience. The extremes of deprivation can compromise not only the timing, pace, and trajectory of language development (Berk, 2004; Kotulak, 2008), but even the overall organization of brain development globally (Perry & Pollard, 1997).

PHYSIOLOGICAL DIFFERENCES AND LANGUAGE DEVELOPMENT

When early developmental differences or trauma are known or suspected, the investigating family law professional may need to receive and review prenatal, birth, and pediatric records. Documentation of early illness, injury, or delay can help to explain present-day functioning and may bear on court-related questions of maturity and competence. Alternately, collecting a comprehensive developmental history can be critically important to formulating legal remedies best suited to a child's specific needs and abilities.[9]

Physiological differences due to prenatal trauma, toxic exposure, peri- and postnatal injury, can impair sensory development, behavior, and temperament and thereby dramatically limit the child's early-language experience. These differences can remain undetected for months and even years. The result can be very much like the result of early neglect, that is, without adequate early-language experience, development may be delayed, idiosyncratic, or completely arrested. Some common physiological impacts on language development are discussed below.

Fetal alcohol syndrome (FAS) is caused by in utero exposure to maternal alcohol consumption. It is strongly associated with cognitive delays, difficulties with vision and audition, shortened stature, learning disabilities, impulsivity, and organ failure. Prominent within this broad and diverse constellation of deficits are global delays in both receptive and expressive language abilities observed by school age (Pellegrino & Pellegrino, 2008).[10]

Early hearing loss can be the result of genetic anomalies, prenatal drug exposure, perinatal trauma, disease (e.g., meningitis), and/or exposure to extremely loud noises. Because an infant's hearing loss or deafness may not be detected until the child's first birthday (Marschark, 2001),[11,12] important language experience and associated neurological development can be compromised (Bowen, 1998) with potential implications for lifelong communication differences.

Articulation deficits. In a similar manner, damage to articulation-related "hardware" (e.g., lips, tongue, mouth, vocal cords) due to genetic anomalies, trauma, or drug exposure can impair early speech production. Because these physical differences are more likely to be visible (e.g., cleft palate), they are often diagnosed and surgically corrected early on (Pope & Snyder, 2004).

Autism and autistic spectrum disorders (ASDs), such as Asperger's syndrome, are often associated with differences in language comprehension and production.[13] These developmental differences can be identified as young as 18 to 30 months of age, in part on the basis of differences in both expressive and receptive language development, most significantly in the use of gesture (Luyster, Kadlec, Carter, & Tager-Flusberg, 2008). Individuals with these developmental differences may be very slow to develop spoken language, tend to be relatively concrete in their language usage throughout life, have difficulties interpreting the nonverbal aspects of spoken language (i.e., prosody), and may find face-to-face interaction aversive (Rogers & Williams, 2006).

Learning Disability and Nonverbal Learning Disability

"Learning disability" (LD) and "nonverbal learning disability" (NVLD) are labels that describe meaningful discrepancies of cognitive functioning within an individual, some of which have direct bearing on language comprehension and/or production.[14] NVLD, for example, refers to a pattern of verbal strengths as contrasted with relative nonverbal (e.g., visual-spatial) cognitive weaknesses. The *Diagnostic and Statistical Manual of Mental Disorders, Fourth Edition* (*DSM-IV*; APA, 1994) defines four specific LDs as well as two additional, language-related diagnoses:

Expressive language disorder and mixed receptive-expressive language disorder. Diagnosis of or suspicion that a child may qualify for any of these difficulties calls for special attention to how the child participates in any family law process. These and similar diagnoses must raise questions as to the child's capacity to understand the limitations of confidentiality and privilege, the child's capacity to accurately and fully report an experience, and his or her ability to accurately relate thoughts and feelings. The thorough family law professional, aware of these differences, consults with concerned speech and language professionals so as to maximize the likelihood that the child will understand and be understood.

SUMMARY

Once upon a time in linguistics, the Whorf-Sapir Hypothesis (Whorf, 1956) was quite popular. According to this hypothesis, we are incapable of considering a concept for which we have no words. It is quite clear today that thought (and feeling) often precede language; that a child who is silent by choice or for lack of conventional expressive abilities may yet understand a great deal. In our work in family law, we must remain mindful of how a child's unique language skills bear on the legal process, mindful that those who do talk may not say what they mean and those who do not talk may yet understand far more than we give them credit for.

NOTES

1. Noting specifically that, "Although many evaluators offer lists of details in figure drawings that purport to indicate sexual abuse, the research shows that a large proportion of children who have not been sexually abused display the same indicators in their figure drawings" (Ellis, 2000, p. 286).
2. See also an excellent and concise summary of typical language development at http://www.literacytrust.org.uk/research/earlylanguage.html
3. Bowen (1998) provides an excellent summary of early articulation milestones. She summarizes, stating that "by 18 months a child's speech is normally 25% intelligible, by 24 months a child's speech is normally

50–75% intelliglble [and] by 36 months a child's speech is noramlly 75–100% intelligible."

4. Young children's experience of their caregivers' emotional states can have a profound physiological affect on the child, as well (e.g., Schore, 2003a, b).

5. Wernicke's region is a neurological structure in the left hemisphere of most people's brains to the rear of the superior temporal gyrus and surrounding the auditory cortex (cf., Tanner, 2007).

6. Broca's region or "the speech motor center" is a minute area toward the back of the inferior frontal gyrus in most people's left cerebral hemisphere. See Grodzinsky and Amunts (2006) to learn more.

7. This is not to say that a young child's provocative language or behavior is necessarily benign, but it is only when an adult responds calmly and without presumption or leading questions that the child's real meaning can be discovered.

8. Some researchers propound a "critical period" hypothesis, the idea that the neurological "door" for language acquisition is only open for a fixed period, after which it slams shut and acquisition is impossible (Lenneberg, 1967) and that "[u]nder dramatic circumstances, environmental factors during the first years of life can be quite decisive for the development of language, social, and other intellectual functions" (Uylings, 2006, p. 59).

9. Whitaker and Palmer (2008) provide a format for and a thorough discussion of a comprehensive developmental history. I make a sample, parent-report developmental history form available for adaptation at http://www.healthyparent.com/DEVHX.pdf

10. The Center for Disabilities, Department of Pediatrics, University of South Dakota School of Medicine provides an excellent handbook on FAS at: http://www.usd.edu/cd/publications/fashandbook.pdf

11. "About one in every 2,700 children is born with profound hearing loss and even more suffer lower levels of hearing loss. Ninety percent of deaf children are born to hearing parents where deafness will be completely unexpected. Too often, hearing loss is not diagnosed until children are 12 months old, when they will have missed out on a crucial year of initial language acquisition." Retrieved November 30, 2008, from http://www.literacytrust.org.uk/pubs/stern.htm

12. The World Health Organization provides an excellent resource for understanding deafness at http://www.who.int/topics/deafness/en/

13. "Although in some cases [of autism] speech never develops fully or never develops at all, in other cases, speech may be present but so inflexible and unresponsive to context that it is unusable in normally paced conversation; often, speech is limited to echolalia or confined to narrow topics of expertise in which discourse can proceed without conversational interplay" (Belmonte et al., 2004, p. 9228).

14. The Individuals with Disabilities Education Act (IDEA; Public Law 94-142) defines a learning disability as "a disorder in one or more of the basic psychological processes involved in understanding or in using language, spoken or written, which may manifest itself in an imperfect ability to listen, think, speak, read, write, spell, or to do mathematical calculations. The term includes such conditions as perceptual handicaps, brain injury, minimal brain dysfunction, dyslexia, and developmental aphasia. The term does not include children who have problems that are primarily the result of visual, hearing, or motor disabilities, or mental retardation, emotional disturbance, or of environmental, cultural, or economic disadvantage."

5   Social and Emotional Development

A mature person is one who does not think only in absolutes, who is able to be objective even when deeply stirred emotionally, who has learned that there is both good and bad in all people and all things.

—Eleanor Roosevelt

The day the child realizes that all adults are imperfect, he becomes an adolescent; the day he forgives them, he becomes an adult; the day he forgives himself, he becomes wise.

—Alden Albert Nowlan

If cognitive development lays the foundation for mature thinking, and language development lays the foundation for mature communication, then social and emotional development lay the foundation on which a mature sense of self and healthy relationships can be built and a responsible place in the community can be constructed.

The infant's experiences of *relatedness*—the give-and-take between self and caregiver—is the crucible in which *self* is forged. This earliest definition of "me" emerges gradually as the reciprocal of the experience of care. In this way, identity and relatedness are understood to develop as complementary parts. One's sense of self shapes how relationships are experienced and one's experience of relationships shapes how *self* is defined. This is the back-and-forth dance of socioemotional development.

Imagine the fetus' preverbal experience in utero as one of idealized immediate gratification. The amniotic sac and the umbilicus deliver nutritional and hormonal answers the same moment that biological questions are asked. Hungry? Food arrives. Tired? Sleep happens. For the soon-to-be-born baby, there is no distinction between what is inside and what is outside, between self and other. This is what Freud (1930/1961) referred to as the neonate's "oceanic sense of self."

A simple visual aid effectively illustrates the distinction between self and other: Dip the tip of a finger in a cup of water and withdraw it slowly. A drip will cling to your fingertip. This drip is well defined. That is, you can see its boundaries or edges—what is drip and what is not-drip. Now move your finger enough to let the drip fall back into the cup. Where is it? The singularity or identity of the drip is now entirely lost. This is how we imagine the neonate's sense of self and experience of the world. Socioemotional development throughout the lifespan is about emerging from boundlessness to define the boundaries and edges of oneself and a means of relating to all that is not-self.

Birth is the trauma of separation, setting the stage for the lifelong process of differentiating self from other and negotiating a relationship between the two. Those first neonatal experiences of physical discomfort and the frustration that occurs when need is no longer instantly fulfilled trigger primitive, reflexive signals.[1] Unfulfilled need and discomfort cause crying. Satiation and relief prompt cooing and later, smiles. Fatigue prompts yawning. These preverbal cause–effect exchanges are the earliest antecedents of language development (see chapter 4).

Just as with the shoemaker described in the introduction to this book, everything to follow is about "goodness of fit" (Thomas & Chess, 1977), the unique and subjective match between the child's cues and the caregiver's responses.[2] Implicit in this concept are variables which include the child's physiological abilities (e.g., the requisite visual, vocal, auditory, and motor skills to signal need), the child's temperament (i.e., innate personality tendencies; Thomas & Chess, 1977),[3] and the caregiver's sensitive/responsivity (McElwain & Booth-LaForce, 2006). This chapter introduces the concept of attachment security, the child's learned experience of each caregiver's sensitive/responsivity. Attachment theory is among the most thoroughly researched, widely respected, and empirically validated concepts in developmental psychology, yet it is only recently finding a footing in both clinical practice and forensic process.

CAREGIVER–CHILD ATTACHMENT IN THE FIRST 2 YEARS

John Bowlby, the patriarch of attachment theory, posited that the infant–caregiver relationship develops in four phases toward a "goal-directed partnership." In the *Preattachment Phase* from birth until 6 or 8 weeks of age, the infant is described as indiscriminately sociable, crying, and cooing, and smiling in response to internal cues.[4] These signals attract caregivers (who commonly misinterpret these as smiles of recognition and, less commonly, as cries of rejection) and open a dialogue that is thereafter communicated through proximity, reciprocal emotional exchange, and preverbal sensory recognition (e.g., scent, texture, taste).

In the *Attachment in the Making* phase, between 2 and 6 to 8 months of age, the infant begins to respond differentially to familiar faces. Recognition of the familiar is accompanied by the infant's first expectations and anticipation built upon experience. The caregiver who provided warmth and smiles and satiation in the past is greeted quite differently than the caregiver whose responses have been cold and harsh and rejecting. This development corresponds with neurological growth, which allows the child to better direct his or her gaze and to focus more accurately (Hamer, 1990) and with Erikson's (1968) description of the onset of trust (see Table 5.1).

In the phase of *Clear-cut Attachment*, between 7 and 24 months, the growing toddler begins to differentiate familiar from unfamiliar and uses his or her newfound motor control and verbal skills to approach and avoid accordingly. Stranger anxiety is manifested in upset associated with the approach of unfamiliar persons and separation anxiety is seen in upset associated with the departure of a familiar figure.

From the beginning of this third phase (and arguably from birth) onward, infants accumulate information about each caregiver's sensitive/responsivity. The result is a constantly accreting, preverbal schema—what Bowlby called an *internal working model* (IWM)—that allows the infant to anticipate care based on experience with each specific caregiver and to respond accordingly.

Caregiver sensitive/responsivity remains a critically important factor in understanding parenting effectiveness and children's development throughout the lifespan, even though the specific form this abstract idea takes must vary to suit the child and his or her developmental needs and abilities. Thus, a National Institute of Child Health study of 5-year-olds clarifies that:

> [s]ensitivity of parents to the child's developmental needs during this time involves whether parents can respect and support the child's autonomous actions, provide a supportive presence, and do so in a positive, nonhostile manner, especially when the child is faced with a challenge...[such that] respect for autonomy reflects the degree to which the parent acts in a way that recognizes and respects the child's individuality, motives, and perspectives..., [and] a parent scoring high on supportive presence expresses positive regard and emotional support to the child. (2008a, p. 898)

Bowlby's third phase in the development of attachment ends by about a child's second birthday, coincident with the development of the Piagetian skill known as *object permanence* (discussed in chapter 3). The interdependence of cognitive, linguistic, and socioemotional developments once again highlights that it is the development of the child—not the development of independent subsystems—that is at issue: "Both Bowlby and Ainsworth proposed that the behaviors through which attachment develops are comparable to Piaget's initial schemata—indeed most of them are the same—and that they develop through processes homologous to those which Piaget described for cognitive development" (Ainsworth, 1969, p. 42; internal references excised).

The fourth of these phases, the *Formation of a Reciprocal Relationship*, begins by 2 years of age. In this phase, the toddler begins to rely upon an internalized sense of a caregiver's availability as emotional fuel, which allows him or her to move away from the caregiver and explore the world.

Table 5.1

ERIC ERIKSON'S (1950, 1959, 1968) STAGES OF PSYCHOSOCIAL DEVELOPMENT

APPROXIMATE	ESSENTIAL	ACHIEVEMENT UPON RESOLUTION
Birth through 18 months	Trust versus mistrust	Can I rely on caregivers to fulfill my needs? Achieves hope and freedom to look beyond self.
18 months through 3 years	Autonomy versus shame and doubt	Is it safe to be separate from my caregivers? Achieves pride and confidence.
3 through 5 years	Initiative versus guilt	How will the consequences of my actions affect me? Achieves self-control and conscience.
6 years through teens	Industry versus inferiority	Am I good at what I do? Achieves competence and confidence.
Teens through 20s	Identity versus role confusion	Am I accepted by my peer group? Achieves new definition of self especially in context of intimate relationships.
20s through 40s	Intimacy versus isolation	Can I establish intimate bonds even at the cost of losing others? Achieves new definition of self and capacity to tolerate loss.
40s through 60s	Generativity versus stagnation	Can I give back to others and is my contribution valued/valuable? Achieves sense of continuity into next generations.
60s and beyond	Ego integrity versus despair	Has my life been worthwhile? Achieves fulfillment.

ATTACHMENT SECURITY

A child's acquired expectations about a specific caregiver's sensitive/responsivity is referred to as the quality of that child's *attachment security*. Born of Bowlby's work (1958, 1969, 1973), attachment theory moved the discussion of socioemotional development away from Freud's earlier and previously dominant drive-related theory toward an evolutionary/biological understanding of development in the interest of survival.

Mary Ainsworth's work to operationalize attachment theory in the laboratory-based *Strange Situation Paradigm* (Ainsworth & Bell, 1970; Ainsworth, Bell, & Stayton, 1971) first allowed reliable measurement of attachment security and launched thousands of subsequent studies, each concerned with understanding the nature and implications of attachment throughout the lifespan (e.g., Cassidy & Shaver, 1999; Nelson & Bennett, 2008).

The Strange Situation Paradigm is a laboratory-based means of assessing the quality of a toddler's attachment security with an accompanying caregiver. In this time- and resource-intensive research measure, the child is observed and videorecorded through the course of seven 3-minute episodes, variously including the accompanying caregiver and a stranger. The child's ability to use the caregiver as a *secure base* from which to explore and take comfort when stressed yields a measure of security.[5]

To think about attachment security and associated behaviors, it is useful to imagine that people require emotional fuel in very much the same way that cars require gasoline. As we grow, our physical and social worlds expand and we develop more and more refueling options. As an adult, you probably get refueled through some combination of work and hobbies and play, friends and family and neighbors, home and recreation (see chapter 17 about emotional refueling, burn-out and the family law professional). Understanding how and where and when adults find their "emotional fuel" can be an important part of any evaluation, keeping in mind the many and varied unhealthy and destructive ways in which many people find their emotional fuel—some, even from their children (e.g., MacFie, Houts, Pressel, & Cox, 2008).[6]

Infants and toddlers have relatively smaller emotional gas tanks, get relatively less efficient mileage, and have relatively fewer alternative sources of emotional fuel. In the conventional intact family, a young child's options are typically limited to Mom and Dad.

In the same way that you may have learned through experience which gas stations offer the best price and service and which ones are open the most convenient hours, children acquire comparable information about their caregivers. Experience teaches them whether Mom (or Dad or sister or nanny...) will respond to their verbal and behavioral signals, whether needs will be fulfilled, discomfort relieved, and emotions calmed. This experience creates expectations specific to each relationship such that a child can be described as more or less securely attached.

Secure Attachment

Secure attachment is evident in a child whose experience has taught him or her to anticipate that a specific caregiver will be sensitive and responsive to his or her needs. Securely attached children typically represent approximately 60% of healthy, middle-class, American toddlers.[7]

The secure child behaves as if he is confident that the caregiver is available to refill his emotional gas tank. He orients to the caregiver for reassurance even while conducting the necessary and natural business of childhood: exploring and discovering and experiencing the surrounding world. When separated, this toddler obviously misses the caregiver, but is quickly developing the psychological resources to negotiate this stress relatively well (improving mileage), all other things being equal.[8] The securely attached child will greet the caregiver warmly upon reunion, may seek contact as if to top off his gas tank, and then resumes healthy play: "Secure attachment and adaptive functioning are promoted by a caregiver who is emotionally available and appropriately responsive to her child's attachment behavior, as well as capable of regulating both his or her positive and negative emotions" (Sable, 2008, p. 22).

In interview,[9] parents of securely attached children are able to discuss their own positive and negative childhood experiences of neediness and care in a coherent and collaborative manner. These caregivers are referred to as *autonomous*.

Insecure Attachment

An *insecure attachment* is evident in a child who has learned that the caregiver will be relatively insensitive, unresponsive, and unavailable when needs arise. This child's emotional gas tank is seldom full, forcing him either to refuel often if inefficiently or to remain aloof and distant, running on empty.

Uncertain that his needs will be met, the insecurely attached child is relatively less successful in exploring the environment, engaging with others, and learning to regulate his or her own physical and emotional experiences (Egeland & Erickson, 1999). Separation from the caregiver can be disabling and his or her return can be cause for either clinging upset or angry rejection. "The experience of early attachment insecurity is not indicative of psychopathology but [rather, a] risk for psychopathology" (Zeanah, 1996, p. 50).

Toddlers can appear insecure in one of (at least) two ways:

Insecure/resistant children compose between 10 and 20% of research samples. They commonly appear to be angry and/or ambivalent toward the caregiver, reaching for and then rejecting comfort. Their play and exploration may be interrupted by a preoccupation with the caregiver as if constantly needing to know that the caregiver is present. Parents of these children are commonly angry, passive, and/or fearful when discussing their own early attachment experiences.

Insecure/avoidant children typically make up another 10–20% of research samples. These children behave as if to anticipate that the caregiver will be rejecting or dismissing and react by remaining distant and aloof. These children may not cry at separation, and turn away from the caregiver at reunion. In interview, parents of these children tend to overvalue their own childhood experiences of attachment and to idealize their childhood caregivers. When queried, these adults are unable to substantiate this idealized picture and may struggle to recall their own childhood experiences of neediness, perhaps because the reality of their caregiver's unavailability is inconsistent with their idealized character.

Disorganized Attachment

Disorganized attachment (Main & Solomon, 1986) describes an extreme disturbance of the reciprocity between child and caregiver. Representing between 5 and 15% of many research samples, these children commonly experience their caregivers as frightening, sometimes unavailable, cold, and harsh and, at other times, as overwhelming and consuming. This child can appear fearful, dissociative, and disorganized, and uncertain and anxious to the point of decompensation when stress arises in the company of this caregiver.

Overextending the emotional fuel analogy, disorganized attachment might be comparable to your experience at a gas station where the attendant sometimes greets you eagerly, pours you a complimentary cup of coffee, changes your oil, and refuses your payment, but other times ignores you, puts water in your tank, and scratches your vehicle in the process. Of course you'd take your business elsewhere. By analogy, the toddler who experiences a caregiver in the same unpredictable, labile manner may have no such alternatives.

Children who evidence disorganized attachment typically have caregivers who themselves report unresolved childhood abuses, neglect, and/or traumatic losses. In interview these adults tend to be scattered, dissociative, and even delusional about their early caregiving experiences.

Stability and Predictive Validity of Attachment Security

A vast cross-cultural literature converges on the idea that the quality of attachment security in the second year of life is strongly related to a wide variety of social, emotional, academic, occupational, and even physical health measures well into adulthood, *all other things being equal* (Shorey & Snyder, 2006; Thompson, 2000; Tarabulsy et al., 2008).

The numbers are very impressive: Greater than 80% of children evidencing secure attachments between 12 and 18 months of age continue to look secure in kindergarten (Wartner, Grossman, Fremmer-Bombik, & Suess, 1994; Weinfield, Whaley, & Egeland, 2004) and as many as 70% remain unchanged at 20 years of age (George, Kaplan, & Main, 1996). Attachment security assessed as young as 1 year of age reliably predicts later cognitive skills (Bretheringon, 1985), social confidence (Laible, Gustavo, & Raffaelli, 2000), leadership skills (Deason & Randolph, 1998), peer relationships (Barnett, Butler, & Vondra, 1999; Schneider, Atkinson, & Tardif, 2001), anxiety (Thompson, 2000), larger family dynamics (Cook, 2000), and marital and sexual satisfaction (Butzer & Campbell, 2008).

The magnitude of these stability coefficients declines, however, as the socioeconomic status of the families declines (Weinfield, Sroufe, & Egeland, 2000), such that the quality of attachment security is least stable for those children who experience the greatest number and intensity of life stressors. In short, real-life stressors—from the birth of a new sibling (Teti, Sakin, Kucera, Corns, & Eiden, 1996) to the onset or intensification of marital conflict (Cummings & Davies, 1994; Laurent, Kim, & Capaldi, 2008; Schermerhorn & Cummings, 2008), divorce

(Kelly, 1988; Lewis, Feiring, & Rosenthal, 2000), death, abuse, and chronic illness (Solomon & George, 1999)—each has been associated with discontinuity of attachment security. Thompson (2002, p. 271) summarizes succinctly:

> [A] secure attachment in infancy sets the stage for subsequent psychosocial achievements if the sensitive, supportive care initially contributing to attachment security is maintained (conversely, insensitive parenting contributes to insecure attachment, and to less optimal later functioning if it also endures over time). If, however, the harmony of the secure parent-child relationship changes and their mutually cooperative orientation is disrupted or lost, there may be no apparent sequelae of the initially secure attachment.

In fact, it makes sense that attachment security can be compromised over time under conditions that would reasonably be expected to cause caregivers to become less sensitive and responsive. On the flip side of - that coin, it makes sense to imagine that insecure attachments can become more secure when caregivers become more sensitive and responsive.

This is precisely the case. Broberg demonstrates that therapeutic interventions with parents intended to improve the sensitivity of caregiving can be "effective in enhancing infant attachment security" (2000, p. 41). Marvin and colleagues (among others; e.g., Bakersman-Kranenberg, Breddels-van Baardewijk, Juffer, Velderman, & van IJzendoorn, 2008; cf., Stolk et al., 2008) have pioneered a program which uses video feedback to improve caregiver sensitive/responsivity and thereby benefit their children's attachment security (Marvin et al., 2002).

Attachment Security Among Highly Conflicted and Court-Involved Families

In theory, there's every reason to expect that children whose parents are intractably conflicted regardless of marital status (Moné & Biringen, 2006), or whose worlds are unpredictable, neglectful, and abusive, are at high risk of developing insecure or disorganized attachments on the one hand (Tarabulsy et al., 2008) or an attachment disorder on the other (Zeanah, 1996).

We won't know how the varieties (or degrees) of attachment security are distributed within the population of highly conflicted and court-involved families unless and until a collection of empirical, ethical, and practical hurdles are overcome, not the least of which is the tremendous practical difficulty associated with recruiting and collecting data from highly contentious, court-involved parties whose every word is subject to discovery, deposition, and cross-examination (Garber, 2009). In fact, although the potential value of attachment measurement tools in child-centered forensic matters has been declared loudly (e.g., Condie, 2003; Kelly & Ward, 2002; Lamb & Kelly, 2001; Riggs, 2003), the extant research suggests that family law professionals generally disregard the quality of parent-child attachment in favor of a focus on the extent of the inter-parental conflict when making custody arguments (Hinds & Bradshaw, 2005).

Landmarks of Continuing Socioemotional Development: Security and Self-Regulation Beyond Age 3

One's experience of emotional security in infancy is shaped and reshaped constantly throughout life, shifting in some yet-to-be-elucidated way from a dyad-specific attribute to become a quality intrinsic to the individual and then, in adulthood, it is reinvested (or reinvented?) in intimate relationships and parenthood. With these transitions, the family law professional's interest is likely to shift from evaluating the quality of the child's particular relationship with one or more caregivers to the larger question of evaluating the child's intrinsic social and emotional maturity.

Socioemotional development is the simultaneous and interactive process of defining self and relatedness along the developmental path toward adulthood. If early attachment experiences help to define the first steps of emerging from the larger pool of undifferentiated self, then the present discussion seeks to define observable variables that can help to gauge a child's socioemotional maturity, a subject that is itself discussed in detail in the context of defining the "mature minor" concept in chapter 14.

Let's switch metaphors: Imagine that the caregiver's primary responsibility is to serve as the child's thermostat, an external means of regulating the often overwhelming experience of the world (Solomon & Biringen, 2001). A sensitive and responsive caregiver is a successful thermostat. He or she reads the child's needs accurately and responds adequately to help the child to reestablish comfort.[10] The child internalizes this success as an association between the particular caregiver and renewed comfort, thus motivating behaviors seen in the Strange Situation Paradigm as attachment security. In effect, the child learns to associate and thereby anticipate a connection between that specific caregiver's presence and stress relief.

Over time, the child is simultaneously learning to monitor and adjust his or her own experience of the world—to internalize the thermostat—toward the goal of self-regulation (e.g., Bronson, 2001; Jahromi & Stifter, 2008; Kopp, 1982, 1991; Post, Boyer, & Brett, 2006; Schore & Schore, 2008). Thus, "between early and middle childhood, adult regulation of children's emotions and emotional expression transforms into adult-child coregulation and ultimately to children's self-regulation" (McHale, Dariotis, & Kauh, 2003, p. 250).

The pace and success of this process is associated with many factors, including the child's physical health and temperament, the caregiver's relative success as a sensitive and responsive thermostat, and the biobehavioral synchrony (Feldman, 2007) between the two. In general, a child who enjoys at least one secure attachment relationship will be more successful than a child who does not in establishing self-regulation and will do so earlier. At the extreme, "children with a disorganized attachment…have not learned effective coping skills to use to soothe and control their feelings and behavior in frightening situations, which leads to problems in emotional and behavioral self-regulation" (Pearce & Pezzot-Pearce, 2007, p. 54).

It is important to be clear that the quality of a child's attachment does not determine the development of self-regulation. Instead, we must look at attachment and self-regulation as they emerge in tandem, both responding to the inter- and intrapersonal developments of the caregiving experience.

Contrasting Concepts: Social Skills Versus Socioemotional Maturity

Consider the case of *reactive attachment disorder* (RAD; e.g., Zeanah, 1996; Zeanah & Smyke, 2008; Zilberstein, 2006).[11] RAD is a condition associated with the extremes of early neglect sometimes experienced in (especially Third World) orphanages and foster care. RAD presents as a constellation of associated linguistic, cognitive, and behavioral difficulties in childhood, but it is most obviously identified as one or the other of two distinct socioemotional profiles. The "inhibited" child with RAD is angry, avoidant, and withdrawn. The "disinhibited" child with RAD is gregarious, engaging, and indiscriminately affectionate.

Which child is socially and emotionally more mature?

Which child is psychologically healthier?

It's tempting to think of a withdrawn and isolating child as socially delayed and the outgoing and engaging child as socially precocious, when in fact both kids are terribly off-course. Although the more outgoing child will be easier to talk to and more likable, neither is socially and emotionally mature. Both have failed to establish the core sense of self associated with early attachment security and the rudiments of reciprocity necessary for developing healthy relationships. Both have a very limited capacity for self-regulation and both have developed a short-term and maladaptive strategy for coping with relationships. The inhibited RAD child cowers in fear and lashes out in rage, certain that nurturance will never be forthcoming. The disinhibited RAD child fawns on anyone at any time, eager to add any little drop of fuel to an empty emotional gas tank.

The extremes associated with RAD—particularly the disinhibited child's presentation—help to put a discussion about social and emotional development in context. We must never mistake a child's social skills for his or her social and emotional maturity (Semrud-Clikeman, 2007). Social skills are the clothes that we wear when we encounter others. They are the acquired or explicitly taught strategies that lubricate social interaction even if they do little to shape how an individual thinks of him- or herself and a relationship partner.

Consider the two cases of a false-positive and a false-negative error:

■ In interview, you find Sam to be a thoroughly engaging, respectful, and polite 10-year-old. He looks you in the eye, shakes your hand, addresses you by your title, and eagerly complies with all of your requests. This impressive display of etiquette may be consistent with genuine maturity, but is not enough. Sam is just as likely to be an adultified child whose family circumstances have taught him that interacting with grown-ups in a peer-like manner earns acceptance and that critical fuel known as affection and approval. In fact, Sam's apparent social skills may be transitory, a performance culminating an intrusive and controlling parent's direct instruction ("Here's what you're going to say to the nice man, Sammy."). This is the risk of a false-positive conclusion: To mistake the adultified and/or coached child for one who is socially and emotionally mature.

■ By contrast, consider Bruno: At 14 years old, Bruno is unkempt, seldom meets your gaze, grunts in response to your questions, and otherwise barely acknowledges you. This type of presentation will quickly mislead many to conclude immaturity, when, in fact, teenagers' anxiety and hostility in interview as part of a family law process are common to the point of being normative and expectable. These children are being torn apart. They are interviewed and observed and assessed and examined endlessly. They blame themselves for the family crisis and they are entirely uncertain about their future. To mistake this hostility and fear for immaturity is to risk a false-negative outcome. Bruno may be quite mature, but those developmental successes are masked by anger and fear and may be compromised by regression (see chapter 6).

A conclusion about social and emotional development based on social skills is as valid and meaningful as a conclusion about maturity based solely on a child's height or a conclusion about a child's intelligence based solely on report card grades. In each case the correlation can be illusory and misleading, a potential source of misinformation and harmful outcomes.

SOCIOEMOTIONAL DEVELOPMENT: AGES 3 THROUGH 13

Much as the quality of a child's early attachment experience has a profound and lasting impact on social and emotional development, attachment theory does not easily lend itself to clinical or forensic application beyond age 3 (Garber, 2009).[12] Social and emotional maturity can be observed, however, in the developmentally appropriate tasks of the years to follow. In the period culminating in adolescence, these are the tasks of self-regulation.

The seeds of self-regulatory skills are planted in the soil of early attachment security and are thereafter facilitated (or hindered) by interpersonal experience, linguistic development, and explicit training, beginning as young as 18 to 30 months (Berk, Mann, & Ogan, 2006; Niles, Reynolds, & Nagasawa, 2006). Subsequent development moves forward such that, "[the] well-regulated children can wait for a turn, resist the temptation to grab a desired object from another child, clean up after a play period with little or no adult prompting, willingly help another child or adult with a task, and persist at a challenging activity. Such children also actively try to control negative emotion, often by talking to themselves ('I'll get a chance soon') or changing their goals (when one activity isn't possible, turning to another)" (Berk, Mann, & Ogan, 2006, p. 74).

The developing capacity for self-regulation has been related to peer popularity (Eisenberg, Fabes, Guthrie, & Reiser, 2000), risk of physical illness (Kligler & Lee, 2004), and quality of academic achievement. As Dickinson and Neuman (2006, p. 16) observe:

> The capacity for self-regulation is increasingly coming to be seen as essential to social development and the ability to learn in school. Preschoolers with effective regulatory skills are better able to form positive relations with peers and teachers...evidence greater social competence in kindergarten...[and]greater behavioral self-regulation skills and achievement.

Self-regulation is seen to have particular meaning for coping under stress, including and especially the stresses associated with divorce:

> Children who are better able to self-regulate may be more likely to delay immediate maladaptive responses to stress, such as acting out behaviorally, and may use active coping strategies more adaptively to change stressful situations. They may be better at sustaining attention and persisting in focusing on problem-solving tasks. They may also be more flexible and adaptable in employing active coping strategies to meet the demands of the situation. (Lengua & Sandler, 1996)

Four particular skills mark a child's social and emotional development through this period. These are: (a) emotional balance—the capacity to recover from upset; (b) impulse control—the capacity to tolerate frustration and delay gratification; (c) empathy—the capacity for emotional perspective-taking; and (d) personal responsibility—the capacity to acknowledge culpability.

Emotional Balance

Recall that the Strange Situation Paradigm (Ainsworth & Wittig, 1969) records a child's behavior across a series of seven, 3-minute episodes, during which the caregiver is present, a stranger enters the room, the caregiver departs, the stranger departs, and then the caregiver returns. Perhaps most telling among the child's many more-or-less subtle, more-or-less distressed behaviors during this process is his or her ability to use the caregiver upon his or her return to calm and resume adaptive play.

This skill carries forward such that the socially and emotionally mature child is relatively less likely to become upset, relatively better able to recover when upset occurs, and gradually better able to achieve these goals independently. This final characteristic—a decreased reliance on caregivers to maintain emotional balance and recover from upset—heralds the development of autonomy and filial maturity, milestones of maturation discussed below.

Emotional balance is composed of unknown proportions of early attachment security, temperamental predisposition, physical health factors, adult modeling, and environmental stability. Thus, if one were to write a recipe for creating an emotionally balanced 8-year-old, for example, it might call for equal parts secure attachment experiences with both of two parents (each of whom is him- or herself emotionally balanced), an easy temperament (Thomas & Chess, 1977), ordinary physical health, and the good fortune to have lived 8 years without exposure to trauma, abuse, neglect, serious loss, or relocation. This idealized child has been variously referred to as "invulnerable" (Anthony & Cohler, 1987; Chowdhury & Chowdhury, 1993), "hardy" (Maddi, 2002), and "resilient" (Garmezy, 1985; Masten, 1999).

Acknowledging that this idealized 8-year-old will never enter any of our offices (if, indeed, he exists at all), it is safe to say that the trauma, chaos, conflict, loss, and abuses associated with the children we do meet put them at relatively high risk of delayed or disturbed social and emotional development.

Impulse Control

Impulse control is at the root of reciprocity and turn-taking, critical elements of healthy relationships. It is the mature skill that allows an individual to take a deep breath, count to three, and consider alternatives and their associated consequences before reacting to a (real or imagined) stimulus. Delayed or disturbed impulse control is associated with antisocial behavior, aggressive acting out, and self-destructive choices.

The roots of the ability to control impulses are evident as young as 18 months of age (Putnum, Spritz, & Stifter, 2002) and continue to grow through childhood (e.g., Xue & Yisheng, 2007). This emerging skill is facilitated by developing expressive language skills (Berk, Mann, & Ogan, 2006) and is subject to peer pressure (Yang & Yu, 2002). The capacity to delay gratification has been referred to as "the key component and skill of children's self-control, the component of socialization and emotional adjustment, and a basic and positive variable of personality" (Yang & Yu, 2002, p. 712).

Schore (1994, 2003a, 2003b) explicitly connects impulsivity (especially the ability to regulate affect and control self-destructive behaviors) in childhood with the quality of early attachment relationships. He proposes that insecurely attached children lack the requisite experiences with which to fully develop the neurological structures for behavioral inhibition, which in turn creates long-term vulnerability to impulsivity, with all its associated social, behavioral, psychiatric, academic, and legal vulnerabilities.

In the context of a secure attachment history and positive self-esteem, impulse control and its related developmental skills contribute to an individual's capacity for selflessness and altruism, qualities that are highly valued in our society. The same skills, however, in a context of depression, feelings of worthlessness, and/or a history of insecure attachment, can contribute to self-deprecation and participation in enabling and abusive relationships.

Empathy

If perspective-taking is the abstract, cognitive ability to see the world from another point of view, empathy is the same skill as applied to understanding another person's thoughts and feelings. Both skills require the ability to decentrate, that is, to see beyond the egocentrism that Piaget attributes to the sensorimotor child. Perspective-taking is often illustrated by reference to Piaget's famous "three mountains" task (Piaget & Inhelder, 1967)[13] and is evident by about 7 years of age (cf., Borke, 1975, with regard to younger children).

Empathy is presumably a more developmentally demanding skill, in that it requires more than imagined physical perspective on a concrete object or event (e.g., Eisenberg & Strayer, 1990). In addition to decentration, empathy requires that a child establish what psychologists refer to as a *theory of mind* (Premack & Woodruff, 1978; Wellman, 1990), the essential understanding that others have an internal mental experience distinct from one's own.

Although theory of mind may be evident as young as 4 years of age for some children, it may never develop for others, thereby delaying or distorting the capacity for mature empathy. Some individuals with autism[14] (Baron-Cohen, Leslie, & Frith, 1985; Hughes, 2008), schizophrenia (Andreasen, Calage, & O'Leary, 2008), or early and extreme deprivation such as that associated with RAD (Colvert et al., 2008), may lack a conception of others as having unique and separate mental experience.

Personal Responsibility

An individual's capacity to take responsibility for his or her own actions can be understood as it develops along two closely related variables. Moral reasoning grows from the infant's concrete, me-here-now perspecive toward an abstract sense of serving the greater good (McGrath & Brown, 2008). This development is most clearly delineated by Kohlberg (2008; see Table 5.2), noting the ongoing controversies, confirmations, and conflicts associated with this theory (e.g., Baird, 2008; Donleavy, 2008; Murphy & Gilligan, 1980).

Personal responsibility is also related to the child's developing ability to distinguish truths from lies. Truth-telling and lying[15] develop only as children become able to anticipate consequences, initially motivated by a wish to avoid subjectively aversive personal outcomes (Ruck, 1996). Thus, many more 7-year-olds than their 3-year-old peers lie, probably simply because younger children are less likely to think ahead to anticipate the associated negative consequences (Talwar & Lee, 2002).

Table 5.2

KOHLBERG'S (2008) STAGES OF MORAL REASONING

Level 1. Preconventional Morality

Stage 1: Obedience and Punishment (A behavior is wrong if it is punished.)

Stage 2: Individualism and Exchange (A behavior is right if it suits one's needs.)

Level 2. Conventional Morality

Stage 3: Interpersonal Relationships (A behavior is right if it conforms to immediate expectations, e.g., earns "good boy" type of praise.)

Stage 4: Maintaining Social Order (A behavior is right if it conforms to rigid rules.)

Level 3. Postconventional Morality

Stage 5: Social Contract and Individual Rights (A behavior is right if it conforms to rules which must themselves be adaptable to people's needs.)

Stage 6: Universal Principles (A behavior is right if it conforms to an individual's larger moral sense regardless of established rules and the behavior of others.)

In the 7- to 11-year-old range, the child begins to consider the beneficiary of the lie as relevant to the process. Thus, 7-year-olds will more readily lie to serve their own needs, whereas 11-year-olds more readily acknowledge that lying can be acceptable if it serves the larger group (Fu & Wang, 2005). This observation has intriguing applications to family law as, for example, when a child considers lying to one parent about (or on behalf of) the other.

In adolescence, lying serves the development of autonomy (Finkenauer, Engles, & Meeus, 2002) and becomes a justifiable choice to the extent that it supports a larger moral belief. Given that teens' moral beliefs diverge from those of their families over time, it is not surprising to find that 15- to 17-year-olds lie to their friends and parents more than do their 12- to 14-year-old peers (Perkins & Turiel, 2007).

Lying and the Self-Serving Bias

Self-serving bias is the normative and expectable tendency in all people to credit themselves with success and blame others for failure (Shepperd, Malone, & Sweeny, 2008) so as "to maintain and protect positive self-views" (Krusemark, Campbell, & Clementz, 2008, p. 511) and/or to "manage the impressions they make on others" (Ross, Smith, Spiel-macher, & Recchia, 2004, p. 61). Children in the preschool/kindergarten age range are prone to simply deny their own negative behaviors, preferring to blame others, including invisible friends. By 9–10 years of age, children may omit any reference to their own negative behaviors in spontaneous dialogue but, when queried, are more likely than their younger peers to take responsibility, albeit with elaborate rationalizations (frequently amounting to "but he did it first!"). Wilson and colleagues (2004, p. 39), summarizing with regard to children's ability to acknowledge responsibility for sibling conflict, report that "children were systematically biased in favor of their own innocence, and older siblings were more self-serving in their use of justifications than their younger siblings. The number and complexity of justifications increased with siblings' age, whereas denials were more frequently relied upon by younger siblings."

The likelihood of denial of one's own culpability increases with perceived threat (Roese & Olson, 2007), in the same manner and for the same reason that lying increases. To the extent that children with secure attachment experiences are less likely to feel threatened and are better able to cope when threat occurs, securely attached children are more likely to acknowledge their own behaviors and to be able to do so at a younger age.

Two studies bear on the question of how to minimize children's self-serving bias in interview:

- Johnston and Lee (2005) examined 5- to 7- and 8- to 11-year-old boys' attribution of blame for negative events. When questions about the responsibility for these events were phrased as if they concerned a hypothetical other child rather than the interviewee himself, their attributions were much more accurate.
- Lyon and Dorado (2008) studied 5- to 7-year-old children with a history of mistreatment. In this study, children who made an explicit promise to tell the truth and who were reassured that truth-telling would not yield harm were more likely to tell the truth than either those who only promised/reassured or those who did neither.

SOCIAL AND EMOTIONAL MATURITY FROM ADOLESCENCE INTO ADULTHOOD

The social and emotional goal of adolescence is the establishment of autonomy—an understanding and acceptance of self as an individual willing and able to function independent of parents (Arnett, 2000; Beyers & Goossens, 2008; Karlsson, Arman, & Wikblad, 2008; Steinberg & Silverberg, 1986).[16] In one dramatic illustration, Supreme Court Justice Stevens asserted the relevant standard that "by definition,...a woman intellectually and emotionally capable of making important decisions without parental assistance also should be capable of ignoring any parental disapproval."[17]

Unfortunately for all involved, the teen's movement away from family—a process referred to as separation-individuation—is characteristically ambivalent and conflicted. This conflict, acted out in the midst of puberty, the movement toward abstract thinking and higher order social/emotional/moral development, the transition into high school, the independence associated with obtaining a driver's license, and a host of other convergent developmental events, expectably stresses the entire family. This period is as much a trap for caregivers who can't tolerate conflict and respond by giving in as it is for those who are threatened by conflict and who respond in kind (Seiffe-Krenke, 2006). The former group—the acquiescors—overindulge their kids so as to minimize upset and, in so doing, fail to teach frustration tolerance even as they incite even greater rage and anxiety, potentially opening the door for drug and alcohol experimentation, sexual acting out, gang membership, and school failure (Dishion, Poulin, & Medici-Skaggs, 2000; National Institute of Child Health, 2008a). Ironically, caregivers who respond at the other extreme—the overprotectors—may be opening the same doors. When adolescent mood swings and rage elicit adult emotion, the child can feel (and may actually become) rejected and unwelcome.

The co-occurrence of teenage rebellion and family conflict is very common and prompts expectable but impossible chicken/egg questions.[18] Is the parent's separation and divorce, or the onset of adult domestic violence, or the sudden occurrence of child abuse or neglect a *response to* the teenager's moodiness and acting out, or, vice versa, is the teenager's moodiness and acting out at least partially the *result of* the family conflict? In the vast majority of cases, both dynamics are simultaneously in force and the search for a first cause and associated blame is worse than pointless; it can be destructive. Both dynamics must be tackled simultaneously and in a coordinated manner if the child is to adequately negotiate this process. When these matters come before the courts, this means that family law and mental health professionals must work hand-in-hand if the child's needs are to be met.

The teenager's experience of a healthy father figure appears to facilitate the movement toward autonomy (Galambos, Magill-Evans, & Darrah, 2008): "fathers' relationships with children may be particularly important in supporting children's self-reliance as they transition to the world outside the family" (National Institute of Child Health, 2008a, p. 903). This affect is quickly compromised, however, when mothers expose their children to negatives about their dads (i.e., alienation; Kenyon & Koerner, 2008).

In Search of "Maturity"

Because psychology tends to view development as a continuous, step-wise progression, neither research nor theory has emphasized the idea of "maturity" as an end state in and of itself. In one early instance, Strang (1953, p. 753) operationalized the concept of matuirty as seven variables:

1. Ability to feel with others, to see things from their point of view, and to be creative and happy rather than antagonistic or indifferent in one's relations with others
2. Objectivity toward one's self, "ability to recognize and accept one's own emotions as natural," to project hypotheses about one's behavior, submit them to test, and, according to the results, further develop or discard them
3. Ability to select suitable, worthwhile, long-term goals and to organize one's thinking and acting around these goals
4. Ability to make adjustments to situations; a certain amount of "role flexibility" is necessary to bring one's concepts into line with reality
5. Ability to meet unexpected stresses and disappointments without experiencing emotional or physical collapse and without abandoning established lines of interest and activity
6. Ability to give as well as to receive affection

7. Ability "to form opinions based on sound reasoning and to stand up for them, without abandoning willingness to accept such compromises as do not violate fundamental convictions"

In contemporary practice, definitions of maturity have focused on autonomy, as in the capacity for "independent decision making, less easily influenced by the advice or urgings of others, and more able to function responsibly in the absence of adult supervision" (Steinberg & Cauffman, 1996, p. 253). Research seeking to understand peer conformity as it relates to gang membership, for example, provides age-specific landmarks with which to observe this process. In one typical study, as many as 87% of 12-year-olds and 55% of 14-year-olds but only 10% of 17-year-olds behave in a manner intended to conform to that of peers (Sullivan, McCullough, & Stager, 1971). The precipitous decline in conformist behavior at 17 years of age seems to suggest an important shift of social and emotional maturity.

This conclusion is supported by studies of teenagers' roles in criminal matters. Grisso and colleagues (2003, p. 356), for instance, observe that "juveniles aged 15 and younger are significantly more likely than older adolescents and young adults to be impaired in ways that compromise their ability to serve as competent defendants in a criminal proceeding...the competence-relevant capacities of 16- and 17-year-olds as a group do not differ significantly from those of young adults. These patterns of age differences are robust across groups defined by gender, ethnicity, and SES [socioeconomic status]."

The autonomy of late adolescence becomes the foundation of continuing socioemotional development in the period of emerging adulthood (Asberg, Bowers, Renk, & McKinney, 2008) and beyond. The next decade, for example, marks the individual's movement toward filial maturity (Birditt, Fingerman, Lefkowitz, & Dush, 2008; Blenkner, 1965), a consolidation of identity that allows the child to understand his or her parents objectively (that is, in a less idealized manner), as separate, fallible people. It is only with the achievement of this socioemotional milestone that children are genuinely prepared to interact with their parents as peers.

SUMMARY

Psychology has its own chicken/egg debate: Which comes first, cognition or emotion? Although the controversy rages on, I contend that socioemotional development precedes all else. It is only in the fertile soil of healthy attachment relationships that language and thought can really grow. The child's experience negotiating these relationships builds his sense of self toward healthy autonomy and opens the door to healthy intimate relationships. With this knowledge it is all that much more humbling to consider the power wielded by the family court system to make or break these early relationships and thereby to shape the course of all that may follow.

NOTES

1. Bonding refers to the mother–child pairing that occurs at birth in some species in the context of the tremendous hormonal burst that accompanies birth (Klaus & Kennell, 1976). Imprinting is a naturally occurring example of bonding that occurs among geese, for example, as illustrated in Lorenz's studies (1937) and the very entertaining movie, *Fly Away Home* (1996, Columbia Pictures). Although courts often order a "bonding assessment" in an effort to garner an expert opinion about the quality of relationship between a child and an adult when, for example, termination of parental rights is at issue, the phrase is most usefully understood to refer to the quality of attachment within the dyad (Barone, Weitz, & Witt, 2005).

2. Family law professionals reasonably read "goodness of fit" as "best interests of the child" (BIC), although this equation has not been formally propounded either in the developmental literature or in the law. The BIC, of course, is the near universal standard for decisions that bear on children's well-being (Bartlett, 2002; van Kreiken, 2005), a standard that I once described as, "…second only to the concept of 'god' as a popularly endorsed beneficence without clear definition, proof of existence or reliable measure. Like the idea of 'god,' the BIC is often invoked in support of self-serving interests in such a way that conflicts are more often exacerbated than quelled" (Garber, 2009).

3. Thomas and Chess (1977) identified three temperament types. Infants who were "easy" were generally positive and adaptable. Those who were "difficult" were relatively fussy, irritable, and tearful. The remaining group were "slow to warm" or cautious, tentative, and only adapted to change gradually. These temperament types have been found to be relatively stable throughout life and common across cultures (Thomas, Chess, Birch, Hertzig, & Korn, 1963), and are questionably related to the

development of later psychopathology (Salekin & Avereet, 2008), perhaps in combination with socioeconomic stresses (Flouri, 2008).

4. Barry Brazelton (Brazelton & Cramer, 1991) identifies the earlier period from birth through one to two weeks post-partum as necessary for the establishment of homeostasis. This refers to the newborn's earliest efforts to tolerate and balance the unfamiliar onslaught of sensation, including light and sound, movement, taste and texture. Brazelton posits that success at this task is a necessary antecedent of the development of attachment. Brazelton discusses subsequent phases in different terms, referring to Prolonging of Attention (2-8 weeks), Testing Limits (3-4 months) and Emergence of Autonomy (4-5 months). About this latter, Brazelton and Cramer write descriptively: "A most common sign of this development can be seen in normal infants at 4-5 months during a feeding, when they stop to look around and attend to their environment. When a mother can allow this and even foster it, she is encouraging her infant's burgeoning autonomy" (p. 117).

5. Although the majority of attachment research refers to discrete categories of attachment security, more recent research suggests that security is a continuous variable that should be discussed as a matter of degree, not type (Fraley & Spieker, 2003). I prefer this continuous explanation, particularly as it helps us to understand how intervening events (e.g., divorce, therapy) can result in greater or lesser security (Marvin, Cooper, Hoffman, & Powell, 2002).

6. There is tragically little research or theory seeking to understand revolving door litigants, those adults who repeatedly seek court intervention for (as one example), post-divorce matters. Nevertheless, the parent coordination movement (Smith-Bailey, 2005) was initiated, in part, to reduce the number and frequency of these recidivists.

7. McElwain and Booth-LaForce (2006), for example, find 56–64% secure, 12–14% insecure/avoidant, 10–13% insecure/resistant, and 14–17% disorganized or unclassifiable.

8. In every instance, we must keep in mind the extent to which situational factors can compromise optimal functioning. These include understanding whether the child is well rested and fed, healthy or ill, and—when studying infants and toddlers—the status of their diapers and pull-ups.

9. The Adult Attachment Inventory (George, Kaplan, & Main, 1996) allows researchers to reliably predict a child's attachment to a parent based upon a structured interview with that parent about his or her own childhood attachment experiences (Fonagy, Steele, & Steele, 1991; Hesse, 1999). Mothers of toddlers who demonstrate secure attachments discuss their own experience of attachment in childhood in a cohesive, realistic, and

emotionally balanced manner (van IJzendoorn, 1995) and are thus referred to as "autonomous."

10. This desirable state of comfort or balance has been referred to elsewhere as homeostasis (Greenspan, 1981).

11. Despite the common use of the word "attachment," RAD and Bowlby's attachment theory have no established relationship beyond describing developments within the child in response to the caregiving environment.

12. There are important and promising exceptions to this observation, most notably potential applications of the Attachment Q-Set (Caldera, 2004; van IJzendoorn, Vereijken, Bakermans-Kranenburg, & Riksen-Walraven, 2004).

13. See http://social.jrank.org/pages/660/Three-Mountain-Task.html or http://projects.coe.uga.edu/epltt/index.php?title=Piaget's_Stages for a full description.

14. Mitchell and O'Keefe (2008) observe that individuals with autism spectrum disorders report that they know their own mental state and that of others equally well. With this in mind (pun intended), we must consider such children's perspectives on their family conflict, chaos, and transition very carefully.

15. Coached or scripted lies (as when a parent instructs a child to report a falsehood to another caregiver) are a different consideration, partly a matter of compliance with authority, partly moral flexibility, and partly the child's wish to please.

16. It is important to note that the movement toward autonomy, perhaps more so than most other developmental landmarks, varies tremendously by culture. For brief descriptions of relevant differences, see, for example, Briggs (2008) and Fulgini (1998).

17. *H. L. v. Matheson*, 450 U.S. 398 (1981) at 425 n.2. Justice Stevens, concurring in the judgment, wrote further: "if every minor with the wisdom of an adult has a constitutional right to be treated as an adult, a uniform minimum voting age is surely suspect. Instead of simply enforcing general rules promulgated by the legislature, perhaps the judiciary should grant hearings to all young persons desirous of establishing their status as mature, emancipated minors instead of confining that privilege to unmarried pregnant young women."

18. As one example, Wymbs et al. (2008, p. 735) finds that parents with children with ADHD are more likely to divorce than parents of children without ADHD, highlighting, "how parent and child variables likely interact to exacerbate marital discord and, ultimately, dissolution among families of children diagnosed with ADHD."

6 The Child's Defense Mechanisms: Regression, Stress, and Impediments to Developmental Capacity

[I]f the challenges are too great and exceed children's capacity to cope, emotional survival begins to take precedence over mastery of developmental tasks, and they begin to show developmental delays (e.g., retarded language development) or regression (e.g., soiling or clinging), as well as other inappropriate coping strategies (e.g., numbing).

—*Lois E. Wright and Cynthia B. Seymour*

Developmental research and clinical and forensic assessments, each in their own way, speak in terms of *capacity*, that is, the upper limits of an individual's (or a class of individuals') functioning in a specific domain. Capacity is contrasted with observed behavior in the same way that one might contrast how much a cup *can* hold with how much that cup *actually* holds.

As further analogy, consider an automobile's advertised capacity to attain a specific number of miles per gallon (mpg). The informed consumer reasonably contrasts this advertised number with the vehicle's actual fuel efficiency in day-to-day driving. No matter what the ads or the salespersons claim, actually attaining the car's advertised mpg will depend upon a great many conditions that are seldom discussed in advance of the sale: speed, weather, number of passengers and load weight, road surface and incline, type of tires, and wind resistance.

Closer to home, parents and teachers concerned with a child's grades will often request that an intelligence test be administered, seldom aware that the test can only speak to the child's *capacity* for learning. When a discrepancy appears between IQ and actual achievement, the conversation must turn to consideration of the relevant impediments to learning—those factors that may be getting in the way of the child fulfilling his or her capacity—including emotions, learning disabilities, teaching methods, and classroom conditions (read more about IQ in chapter 3 and IQ testing in chapter 15).

Closer still, most family law professionals are familiar with the dilemma that can arise when the courts order an assessment of an individual's "parenting capacity" (Otto & Edens, 2002). Those procedures and tests intending to measure this concept (e.g., Ackerman, 2005; Bow, Flens, Gould, & Greenhut, 2006; Bricklin & Halbert, 2004; Flens, 2005) are abstract and hypothetical. Just like the car's advertised mpg and the child's IQ, a great many limitations may stand between a parent's actual caregiving practices and his or her abstract capacity.[1]

When a measure has established reliability and validity (see chapter 2) but overestimates actual performance, we must talk instead about performance impediments. These are the incline of the road as it limits the car's fuel efficiency, the experience of bullying as it limits a student's application of his or her native intelligence, and the sixth sleepless night up with a baby's croup as it frustrates the adult's well-intended parenting behavior. In the context of child development, performance impediments include those stresses that hinder a child's ability to think and behave to his or her mature best. These can include state-related discomforts (e.g., fatigue, hunger, heat, cold) and acute physical illness or injury (e.g., flu or broken bone), transitory stresses (e.g., acute conflict, interruptions of routine), and profound stresses (e.g., abuse, neglect, loss, severe injury, chronic illness).

This chapter discusses defense mechanisms, those natural and necessary psychological tools with which we each manage the stresses that would otherwise drown us in sensation and information and emotion. Among the defense mechanisms, developmental regression poses a particular paradox to investigating family law professionals. In short: If the stresses that bring a child before the court compromise his developmental capacity, and if the stresses that we impose through interview, observation, and assessment compound this effect, how are we to reasonably understand the child's genuine strengths and weaknesses so as to make useful recommendations for his future?

PSYCHOLOGICAL DEFENSE MECHANISMS IN OVERVIEW

Freud (1937/1964) discusses the idea that we each filter and distort our experience of reality in the interest of protecting self (ego) from anxiety. The mechanisms that serve this purpose develop over time in concert with the growth of cognition and social and emotional functioning and are shaped by experience. They are deemd to be more or less adaptive (and, in the extreme, even pathological) to the extent that they facilitate or impede healthy functioning.

Consider the development of defense mechanisms by analogy to any of the many aggressive video games available today. The eager player enters the game with a minimum number of basic resources. By conquering progressively greater and greater challenges, the player's arsenal gradually grows to include more and more sophisticated and powerful weapons. At some point in the game, the player reaches his limit. Faced with an insurmountable challenge, he procedes to exhaust first his most sophisticated weapons and then gradually falls back on his less powerful, less sophisticated armaments until his last, most primitive protection is finally defeated. Game over.

Our psychological defenses are accumulated over time and implemented in the same way. At birth the infant has only the most primitive means to cope when overwhelmed. Development and experience augment her defenses. If and when she faces overwhelming stress, she'll rely first on her most recently acquired and most mature functioning, but, failing that, she'll fall back upon less and less mature means of coping. This is regression.

Table 6.1 presents an overview of many of the commonly discussed defense mechanisms, from the least to the most developmentally sophisticated.

Table 6.1

PSYCHOLOGICAL DEFENSE MECHANISMS AS THEY COMMONLY EMERGE IN DEVELOPMENTAL SEQUENCE

DEFENSE MECHANISM	DESCRIPTION
Infantile Defenses	
Conservation Withdrawal	When signaling (crying, cooing) fails to find relief, the child shuts down in sleep
Childhood Defenses	
Denial	Failure to acknowledge an anxiety-inducing experience
Distortion	Re-forming of an anxiety-inducing experience to fit existing beliefs
Regression	Stress-induced abandonment of most current and sophisticated development in favor of earlier levels of functioning
Adolescent Defenses	
Fantasy	Retreat into a false world internally (as fantasy) or externally (e.g., video games, fiction, movies)
Passive Aggression	Inaction that covertly expresses rage
Idealization	Attributing to someone unrealistically positive qualities; failing to recognize someone's weaknesses or faults
Acting Out	Behavior that expresses a strong emotion without understanding or acknowledgement that that feeling exists
Somaticization	Expression of strong emotion indirectly through bodily (somatic) complaints (e.g., gastric upset, headache)
Projection	Disowning one's own strong emotion and attributing it instead to someone else
Adult Defenses	
Displacement	Redirection of strong feelings from their actual source to another, less threatening source
Dissociation	Separation of strong emotion from self, sometimes expressed as a "not me" experience
Intellectualization	Acknowledgement of an anxiety-inducing event without emotion
Reaction Formation	Distorting an unacceptable emotion into its opposite (e.g., the thief who becomes a police officer)
Compartmentalization	Distancing oneself from threatening emotion by locking associated events into accessible but separate experiences
Rationalization	Imposing reason so as to excuse or make sense out of otherwise unacceptable and threatening emotion

Defense mechanisms may help us to consider how children cope both with the stresses of family conflict and those inherent in family litigation, but they remain intangible psychoanalytic constructs that defy measurement, have escaped consensual validation, and fall far short of falsifiability. As such, recommendations delivered to the court based upon inferences about a child's defenses generally fail to meet *Daubert* standards.

Particularly notorious among these inadmissible arguments are those based upon denial. The quasi-psychological suggestion that an individual's denial of a particular act is no different than an admission of the same act is farcical, but sadly familiar. Meier (2009, p. 11), illustrates this point with regard to the controversial construct known as Parental Alienation Syndrome (PAS): "Because PAS theory is so circular, deeming all claims, evidence and corroboration of abuse allegations merely to be further evidence of the 'syndrome,' direct rebuttal is virtually impossible." Read more on this subject in chapter 2.

UP THE DOWN STAIRCASE: THE PARADOX OF DEVELOPMENTAL REGRESSION IN CHILD-CENTERED LITIGATION

Imagine that the stages of development are built, one upon another, like a flight of stairs that leads up from the most primitive, need-driven, me-here-now infantile state, toward the ideals of abstract thought and autonomy. In this way, development can be understood as the process of cautiously climbing from one step to the next. When stress occurs, growth can pause and even retreat back down the staircase of development. The backward movement toward more primitive levels of functioning and emotional defenses is called *regression*.

Regression is a primitive defense mechanism, a sort of fail-safe escape when other, more mature functioning is overwhelmed by stress. Given the present metaphor, stress is the wind that blows down from the top of the staircase of development. Sometimes it is little more than a refreshing breeze. Other times, stress arrives with hurricane-like pressure, forcing the child backward despite his or her constitutional resilience and supports. The child's subjective experience of stress will be due to some combination of his or her interpretation of events and/ or their objective severity, frequency, and duration. Regression can be minimal, brief, and transitory, as when an otherwise macho teenager curls up in his mother's arms seeking comfort in the aftermath of his first broken heart, or it can be profound and long-lasting, as is sometimes the tragic outcome when a parent dies or in the aftermath of abuse, grievous injury, or war. In some of these circumstances, regression coincides with the appearance of post-traumatic stress disorder (PTSD; see the related discussion of vicarious traumatization in chapter 17).

DEVELOPMENTAL CAPACITY, REGRESSION, AND FORENSIC EVALUATION

Recognizing that the circumstances under which children come before the courts are, by definition, quite stressful and that stress can compromise mature functioning, how can the family law professional understand an individual's genuine developmental capacity?

It's All About Rapport

Across all that has been written about forensic interviews (and, for that matter, about psychotherapy) with children, time and again the quality of the interviewer's rapport proves to be critically important. Taking the time to establish a modicum of trust and familiarity up front will always make the remainder of the process more time efficient, more productive, and less stressful. The unfamiliar guardian ad litem or child protective worker who swoops into a school and has a child excused for an emergency interview in an empty classroom must expect to see that child at his most anxious. Defenses piqued, this child is unlikely to be at his developmental best, never mind open, honest, and forthcoming.

Although some emergency circumstances may call for such abrupt confrontations, the most valid and informative interviews occur when the child is at ease. Stress is diminished and defenses are taken off red alert. This calls for a carefully scripted introduction, a cautious, developmentally appropriate approach, clear definition of the nature and limits of the relationship and its purpose, and a pace suited to the child's needs. It may be important, for example, to:

1. *Describe who you are and what your purpose is in advance of your first meeting with the child.*[2] This often includes clarifying that you are the child's (or the court's) helper, that the child can speak freely with you, and whether and under what circumstances you will share what you learn from the child with others. Having set the stage carefully, it is then impingent upon the evaluator to check in with the child to assure that this message is fully understood.

2. *Conduct the interview in a place and at a time best suited to the child's needs and interests.* The child who is forced to miss a preferred activity, who is publicly excused from a peer group and fears associated stigma, who is interviewed in an austere and formal setting or who is otherwise uncomfortable, embarrassed, and ill at ease is likely to be least cooperative and most defensive.

3. *Conduct the interview flexibly, in a manner and at a pace best suited to the child's apparent needs as the process unfolds.* This can include, for example, playing a board game, discussing teen idols, taking a walk, sharing a treat, and the flexibility to take a break and return to a sticky issue later, when the child is ready. These alternatives call not only for flexibility, but a willingness and ability to read the child's apparent emerging need and the creativity and resources necessary to respond accordingly. The good news is that most children today advertise their interests on their shoes, their caps, and emblazoned across their tee-shirts. The astute interviewer who expresses some interest in and knowledge of the athletic team, Disney character, or musical group advertised on a child's clothing has a far greater chance of getting beyond the child's defenses than the rushed and unresponsive interviewer who proceeds otherwise.

Collateral Resources

Contemporaneous observations alone are vulnerable to one of two logical errors. To assume that the tearful and clingy 11-year-old is socially and emotionally immature is to ignore the impact of regression and thereby to underestimate her genuine developmental capacity. On the other hand, to assume that regression is at work and that, once the family stresses have subsided, she'll resume a more age-appropriate level of functioning, is to risk missing critical developmental differences of an entirely different nature. In neither case will the corresponding recommendations be appropriate to the child's needs.

These are among the reasons why the evaluating professional must gather a comprehensive history from as many sources as possible (see

Table 6.2

POTENTIAL COLLATERAL RESOURCES WITH WHICH TO BETTER ASSESS A CHILD'S DEVELOPMENTAL COURSE AND PRESENT CAPACITY

Pediatrician	Records from conception through delivery and healthy child check-ups offer invaluable clues to developmental course.
School records	Grades provide clues to cognitive functioning. "Effort" and "conduct" marks often reflect social and emotional functioning. Teacher comments can be particularly valuable indicators of developmental capacity and corresponding concerns.
Scout leaders, coaches, Sunday School teachers, and similar extracurricular mentors	Particularly when these resources' knowledge of the child antedates the family stress and the litigation, information about the child's strengths and weaknesses can put a child's functioning into a broader perspective.
Psychotherapist	A child's psychotherapist may be willing and able to answer developmentally informed questions without breaching the child's confidences.
Parents' references, child's friends' parents, and neighbors	When the investigation calls for parents to provide personal references, these often include other parents who have had direct and longstanding experience of the child's functioning.

Table 6.2). A developmental history for each child and from each caregiver can clarify the nature and extent of the stresses that the child has endured; the progression of his or her physical, cognitive, linguistic, social and emotional development prior to and since the start of the acute family stressors;[3] and the extent to which regression may be at work.[4] This argument may be particularly important in the context of adoption in that neither the parents nor the court may not have access to a child's developmental history (Silverman, 2001).

Autism Spectrum Disorders: A Special Case of Regression

Regression can also be triggered by neurological causes. This may be the case for some young children who go on to be diagnosed with autism and autism spectrum disorders.[5]

The developmental course of the child who is later diagnosed with autism or an autism spectrum disorder may be quite unique. Although this child's early cognitive, linguistic, social and emotional development may be indistinguishable from those of his healthy peers, sometime between 15 and 30 months of age development goes awry (Bernabei, Cerquiglini, Cortesi, & D'Ardia, 2007; Stefanatos, 2008). Spontaneous regression occurs as a loss of social interest and socioemotional capacities (Luyster et al., 2005), of mature behaviors (Young, Brewer, & Pattison, 2003), and of language abilities (Loucas et al., 2008; Williams, Botting, & Boucher, 2008). Although promising and impressive psychosocial, sensory, and academic interventions are newly becoming available (e.g., Hollander & Anagnostou, 2007; Matson & Minshawi, 2006), many autistic children never fully resume their climb up the typical staircase of development. Thus, the developmentally informed family law professional must be particularly astute, relying on expert medical opinion, to differentiate an otherwise healthy toddler's regression in the face of family stresses from the unique and tragic case of the autistic child's regresssion.

SUMMARY

A useful understanding of child development must include consideration of the ways in which we protect ourselves from stress. In particular, our efforts to craft developmentally sensitive parenting plans must account for the likelihood that regression in response to family conflict, transition, loss, and even litigation itself can mask a child's genuine developmental capacities. Armed with this understanding, we must take every opportunity to look beyond the child's immediate presentation. This includes shaping the interview process to each child's needs in the interest of building rapport and thereby minimizing defensiveness and incorporating collateral resources into the final formulation of the child's best interests.

NOTES

1. See Yanez and Fremouw (2004) for a discussion of parenting capacity instruments under *Daubert*.
2. Among the first items in my standard guardian ad litem (GAL) contract is the following: "Because the GAL will need to observe and/or meet with

and interview the child(ren), it is important to agree in advance how to describe the GAL's role to the child(ren): The GAL is a 'helper.' The GAL's job is to help ['the court'], ['the judge'] ['mommy and daddy'] to make decisions. The child(ren) must be reassured that it is completely okay to speak openly to the GAL and that there will be no negative consequences ('get in trouble') for doing so. It is important that no one tell the child(ren) what to say, script the child(ren)'s words or otherwise contaminate the child(ren)'s view in speaking with the GAL. It is important that no one try to debrief or otherwise interrogate the child after meeting with the GAL. It is important that no one mislead the child regarding confidentiality or privacy. The GAL cannot promise the child that his or her words will not be repeated. Finally, it is important that this document and its contents not be shared with the child(ren)."

3. Take great care not to confuse the date an action is filed with the court, a hearing is held, or a ruling received as the start of the relevant stressor. The paperwork and formalities of the legal system are only landmarks and often occur long after the matter first began to bear on the child's well-being.

4. I make my own developmental history questionnaire available at: http://www.healthyparent.com/DEVHX.pdf

5. Acknowledging that, although the evidence is far from conclusive, many people believe that the regression associated with the onset of autism spectrum disorders is due to environmental causes, including the MMR immunization (see, for example, the National Institutes of Health discussion at http://www.nichd.nih.gov/publications/pubs/autism/mmr/ ; cf., Gillberg & Heijbel, 1998).

7 Developmental Asynchrony and Décalage

In all cultures, there are children who progress through the intellectual mile-stones at a more rapid rate than their peers. While others look upon the gifted as being advantaged in a race for personal gain, the experience of being different in cultures that value sameness, coupled with acute awareness of the pain and suffering in the world make the gifted feel distinctly disadvan-taged. Gifted children do not see themselves as winners of the competition, but bearers of the burden to make this a better world for all.

—*Linda K. Silverman*

"I can't help it," said Alice very meekly: "I'm growing."
"You've no right to grow here," said the Dormouse.
"Don't talk nonsense," said Alice more boldly: "you know you're growing too."
"Yes, but I grow at a reasonable pace," said the Dormouse: "not in that ridiculous fashion."

—*Lewis Carroll,* Alice in Wonderland

Each spring a local charity hosts a very popular ironman triathlon. Premiere athletes gather to compete in an amazing contest of speed and endurance. The winners predictably credit their successes to intense training in all three areas of the event while the rest of the pack typically smile and say something about their strength running and biking, but the need to improve their swimming skills. In effect, these committed super-athletes are talking about the synchrony or symmetry of their (physical) development. To a triathlete, the observation that one skill is relatively weaker than others means defeat. To the developmental psychologist, the same observation defines décalage.

In the context of child development, décalage describes important developmental differences within an individual. For Piaget, the idea of horizontal décalage captures the "systematic and necessary" (Feldman, 2004, p. 175) fact that a single cognitive capacity is evident in one functional domain much earlier than it is evident in others. For example, children arguably manifest the cognitive skill known as permanence (see chapter 3) much sooner with regard to objects than they do with people (Slaughter & Boh, 2001). As another example, a child's conservation of matter may be evident by 6 or 7 years of age, even though conservation of weight doesn't appear until age 9 or 10 and conservation of volume isn't evident until age 11 or 12 (Montangero & Maurice-Naville, 1994).[1]

These developmental asynchronies are due, in part, to differences in domain-specific opportunity, experience, salience, and instruction. Thus, the experience of living in South Africa likely bears on the observation that South African 4- to 12-year-olds understand the physics of heat well before they demonstrate an understanding of the physics of cold (Slaughter & Boh, 2001). Several authors (e.g., Ari, Bal, Turgul, Uzmen, & Ydogan 2000; Onyehalu, 1983) demonstrate that explicit training can facilitate a child's use of conservation or seriation skills across domains, thereby decreasing décalage, an achievement that facilitates educational outcomes, such as math grades (Strickland, Jane, Moulton, White, & Schou, 2008). Even a child's understanding of pretend in play can be similarly facilitated (Rakoczy, Tomasello, & Striano, 2006).

The idea of décalage can be interpreted more broadly—with apologies to Piaget—to refer to differences within the individual across different domains of development.[2] Rather than speaking about domain differences within cognitive development, this alternate application of the concept describes asynchronies between areas of development within the individual (Silverman, 1997). Like the triathlete whose biking skills far exceed her swimming and running skills, this sense of décalage might describe a child whose language skills far exceed her cognitive, social, and emotional skills. Using the concept of décalage in this sense opens the door to discussing an individual's unique profile of developmental strengths and weaknesses, to conceptualizing relevant family and social dynamics, and to applying developmental theory to the many dilemmas of family law.

This chapter describes several profiles associated with developmental décalage and their relevance to family law process. I propose that children's interests are best served by forensic outcomes that speak to their relative developmental weaknesses, rather than to their strengths. These issues are of particular importance when the court accords "mature" minors special privileges relevant to family litigation, a topic addressed in detail in chapter 14.

THE PRECOCIOUS OR DELAYED CHILD AND THE FAMILY SYSTEM

Both precocious and delayed development can have a deleterious impact not only the individual child's emerging sense of self but on the family system in which he lives, as well (Seligman & Darling, 2007). Identification of precocious potential can be as much a source of family upheaval, coparental conflict, economic hardship, sibling anger, guilt, jealousy, and resentment, as the diagnosis of a child's developmental delay (Rogers & Nielsen, 1993; Webster, Majnemer, Platt, & Shevell, 2008).[3]

Healthy siblings will experience both benefits and costs associated with a brother's or sister's developmental difference (Mulroy, Robertson, Aiberti, Leonard, & Bower, 2008), often creating "amplified ambivalence" (Waite-Jones & Madill, 2008), the intensification of the typical and expectable sibling conflicts in response to the identified child's special needs and the family's disproportionate investment of time, attention, emotion, and money in that child's needs.[4]

In the words of one child, "Non-handicapped kids can get pushed aside when their brothers or sisters have handicaps. Andrew seems to get help naturally—it's like attention to his needs is 'built into the system.' I'm the bad one, but he can do no wrong. He makes all the messes, but I get into trouble if I don't empty the dishwasher" (as quoted in Binkard, 1987, p.10).

The impact of these systemic stresses is mediated by the quality and availability of social supports (Bugental, 2003) and access to proper rehabilitation services (Rogers & Hogan, 2003), but can have far-reaching effects throughout the course of individual and family development. In one familiar dynamic, a child's dramatic developmental delay sparks

rage, guilt, and depression that resonates throughout the family, impeding the caregivers' sensitive and responsive availability and thereby
compromising not only the identified child's attachment security, but
that of the other children as well. This effect may be more pronounced
for fathers than mothers (Pelchat, Bisson, Bois, & Saucier, 2003), but
the emotions ricochet among the family members regardless, impacting
every individual and every subsystem within the group.

We know that families with children with disabilities are generally
more likely to experience marital separation, divorce, and lower incomes
than matched families with healthy children (Hodapp & Krasner, 1994).
These outcomes, in turn, exacerbate the differently abled child's social
and emotional difficulties, limit his access to resources, and create a
downward spiral for the entire family system (Perryman, 2005).

But not all patterns of décalage are created equal. The nature and
extent of the child's developmental difference is relevant to understanding its impact on the child and the family system. Thus, the sections
that follow discuss the most common profiles of décalage, their causes,
associated attributes, and corresponding family dynamics as these may
bear on better understanding and meeting the needs of court-involved children.

PATTERNS OF DÉCALAGE AND THEIR CORRELATES

Any important discussion about human development and relationships
should begin in the mirror: How do you see your own development?
In what areas do you consider yourself to be more or less mature?
What are your developmental strengths? Your developmental weaknesses? (See chapter 17 for discussion of the family law professional's
unique developmental course.)

We can conceptualize an individual's developmental strengths and
weaknesses relative to chronological age as a simple bar graph. Figure
7.1, for example, graphs the developmental profile of a hypothetical
child whose cognitive, linguistic, physical, and socioemotional development are all entirely consistent with his chronological age (as represented by the horizontal black line). This is the unlikely case of complete
developmental synchrony, a profile entirely without décalage.

Understanding décalage requires that we ask two questions, both
of which can be answered from a graph of this sort, but only the second
of which bears on chronological age:

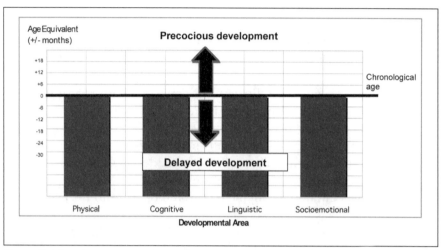

Figure 7.1 Developmental profile of a hypothetical child with no evidence of décalage.

1. *What are the child's intrapersonal developmental strengths and weaknesses? That is, relative to his or her own development, which area(s) of growth are strongest and which are weakest, without regard for chronological age?* The hypothetical triathlete might know, for example, that he is far stronger in the water than on land and with this knowledge decide to increase his running and biking training and cut back on his swimming. This choice may help to even out his skills (that is, decrease his athletic décalage), but until he competes, he will have no idea whether his weakest run is faster than those of all of his competitors or his strongest swim might be far slower than that of even the worst of the contenders. His awareness of his own intrapersonal skills is valuable, nonetheless, to the extent that it helps to guide his future training.

2. *What are the child's developmental strengths and weaknesses relative to age and developmental norms? That is, relative to his peer group, where does he stand?* Our hypothetical triathlete answers this question by comparing his speeds with others' documented speeds or by actually entering a competition. This is where he learns where he stands in the pack. Could it be that even his slowest run is fast enough to win that segment of the competition? Or is it possible that his fastest swim doesn't even qualify to enter? For the child, the question then concerns his or her development in each domain relative to age-specific norms. Although Billy's cognitive development may be far in advance of his social, emotional, and physical development, for example, how does his cognitive development compare to that of his typical peers?

Figures 7.2a and 7.2b illustrate this question with regard to development. If the dark horizontal line in each refers to typical or expectable development among peers, then we can identify children for whom décalage is evident within a generally precocious developmental profile (Figure 7.2a) as well as those for whom décalage occurs within a generally delayed profile (Figure 7.2b).

Plotting a child's developmental profile relevant to his peers bears not only on plans for support and intervention, but on how we might anticipate and attempt to modify his experience. This is where the ironman analogy fails: Whereas the triathlete who discovers that his best swim barely makes the grade can give up running and biking and, by devoting all of his energies to the pool, have a better chance to win at something, the child can hardly abandon physical, linguistic, and socioemotional development in favor of cognitive development. Instead, understanding décalage relative to developmental norms can help concerned adults help the child to succeed as well as possible in every area of development.

The concept of décalage allows us to map a great variety and depth of developmental research onto the hypothetical profiles of children with distinct strengths and weaknesses. These profiles and their associated risk statements are necessarily oversimplified, but serve as excellent starting blocks from which we can begin to ask important questions in the interest of both intervention and the legal remedies discussed in the third and fourth sections of this book.

THE PHYSICALLY PRECOCIOUS OR DELAYED CHILD

"Adolescence," observed Alexander and Strang (1953, p. 756), "is as if the biological functions of mature sexuality were foisted upon an organism which emotionally is not fully prepared for it....A full-grown body is entrusted to an inexperienced mind."

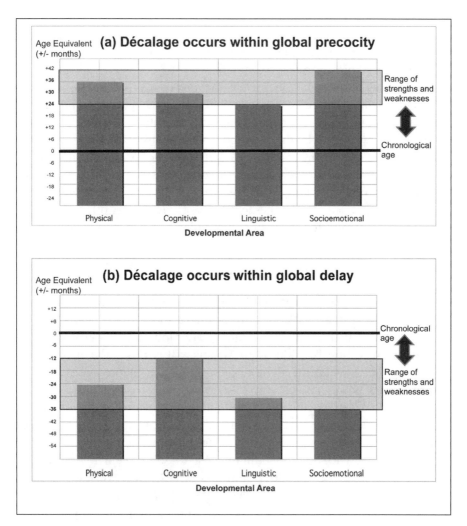

Figure 7.2 Profiles representing developmental strengths and weaknesses for (a) a globally precocious and (b) a globally delayed child.

Physical maturation from conception through later adulthood follows a course determined by DNA and altered—sometimes subtly and other times quite radically—by a variety of environmental factors, including stress,[5] nutrition, medication, and toxic exposure. All other things being equal (which never actually occurs), the best predictor of a child's stature, coordination, and age of onset of puberty (as three among many physical aspects of development) are the same-sex biological parent's comparable achievements.

Figures 7.3a and 7.3b profile the physically precocious and the physically delayed child, respectively. Compared to those children with different patterns of décalage, these children literally stand out in the crowd. They tend to be the kids about whom parents remark spontaneously when examining a child's class pictures. Some are tall and gangly, others are very short. Some have the obvious signs of puberty—facial hair and broad musculature in boys; breast development in girls; acne for both—in a sea of prepubescent faces or, vice versa, others look like little kids surrounded by their much older brothers and sisters.

Physically Precocious Children

In the United States, girls on average achieve menarche by 12.5 years of age. Fewer than 10% of girls begin to menstruate before age 11 and 90% are menstruating by age 14 (Kaplowitz & Oberfield, 1999; Gluckman & Hanson, 2006). Physicians will typically diagnose precocious puberty when the signs of puberty appear before age 8 in a girl or $9^1/_2$ in a boy.

Physically precocious boys and girls tend to travel different social, emotional, and academic/occupational paths (Mazur, 1999; Money & Lewis, 1990). Although the early onset of puberty is often associated with teasing, with its concomitant cost to self-esteem for both boys (Ge, Conger, & Elder, 2001) and girls (Ge, Conger, & Elder, 1996), boys tend to fare better. Early developing boys are captains of the team, class leaders, and social magnets. Early developing girls, by contrast, are at higher risk in many areas of development, particularly for social withdrawal, depression and somatic complaints (Xing-xing, Zhu-wen, Jian-jiang, Xiu-yin, & Xi-qiang, 2005), substance abuse and dependence (but see Biehl, Natsuaki, & Ge, 2007), multiple sexual partners, unwanted and early pregnancy, serial relationships, and associated costs to academic and occupational outcomes (Graber, Lewison, Seely, & Brooks-Gunn, 1997; Mendle, Turkheimer, & Emery, 2007; Sonis et al., 1985).

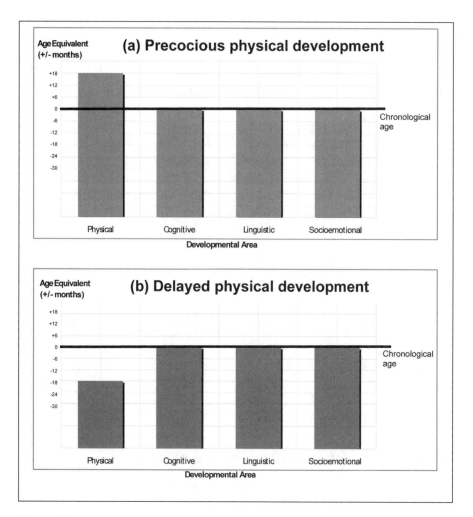

Figure **7.3** Developmental profiles representing a hypothetical child with (a) precocious physical development and (b) delayed physical development.

Physically Delayed Children

Because the pace of physical development is quite variable, parents, health care providers, and peer groups are slower to identify a child whose physical development is delayed than one whose physical development is accelerated. The reasons for delay are extremely varied, from endocrine dysfunction to chromosomal abberation to malnutrition and toxic exposure. Short stature, delayed pubescence, and dyscoordination can also appear among clusters of symptoms associated with a number of genetic syndromes, notably Turner syndrome (Christopoulos, Deligeoroglou, Laggari, Christogiorgos, & Creatsas, 2008).[6]

The evidence for social and emotional difficulties associated with physical delay among otherwise healthy children is ambiguous. Gilmour and Skuse (1999), for example, find that stature is unrelated to emotional and behavioral measures, whereas Sandberg (1999) suggests that these children are commonly subjected to "stigmatization and juvenilization." By the same token, we might guess that children who are slower to develop physically may be more vulnerable to a needy parent's infantilization.

THE COGNITIVELY PRECOCIOUS OR DELAYED CHILD

Figures 7.4a and 7.4b illustrate two instances of décalage, each of which is notable for cognitive differences. While the needs and remedies suited to the two children described by these profiles are quite different, they share more than one might expect. Both the "gifted" and the cognitively delayed[7] child commonly feel out of place in their usual environment (Peterson, 2006),[8] but one is at far greater risk of social and emotional difficulties than the other.

Factors That Influence Cognitive Development

A diverse collection of variables are known to affect cognitive development. These include:

1. **Environment** in general has been shown to have a tremendous impact on cognitive development. In one well-known study, identical twins adopted into different homes before 6 months of age were found to have IQ differences of as much as 16 points (that is, a full standard deviation; Capron & Duyme, 1989). In the extreme, early neglect, abuse, and trauma can be associated with lifelong cognitive (Behen et al., 2008) and socioemotional (Zeanah & Smyke, 2008) impairments. More specifically, the nature, composition, and functioning of the

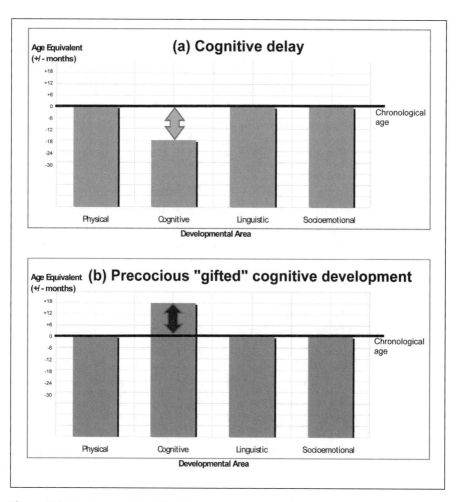

Figure 7.4 Developmental profile of a hypothetical child with (a) significant cognitive delays and (b) precocious cognitive strengths (i.e., "gifted").

family has been associated with children's cognitive functioning (Grigorenko & Sternberg, 2001).

2. **Socioeconomic status:** All other things being equal, growing up in a wealthy home is associated with higher IQ scores than growing up in a poor home by at least 5 years of age (Duncan, Brooks-Gunn, & Klebanov, 1994). Poverty is associated with lower cognitive functioning, especially in nonverbal IQ (Espy,

Molfese, & DiLalla, 2001; see also Noble, Norman, & Farah, 2005).

3. **Parental (particularly maternal) depression:** Maternal depression is associated with a variety of negative childhood outcomes as a function of duration, severity, and the child's age, notably lower IQ scores beginning in grade school. These include compromised cognitive outcomes in infancy and the toddler years, decreased creative play, ADD-like behaviors in the early grade school years, anxiety, and depression in adolescence (Duncan et al., 1994).

4. **In utero maternal stress:** The hormones associated with severe and prolonged stress can have a deleterious impact on the child's development in utero, as illustrated by the observation that, "prenatal exposure to a moderately severe natural disaster is associated with lower cognitive and language abilities at 5 1/2 years of age" (LaPlante, Brunet, Schmitz, Ciampi, & King, 2008, p. 12).

5. **In utero drug exposure:** Maternal drug use can cause idiopathic damage in utero. For example, fetal cocaine exposure has a clear detrimental impact on IQ, most prominently for males (Bennet, Bendersky, & Lewis, 2008).

6. **Maternal intelligence:** Standarized psychological testing seldom finds a reliable relationship between maternal (or more generally, parental) cognitive functioning and child cognitive functioning (Aunos & Feldman, 2007; McConnell, Llewellyn, Mayes, Russo, & Honey, 2003). Nisbett (2009, p. 22) summarizes, stating that, "genes are far from being completely determinative of intelligence and that the environment can make a huge difference."[16]

7. **Father presence:** A father's presence is associated with better cognitive outcomes in early childhood, especially for boys and especially for developmentally delayed boys (Bronte-Tinkew, Carrano, Horowitz, & Kinukawa, 2008; Clarke-Stewart, 1980).[17]

8. **Nursing:** Breastfeeding is associated with higher cognitive functioning. Kramer et al. (2008), in particular, find, "strong evidence that prolonged and exclusive breastfeeding improves children's cognitive development" by 6.5 years of age. Contrary to popular wisdom, however, breastfeeding does not impart

any measurable benefit in terms of the child's height, risk of obesity, or risk of high blood pressure (Kramer et al., 2007).

9. **Nutrition:** Early malnutrition predisposes children to cognitive deficits that, in turn, are related to externalizing and antisocial behavior through adolescence (Liu, Raine, Venables, Dalais, & Mednick, 2004). Conversely, healthy nutrition is associated with cognitive gains through childhood (Sigman & Whaley, 1998). Iron deficiency is identified as a continuing dietary concern that is strongly related to intelligence scores (Lozoff, Jiminez, & Smith, 2006),

10. **Toxic exposure:** Neurotoxin exposure (e.g., lead poisoning; Chiodo et al., 2007) is associated with impaired attention and lower IQ, increased impulsivity, personality changes, debilitating physical illnesses (Singer, 2008) and death.

11. **Attachment security:** Secure mother–child attachment at 2 years of age is associated with higher IQ scores in kindergarten (van IJzendoorn & Van Vliet-Visser, 1988; see also O'Connor & McCartney, 2007).

12. **Daycare/preschool enrollment:** The *compensatory hypothesis* (Spieker, Nelson, Petras, Jolley, & Barnard, 2003) suggests that the negative impact of insecure attachment experiences can be mitigated by exposure to healthy, appropriate, and consistent care, as can be provided by enrollment in daycare (Broberg, Wessels, Lamb, & Hwang, 1997; Caughy, DiPietro, & Strobino, 1994).

13. **Birth order/sibling presence:** Zajonc (2001, p. 523) reports unambiguously that, "As the number of siblings increases, the intellectual environment declines in its relative quality." The case for intelligence as a function of birth order is far less compelling. Cross-sectional studies have traditionally suggested that birth order affects IQ (Zajonc, 2001). Longitudinal studies, however, suggest otherwise, clarifying only that larger sibling groups deplete resources and may therefore be associated with lowered IQ (Rogers, Cleveland, van der Oord, & Rowe, 2000).

14. **Divorce:** A number of studies support Guidubaldi and Duckworth's (2001, p. 106) observation that "children's cognitive performance is adversely affected by parental divorce." However, none of the related research—nor the general discussion

of divorce—distinguishes between the child's experience of coparental conflict and divorce itself (Garber, 2008a).

Cognitively Precocious Children

The cognitively precocious child[9] may feel understimulated (which is often expressed as boredom) and different than his or her peers, but is likely to have the social and emotional resources to cope adequately with these experiences. Gifted kids are found time and again to be at no greater risk for psychopathology than their cognitively typical peers (Gallucci, 1988; Jackson & Peterson, 2003), even if their risk of perfectionism and associated anxiety might be greater (Neihart, 2002a, 2002b; Peterson & Ray, 2006a, 2006b; Peterson & Rischar, 2000). Despite conventional wisdom (and stories dramatized in the media) to the contrary, cognitively precocious children are no more vulnerable to self-destructive acts and suicide than others, allowing that the exceptions do garner a great deal of attention (Cross, Gust-Brey, & Ball, 2002). In fact, research suggests that gifted children as young as 10 years of age tend to develop assertiveness, dominance, creativity, self-sufficiency, positive self-esteem, and internal locus of control[10] (Haier & Denham, 1976; Lehman & Erdwins, 1981, 2004) well in advance of their peers, attributes that are associated with psychological resilience (Ciccehetti & Garmezy, 1993).[11]

The concept of resilience in psychology refers to the search for those elements of personality, relatedness, and experience that together determine who will manage stress successfully and who will not (Rutter, 2007). Waugh, Fredrickson, and Taylor (2008, p. 1031) describe resilience as the ability to "maintain psychological stability and experience fewer mental health problems" in the face of negative life events. In addition to a solid foundation of empirical study of childhood resilience in the face of family stresses (Emery & Forehand, 1996; Li, Nussbaum, & Richards, 2007; Luthar & Zelazo, 2003; Masten & Reed, 2002), interest in the concept of resilience has blossomed in response to contemporary Western concerns with terrorism, war, and natural disaster (Garbarino, 2008).

From a family systems perspective, the child whose décalage favors thinking above all else is at risk of a very specific type of anxiety. This child is capable of understanding a great deal more than he or she can cope with emotionally. Like a person who chews and swallows a meal but cannot digest it, this child is vulnerable to become overwhelmed. He or she is vulnerable to excessive worry and OCD-like behaviors (Garber, 2008a). In the company of a needy, self-absorbed, or unsophisticated caregiver, this child's obvious intelligence may be mistaken for global maturity, opening the door to role reversal in the form of adultification, parentification, and even sexual abuse (Burton, 2007).[12]

Cognitively Delayed Children

The cognitively delayed child may, like his precocious peer, feel out of place among his or her typical age-mates, but likely lacks the social and emotional (and in some instance, also the linguistic and physical) skills to manage these experiences. This child is at a tremendously higher risk for social rejection (Pijl, Frostad, & Flem, 2008) and for developing psychopathology. Einfeld and Tonge (1996) observe that, "40.7% of those with [intellectual disability] and aged between 4 and 18 could be classified as having [a] severe emotional and behaviour disorder or as being psychiatrically disordered."[13]

The nature and severity of the social and emotional deficits that can accompany cognitive delay rest, in part, on the child's capacity for frustration tolerance and impulse control. These two skills (first discussed in chapter 5) normatively develop in the context of the family from the infant's natural and necessary inability to tolerate any frustration or inhibit any impulse, toward a state of progressively greater volitional control of both. However, when cognitive and linguistic resources are limited and/or when opportunity and social reinforcement are inadequate,[14] externalizing (that is, defiant, demanding, and aggressive) behavior can persist unchecked.

Some causes of cognitive impairment are associated with predictable constellations of social and emotional dysfunction.[15] Children with fragile X syndrome, for example, have an extremely high co-occurrence of cognitive deficit and externalizing psychopathology (von Gontard et al., 2002). Children with fetal alcohol syndrome commonly have significant cognitive impairments associated with hyperactivity, distractibility, and a very high degree of impulsivity, sometimes (mis-)diagnosed as attention-deficit disorder (ADD or ADHD).

Among children with autism, the quality of cognitive functioning as measured by IQ is strongly related to comorbid psychopathology, such that higher cognitive functioning is associated with internalizing (e.g., withdrawal, isolation, depression, and anxiety) whereas lower cognitive functioning is associated with externalizing behaviors (Estes, Dawson, Sterling, & Munson, 2007). This is likely a function not only of intellectual ability in general, but of language capacity more specifically.

By contrast, although both Prader-Willi syndrome and Down syndrome are associated with significant cognitive deficits, the appearance of comorbid social and emotional deficits, if any, appears to be entirely idiosyncratic (Reddy & Pfeiffer, 2007; McCarthy & Boyd, 2001, respectively).

Finally, in the same manner that the cognitively precocious child may be vulnerable to adultification, the cognitively delayed child may be vulnerable to infantilization, the destructive family dynamic in which a self-serving caregiver inhibits a needy child's otherwise natural growth toward autonomy (Sharlin & Polansky, 1972).

Parents, guardians, and the courts sometimes face the dilemma of prodigy. The dilemma here is the choice between investing finite resources (time, effort, and money) to build a child's (assumed) potential for genius in a single, narrow area versus investing more generally in the interest of diminishing décalage. The former is associated with child movie stars, athletes, and musical talents (Feldman, 1993; Fingelkurts & Fingelkurts, 2002), one of whom famously wrote,

> Having been built in the fashion I was as a child—created and then deflated—has left me with a distinct feeling of failure....Designating children as gifted, especially extremely gifted, and cultivating that giftedness may be not only a waste of money, but positively harmful. (Quart, 2006)

By contrast, the latter strategy, seeking to diminish the décalage, is often thought to contribute to a child's overall psychological health even if the cost is a lost opportunity for genius.

THE LINGUISTICALLY PRECOCIOUS OR DELAYED CHILD

Just as one would never assume that a taller child is more intelligent or more emotionally mature simply by virtue of his or her physical development, we must be careful to look beyond a child's verbal skills for other clues to social, emotional, and cognitive development (Cohen, 2001). Nevertheless, we can reasonably make two assumptions about language that bear on this discussion of décalage.

First, because language is built upon the scaffolding of cognition, it is fair to assume that a child's intellectual development is at least on par with his or her genuine linguistic development.[18] Thus, a verbally precocious child is probably also intellectually precocious, although the converse is not necessarily so. That is, there is no necessary association between cognitive development and linguistic delay.

Second, because language comprehension routinely develops in advance of expression (see chapter 4), a child's expressive skills are reasonably assumed to mark the least of his or her comprehension. In this instance, the converse does apply. That is, a measure of a child's verbal comprehension sets the upper limit on his or her expressive abilities, with one important exception. The exception is discussed below as "The case of words gone awry."

Because the toddler's first words, the preschooler's ability to follow directions, and the grade-schooler's reading and writing skills seem to be loud-and-clear landmarks of developmental status, both parents and professionals pay a great deal of attention to early evidence of language precocity and delay. We know that children whose language differences are identified and remediated early and who have their parents' active support have the best chance of healthy outcomes. Moeller (2000, p. e43) makes the point concisely that "limited family involvement was associated with significant child language delays at 5 years of age, especially when enrollment in intervention was late." When a child's language differences persist beyond age 5 ½ and into the school years, children are statistically at the highest risk of associated attentional, social, and emotional difficulties (Snowling, Bishop, Stothard, Chipchase, & Kaplan, 2006).[19]

Significant Expressive Language Delay

Figure 7.5a represents a hypothetical child whose expressive language skills fall short of his or her development, in general, and his or her language comprehension, in particular (Weismer, 2007). Because comprehension is often mistakenly inferred from expression, this child is at very high risk of being mistaken as cognitively delayed.[20] Proper identification may require thorough speech/language and/or neuropsychological assessments.

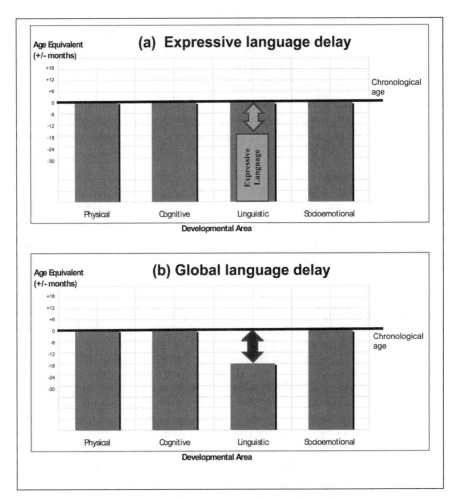

Figure 7.5 Developmental profiles of four hypothetical cases of language décalage: (a) significant expressive language delay and (b) global language delay; (c) precocious language comprehension and (d) precocious global language ability.

Developmental expressive language delay (as opposed to expressive language delays acquired as a result of head injury, toxic exposure, or illness, for example) may be evident in the vocabularies of children as young as 10 to 12 months of age (Stein, Parker, Coplan, & Feldman, 2001) and can persist to varying degrees well into grade school. They may be as pervasive and profound as a complete absence of expression

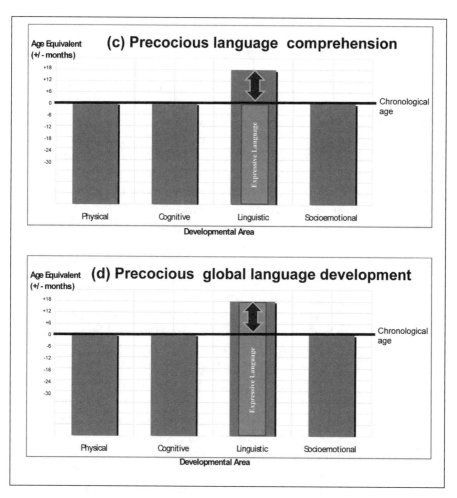

Figure 7.5 *(continued)*

in all media (spoken, written, and electronic), as can occur due to genetic differences (Vodopiutz, Item, Häusler, Korall, & Bodamer, 2007), can be situationally defined (as is often the case with selective mutism[21]), or limited to specific forms of speech. In some instances, a child's speech is unremarkable save a persistent failure to use pronouns (*he, she*) or persistent syntactic errors (*"I out go"*).

Developmental expressive language disorders occur among 10 to 15% of children under 3 years of age, and in 3 to 7% of grade-school kids. They are diagnosed two to five times more often in boys than in girls. Both the *DSM-IV* and the *International Classification of Diseases (ICD-10)* recognize and categorize these disorders (codes 315.21 and F80.1, respectively).

Research agrees that "even in the very early years (21–31 months), children who lag behind others in their expressive language are more likely to experience depression and withdrawal, and show less social relatedness and interest in play than their typically developing...peers" (Farmer, 2006, p. 74; see also Irwin, Carter, & Briggs-Gowan, 2002; Ross & Weinberg, 2006). Related studies find a strong relationship between global language delay and aggressive acting out between kindergarten and third grade (Hooper, Roberts, Zeisel, & Poe, 2003). Most recently, questions have been raised suggesting that vocabulary delay (as one particular subtype of expressive language delay) may be associated with parental underinvolvement and understimulation in the home (Desmarais, Sylvestre, Meyer, Bairati, & Rouleau, 2008), suggestive of neglect. In a complementary fashion, daycare enrollment "mitigates the adverse effects of insecure attachment on cognitive and language development of low-income children by providing children with a more stimulating environment than would have been experienced at home with mothers" (Spieker, 2003, p. 326).

In one further variation on this type of décalage, Sowell (2001) refers to the "Einstein syndrome." This colloquial (nondiagnostic) label seeks to capture the experience of the cognitively precocious child whose early expressive language skills are significantly delayed. These children—identified as mostly boys—are said to have extraordinary intellectual potential. Whether and to what degree these children might more accurately be diagnosed with Asperger's syndrome or Down syndrome remains a matter of debate.[22]

Significant Global Language Delay

Significant delays of both expressive and receptive language are more common in boys than in girls. Quite different than delays associated only with expressive language, global language delays are associated with a number of quite serious and non–mutually exclusive causes, including hearing loss, blindness, mental retardation, trauma, and genetic anomolies, each of which must be ruled out by a qualified professional (e.g., audiologist, ophthalmologist, neurologist, geneticist). Among possible genetic causes, autism, pervasive developmental disorder, and Landau-Kleffner syndrome[23] are notable.

Early global language deficits have been identified as among the first evidence of HIV-related neurological dysfunction among prenatally exposed children (Baillieu & Potterton, 2008; Coplan et al., 1998).

Global language delay seldom occurs without moderate to severe social, emotional, and behavioral concomitants (Tervo, 2007). Redmond and Timler (2007, p. 185) observe that, "children with developmental language impairments…contend with high levels of peer neglect, rejection, or abuse. They may even experience the consequences of pejorative teacher evaluations of their intellectual or social competence."

When no productive language is evident by 18 months of age, a comprehensive developmental screening is necessary. Genetic screening may also prove important. Figure 7.5b depicts global language delay as a matter of developmental décalage.

Precocious Language Skills

Figures 7.5c and 7.5d capture the profiles of two children who fall under this heading—the child with precocious language comprehension (even if expressive skills are relatively delayed) and the child with precocious global language abilities, respectively.

What is precocious language development? Harris (1992) reports that among her group of early developing toddlers, the most precocious produced his first words at 10 months of age and had a functional vocabulary of at least ten words by 15 months, whereas typically developing children achieve these milestones no earlier than 12 and 18 months, respectively.[24]

As is the case in any area of development, language is most likely to advance precociously when the environment values and enables its growth. Thus, language develops earlier among children whose parents are themselves verbally expressive and engage their children in verbal play from birth (and even earlier). Language acquisition is further facilitated when caregivers match their words with actions; thus, "mothers who ask questions, give instructions and generally comment on their toddler's ongoing activity have children with more precocious language development" (Spencer & Harris, 2006, p. 73). Understandably, these interactions are associated with more sensitive and responsive caregiving, such that "secure attachment proved to be a developmental benefit with regard to understanding spoken language (but not more general cognitive development or the ability to express oneself)" (Grossman, Grossman, & Waters, 2005, p. 86).

Sieratzki and Woll (1998) and others (Bénony, Golse, Larome, & Bénony, 2004) observe that among severely motor-impaired children, language sometimes develops precociously as a means of compensating for other developmental deficits. The décalage between physical and language development for these children can be quite astonishing.

Words Gone Awry: When Expressive Language (Seems to) Precede Comprehension

Language acquisition, like the acquisition of so many other skills, is a process of trial and error. The would-be bicycle rider, for example, has to be willing to fall down, scrape a knee, get up, and try again. In like manner, the would-be communicator makes many errors in both comprehension and expression along the way toward fluency. These are the misunderstandings and misstatements that make parents smile throughout the toddler years and that may be associated with peers' taunts and bullying throughout the grade-school and high-school years, all of which, one way or another, help to shape a child's language understanding and usage.

Because language development (like development in every area) must be understood as it occurs in an interpersonal context, the young speaker's expressive errors[25] necessarily reflect this context. A word is overheard and then used or misused, often intentionally as a means of determining its meaning and/or to elicit its associated observed emotional impact. These matters were discussed briefly in chapter 4.

In some family circumstances, a child's necessary and natural experimentation with words will resonate with a caregiver's selfish needs. Rather than issue a correction of any kind, the caregiver takes the child's ambiguous utterances as self-serving validation; as an expression of super-mature empathy, peer-like support, or confirmation of a lingering fear. Linguistically, the result is a situation in which a child's expressive skills appear to grow in advance of his or her language comprehension skills. Systemically, this common and otherwise innocuous process can spark family court conflagrations that consume fortunes and years, which turn otherwise manageable legal skirmishes into nuclear wars, and that can culminate in broken relationships and even imprisonment.

In some instances the child's expressive language errors add bricks to the foundation on which a parent will rationalize a role reversal. "My 7-year-old gets it. Why shouldn't I talk to her about the divorce?" In other cases, this is the tinder with which the fires of inaccurate claims of abuse are built.

It begins simply. Five-year-old Billy overhears something sexual. The original source is as likely to be the playground or the neighborhood or the school bus as Mom's house or Dad's. The words are unfamiliar but intriguing and the intended listener (not Billy) has a reaction that gives the words emotional power. Intrigued, Billy repeats the words at Mom's house.

Mom is angry and lonely and scared. The man she once married has turned out to be a stranger. She no longer knows what he's capable of. She genuinely hears Billy's words as an expression of her worst fears come true. She asks leading questions that Billy, caught like a deer in the headlights of this abrupt emotional reaction, fumbles through more in an effort to make his mom happy and to escape her intense scrutiny than to express any real meaning or memory. Her tears may even elicit his tears, which she takes, in turn, as evidence of trauma. The police are called. Child protective services intervene. The rest is tragically familiar to us all. Reverse the gender roles and nothing changes. Replace "parent" with teacher or clergyperson or coach, and nothing changes.

No one knows how often this scenario plays out. One kind of thinking would have us credit Mom with malicious intent in this scenario and think of this dynamic in terms of parental alienation (Gardner, 1999b). One hopes the vast majority of these potential legal–emotional conflagrations die out long before the worst damage is done, either because a well-informed family law professional is able to defuse it or because the caregivers involved find a way to see past their own emotions to better understand and respond to the child's needs.

Does this mean that a child's apparent report of abuse or neglect should be ignored? Of course not. Abuse and neglect (and coparental alienation) are very real. As developmentally and systemically informed family law professionals, however, we must be alert to all of the ways in which these matters can emerge, including the case of the child who may be saying more than he or she understands.

PRECOCIOUS AND DELAYED SOCIAL AND EMOTIONAL DEVELOPMENT

Remember the 6-year-old who shakes your hand, looks you in the eye, compliments you on your tie, and greets you by saying, "Good afternoon. How are you today?"

By distinguishing between social skills and socioemotional maturity (see chapter 5), we recognize that this pleasant and charming second-grader may indeed be socially and emotionally mature, but is at least equally likely to have been adultified, parentified, or explicitly coached in advance of your interview. With this in mind, a discussion of socioemotional décalage must look beneath the child's charming veneer (or, at the other extreme, beneath the child's enraged and enraging armor) to try to understand her genuine socioemotional capacities both in comparison to her physical, cognitive, and linguistic development and in comparison to her peers' development. Using the concrete terms defined in chapter 5, this means trying to assess a child's attachment security, emotional balance, impulse control, empathy, and capacity for personal responsibility. Figures 7.6a and 7.6b illustrate this discussion.

Socioemotional development is particularly important to the extent that peer group acceptance opens doors for further growth, increased breadth of experience, and reinforcement of self-esteem,[26] particularly among girls (Thomas & Daubman, 2001), and particularly as adolescence approaches.. Thus, the child who fits in among her peers and copes adequately with the stressors in her life will bootstrap her way through development, making each new opportunity and invitation into more of the same across the years. These children will be more academically successful (Erath, Flanagan, & Bierman, 2008) and generally well adjusted (Waldrip, Malcolm, & Jensen-Campbell, 2008). As one study concluded,

> Children who had more positive experiences with peers in childcare had better social and communicative skills with peers in third grade, were more sociable and co-operative and less aggressive, had more close friends, and were more accepted and popular. Children with more frequent negative experiences with peers in childcare were more aggressive in third grade, had lower social and communicative skills, and reported having fewer friends. (National Institute of Child Development, 2008b, p. 419)

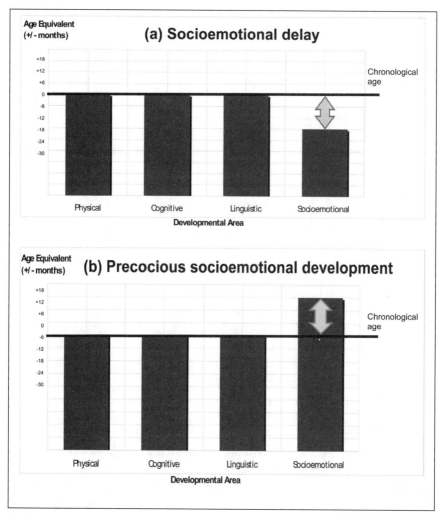

Figure 7.6 Developmental profile of a hypothetical child with (a) significant socioemotional delays and (b) precocious socioemotional skills.

Social and Emotional Delay

Limited experience, psychopathology, trauma, and neurological anomolies singly and in combination can contribute to delays of socioemotional development. Experiential differences can result from cultural and religious prohibitions atypical of the surrounding community, from intentional neglect, or from undiagnosed sensory difference (e.g., deafness[27]). Psychopathology (particularly in the form of social anxiety) and aftershocks of trauma can further restrict a child's social experience. Genetic and neurological anomalies that impact a child's behavior causing him or her to be ridiculed and/or to withdraw in anticipation of social rejection can do the same. No matter the cause, the effect is the same. This type of décalage is illustrated in Figure 7.6a.

Much as linguistic, cognitive, and physical differences may contribute to conditions that can be associated with social and emotional delay, the converse is less often the case. Social and emotional delays have no empirically demonstrable impact on these other areas of development. Nevertheless, we all know anecdotally at least about the risks that the withdrawn, avoidant child is likely to face academically and later, occupationally.

Consider the dilemma of the child with ADHD. He or she may be intellectually, linguistically, and physically indistinguishable from his (or her) peers, but by definition will appear less attentive, more impulsive, and demanding in the classroom. He may have greater difficulty decentrating and recovering from upset in his peer group. As a result, these kids "often have conflicts with adults and peers, and suffer from unpopularity, rejection by peers, and a lack of friendships" (Nijmeijer et al., 2008, p. 692). Although ADHD is diagnosed more often in boys than in girls, the detrimental social impact of diagnosis is not at all gender-specific (Ohan & Johnston, 2007). The good news is that these effects appear to diminish with proper medication (Abikoff et al., 2007).

In like manner, but presumably for very different reasons, children with autism, autism spectrum disorder (ASD), and pervasive developmental disorder (e.g., Asperger's syndrome) tend to be socially and emotionally delayed (Dunlop, Knott, & MacKay, 2008). From the earliest months of life, these children typically have difficulty making and maintaining eye contact, may be minimally responsive to their name, lack early pretend play, fail to imitate caregiver motor movements, and quickly fall behind in both verbal and nonverbal communication. Whereas children with fetal alcohol syndrome may be similarly delayed and interpersonally inappropriate, fetal alcohol kids eagerly seek out social interaction, whereas children with ASD shun it (Bishop, Gahagan, & Lord, 2007).

At the crux of this difficulty is the ASD-diagnosed child's delayed or deficient theory of mind—the understanding that others have a unique internal world apart from one's own that underlies much of socioemotional maturation (Kaland, Callesen, Moller-Nielsen, Mortensen, & Smith, 2008).[28] Curiously, children with early extreme deprivation and neglect (children with disinhibited reactive attachment disorder, for example) seem to suffer similar deficits with similar results (Colvert et al., 2008).

No matter the cause or the associated diagnosis, developmental asynchronies favoring cognitive maturity over socioemotional maturity are likely to be a continual source of internal tension, frustration, and confusion within all but the most severely disturbed children. Children as young as 3 and 4 years of age know what behavior is expected, and recognize (even if they seldom vocalize) their relative inability to fulfill these expectations. From 7 years of age and on through high school, the awareness that others make and keep friends, follow rules, and are rewarded for the effort can exacerbate these children's loneliness, anger, and perceived isolation. These experiences are compounded by the constant criticism of adults who take these children's impulsivity, inability to delay gratification, failures of empathy, and relative inability to recover from upset as manipulative choices in need of discipline. Thus, in the same way that the socially and emotionally mature child's behaviors open doors that build greater and greater maturity, the socially and emotionally delayed child's behavior can appear to slam and lock these same doors shut, denying growth opportunities while age-mates continue to mature, thereby increasing the painful décalage.

Social and Emotional Precocity[29]

The child whose social and emotional maturity outstrips his or her cognitive, linguistic, and physical development is most likely female, an only or an eldest child, and/or has grown up among significantly older individuals (Herer & Mayseless, 2000; Suitor & Pillemer, 2007). For these children especially, experience and social necessity work in tandem to foster advances of empathy, perspective taking, impulse control, and personal responsibility. This type of décalage is illustrated in Figure 7.6b.

Precocious social and emotional development can have its benefits. Especially among girls, these children tend to be leaders and popular among their peers (Nowicki & Duke, 1992) and are overrepresented among the young adults intending to enter the helping professions.[30] In some social situations, however, these same children are also at risk for peer isolation, rejection, and the development of depression (Gest, Sesma, Masten, & Tellegen, 2006).

In the context of a dysfunctional family, the socially and emotionally precocious child is at particularly high risk for role reversal in any of its many destructive forms. This includes adultification, parentification, and sexual abuse (Burton, 2007; Byng-Hall, 2007; Chase, 1999; Jurkovic, 1998), as well as the associated difficulties of adult intimacy and reciprocity (Castro, Jones, & Mirsalimi, 2004; DiCaccavo, 2006; Hooper, 2007; Jurkovic, Thirkield, & Morrell, 2001; Neuenschwander & Pistole, 2008).

Is there a correspondence between a child's precocious development and legally sanctioned autonomy, as when a minor is granted emancipated status?[31] The research is yet to be done. It makes sense that the court would emancipate those minors who have achieved social and emotional maturity, but the opposite is more likely the case. Emancipation is one among many legal outcomes often associated with a child's long history of delinquency, school refusal or failure, family conflict, and abuse and/or neglect, circumstances that are unlikely to foster maturity even if they do force a child to function independently. As such, there is a strong correlation between self-declared and legally sanctioned emancipation and subsequent depression (Paunesku et al., 2008), criminal activity, and drug- and alcohol-related problems.

NORMATIVE DÉCALAGE? THE CASE FOR MATURITY OF JUDGMENT

This discussion has proceeded as if development within a child is normatively synchronous, with the various, successive stages of physical, cognitive, linguistic, and socioemotional maturation somehow emerging in lock-step. In fact, because developmental research tends to be domain-specific, there is very little data with which to determine whether this is the case.

Intuitively, one might just as easily argue that décalage is the norm and that developmental synchrony—what Piaget referred to as equilibrium—is the exception. Development in each domain is, after all, relatively facilitated or impeded by opportunity and experience. Thus, one would expect that a child raised in a linguistically rich environment, for example, would lead with language and pull cognitive, socioemotional, and physical development behind in its wake.

Even dismissing differential environmental opportunities, there is no reason to assume that development is biologically predisposed to synchrony. Just as development within each domain is marked by expectable stages or plateaus, we might reasonably imagine that the normative course of development across domains is marked by expectable periods of asynchrony. These would presumably be the stormiest periods of growth, periods during which the child feels unsettled both within him- or herself and between self and the world in which he or she is struggling to fit.

Are the fabled "terrible twos," for example, at least in part the result of the asynchrony that occurs when cognition leaps ahead into preoperational thought even while the child remains socially and emotionally infantile, physically vulnerable and communicatively limited?

In fact, there is reason to believe that just such a normative décalage occurs in the latter portion of adolescence, a period during which, "pseudoindependence signified defensiveness and not maturity" (Nelson & Bennett, 2008, p. 3; see also Galambos, Turner, & Tilton-Weaver, 2005; Tilton-Weaver, Vitunski, & Galambos, 2001). In the context of studying the adjudication of minors to be tried as adults in criminal matters, Cauffman and Steinberg (2000a, 2000b; Steinberg & Cauffman, 1996) define a constellation of cognitive and socioemotional factors that they refer to as maturity of judgment. This includes achievement of the Piagetian stage of Formal Operations, and three others factors[32] defined as follows (Steinberg & Cauffman, 1996, p. 252):

1. **Responsibility:** "Healthy autonomy, self-reliance and clarity of identity"
2. **Temperance:** "The ability to limit impulsivity, avoid extremes in decision making and to evaluate a situation thoroughly before acting"

3. **Perspective:** "Being able to acknowledge the complexity of a situation and to frame a specific decision within a larger context," including the ability to decentrate

Cauffman and Steinberg (2000a) assessed the emergence of these three components of maturity among more than 1,000 eighth-, tenth-, twelfth-grade, and college-age students, spanning an age range of from 13.7 to 25.0 years. They observe that "the period between 16 and 19 marks an important transition point in psychosocial development that is potentially relevant to debates about the drawing of legal boundaries between adolescence and adulthood" (Cauffman & Steinberg, 2000a, p. 756). Whereas the youngest teens had achieved the cognitive skills presumed necessary to anticipate the outcomes of their choices, the three relevant social and emotional developmental milestones typically lagged at least 2 years behind.

Using these same measures of maturity of judgment Modecki (2008, p. 78) confirms that "adolescents (ages 14–17) display less responsibility and perspective relative to college students (ages 18–21), young-adults (ages 22–27), and adults (ages 28–40)."

These data, together with the results of studies of socioemotional developmental milestones discussed earlier (see chapter 5), converge to suggest that the period from 14 to 16 years of age is marked by expectable décalage. Although the 14-year-old may achieve Formal Operations and thereby the cognitive maturity to foresee abstract possibilities and their contingent outcomes, it's not until age 16 that he or she is likely to have the socioemotional maturity to cope with the impact of these possible future paths (see Figure 7.7). As one editor summarizes simply: "Adolescents may have mature thought processes sometimes but not at others" (Rosado, 2000, p. 22).

SUMMARY

It is far too easy and too frequent that a child's maturity is equated with the superficial signs of physical growth, linguistic competence, academic achievement, or social engagement alone. Understanding that development encompasses many simultaneous, but seldom synchronous, threads allows us to look beneath the surface, to look for a

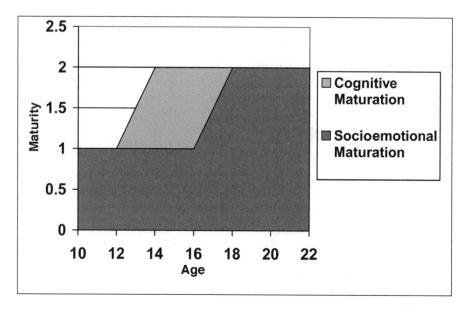

Figure 7.7 Illustration of the hypothetical course of cognitive and socioemotional development, ages 13 to 25 years, in support of Cauffman and Steinberg's (2000a) data.

child's relative developmental strengths and weaknesses, and to make recommendations to the court accordingly. With this understanding, we can begin to consider children's experience in the many dilemmas thrust upon them when their families transition and conflict. We return directly to this discussion in the final chapter, by examining décalage in our own development as family law professionals.

NOTES

1. Montangero and Maurice-Naville (1994, pp. 88–89) illustrate: "If a child is shown two balls of clay, A and B, of the same size, he or she admits that there is the same amount of matter ("the same thing to eat") in the two balls. While the child watches, ball B is then rolled out into a sausage shape. At the age of 5 or 6, a great number of children give a nonconservation response: a child judges that there is more matter ("more to eat") in the sausage than in the ball. From about the age of 7, most children give correct judgments, namely that there is the same amount of mat-

ter...." Thus, the underlying cognitive ability known as conservation is achieved in different domains at different ages.

For even more vivid accounts of preconservation thinking about matter and number, see student videos uploaded to www.youtube.com (e.g., http://www.youtube.com/watch?v=MpREJIrpgv8 or http://www.youtube.com/watch?v=qYtNhNP69lk&feature=related).

2. Smith (1982) takes a similar liberty by introducing the fascinating concept of "family décalage " to refer to "uneven cognitive development among family members" (abstract) as a variable relevant to resolving intrafamilial conflict.

3. Gottfried, Bathurst, and Guerin (1994, p. 151) find that "marital stability or disruption is unrelated to [children's] intellectual differences by age 8" even while noting that other studies have reached different conclusions.

4. Read an intriguing first person account of growing up with an intellectually disabled sibling by Cameron (2008). Also of value are the videos, "Understanding brothers and sisters on the autism spectrum" (www.coultervideo.com).

5. Quinlan (2003, p. 376) offers startling observations: "Divorce/separation between birth and 5 years predicted early menarche, first sexual intercourse, first pregnancy, and shorter duration of first marriage. Separation in adolescence was the strongest predictor of number of sex partners. Multiple changes in childhood caretaking environment were associated with early menarche, first sex, first pregnancy, greater number of sex partners, and shorter duration of marriage. Living with either the father or mother after separation had similar effect on reproductive development. Living with a stepfather showed a weak, but significant, association with reproductive development, however, duration of stepfather exposure was not a significant predictor of development. Difference in amount and quality of direct parental care (vs. indirect parental investment) in two- and single-parent households may be the primary factor linking family environment to reproductive development."

6. Regarding educational resources and remedies for children with Turner syndrome (and other, similar conditions), see Wodrich and Tarbox (2008).

7. Colloquial use of the label "retarded" has fallen out of fashion in professional use except as defined by the *Diagnostic and Statistical Manual, Fourth Edition (DSM IV*; American Psychiatric Association, 1994). *DSM-IV* defines the following categories based on standardized IQ measurements (as indicated in parentheses):

■ Mild Mental Retardation (50–75) comprises approximately 85% of the cognitively delayed population;

- Moderate Mental Retardation (35–55) comprises approximately 10% of this population;
- Severe Mental Retardation (20–35) comprises 3–4% of this population; and
- Profound Mental Retardation (under 20) comprises 1–2% of this population.

For more information about mental retardation and associated deficits, see American Academy of Child and Adolescent Psychiatry (1999).

8. "At both ends of the school-ability continuum, students have a difficult time connecting to interaction and instruction in a heterogeneous classroom unless a high level of differentiated curricula is in place" (Peterson, 2006).
9. See Jarosewich, Pfeiffer, and Morris (2002) for a review of instruments that purport to identify giftedness among students.
10. "Locus of control" (LOC) is a concept related to attribution theory and implicated in some models of depression. LOC refers to whether an individual attributes the experience of success and failure to self or to chance. Depressed individuals, for example, commonly attribute success to chance and failure to self in a manner that tends to reinforce their depressed state.
11. Vanderbilt-Adriance and Shaw (2008) find that early childhood measures of " IQ, nurturant parenting, and parent-child relationship quality" together determined which among their sample of disadvantaged urban youth became socially successful adolescents.
12. Burkett (1991) finds that parents who were themselves sexually abused as children are at high risk for seeking parent-like nurturance from their children.
13. Take care not to infer causality in these findings. Although cognitive delay may cause circumstances that indeed cause social and emotional distress, it is at least equally likely that both cognitive delay and social/emotional dysfunction are born of the same underlying cause.
14. In one dramatic clinical example, a 12-year-old girl was presented for psychotherapy by her single mother. Mother was an extremely successful businesswoman who had raised her daughter alone from birth largely by giving in. As a result, the child had every toy and gadget imaginable but no friends, failing grades, and an utter inability to tolerate frustration and inhibit impulses. She had been taught that demanding and tantruming were successful coping strategies. Although quite intelligent and linguistically competent, this child was socially and emotionally still an infant. Unfortunately, psychotherapy failed because Mom characteristi-

cally demanded that the answer had nothing to do with her parenting or the mother–daughter relationship, but that the child should be medicated.

15. Although many people have significant cognitive deficits of unknown causes and up to 50% of those with any identified cause have multiple causes (Luckasson et al., 1992).

16. Nisbett (2009) provides an intriguing and simple table illustrating the relation among child and parent and sibling IQs raised together and apart. He asserts that the correlation between a child's IQ and the average of his or parents' IQs when raised together is .50.

17. See also http://www.healthfinder.gov/orgs/hr2906.htm

18. Keeping in mind the false positive impressions associated with mimicry and coaching as discussed in chapter 4.

19. Miniscalco, Nygren, Hagberg, Kadesjo, and Gillberg (2006, p. 361) more specifically find that "children in the general population who screen positive for speech and language problems before age 3 years appear to be at very high risk of autism spectrum disorders or ADHD, or both, at 7 years of age. Remaining language problems at age 6 years strongly predict the presence of neuropsychiatric or neurodevelopmental disorders at age 7 years."

20. Familiar and most dramatic is Helen Keller's story: Because she was mute, her family inferred that she understood nothing and was severely cognitively impaired.

21. Learn more at http://www.selectivemutism.org/ or read Hayden's fascinating account in *Twilight Children: Three Voices No One Heard Until a Therapist Listened* (2005, New York: HarperCollins)

22. One blogger presents this discussion eloquently: "So there you have it...whether your child has 'Einstein syndrome' or Down syndrome...expect great things from your child, pretend he has 'Einstein syndrome,' show him your excitement with each new achievement, and he will surprise you with the things he can do and learn. He will probably even teach you a few things" Retrieved January 3, 2009, from http://www.about-down-syndrome.com/einstein-syndrome.html

23. Formerly known as "epileptic aphasia;" learn more at: http://www.nidcd.nih.gov/health/voice/landklfs.htm

24. The Literacy Trust provides an excellent and concise summary of language learning milestones and relevant developmental variables at http://www.literacytrust.org.uk/research/earlylanguage.html

25. That is, errors of meaning as opposed to errors of articulation. The latter—including stutter, stammer, lisp, and those articulation errors attributable to physical deformity, neurological differences and/or impaired motor control—will not be addressed in this text. The interested reader is di-

rected to the American Speech-Language-Hearing Association at http://www.asha.org/default.htm or to Bernthal, Bankson, and Flipsen (2008).

26. Curiously, note Bishop and Inderbitzen's (1995) conclusion that self-esteem among ninth-grade students increased so long as a child had at least one close friend, but showed no improvement as the number of close friends increased.

27. The *Journal of Deaf Studies and Deaf Education* makes free articles available, including the following regarding social maturity and hearing deficits: "Social processes and outcomes of in-school contact between deaf and hearing peers" [Summer 2002, 7(3), 200–213]; "Promoting social competence in deaf students: The effect of an intervention program—a study on the effects of a social skills training program for mainstreamed deaf students" [Fall 2000, 5(4).323–333]; "Theory of mind: Deaf and hearing children's comprehension of picture stories and judgments of social situations" [Summer 2000, 5(3), 248–265]; and "The social adjustment of deaf adolescents in segregated, partially integrated, and mainstreamed settings" [Winter 1996, 1(1), 52–63].

28. In fact, individuals diagnosed on the autistic spectrum may not even know what they themselves know (Mitchell & O'Keefe, 2008)!

29. As throughout the discussion of décalage, delay and precocity are relative terms. I note, for example, the United States Supreme Court's consideration of relative social precocity and mental retardation as mitigating factors in *Penry v. Lynaugh* [US 492 U.S. 302 (1989)]: "he intellectually functions at an age between six and seven and functions in a social environment at age between nine and ten."

30. These outcomes may be quite culturally dependent (Türetgen, Unsal, & Erdem, 2008).

31. For a state-by-state directory of emancipation legislation, go to: http://www.jlc.org/factsheets/emancipationus/

32. These factors map onto the four-factor model discussed earlier quite closely: "Personal Responsibility" and "Responsibility"; "Temperance" and "Impulse Control"; and "Perspective" and "Empathy." The fourth variable introduced here, "Emotional Balance," may be conceptually related to "Temperance" or may instead highlight an independent factor closely related to the larger concept of self-regulation.

In the Best Developmental Interests of the Child: Topics in Separation, Visitation, and Reunification

It is cardinal with us that the custody, care and nurture of the child reside first in the parents.

—*Prince v. Massachusetts*

Family law scholars and psychologists agree that a child will best develop his potential and will make the greatest gains in physical and mental health if he has a healthy relationship with both parents.

—*Aviva Orenstein*

Family law has always sought to answer questions about the nature, quality, frequency, and condition of children's relationships with others, most particularly with caregivers in their various roles. But family law in the age of DNA testing and PDA messaging, donor eggs and gestational surrogates, gay marriage, no-fault, divorce, and emancipated minors suddenly faces questions (and potential answers) never before considered.

Fortunately, the fundamentals of child and family development remain unchanged. Our task in the chapters that follow is to map these principles and theories and findings onto the brave new world of 21st-century technology and morality and law so as to answer a single question: What is in the best developmental interests of today's child?

8

A Child's Understanding of Time, Separation, and Loss

When it cries with hunger, the baby has its first experience of duration.

—Jean Piaget

The future is something which everyone reaches at the rate of 60 minutes an hour, whatever he does, whoever he is.

—C. S. Lewis

In its necessarily adult-centered view, the law has a wide variety of names and procedures for what are, from the child's perspective, variations on the single theme of parent–child separation. This chapter discusses the developmental research and family systems dynamics associated with separation, loss, and reunion as common foundation for subsequent discussions of specific family law matters: custodial schedules and infant overnights, visitation resistance and reunion, relocation, and reunification and termination of parental rights. By carefully setting forth this foundation at the outset, I hope to provide you with tools with which to approach any of the many other specific instances in which the court must address matters of parent–child separation, including (as examples) matters of foster care, adoption, and grandparents' rights (e.g., Riggs, 2003).[1]

THE DEVELOPMENT OF A SENSE OF TIME

The experience of separation and loss can only exist as a function of time. It may be common knowledge that the experience of loss changes over time, often following a pattern of shifting emotions from initial shock to a painful crescendo and then falling back to a dull ache that for some may never disappear. It may not be common knowledge, however, that the time course of this process varies for individuals by circumstance (Archer, 2008; Maciejewski, Zhang, Block, & Prigerson, 2007 [cf., Weiner, 2007]; Murray-Parkes, 2006) and with the cognitive and socioemotional development of the experience of time (Busby & Suddendorf, 2005).

Children experience the passage of time quite differently as they grow. Piaget (1927/1969) observed a succession of stages in the understanding of time built upon the child's experience of velocity and travel across physical distance. To oversimplify, I have suggested elsewhere (Garber, 2008a) that we can understand an individual's subjective experience of a given period as a proportion of his or her total experience, a quantity most easily gauged as a function of chronological age.[2] Thus, one year is a full 20% of a 5-year-old's experience and an inconceivably long period for that child to understand, never mind to wait for Mommy to come home. The same 365 days is, however, only 2% of a 50-year-old's life and can, in some circumstances, be experienced as a tolerable, even a fleeting moment.

Let me illustrate the importance of working within a child's sense of time with a clinical example: To motivate behavior change, I often recommend to parents that we establish incentives or rewards for the child. It is commonly the case that one or both parents present this reply, "We tried that. It didn't work." Upon further discussion, this usually means that Mom and Dad have told their impulsive and immature 5-year-old that if he makes his bed every day for a week, he can earn a reward on Sunday.

Why did the child make his bed on Monday, then half-heartedly on Tuesday, but not at all the rest of the week? Chances are that on Monday he had the reward fresh in mind. On Tuesday, the salience of that same reward had eroded so that by Wednesday, the eventuality of success seems far, far too distant. Assuming that he values the promised reward, the answer is that he couldn't manage the time interval. For this child, working toward something 1 week distant is like offering his mom or dad a job for which they'd be paid only once every 2 or 3 years. The temporal connection between today's behavior and the desired outcome is far too weak.

The same principle applies to family law matters: Contact with an absent parent, for example, is often scheduled to occur on alternating weekends to accommodate adult needs, with little consideration of the child's needs. A preschooler may experience a 2-week separation the way you or I would experience a period of months or even years, whereas a teenager might complain that the same alternating-week schedule gets in the way of his or her social life.

The law has occasionally recognized developmental differences in the subjective experience of time. *The Model Statute for Termination of Parental Rights* (as discussed in Ezzo, Evans, & McGovern-Kondik, 2004, p. 33), for example, acknowledges that "a child's sense of time and urgency is quite different than an adult's. A short wait for an adult can be an intolerable separation for a young child."

The development of the sense of time is associated with the growth of critical socioemotional capacities introduced in chapter 5, namely, the ability to delay gratification and the ability to tolerate frustration. Together, these interwoven developments bear directly on understanding a child's conception of and reaction to separation and loss.

From the earliest emergence of object- and person-permanence sometime in the sensorimotor period (4–7 months of age), the emotionally secure child gradually learns to tolerate longer and longer periods of separation from his or her primary attachment figures. By contrast, the experience of inconsistent and chaotic caregiving can interfere with a child's reaction to separation, causing some to become almost instantly crippled with distress and others to disengage in a manner that suggests indifference or rejection upon separation (e.g., Ainsworth & Wittig, 1969; Zilberstein, 2006).

Even the most secure children normally go through periods of more intense separation anxiety. This typically peaks between 18 and 30 months of age. In atypical cases, separation anxiety can persist into adolescence (Foley et al., 2008) and may be a harbinger of adult panic disorder and depression (Lewinsohn et al., 2008).

The normal course of development can be significantly and even permanently disrupted when a parent and child are abruptly separated, when a child's contact with an absent parent is either too distant in time or unpredictable and/or when the separation is extended beyond the child's cognitive and emotional tolerance: "A disruption of this attachment, and repeated uprooting of a child...[is] seriously detrimental to their physical, mental and emotional well-being" (Ezzo, Evans, & McGovern-Kondik, 2004, p. 33). At the extreme, the child's experience of separation is indistinguishable from the child's experience of death. Grief sets in with its panoply of expectable emotions:

> [G]rief and mourning occur when the attachment figure is repeatedly unavailable, thereby activating the child's attachment system in the form of crying behavior....continual parental absences could leave a child with an inability to form deep relationships. (Bowlby's work as summarized by Nelson & Bennett, 2008, p.3)

TRANSITIONAL OBJECTS AND INTERIM CONTACTS

Earlier, I described caregivers as the source of the child's emotional fuel. As the healthy child grows, his or her fuel tank and fuel efficiency grow. All other things being equal, one unit of Mom or Dad's love might carry the healthy toddler through a half-hour of play, the healthy grade-schooler through a full school day, a healthy high-schooler through a week or 2 of summer camp, and a healthy young adult through the years that lead toward becoming a parent him- or herself.

With the introduction of stress, fuel efficiency plummets. At any age, healthy individuals turn from stress back to their emotional anchors in search of refueling (read about regression in chapter 6). Once basic representational thought is developed, we can facilitate a child's independent functioning, the ability to tolerate frustration, the ability to delay gratification, and thereby the ability to manage separation through the use of transitional objects.

A *transitional object* is anything that represents the security that a caregiver providers in his or her absence (Ikeuchi & Fujihara, 2004). Pacifiers and thumb-sucking may be among the most primitive transitional objects, helping the infant and toddler to self-soothe by providing a sensorimotor (prerepresentational) substitute for the security associated with nursing. Later in development, many toddlers and preschoolers spontaneously develop their own transitional objects. These are the treasured blankets and stuffed animals that become shredded and filthy even as they become more and more beloved.[3]

We can help children to better understand and manage the experience of separation by making the experience more concrete and by providing transitional objects. For example:

1. Make time concrete and visible. Many children who see an absent parent on a fixed schedule (in the context of, for instance, divorce, incarceration, or hospitalization) struggle to understand and thus to manage the interval between contacts. Like the back-seat voice that constantly begs "Are we there yet?" these kids need help to conceptualize the passage of time. This is expected of toddlers and preschoolers, but may be equally true of grade-schoolers, who may have the requisite cognitive and socioemotional tools, but are unable to use them in these distressing circumstances because of regression.

These children can benefit from the institution of a new suppertime or bedtime ritual. A large wall calendar is color-coded so that contact days with the absent parent are clearly visible. Each evening, the present day is crossed out and the number of days remaining until contact is recounted. When parents are divorced and the child spends (subjectively) long periods in both homes, identical calendars and rituals in each will help the child to grasp the time frame.

The same principle applies to shorter periods. An hour visit with Dad at the prison or the hospital once a week can be intolerably brief. Well-meaning adults who point to their digital watches or clocks and offer "10 minutes until we have to go" reminders may be simply supplying insufficient data. Analogue-face clocks help children to physically see the time pass as the big hand approaches an identified digit (or even better, the fat red line drawn on its face). Egg timers can accomplish the same goal.

We can sometimes communicate duration best when we express the time in the child's language of familiar events rather than in our own abstract language of minutes, hours, days, and weeks. Rather than refer to the next visit with Dad as a number of days in the future, young children will understand the same period expressed as a number of "sleeps," as in, "we'll come back and see Daddy again in three more sleeps." Younger grade-school children can understand the same period as occurring after two more swim lessons, or the next time a favorite weekly television show is on.

Older children may be calendar- and clock-competent in classroom exercises, but the stresses associated with family matters can compromise these brand new skills (read about regression in chapter 6). It's always better to speak too simply to a child and tolerate the resulting roll-of-the-eyes than to assume understanding only to discover later that your meaning was misunderstood.

---

2. A dose of Dad (or Mom). Our first and most basic experience of caregiving is experienced through our most primitive senses: smell (olfaction), texture (tactile input), sound (audition), and taste (gestation). The most effective transitional objects for the most needy and least socioemotionally mature children communicate to these same senses. When father and son must be apart for an extended period, can Billy have Dad's unwashed tee-shirt to wear as pajamas or made into a pillowcase? An audio recording of Dad reading bedtime stories that a child can listen to at bedtime in his absence? A drop of Mom's perfume on the child's pillow? A video recording of the parent and child at play?

More developmentally sophisticated transitional objects rely on a child's thinking and verbal skills and less on primitive senses: A note or a photograph taped inside a lunchbox; a message in a locket or in the secret compartment of a little boy's wallet.

Transitional objects can give the child an outlet for expression, as well. In some instances, it's useful for the child to have a "Daddy box" in Mom's home and a "Mommy box" in Dad's home so that found treasures, pictures drawn, and notes written can be collected over time and then delivered to the intended recipient later. Older children can use a journal or a diary similarly.

3. The benefits and burdens of media. Live contact with an absent parent via any of the many amazing digital media now available can help to ease a child's experience of separation when used carefully (Gottfried, 2002; Samuels & Friesen, 2004). When misused, these media cannot only make the child's experience of separation more painful, but can interfere with daily routines, responsibilities, and healthy functioning.

When phone calls (or instant messaging, texting, video chat, etc.) are predictable, the child can break down an otherwise intolerable period of separation into smaller chunks between media contacts, usually to his benefit. When these contacts are unpredictable for any number of reasons, some children will become distracted and hypervigilant waiting for the next call. When these contacts are random, as can result from a well-intended court's order allowing a child "unmonitored and unimpeded cell phone access with his absent parent," authority in the child's home can be disrupted and undermined.

4. The protective value of siblings.[4] A sibling may be a child's best transitional object (Beaudry, Simard, Drapeau, & Charbonneau, 2000; Bush & Ehrenberg, 2003). In most instances, postseparation and postdivorce custody arrangements which separate siblings serve the contesting parties' wishes more than the children's best interests (Kaplan, Hennon, & Ade-Ridder, 1993). By the same token, foster and adoptive care arrangements that separate siblings can work against their mutual well-being (Seifert, 2004; Wulczyn & Zimmerman, 2005).[5] Badeau (2004, p. 176) takes a very strong position:

> Even when a child clearly will not be well served by returning home, and no relatives are available to provide a permanent home for the child, children must be allowed to maintain the connections that have been significant in their lives. Sibling relationships, in particular, should be carefully preserved in all but the most extreme circumstances.

Poehlmann and colleagues (2008, p. 6) observe that "separation from siblings may be traumatizing for young children in the context of maternal incarceration." Siblings can be one another's greatest supports, no matter how disruptive their natural and necessary rivalry.

Whereas as recently as 1995, "Case law specifically addressing siblings' rights to visitation [was] sparse…[and] courts which have heard such cases have generally abided by a 'no statute–no standing–no right to visitation' rule" (Williams, 1995), in recent years many jurisdictions have adopted standards similar to New Jersey's:

> [T]his Court finds that the relationship between a child and his/her siblings is a significant and unique one, from which a myriad of benefits and experiences may be derived. The bonds which develop between brothers

and sisters are strong ones, and are, in most cases, irreplaceable....The time has come for this State to take its place among those which recognize the necessity and importance of the right of siblings to visit with one another. *Therefore, this Court finds that siblings possess the natural, inherent and inalienable right to visit with each other.* This right is, of course, subject to the requirement that such visitation be in the best interest of a minor child, for it is that which is of paramount concern to this Court. (*L., K., C., B. and H.K. v. G. and H.*, 497 A.2d 215; N.J. Super. Ct. Ch. Div. 1985)

In fact, some family law professionals (Ferraris, 2005; Grob, 1993; Shlonsky, Bellamy, Elkins, & Ashare, 2005) recommend creation of "a constitutionally protected right of association among siblings."

ONE MODEL WITH WHICH TO OPERATIONALIZE PARENT–CHILD SEPARATION

Unfortunately, children's needs cannot be postponed while empirical data is collected, validated, and published in peer-reviewed journals. In the best of circumstances, family law professionals apply relevant –if generic—research findings to current problems to the child's benefit. More commonly, we are left to speculate about how to apply incomplete and often tangential data to a child's unique circumstance.

The latter is the case with regard to court-mandated parent–child separations. I have proposed a simple heuristic as a starting point for consideration of the period of separation as may be appropriate, for example, to postdivorce custody considerations (Garber, 2008a). All other things being equal:

1. The plan must be built around the child's needs and abilities, not the child's wishes or the parents' needs or wishes.
2. The plan should anticipate developmental change and adjust accordingly, rather than emplace a schedule suited to the child's present functioning and require that parties return to court as that schedule is inevitably outgrown.
3. The plan must facilitate the child's opportunity to create and maintain a healthy relationship with both of his or her parents, acknowledging that "it is important for children that their non-residential parent continue to act like a 'full-service' parent rather

than taking trips to Disneyland or McDonalds" (Clarke-Stewart & Hayward, 1996, p. 260).

4. As an outer limit, the plan must avoid separating the child from a parent for a number of consecutive nights in excess of twice the number of years in his or her age. Thus, a 2-year-old might manage a 4-night separation and a 12-year-old might manage as many as 24 consecutive nights away. In routine instances, the schedule should avoid separation for a number of consecutive nights in excess of the child's age in years. This more conservative rubric recommends that a 2-year-old should have no more than 2 consecutive nights away.[6]

SUMMARY

In our own pressured, rushed efforts to do this very difficult work, it is far too easy to forget that children speak another language. Their thinking is likely to be concrete, immediate, and self-centered due to a combination of cognitive immaturity and regression caused by stress. We must always take the time to explain time and separation from important others, including siblings, in terms that children can understand and to structure time in a manner that children can manage. Building on this bedrock, we can now procede to consider how best to tailor parenting plans for young children.

NOTES

1. The Superior Court of Maricopa County, Arizona, USA, provides an impressive and useful bibliography of current sources on these and related issues at: http://www.superiorcourt.maricopa.gov/lawlibrary/Docs/PDF/Bibl iographies/Visitationrev2.pdf

2. Certainly the contents (Droit-Volet & Meck, 2008) and emotional meaning (Droit-Volet & Meck, 2008) of the period in question both have a large impact on the individual's perception of time, as well.

3. Two wonderful children's books can help parents and their children talk about transitional objects and emotional security. For younger children: *The Kissing Hand* by Audrey Penn (Child and Family Press, 1993). For preschool and grade-school children: *The Velveteen Rabbit* by Margery Williams, 1922, Doubleday).

4. For an excellent bibliography regarding siblings in the context of family law, see the Australian government's site at http://www.aifs.gov.au/afrc/bibs/siblings.html
5. The case of *Nelson v. Horsley* (NH Supreme Court, 2003-433) presents a fascinating case in which the legalities of parent–child relationships trumped the emotional bonds, arguably to the child's detriment (see http://www.courts.state.nh.us/supreme/opinions/2003/hors1075.htm).
6. This heuristic frequently generates conclusions consistent with the specific recommendations of independent professionals. For example, all other things being equal, "[b]y the time children reach age 2 they can manage two consecutive overnights with each parent without stress....For a pre-schooler, an extended weekend in each parent's home as well as overnights during the week, is quite tolerable but separations from either parent should last no more than three or four days....At school age, and certainly by age 7 or 8, children can manage 5- to 7-day separations from parents as part of a regular schedule as well as two weeks vacation" (Altobelli, 2005, pp. 34–36).

9 Custodial Schedules and Infant Overnights

Overnight visits are likely not to be in the child's best interests, because infants' eating and sleeping arrangements should be as stable as possible.

—*W. F. Hodges*

If infants can tolerate sleeping away from both parents during nap time at day care centers, on what basis can we argue that sleeping away from one parent, in the familiar home of the other parent, would harm children?

—*R. A. Warshak*

Rock-a-bye baby, in the tree top.
When the wind blows, the cradle will rock.
When the bough breaks, the cradle will fall,
And down will come baby, cradle and all.

—*Mother Goose/ British nursery rhyme, circa 1700*

The question of infant overnights in the context of marital separation and divorce is among the most hotly contested of the frequently red-hot issues that arise in family law.[1,2] As narrow as this topic may appear, it has fostered a tremendous literature, the best of which relies on sound empirical data to reach one or the other of two divergent conclusions:

Infants can and should or cannot and must not do overnights with their fathers (Biringen et al., 2002; Ram, Pinzi, & Cohen, 2002; Pruett, Ebling, & Insabella, 2004; Solomon, 2005; Warshak, 2002).

The gender specificity of this statement applies with little exception. The arguments for and against infant overnights routinely occur with regard to a child 2 years of age or younger who resides largely or exclusively with Mom while Dad argues more or less vehemently, more or less cogently, for at least day contacts with his new child in the interest of building a secure attachment (usually voiced before the court as "bonding"), and more usually for overnight care at least once each week. Mom counters that the baby won't sleep well while away, that his routine will be upset, that she's nursing, and/or that Dad has no experience with infants.

Throw into this mix the intense emotions stirred in part by the hormones associated with birth for both parents (see, e.g., Cox, 2005), strong opinions about nursing versus expressing breast milk versus formula, the powerful emotions harbored by parties whose relationship failed to survive pregnancy, and the well-intended but seldom constructive partisan support of friends and families. The result is a helpless newborn left sitting atop a powder keg.

The tragic irony is that the legal processes intended to remedy this conflict can last far longer than the developmental period in question. Thus, by the time the court rules on Dad's motion for overnights with his new son, the child has become a toddler, the parties are far more acrimonious, the extended families are far more polarized, everyone is deeply in debt, and the quality of the child's experience in *both* homes has been compromised by the process.

Like the disputing parties, both sides of the associated empirical/philosophical debate can be heard loud and clear. On one side of the coin are those researchers who promote overnights in the interest of building infant–father attachments (e.g., Kelly & Lamb, 2000; Kelly & Lamb, 2001). Others go to the opposite extreme (e.g., Awad & Parry, 1980).[3] Perhaps representative of the latter is the recommendation that overnights should not begin until 2 to 3 years of age (e.g., Garrity & Baris, 1994; Hodges, 1991; Skafte, 1985).

Most reasonable are those moderating voices that recognize that there cannot be a single, universal answer to this question; that, instead, we must learn to recognize the conditions which are either conducive or contrary to infant overnights. For example,

[W]hen parental conflict is high and parent communication about the child is low, overnight separations from the primary caregiver should be avoided at least through the 3rd year of life. Conversely, we believe that a variety of overnight access schedules can work when parent communication is high and parents are able to work flexibly together on the care of their young child. Even separations of a few days from the primary caregiver seem to be well tolerated when conditions are supportive." (Solomon & Biringen, 2001, p. 361)

In this chapter, the basic tenets of child and family development are put to the test. The question of infant overnights proves to be the crucible in which a thorough understanding of the growing infant's cognitive, social, emotional, and linguistic capacities—in particular, those conditions that work for and against establishment and maintenance of attachment relationhships—are tested. Just as importantly, the question of infant overnights tests our own deepest (and often least rational) feelings about a child's need for a healthy relationship with his or her mother.

What conditions are conducive to shared parenting?

The creation of any parenting plan is a balancing act worthy of Ringling Brothers, Barnum and Bailey. Mom's wishes versus Dad's wishes. The child's needs versus the child's wishes. The strengths of each parent versus his/her weaknesses. The strengths and weaknesses of one parent versus those of the other.

We approach this incredible feat in a legal environment that supports the child's continuing relationship with both parents, a presumption which is wholly consistent with the developmental literature, even if near impossible on a case-by-case basis. Much as we might hope to balance the child's opportunity to benefit from each parent's strengths, we must be mindful of the very real (if politically incorrect) "accumulative risks for children whose care is divided between parents who lack the core relational infrastructure to support a healthy environment for shared care...particularly for young children who experience divided care in a hostile climate" (McIntosh & Chisholm, 2008, p. 37).

Johnston (1995, pp. 422–424), describes six criteria with which to begin to determine postseparation care schedules. In short, these include:

1. Assuring the child has access to "warm, affectionate, and responsive parent–child relationships, with appropriate parental expectations and control" (and)
2. Parents who are "relatively free of psychological disturbance or substance abuse" (then)
3. The parenting plan must protect the child from violence and minimize the opportunity for coparental conflict.
4. For highly conflicted caregivers, a "clearly specified, regular visitation plan is crucial, and the need for shared decision making and direct communication should be kept to a minimum."
5. "[I]t may be appropriate to give more weight to providing the child with continuity in relationships with supportive others (such as grandparents, child care persons, and peers) and stability of place (such as neighborhood and school)."
6. "If there is a current threat of violence, or if there is ongoing/episodic violence, then (other factors being equal) the nonviolent parent should have sole custody and the violent parent's access to the child should be supervised."

McIntosh and colleagues (Altobelli, 2005; McIntosh and Chisholm, 2008; McIntosh & Long, 2006, 2007; Parkinson, 2006; Smyth, 2004; Smyth & Chisholm, 2006) studied high-conflict families who appeared before the Australian family courts. McIntosh and Chisholm (2007, p. 9) conclude that "substantially shared care arrangements may entail risks for children's healthy emotional development in families that have the following specific factors, especially in combination.

Parent factors:

1. Low levels of maturity and insight;
2. A parent's poor capacity for emotional availability to the child;
3. Ongoing, high levels of [coparental] conflict;
4. Ongoing significant psychological acrimony between parents;
5. Child is seen to be at risk in the care of one parent.

Child factors:

6. Under 10 years of age;
7. The child is not happy with the shared arrangement;
8. The child experiences a parent to be poorly available to them.

WHAT CONDITIONS ARE SPECIFICALLY CONDUCIVE TO INFANT OVERNIGHTS?

Given that infants have the fewest physical, cognitive, social, and emotional resources with which to cope with stress, and given what we know about the development of language, thinking, and early relatedness, we can prescribe some of the conditions that are congruent with a parenting plan including overnights with Dad. Above and beyond the more general conditions described previously, the infant should have:

1. A high degree of consistency across caregiving environments. This calls for frequent, constructive, and child-centered coparent communication so as to assure that the child has similar experiences in the two homes, including:
   (a) Consistency of routines (e.g., waking, napping, diapering, mealtimes);
   (b) Consistency of sensory experiences[4] (e.g., bedding and clothing textures as a factor of manufacturer and detergent, tastes and the succession of new foods, ambient sounds and media volume, room temperature and lighting);
   (c) Consistency of limits, expectations, and discipline.
   (d) Consistency of auxiliary caregivers. When a nanny, babysitter, or daycare is required by either parent, that caregiver should be available to the child across environments. This specifically requires that parents refrain from inducting such caregivers into their conflict, assuring that the caregiver is allied with the child, not with either adult or either home.
2. An absolute minimum of exposure to adult conflict, namely, that "caution be exercised in relation to substantially shared care for children under 4, especially when there are high levels of parental conflict" (Altobelli, 2008, p. 13). This requires that each parent have the impulse control and socioemotional maturity to contain whatever negative emotions arise regarding and in the presence of the child's other parent, fully aware that the infant will respond to the caregivers' physiological signs of stress (e.g., heart rate, respiration, muscle tone) at least as much as the caregiver's words and actions. As a practical matter, this may call for:

(a) One or both parents to be in psychotherapy, at least, so as to have a contained place to vent and a skilled helper with whom to develop strategies to manage these strong feelings so as to better protect the infant from vicarious exposure to coparenting stress;

(b) Scripted transitions (Garber, 2008a) intended to minimize the eruption of conflict in the child's presence;

(c) Emplacement of effective dispute-resolution pathways for the purpose of reassuring the parents that conflicts will be resolved promptly and in a child-centered manner, thereby minimizing the duration of the associated stresses and recognizing that most (if not all) infant-related conflicts demand immediate resolution. This might include mutual participation in a facilitated coparenting intervention, mediation, or the appointment of a Parenting Coordinator.

3. The opportunity to establish and maintain a secure attachment with each parent (Aaronson, 2007) uncontaminated by other adults' potentially alienating, negative messages.

4. A predictable schedule which strikes a child-centered balance between continuity of care with one parent and the loss associated with separation from the other, taking into accouint the child's sense of time (see chapter 8)

A DEVELOPMENTALLY INFORMED MODEL OF INFANT'S SHARED CARE

Building on these observations, I offer the following synthesis and recommendations as a place to start the conversation regarding each specific infant's care in the context of separation and divorce:

1. Presume that the child's time will be shared, including overnights, unless and until:

(a) The coparents' communication fails, such that the two home environments and parenting practices become inconsistent, particularly if one or both parents refuse to comply with established structures for communication (see www.ourfamilywizard.com, a Web site that helps separated parents coordi-

nate communication, schedules, and other parenting duties) ;
(b) The coparents' conflict erupts in the child's presence despite efforts to script the adults' face-to-face encounters, despite education about the deleterious impact of such experiences on the child, and particularly if one or both parents fail to successfully comply with recommended remedies (e.g., psychotherapy, medication);
(c) There is reason to believe that one parent is insensitive and/or unresponsive to the child's needs,[5] particularly if this parent is unresponsive to this feedback and/or unwilling to successfully comply with associated remedies (e.g., Marvin et al., 2002);
(d) The existing care schedule proves impractical (e.g., with regard to work schedules, transportation time between homes, conflicts with the child's schedule) and/or is disregarded by one parent without the other parent's foreknowledge and consent;
(e) The child's health and well-being are compromised by the arrangement; or,
(f) Either parent is abusive, neglectful, or violent or acts to alienate the child from the other parent.

2. Under these conditions, a default schedule is established, based on the heuristic offered in the preceding chapter; that is, the child will not be separated from a parent for a number of nights in excess of twice the number of years in his or her age and, in the routine, should not be separated for a number of nights in excess of the child's age in years.

3. A dispute resolution pathway is in place and endorsed by the co-parents (e.g., a Parenting Coordinator [Association of Family and Conciliation Courts, 2006; Kirkland & Sullivan, 2008]).

4 The means of evaluating the plan's continuing utility are in place so as to make schedule changes associated with development (as per item 2) child-centered, predictable, and as cooperative as possible.

Does this approach create an incentive for conflict? No. Had I worded this presentation as a mother-default plan (as in "unless Dad..."), then self-serving mothers might purposefully not communicate and cooperate in the interests of winning a majority share of their child's time. This plan does nothing to increase whatever incentive already exists for high-conflict coparents to conflict.

What this recommendation does, instead, is provide a default child-centered position that is consistent with both developmental theory and the law in most jurisdictions and the means with which to determine whether and how that default might be applied to a particular child's needs.

What this plan does not do is provide the standardized means with which to measure the contingent variables of consistency, communication, and conflict. In this regard, I share Altobelli's (2008, p. 9) lament that neither the courts nor the social sciences have as yet invented a "toxicity barometer which accurately measures the level of the toxicity in parental relationships and provides us with a reading that enables us to make informed judgments about the best type of parenting order to make for children."

Neither does this plan provide guidance as to best next steps if and when the contingent variables are breached. Should one parent be unable or unwilling to fulfill these criteria, does that mean a decrease in the number or frequency or duration—or perhaps a total cessation—of overnights? If so, for how long and subject to what remedies? Where are the thresholds for noncompliance? Surely one act of abuse has an entirely different meaning than one failed communication or late pick-up, but as Johnston (1995) points out, we must have some means of accounting for the severity, frequency, and impact of these acts. To the extent that high-conflict coparents are, by definition, relatively unable to meet the criteria I have set forth, these many questions require immediate empirical research and associated jurisprudence.

Breastfeeding and Infant Overnights

On the one hand, breastfeeding is an incredibly important experience for all involved. Lactation confers innumerable medical benefits on the mother. Breast milk (at least through 6 months of age) confers well-documented medical and psychosocial benefits on the infant. Thus, the American Academy of Pediatrics[6] (AAP; 2005, pp. 498–500) strongly advises that:

> Pediatricians and other health care professionals should recommend human milk for all infants in whom breastfeeding is not specifically contrain-

dicated and provide parents with complete, current information on the benefits and techniques of breastfeeding to ensure that their feeding decision is a fully informed one.

On the other hand, father involvement from a child's earliest days is a strong predictor of continuing father involvement throughout the child's development, which in turn is associated with numerous and important cognitive, psychosocial, occupational, and educational outcomes (Almeida, & Galambos, 1991; Borke, Lamm, Eickhorst, & Keller, 2007; Bronte-Tinkew & Moore, 2006; Carlson & McLanahan, 2004; Clarke-Stewart 1980; Day, & Lamb, 2004; Flouri & Buchanan, 2004).

With the parents' separation, a choice must be made. Fortunately, the vast majority of coparents are able to put aside their differences to work flexibly around their child's needs. For the infant, this may mean that Mom makes accommodations so that father and child can be together often and meaningfully while Dad makes accommodations so that mother and child can nurse regularly.

For the persistently high-conflict minority (many speculate 10%) among separated and divorcing parents, the infant's time with Dad and the infant's opportunity to breastfeed may be mutually exclusive. In these infants' best interests, we are forced to make a well-informed judgment. The fact is that the benefits of consuming expressed breast milk are no less than that of nursing. True, when Dad bottle-feeds breast milk, the baby has fewer opportunities to enjoy the socioemotional experience of feeding with Mom, but he or she can benefit from sharing similar physical intimacies with Dad. Intact families function this way when Mom works third shift, when she travels, is active in the military, or is hospitalized. In fact, the same AAP recommendation quoted above goes on to say:

> [W]hen direct breastfeeding is not possible, expressed human milk should be provided...Should hospitalization of the breastfeeding mother or infant be necessary, every effort should be made to maintain breastfeeding, preferably directly, or pumping the breasts and feeding expressed milk if necessary.[7]

I note, finally, this comment from Dr. Robin Deutch (2009, p.3), past-president of the Association of Family and Concialition Courts (AFCC), in her Pesident's Message:

[U]ntil the early part of this century, it was commonly believed that infants and toddlers should not be separated from their mothers and that overnights with their fathers would be harmful to the children. More recently, research suggests that infants and toddlers need contact with both parents to form a secure attachment to both, and that there is nothing magical about overnight contact. The issue is to avoiding stressing the child with too lengthy a separation from an attachment figure.

SUMMARY

The argument in favor of infant overnights challenges a long cultural history, if not a deeply ingrained human belief, that mothers offer babies something unique and irreplaceable; moreover, that even a single night away from mother can be deeply damaging to the young child. This belief may once have been culturally adaptive, but the evidence available to us now is compelling. For those infants who have the opportunity to establish and maintain healthy attachments with more than one caregiver, parenting plans that provide each with a full spectrum of caregiving, including overnights, lays the foundation for lifetime relationships and the child's greater well-being.

NOTES

1. "Family courts face a no more vexing problem than developing residence and access plans for infant children when divorcing and separating parents live apart" (Schepard, 2001, p. 349).
2. The Scottish government provides a useful compilation of international child custody law at http://www.scotland.gov.uk/Publications/2007/10/25160036/3
3. For a thorough and balanced review of this literature, see Altobelli (2005).
4. The infant's need for environmental consistency is well-suited to parents who are amenable to a nesting schedule (e.g., Flannery, 2004, 2008). In this arrangement, the child remains in one environment and the parents move in and out. However, I note Flannery's observation that "there is not a single instance of birdnesting discussed within the legal literature, including all federal and state published opinions, in which the birdnesting arrangement has worked" (personal communication, February 1, 2009).
5. "[R]epeated overnight separations from the primary caregiver are associated with disruption in mother–infant attachment when the conditions

of visitation are poor, i.e. when parents are unable to provide adequate psychological support to the child" (Solomon & George, 1999, p. 2).

6. The American Academy of Pediatrics provides extensive information and valuable links regarding breastfeeding practices at http://www.aap.org/breastfeeding/. Further information is available from Womenshealth.gov at http://www.4women.gov/breastfeeding/index.cfm?page=Campaign

7. Lori Rempel, RN, PhD, Chair of the Department of Nursing, Brock University, Ontario, responds (personal communication, February 10, 2009): "I am reluctant to support overnight visits until the infant has stopped breastfeeding at night....Thus, although feeding expressed milk is not directly harmful, it is possible that the disruption of night-feedings before the infant is ready might undermine their nutritional status because of the potential effect on milk production. Although it is laudable to encourage night visits with dads, it might be best to encourage these dads to make significant efforts to interact with their infants during the day until their infant is sleeping through the night. In situations where an infant continues to require a night feeding once the infant is eating a significant amount and variety of complementary foods, the issue of milk production at night might be argued to be somewhat less important and the question could be revisited.

10 On Visitation Resistance and Refusal

[A] court simply cannot order a parent to love his or her children or to maintain a meaningful relationship with them.
—*Mitchell v. Mitchell*, No. 2-00-0005 Illinois App. Ct.

What we do know is that geography, remarriages, emotions, diversity, and time are all important factors that impact on the quantity and quality of noncustodial parent/child relations.
—*D. Pollack & S. Mason*

The degree to which a child complies with the terms of his or her parents' shared custodial schedule must be simultaneously understood as a legal, a developmental, and a family systems matter. Unfortunately, any incident even vaguely suggestive of visitation noncompliance far too easily and too often becomes the match that ignites accumulated tensions within the family (Garber, 2007a) and within the larger ecosystem of forensic professionals (Grossman & Okun, 2006, 2007).

The subject of visitation resistance and refusal has received limited attention in the literature (e.g., Johnston, 1993; Racusin, Copans, & Mills, 1994; Renouf, 1985; Trinder, Beek & Connolly, 2002), seldom with any focus on developmental factors (but see Freeman & Freeman,

2003), and is all too often viewed through the singular lens of parental alienation—as when, for example, authors have cautioned that "[It is] important for noncustodial parents to understand that their child's behavior may not be as much a rejection of them as an adoption of a new set of rules for navigating the rough waters of divorce" (Stoltz & Ney, 2002, p. 225).

This chapter plots a sequential course through the rough waters of visitation rejection and refusal, recommending a stepwise process of evaluation from the most benign and expectable to the more destructive and pathogenic causes of this phenomenon. Working under the harsh lights of litigation, the family law professional will always be wise and the child's needs will always be best served taking this most parsimonious course.

A CAUTIOUS APPROACH TO VISITATION RESISTANCE AND REFUSAL

Much as the Stoltz and Ney (2002) observation may be correct, it is premature. The developmentally informed family law professional who hears complaints about visitation resistance and refusal must first consider each of a succession of mutually compatible questions originally summarized elsewhere (Garber, 2007a) and reformulated here.

Is the Child Saying What the Listener Wants to Hear?

Children are highly suggestible to begin with (Garber, 2007b). Children whose parents are conflicted, separated, and divorced are at particularly high risk for becoming chameleons, compromising emotional maturity in the short-term interest of fitting in to each of two or more disparate environments. In these circumstances, one particularly dangerous dynamic may be at work: The child who has had to learn to read his socioemotional environment will register the sending parent's (unconscious?) ambivalence about his imminent departure and respond congruently, "Do I have to go to Dad's tonight?" The parent, in turn, will read the child's question as confirmation of her selfish view that the other parent is inappropriate in some fashion and degree. Together, parent and child tumble down the rabbit hole, each cementing the other's ambivalence until a big, bad, horrible something is manufactured out of nothing at all.

This dynamic can be insidious and destructive, resulting in false allegations of abuse, ex parte orders for supervised contact (or worse, the cessation of parent–child contact) and the wholly circular apparent confirmation that a parent whose contact with a child is supervised must indeed require supervision (Crook & Oehme, 2007; Birnbaum & Alaggia, 2006).

Does the Child Resist Separation From the Sending Parent in General?

Jumping to the conclusion that a child's visitation resistance is either a reflection on the receiving parent or due to the malicious undermining of the sending parent (or both), overlooks a host of other, much more benign causes for this behavior. In some cases, the child will be found to resist most or all separations from the sending parent, not simply those that are associated with a transition of care. For some children, this may be symptomatic of separation anxiety, entirely typical and appropriate at some ages (see chapter 5) and entirely expectable (even if atypical of the developmental level) as a function of regression in the face of stress (see chapter 6). Certainly these children have a great deal of stress.[1]

For some children, difficulty separating from the sending parent may be symptomatic of an undiagnosed anxiety disorder, depression, or another psychiatric difficulty (e.g., Lewinsohn et al., 2008). Alternately, the same symptom may be a clue to a destructive role reversal occurring between the child and the sending parent, as when a parentified child fears for the well-being of the sending parent once they're apart. Take, for example, the following trial testimony regarding 10-year-old Yve:

> She says that she wants to be with her mom, because her mom needs her. She wants to make her mom happy. That's a very big burden for a 10-year-old girl. It's really hard for her to take care of herself, much less feel the responsibility of having to take care of her mom. (373 Md. 551 In Re: Yve S.)

This dynamic is captured well by Hulett (2004, p .2):

Some children become the emotional props of their distressed parents, but are unable to express, or attend [to], their own needs. This parentification of children may interfere with separation–individuation developmental tasks, and has the potential of causing significant psychological damage.

It is tragically the case that these three possibilities—separation anxiety, psychiatric illness, and role reversal—are not at all mutually exclusive.

Does the Child Resist Contact With the Receiving Parent in General?

The child who separates from the sending parent generally resists separation to transition into her other home, but may yet be communicating something that is entirely benign and innocuous. She may be avoiding having to sleep in an uncomfortable bed or having to face a scary shadow, to avoid an intimidating new pet, or cope with a noisy roommate. Whether the child is aware of and able to voice these concerns is a separate matter. Even with the requisite language skills, mustering the emotional maturity to voice them constructively can be quite a feat for some children: "Forensic evaluators have a responsibility to learn as much about the particulars of visitation as possible, because younger, less mature, less articulate, and/or more anxious children may be relatively unable to express these concerns directly" (Garber, 2007a, p. 591).

Children who have seen their parents fight, separate, and divorce, who have been removed from one home and placed forcibly in another, who have been adopted and who have seen step-parents come and go, reasonably learn that love can break. They often come to associate anger with rejection, loss, and abandonment. As a result, these children can find the prospect of healthy self-advocacy, direct expression of feeling, and assertiveness terrifying.

It is not at all uncommon to find that a child would rather cling to Dad than tell Mom how scared he is of sleeping alone in his new room, of Mom's new dog, of Mom's new husband, or of their new neighbors. Given the opportunity (e.g., in therapy), he might reveal that he knows that "When Mommy got mad at Daddy, she stopped loving him" and, therefore, "If she gets mad at me, she'll stop loving me, too."

When this dynamic is in force, three remedies are called for. First, caregivers must craft a script that explains the adult relationships as distinct from the child's relationship with her caregivers. For example, "adult love can break, and ours did. Parent–child love cannot break, and ours won't." Second, enrolling the child in outpatient psychotherapy both as a "port in the storm" and explicitly to improve assertiveness and self-advocacy skills may also be necessary. Third, caregivers must genuinely understand and model for their kids that anger is not the antithesis of love, that it is, in fact, a healthy part of a loving relationship.

Is the Receiving Parent More Strict or Demanding?

What child wouldn't resist leaving a less structured, less demanding home to go to a more structured, more demanding home? Routine differences in the number and types of chores, behavioral expectations and consequences, bedtime, media access, and parenting style can contribute to visitation avoidance and refusal no less than transitory differences, as when a child is aware that a restriction or punishment accrued during the last visit will be enforced upon his return.

Is the Receiving Parent Sensitive and Responsive to the Child's Needs?

A parent's sensitive/responsivity or attunement to the child's signals and needs is the characteristic most often associated with the quality of the child's attachment to that parent (Bornstein, Gini, Suwalsky, Putnick, & Haynes, 2006). Research has documented an association between a child's contact resistance and a parent's relatively insensitive/unresponsive manner (Johnston, 2003).[2]

As it affects visitation resistance, a child's experience of a parent's sensitive-responsivity may be a very practical matter. Some children will resist transitioning into the home of a parent who has remarried, particularly if they have to share that parent not only with a new partner but with a new gaggle of children, as well. Resistance transitioning into this environment can be due to some combination of (a) the parent's genuine insensitive unresponsivity, (b) diminished access to a parent who is sensitive and responsive, and/or (c) the child's unfamiliarity coping as one among a (suddenly integrated) brood of quasi-siblings, particularly when the peer relationships are strained and shared resources (everything from bathroom access to breakfast cereal) are limited.

Is the Sending Parent Supportive of the Receiving Parent?

More malignant are those instances of visitation resistance and refusal that are due to an adult's selfish and destructive efforts to communicate that the receiving parent is somehow bad or not worthy of the child's love. When a child overhears or is directly instructed by mom that dad is dangerous, that going to him means rejecting or abandoning her or—most potently—that loving him means not loving her, then alienation is at work. Discussed in detail in chapter 16, alienation is an act of abuse tantamount to the excruciating dilemma portrayed in William Styron's *Sophie's Choice*. Whereas Styron's protagonist had to choose between her children, in this everyday, real-life drama, children are made to choose between their parents. The result can entail not only visitation resistance and refusal, but a complete psychological disownership of the targeted parent.

Is the Receiving Parent Supportive of the Sending Parent?

The converse can also contribute to visitation resistance. In this case, a child anticipates and then acts to avoid being in the company of a parent who damns his or her other parent. In both this case and the last, the child is caught in the middle of his or her parents' immature, selfish and destructive tug of war (Garber, 2008a).

POTENTIAL REMEDIES FOR VISITATION RESISTANCE AND REFUSAL[3]

As with most (if not all) of the dilemmas that come before the family courts and are addressed in this book, the problem when a child resists or refuses contact doesn't reside within one person or another the way cancer can be isolated and treated within an individual patient. In family law matters, the problem is a dynamic that exists within a complex relationship. The word *dynamic* is carefully chosen here for its implication of movement and change. These issues are far from static. When we seek change, we must aim at a moving target.

For these reasons, it would be pointless to respond to concerns about visitation resistance and refusal with one party alone. It is unlikely that psychological assessment of mom or court-ordered therapy for dad or a divorce support group for their daughter will be sufficient. In a like manner, the court's orders, sanctions and threats may be necessary, but are seldom enough. What is necessary, instead, is a coordinated, multifaceted intervention built on a sound understanding of the dynamic family system and the developmental factors at work therein.

The child-centered matters that come before the family courts routinely call for developmentally informed, systemic assessment and intervention. To attempt to understand and remedy any of these matters by looking exclusively at one individual or by looking at two or more individuals in isolation, without understanding their relationship—the fit among them—is not only impractical and inefficient, it may breach professional ethics.[4] Chapter 15 amplifies this idea as it bears on the role of psychological testing in custody matters.

The American Psychological Association, for example, strictly prohibits psychologists from speaking to a child's custody without having conducted a comprehensive evaluation of the family system (American Psychological Association, 1994, 2009).

In the case of visitation resistance and refusal, the family law professional who interviews the targeted parent in an office setting and thereby concludes that the child has no reason to resist contact ("He's a great guy and loves his kid a lot!") is reminiscent of the doctor who examines the patient's knee and pronounces him healthy and well. The knee is part of a dynamic, developing system no less than the father. In neither instance can an understanding of one part be allowed to substitute for an understanding of the whole.

Four potential remedies for mild to moderate visitation resistance and refusal are discussed below. When the dynamics become intractable and entrenched, however, two further remedies are often considered. The topic of reunification after a parent–child relationship has been severed is discussed in chapter 12.

Is the Schedule of Contact Developmentally Appropriate?

A schedule of contact that requires the child to be apart from one home or caregiver longer than the child has ever ventured away from home previously, which places the child with little or no transition or introduction into a starkly new environment, which separates the child from all things familiar and/or at a great distance and/or for a long period away from his or her other home may be a setup for failure (Dember & Fliman, 2005). Much as parents complain that alternate, more child-centered schedules are inconvenient or "unfair" (which translates as, "my ex-partner gets more than I do!") our goal is not to please the contesting parties. Our goal must be to meet the child's needs.

Some of these factors may be ameliorated by making the plan as concrete, predictable, and minimally stressful for the child as possible. Provide the child with photos or video of the new home, a map with which to better understand the distance to be traveled, and a calendar with which to count off the days before leaving and the duration of the separation. Build the child's sense of "ownership" of the destination by allowing him or her to choose the color that the bedroom walls will be painted, its decorations, bedding, and layout. Strategies as simple as allowing the child to record the outgoing answering-machine message, plant a garden, or care for a pet may help to sidestep the visitation battle by focusing on something exciting instead.

A schedule that places the child with one parent in excess of the heuristic recommended in chapter 8 (that is, for more consecutive nights than twice his age in years) may be developmentally inappropriate and an invitation at least to distress and transitional difficulties, if not resistance and refusal. By the same token, a schedule that requires frequent transitions and brief stays in each location will wear on many children, as well. Finding the right balance between duration of stay and frequency of transition is a very difficult, individually determined task that, once achieved, will need to be worked out anew in response to developmental change.

Helping the child to anticipate the positives that follow transition rather than focus on the subjective experience of loss and anxiety associated with the transition itself can sometimes be sufficient remedy. This need not be an invitation to the destructive "Disneyland Dad" split in which one parent enforces all of the rules while the other has all of the fun. Instead, establishing an enjoyable thread that runs continuously across contacts can be sufficient. A jigsaw puzzle that is completed one piece per visit and remains uninterrupted in the in-between. A chess game that is played one move per contact or an airplane model that is assembled one piece per contact serves the same purpose.

In a like manner, a child can be helped to overcome anxiety associated with transition that might otherwise generate resistance by establishing social connections with others in the destination home. Can 10-year-old Billy establish an e-mail or text "pen pal" in dad's new neighborhood in advance of the transition? Can 15-year-old Sally attend a school dance with her new step-sisters while she's there? A babysitting or dog-walking or leaf-raking job for the neighbor can work the same way.

Use of Transitional Objects

Transitional objects were discussed in chapter 8 with regard to separation more generally and have invaluable potential with regard to visitation resistance, in particular. Assuring that the child can take developmentally appropriate and individually meaningful tokens of the security she associates with the sending parent can help her to better manage the anxiety associated with transition.

Flexible Versus Rigid Schedules

Flexible visitation schedules are those that give the parents room to negotiate the child's schedule from one day to the next and/or give the child the discretion to dictate which house he or she wants to be in at any given time. The former may be well-suited to busy adults who are excellent communicators. The latter is often recommended as respectful of the child's wishes (as distinct from his or her needs). In fact, for the population of high conflict caregivers whom we serve, both are invitations to visitation resistance and refusal, increased coparental discord and the child's escalating distress.

A schedule that must be negotiated between the coparents one day to the next sounds good. It may seem to be an opportunity to capitalize on opportunity ("Hey, I got tickets to the game! Want to go?") and convenience ("Can you keep her? I've got a last-minute meeting"), but if these parents were able to communicate constructively in the first place, we would probably never have met them. Instead, a flexible schedule that requires cooperation is more typically an invitation to do battle, a constant source of anxiety for the child ("whose picking me up today?") and a crisis waiting to happen.

In a similar manner, a schedule that allows the child to hold the decision-making reins is a setup for guilt and the parents' competition for the child's time and attention. "Will you be here for supper, honey?" one parent asks cautiously. "I'm not sure," the 12-year-old replies. "What are you making?" These schedules are often established under the aegis of a "mature minor" standard (see chapter 14) with or without the added rationalizations of "she's old enough to decide," "we have to show her that her voice matters," or "he's big enough that no one can make him go." All three are simply abdications of adult authority.

True, when parents can work together in their children's best interests, a flexible schedule can take advantage of unanticipated and spontaneous social, familial, recreational and learning opportunities. And true, an inflexible parenting schedule may mean lost opportunities. But on balance, the benefits of a last minute museum trip or a sudden vacation opportunity pale by comparison to the constant aggravation associated with a plan that requires that two people who dislike one another negotiate. For these parents—the parents who fill our offices, clinics, and courtrooms—a flexible parenting schedule is a setup for a child to believe that he is the reason his parents are always arguing ("after all, they wouldn't be arguing if I didn't exist!") and fertile ground for the appearance of visitation resistance and refusal.

Therapeutic Visitation

Whereas the court may order that a parent who is thought to be violent, a predator, or a flight risk be restricted to supervised visitation, (James & Gibson, 1991; Strauss, 1995; Tortorella, 1996), *therapeutic visitation* serves a complementary and distinct purpose. Therapeutic visitation calls for a child to establish a trusting rapport with a mental health professional explicitly for the purpose of diminishing visitation resistance or—in those more extreme circumstances discussed in chapter 12—for the purpose of reunification.

In that the professional facilitating therapeutic visitation is treating the damaged parent–child relationship, this service cannot suffice for the individual support parent and child may each need.[5] Indeed, the process of therapeutic visitation often calls for both the parent and the child to have their own therapists with the understanding that all professionals involved will be free to collaborate in the best interests of the child.

Unfortunately, there is very little literature on the use of therapeutic visitation (but see Hulett, 2004; Scharff, 2006; Tuckman, 2005). Many state child protective agencies advertise "therapeutic visitation" programs among their services,[6] offering varying purposes and processes. In some instances, the parent–child contact may be restricted to the period that the mental health professional supervises, very much like conventional supervised visitation. In other applications, therapeutic visitation can be used as a means to transition into, transition out of, or to "sandwich" the dyad's time together.

In one variation (Garber, 2008a), therapeutic visitation can be scheduled explicitly to respond to mild or moderate visitation resistance. Used in this manner, the child is scheduled to spend 90 minutes with the therapeutic visitation facilitator. The sending parent (the caregiver with whom the child has most recently resided) delivers the child to this meeting and spends the first 30 minutes, then departs. Child and facilitator strategize together in anticipation of the receiving parent's arrival 30 minutes later. The receiving parent spends the final 30 minutes with the child and facilitator and then the dyad departs for a scheduled visit. For some children, the middle half-hour serves as a transition buffer, a middle ground that allows him or her to shed one persona and prepare the next without suffering the pressures of having to wear both simultaneously, pressures that can, among other things, create visitation resistance and refusal.

In another variation, the therapeutic visitation facilitator uses video recording and subsequent feedback to help the parent–child dyad recognize and change how they interact. Marvin and colleagues' (e.g., Bakersman-Kranenberg et al., 2008; cf., Stolk et al., 2008) use of video feedback to help parents of very young children become more sensitive and responsive in the interest of attachment quality might be construed as facilitating a similar goal.[7]

SHOULD CHILD SUPPORT BE CONTINGENT ON VISITATION?

Wisely, in my opinion, the law totally dissociates payment of child support from visitation. Even financially deadbeat parents, for example, can and should spend time with their kids.

—*Aviva Orenstein*

It has never been our law that support payments were conditioned on the ability to exercise rights of visitation or vice versa. The duty to support is wholly independent of the right of visitation.

—*Raymond v. Raymond*, 165 Conn.735, 742, 345 A.2d 48

With little exception (Ellman, 2004),[8,9] the law is quite clear and consistent in stating that a nonresidential parent's responsibility to pay child support is independent of the condition, exercise, or frequency of visitation. Thus, the interruption, diminution, or cessation of visitation for any reason, including a child's resistance, is seldom if ever reason for the absent parent to withhold support (Raymond, 1988).

Recognizing the child's developmental needs, the courts are ever more likely to clarify that visitation is not a privilege to be exercised as the parents see fit, but a critical responsibility for the parents to fulfill (Pollack & Mason, 2004). Nevertheless, money has sometimes entered the formula. In one instance, for example, the court insisted that a residential mother put up a surety to be held against the possibility that she would discourage her 11-year-old's contact with his nonresidential father (Harris, 2005). In another situation, the Court imposed a fine intended to be incurred each time the nonresidential father missed a scheduled visit.[10]

Unfortunately, neither of these practices is necessarily child-centered or effective when pathologically polarized parents insist on using their children as weapons in their intractable battles. The child who learns that one or the other parent has a financial incentive to visit is likely to feel unvalued for him- or herself ("You're only here because it costs you money if you don't come!")—a dynamic that can paradoxically fuel visitation resistance rather than remedy it. The court has recognized this in stating, for example:

> We are not convinced that forcing the children to spend time with a parent who views the visit as a punishment or obligation would truly be in the children's best interests. Any feelings of abandonment the children may have might actually be reinforced by the realization that their father (or mother) was seeing them only to avoid being jailed for contempt of court. (*Mitchell v. Mitchell*, No. 2-00-0005; Illinois App. Ct. [2001])

SUMMARY

It is only armed with a sound understanding of the norms and processes of child and family development that we can begin to genuinely serve the best interests of court-involved children. This discussion of visitation resistance and refusal is a case in point: The developmentally uninformed family law professional is at risk for prematurely concluding that child's contact refusal as certain evidence of the failure of one parent or another. By approaching the problem in a parsimonious and developmently informed manner, instead, there is a far stronger likelihood that it can be effectively remedied without inadvertently inflaming what is likely to already be a hotly contested issue.

NOTES

1. McIntosh and Chisholm (2008), for example, find that 21% of one sample and 28% of a second sample of Australian children whose parents were highly conflicted evidenced "a higher than average rate of clinical anxiety."
2. Although, intuitively, it makes more sense to understand visitation resistance and refusal in terms of the child's experience of the entire family system. Thus, each parent's absolute degree of sensitive/responsivity would be less a factor than the child's experience of differences between the two parents.
3. For a comprehensive list of relevant case law in the U.S., Canada, Australia, and England, go to: http://www.justice.gc.ca/eng/pi/pad-rpad/rep-rap/2001_8/cas.html
4. Dr. Ken Pope has assembled links to every mental health guild's unique ethics code at http://kspope.com/ethcodes/index.php

5. It is very likely a conflict of interests and a breach of professional ethics for one mental health professional to serve in two or more of these roles, e.g., as the child's therapist and as the therapeutic visitation supervisor (see, e.g., the American Psychological Association's [2002] revised ethical code 3.05 regarding multiple relationships).

6. California's program, for example, is described briefly at http://www.cysfresno.org/tsv.htm

7. Noting the practical and legal hurdles associated with recording interactions, video feedback proves time and again to be a very powerful tool with which to improve relationships. Buggey (2005), for example, discusses video feedback as a useful tool for social skills training with autistic spectrum disorder–diagnosed children.

8. For example, in *Sampson v. Johnson* (Nos. 00-FM-183, 00-FM-689, and 00-FM-1697, Court of Appeals of District of Columbia, 2004), the court notes, "The principle animating the foregoing authorities is not an unyielding one. [In] *Raible v. Raible*, 219 A.2d 777, 781-83 (Md. 1966), for example, the father was a millionaire who had nevertheless developed an arrearage of $ 38,750 in child support. The father did not deny that he was able to make the court-ordered support payments, and he had twice been held in contempt of court for noncompliance with a support order. On this factual scenario, the court concluded that the welfare of the children would be promoted by conditioning further visitation on the father's satisfaction of the arrearage." (available online; retrieved February 7, 2009 at: http://www.plol.org/Pages/Secure/Document.aspx?d=Gy5Txjxl1P 7be%2b fK%2bmGjOA%3d%3d&l=Cases&rp=4).

9. Curiously, Fields et al. (1997, p. 49) observe that "[n]oncustodial parents are often denied access to their children on the grounds that they have failed to comply with court mandated child support payments."

10. In *Gilman v. Gilman*, Docket No. 385930, New Haven Super. Ct. May 14, 1997, WL 276459, a Connecticut court writes, for example, "the court has serious concerns as to whether the plaintiff fully appreciates the importance of complying with the court's orders and the consequences for not doing so. It is fundamentally important that the children have visitation with their father according to the court's schedule. In order to insure that visitation occurs when scheduled, the court imposes a fine of $150 for every visitation missed, now and in the future, due to the plaintiff's willful actions.

Growing Up Apart:
Child–Parent Separation

A child who lives with one parent has, under the best of circumstances, a difficult time sustaining a relationship with both its parents.

—*Bowen v. Gilliard et al.*, 483 U.S. 587 appeal (1987)

Regardless of the cause of the separation (e.g., parental death, divorce, military service, incapacity, or incarceration), it has a profound effect....We know that, depending upon the child's age and length of separation, reactions can include such things as inability to form later attachments, woebegone searching, numbing, self-blame, anger, depression, regression, and antisocial behaviors.

—*Lois E. Wright and Cynthia B. Seymour*

Against the backdrop of our understanding that children benefit from the opportunity to establish and maintain a healthy relationship with both parents, four common circumstances arise that can deprive children of this opportunity: relocation, incarceration, active military duty, and hospitalization. One critically important tenet ties these otherwise disparate circumstances together and must underlie our work as family law professionals: The reason for a parent's absence is far less important than the simple fact of the parent's absence, how it is explained, and how we help (especially young) children to manage it.

At one developmental extreme, it is obvious that infants are incapable of understanding explanations that otherwise justify a parent's absence and make sense to our adult ears. As long as the child's verbal comprehension remains primitive and cognitive functioning remains entirely me-here-now, the distinctions among "Mommy's in prison" and "Mommy's in the hospital" and "Mommy's in Iraq" are meaningless. The infant who once had a relationship with the absent caregiver will grieve the absence no matter its cause, his or her internal working model of the absent parent eroding to the point that that parent is likely to be greeted upon his or her return as a stranger. "[W]hen there is less frequent contact due to geographical distance, there will be a weakening of the emotional relationship with the young child. If there is an interstate separation from an infant, it may have the effect of extinguishing the attachment bond with the noncustodial parent" (Austin, 2000a, p. 197).

At the other developmental extreme, a globally mature teenager will understand the differences between absence of one kind versus another and, armed with sophisticated verbal, cognitive, social, and emotional coping tools, fortified with transitional objects and high tech interim media communications, he or she will maintain the absent parent's emotional presence and tolerate the absence much longer. Seapartion can take its toll even on this impressive teenager, however, sooner or later resulting in a similar process of grief and mourning (Bowlby, 1973; Snyder, 2005). After a long enough period, the reason for the absence will matter as little to the sophisticated teen as it does to the infant.

Although the duration of this path toward grief will differ by child and circumstance, the landmarks along the way are likely to be quite similar. No matter whether the parent is in prison, the intensive care unit, or at war, children's responses vacillate between sadness and anger and indifference. No matter how much the child seems to understand, no matter how much the child denies or minimizes or rationalizes the loss ("That's okay, my friends are all that matter to me"), at some level he is likely to blame himself for the separation (Feiring, Simon, & Cleland, 2009; Buehler, Lange, & Franck, 2007). Unrecognized and unremedied, self-blame can deteriorate into clinically significant internalizing (e.g., depression and/or anxiety) and externalizing (e.g., aggressive and/or destructive) behaviors (Fosco & Grych, 2008).

In some of these situations, transitional objects (see chapter 8) and/ or media-facilitated contact can help to diminish the child's experience of loss and the onset of grief (Gottfried, 2002; Samuels & Friesen, 2004), but research has yet to agree on the effectiveness of these interim measures. With this foreknowledge, we approach each of these and similar dilemmas of separation seeking to best serve the needs of the children so affected.

This chapter discusses the developmental, family-systems, and legal dilemmas of child–parent separation as it arises for: (a) the child whose parents move apart, (b) the child whose parent is incarcerated, (c) the child whose parent is in military service, and (d) the child whose parent is physically incapacitated or hospitalized. For all of the important differences that make these various circumstances unique, the same basic principles pertain to all. Our job as family law professionals is to understand the child's developmental needs and to apply this under-standing in helping the court to identify and meet children's needs in each.

RELOCATION AND MOVE-AWAY PARENTS

A residential parent's wish to relocate a significant distance from his or her child's other parent necessarily impacts at least the travel time associated with visitation, and commonly impacts the frequency, dura-tion, and expense of parent–child contact.[1] Relocation has likely reper-cussions not only on the child's access to one or both of the parents, but upon access to familiar places and significant other people, particu-larly the child's peer group. It imposes short-term and potentially power-ful stressors and longer-term losses. If and how these factors are to be balanced against the financial, familial, geographic, and climatic reasons that motivate the adult's wish to move is the question that family law professionals face time and again (Braver, Ellman, & Fabricius, 2003; Fabricius & Braver, 2006; Stahl & Drozd, 2007).[2]

Two California Supreme Court decisions have established relevant precedents.[3] In the case of *In re: Marriage of Burgess* (13 Cal. 4th 25, 28-29 [1996]), the court established that the parent wishing to relocate need *not* demonstrate that the move is "necessary," but instead "has the right to change the residence of the child, subject to the power of the court to restrain a removal that would prejudice the rights or welfare of the child." In short, the Burgess court created a rebuttable presumption in favor of allowing a custodial parent to relocate.

Subsequently, the California Supreme Court, in *In re: Marriage of LaMusga* (32 Cal. 4th 1072 [2004]), upheld the trial court's decision to grant a previously noncustodial father primary residential care in light of the mother's decision to move across country. In affirming this decision, the court repeatedly highlighted the mother's historical failure to support the children's relationship with their father:

> The situation might have been far different had the parents shown a history of cooperative parenting. If that had been the case, it might have appeared more likely that the detrimental effects of the proposed move on the children's relationship with their father could have been ameliorated by the mother's efforts to foster and encourage frequent, positive contact between the children and their father.

Further, the California court determined that:

> [T]he noncustodial parent bears the initial burden of showing that the proposed relocation of the children's residence would cause detriment to the children, requiring a reevaluation of the children's custody. The likely impact of the proposed move on the noncustodial parent's relationship with the children is a relevant factor in determining whether the move would cause detriment to the children and, when considered in light of all of the relevant factors, may be sufficient to justify a change in custody.

The Arkansas Supreme Court is even more definitive:

> We agree and hold that relocation of a primary custodian and his or her children alone is not a material change in circumstance. We announce a presumption in favor of relocation for custodial parents with primary custody. The noncustodial parent should have the burden to rebut the relocation presumption. The custodial parent no longer has the responsibility to prove a real advantage to herself or himself and to the children in relocating. (*Hollandsworth v. Knyzewski*, 02-720, 109 S.W.3d 653 [2003])

However, the Oklahoma Supreme Court has most recently ruled that:

> [T]he custodial parent has the initial burden of showing that the proposed relocation is made in good faith. If that is shown, the burden of proof

then shifts to the noncustodial parent to show the proposed move is not in the best interest of the child. In reaching its decision as to whether the relocation is in the best interest of the child, the trial court is required to consider numerous specific personal factors. (*Harrison v. Morgan*, 191 P.3d 617 [2008] OK CIV APP 68; Okla. Civ. App. [2008])

These factors have been enumerated by the New Jersey Supreme Court (*Baures v. Lewis*, 167 N.J. 91 [2001])[4] and discussed in terms of a relocation risk assessment model by Austin (2000a, 2000b, 2000c; 2005; 2008a, 2008b). These and related standards are synthesized[5] here and presented with regard to relevant developmental and family systems considerations:

1. What is the quality of the child's relationship with the noncustodial parent? Although Austin frames this in terms of the noncustodial parent's history of involvement in the child's life (e.g., attending ball games, keeping doctors' appointments), the critical variable might be seen as the child's experience of that parent's sensitive/responsivity as captured in his or her internal working model and evident as attachment quality.

Many questions remain unanswered with regard to how we balance or integrate our experience of secure and insecure and disorganized attachments (e.g., Garber, 2009). For present purposes, I suggest that it is reasonable to postulate that to the extent that the noncustodial parent is a secure attachment figure, any plan that diminishes the child's experience of that parent may not be in that child's best interests.

Is that postulate even more important if the noncustodial parent is the child's only secure attachment? Perhaps this is what the *LaMusga* court implicitly captured by highlighting the critical relevance of the custodial mother's failure to support the children's relationship with their father. As an empirical question, however, the data are not yet available.

2. What is the impact of the geographical distance on the child's access to the noncustodial parent Austin and others (e.g., Heatherington & Kelly, 2002[6]; Pollack & Mason, 2004) emphasize distance as it bears on the frequency and duration of parenting time and involvement especially for younger children, such that, if the child or the noncustodial parent could instantaneously disapparate Harry Potter–like into one another's presence, distance would be irrelevant.

One could argue, in fact, that distance is increasingly irrelevant. Doesn't digital wizardry allow a child and parent who are separated by a single wall or by an entire continent to see and hear (even if not to touch or smell or taste) one another in real time (Gottfried, 2002; Samuels & Friesen, 2004)? In fact, these electronic umbilici sometimes work against the child's need to adapt to the reality of the adult separation, let alone the physical distance between his or her homes (Garber, 2008a). Here, too, the data is not yet in. We are yet to determine to what degree contemporary media obviate the potential negative impact of geographic distance when relocation is at issue.

3. Is the child developmentally prepared to understand and cope with the relocation? Austin posits that children who are more cognitively, socially, and emotionally mature and those without identifiable psychopathology may adjust to one parent's relocation better than their less mature, impaired peers.

It stands to reason that a child whose footing is firmly planted in (Piagetian) Formal Operations (or at least has a firm hold on Object Permanence), who demonstrates a strong capacity to delay gratification and to tolerate frustration is better prepared to cope with relocation than others who are not. It's not clear, however, why one might venture that "children with higher IQ scores may adapt better" (Austin, 2000a, p. 200). Here, as with the concept of the mature minor (see chapter 14), it is a mistake to impute global maturity from intelligence, and thus fail to recognize the asynchronies that characterize much of development.

4. Is the custodial/relocating parent reasonably expected to support the child's relationship with the absent parent? This is the critical question voiced in *LaMusga*: To the extent that one parent speaks or acts to or around a child in a manner that undermines the child's security with another parent (i.e., alienation; see chapter 16), the best remedy for the child is likely to be corrective experience in the form of frequent, predictable, and healthy experiences with the targeted parent (Garber, 1996, 2004a, 2008a). Some have gone so far as to recommend in response to those most extreme circumstances that the child be placed with the nonalienating parent (Gardner, 2001). Any parenting plan that unnecessarily limits the child's experience with the targeted parent—including, but not limited to relocation, and acknowledging the uncertain benefits of digital contacts—risks enabling the custodial parent's alienating message and costing the child a healthy parental relationship.

5. Does the proposed relocation facilitate a child's relationships with extended family? The New Jersey standard explicitly calls for consideration of this variable, presumably in the interest of maximizing the child's social and emotional support. In fairness to the child, however, one must further take into account the *quality* of the child's relationships with the extended family in question, the support that the relocating parent might experience from this extended family, the indirect benefit the child might thereby accrue, and the imponderable question of how to balance relationships gained versus relationships lost in the process.

As if these considerations weren't enough, a systems perspective requires that consideration of the quality of the relationships gained must include those parties' willingness and ability to support the child's relationship with the absent parent. As I have pointed out with regard to visitation resistance and refusal (Garber, 2007a) and alienation (2004a), anyone with a secure attachment with the child—extended family, teachers, therapists, neighbors—may have the emotional leverage to encourage or inhibit the child's relationship with a targeted parent.

6. Does the proposed relocation provide the child with at least comparable social, emotional, educational, health, and leisure opportunities? This standard is as much common sense as it is amorphous and unquantifiable. Certainly we'd agree that, all other things being equal, an environment that provides a child more opportunities to learn and grow is more desirable than an environment that provides such opportunities. But how is one to compare, for example, a home that provides easy access to libraries to a home that is situated in a relatively successful school district to a home that is surrounded by scores of same-age neighbors?

What may be manageable are comparisons of resources vis-à-vis a child's known interests, skills, and needs. Relocating a child with established athletic interests to an area reputed for its athletic opportunities, for example, is defensibly a move in the child's best interests, perhaps even when that means moving away from a home that provides rich cultural, musical, and/or social opportunities.[7] However, trying to weigh this against associated changes in the child's contact with the nonresidential parent returns the discussion to the realm of things amorphous and unquantifiable.

There is, however, one developmental consideration with which to anchor this otherwise unwieldy factor: A child's need for and value derived from various extrafamilial opportunities increases with healthy development. Thus, proximal resources are likely to be relatively unimportant for a healthy infant as compared with a grade schooler for whom this factor is still somewhat less important as compared with an older teen. Wallerstein alludes to this idea in an *amici curae* brief submitted in *Burgess*, stating that "[for] reasonably mature adolescents, i.e., those who are well adjusted and performing on course in their education and social relationships...stability may not lie with either parent, but may have its source in a circle of friends or particular sports or academic activities within a school or community" (1996, p. 506).

7. How recent is the separation, divorce, and establishment of the present parenting plan? Austin (2008b, p. 358) argues that relocation concurrent with or within two years of the divorce poses higher risk to the child, all other things being equal: "relocation occurring at the time of divorce will be more likely to contain higher conflict, less authoritative parenting, greater parental stress, and poorer adjustment by the children."

From the child's perspective, it seems unlikely that divorce would be the relevant landmark by which to gauge this recommendation. If indeed a "familiarity hypothesis" is relevant, as Austin suggests, the measure should instead be one of continuity in the child's life. Thus, parents who establish a caregiving schedule at the time of separation and maintain it through the process of divorce may be well beyond Austin's proposed 2-year window by the time the final decree is delivered. By the same token, many revolving-door litigants effectively restart the clock many times postdecree, some in a manner which might never give the child as long as two years of stability.

For all of its implicit sense, however, Austin's recommendation is yet to be validated empirically. To the extent that delivery of a divorce decree does correspond to a major change in the child's life, one might argue that this is the best time to relocate. Why, after all, ask the child to make two stressful transitions in as many years when a single transition (separation, divorce, and relocation) might occur simultaneously and thereafter maximize the child's opportunity for stability?

8. If the child's preferences are known, is the child sufficiently informed to speak to the issue and, if so, are these wishes reasonably understood to reflect the child's genuine feelings? Just as parents and family law professionals are ill-advised to explicitly request that a child choose between his or her parents at the time of divorce, forcing a similar choice in the context of relocation is needlessly stress-inducing and therefore contraindicated (Garber & Landerman, 2006). When a child's preference is known, however, it must be treated with equal amounts of respect and suspicion.

We treat a child's seemingly well-informed preference regarding relocation with respect in an effort to communicate that his or her thoughts and feelings are important and will be taken into consideration, even though they will not be dispositive. We treat the same utterances with suspicion because the likelihood that the child's preference has been either unwittingly influenced and/or explicitly coached by one or both parents is tremendous. The child's wish to please; his or her fears of loss, rejection, and abandonment; promises of a new house and new friends; threats about losing ground in school are among the myriad factors that must temper how we hear the child's preferences.

9. Is the child cognitively, socially, and emotionally mature enough to understand and speak to his or her own best interests? Weighing out the potential plusses and minuses of a hypothetical relocation is a sophisticated intellectual task. Making this challenging balancing act work once the associated emotions of loss and change are thrown in calls for a great deal of socioemotional maturity. Distilling these many conflicting factors so as to speak to one's own needs is certainly beyond the ability of most children and perhaps many adults, as well. Chapter 14 discusses this in terms of "mature minor" standards.

10. Has the child's stated preference been unduly influenced by others? At one extreme, have one or both parents instructed the child in what to say, or promised or threatened outcomes that bear on his or her position? At the other extreme, is the child's stated preference subject to an unhealthy concern for a parent who might become ill or self-destructive, or simply disappear if the child is absent?

INVOLUNTARY SEPARATION: THE INCARCERATED, ENLISTED, INCAPACITATED, OR HOSPITALIZED PARENT

A parent can be separated from his or her child for any of a handful of reasons that fall beyond the jurisdiction of the family courts, but which may yet call for the opinion of a developmentally informed mental health or family law professional. These matters arise largely when parent and child are involuntarily separated, risking damage to the relationship and the stress of instability, loss, and traumatic change to the child.

As different as the causes of these separations are, children's experiences prior to, during, and following each can be quite similar. We know, for example, that compared to children with no trauma history, children with a history of abuse or neglect, family violence, and/or substance abuse are at greater social, emotional, cognitive, academic, and occupational risk when a parent is incarcerated (Poehlmann, 2005a), when an active duty or reservist parent is deployed (Lincoln, Swift, & Shorteno-Fraser, 2008), and when a parent is incapacitated or hospitalized (Leedham & Meyerowitz, 2000).

We know that the separation and stresses associated with each of these circumstances can prompt developmental regression, causing some children's socioemotional development to stall for months and even years pending reunification (Faber, Willerton, Clymer, MacDermid, & Weiss, 2008) and creating immense décalage within the child.

We know that the parent's absence inevitably throws the family's prior roles and interpersonal boundaries out of balance, no matter whether the cause is illness (Rolland, 1999a,b), imprisonment (Pimlott & Sarri, 2002), or military service (Faber et al., 2008). In each of these cases, and in many others of the same sort, the remaining family members must more or less spontaneously adapt to the missing parent's absence by taking on new roles in each other's lives. Whereas "families that frequently have a member absent for periods of time due to work (such as employment as an oil rigger or as an active duty military member) may have learned to tolerate ambiguous loss without boundary ambiguity" (Faber et al., 2008, p. 223), others struggle with the imbalance, putting children at risk for parentification, adultification, and neglect (Boss, 2002; Boss & Greenberg, 1984).

And we know that across these circumstances, some parent–child relationships will become permanently scarred beyond repair; that when the absence is long enough, the stresses intense enough, and the supports weak enough, the parent–child relationship can spontaneously break (e.g., Drummet, Coleman, & Cable, 2003; Smyth & Ferro, 2002) or be broken by others. These are among the cases that can come before the family courts.

Each of these three topics deserves a developmentally informed, family systems–oriented treatment unto itself. For present purposes, I offer a brief discussion of each topic as it might be relevant to family law professionals, as well as detailed bibliographies and associated resources on each subject in Appendix III.

The Children of Incarcerated Parents

Children of incarcerated parents typically are among the highest-risk children in the population, even prior to the parent's incarceration. These children are commonly exposed to drugs and alcohol from conception onward, are witnesses to and victims of multiple (if not chronic) acts of violence, sexual behavior, neglect, and abuse. They live transient lives marked by frequent, sometimes abrupt and forcible relocations, discontinuities of care, interruptions of schooling, and fleeting friendships. The combined impact of these experiences is measured in terms of school drop-out and failure rates, addiction, crime, unemployment, and perpetuation of the cycle of incarceration from one generation to the next (Poehlmann, 2005a, 2005b, 2005c).[8]

It is only since 1972 (*White v. Rochford,* 592 F2d 381; 7th Cir. [1979]) that the law has required that an arresting officer must "lend aid to children endangered by the performance of official duty." Where previously these children were essentially abandoned both by the arrested parent and by the arresting agency alike, social service agencies have since sought means to respond to their needs in their parents' absences. As a result, hundreds of thousands of children are now shuffled off each year into kinship care[9] and, when necessary, into our impoverished and overburdened foster care system:

> 1.3 million children in the United States have mothers under correctional supervision, and most affected children are less than 10 years old...whereas 90% of children remain with their mothers when fathers are incarcerated, grandparents are most likely to assume responsibility for children when mothers go to prison...only 10% of children with imprisoned mothers are placed in traditional foster care. (Poehlmann 2005b, p. 679)

More than 60% of incarcerated women and more than 50% of incarcerated men have children below 18 years of age. As many as 25% of newly incarcerated women are pregnant or have recently given birth

(Satyanathan, 2002). With little exception, however, prisons and prison policies are blind to the needs of the children of their inmates (Smyth & Ferro, 2002; but see Costa, 2003). The difficulties associated with the distance, time, and costs of visits, together with the unresolved emotions about the parent's arrest, the stigma,[10] the physical discomforts of visiting in environments that are seldom child-friendly (Hairston, 2002; Poehlmann, 2005c), as well as expensive and unpredictable telephone access and interim caregivers' efforts to undermine the child's relationship with the absent parent (Enos, 2001) can conspire to create both an implicit double jeopardy for the adult—punishment for their crimes *and* loss of their children—and an entire class of children who are punished for their parents' mistakes. In fact, only about 10% of imprisoned mothers see their children on a regular basis (Satyanathan, 2002) and "more than half of incarcerated mothers do not receive any visits from their children while they are in prison" (Simmons, 2000, p. 4). This, despite the well-established finding that:

> Studies of prisoners consistently show that those who maintain strong family and friendship ties during imprisonment and assume responsible marital and parental roles upon release have lower recidivism rates than those who function without family ties, expectation and obligations. (Pimlott & Sarri, 2002, p. 27)

Satyanathan (2002) incisively identifies several ways in which the justice system and the social service system fail to communicate, thereby doing harm to the children of incarcerated parents. As one example, The Federal Adoption and Safe Families Act (ASFA) of 1997 mandates that social service agencies must commence permanency planning for children held in foster care within 12 months, even though a woman's average period of incarceration is at least twice that. As a result, a mother's absence due to incarceration may be considered abandonment and her parental rights terminated without proper notice or access to legal counsel.[11] To add insult to injury, for those who do return from prison to care for their children, The Personal Responsibility and Work Opportunity Reconciliation Act of 1996 precludes the three-quarters of former prisoners who have been convicted on drug-related charges from receiving Temporary Aid for Needy Families (TANF), thus contributing to the renewed cycle of extreme need, chaos, and instability.

The Children of Military Personnel

As of 2005, there were approximately 1.2 million school-age American children with at least one parent on active military duty (Horton, 2005). The numbers today may be much higher. These children live a unique lifestyle, commonly relocating to bases across the globe, living among other military transients, and more or less accustomed to one or both parents' absences of 6 months and longer when deployed. Although likely to have more resources than children whose parents become incarcerated, the two groups share the burdens (and the blessings[12]) of a transient life.

What some writers have referred to as "military family syndrome" (LaGrone, 1978; cf., Morrison, 1981) we might more conservatively identify as the emotional cycle that families endure through the course of successive separations and reunions. Pincus, House, Christenson, and Adler (2008) describe the impact of this cycle on the children of military personnel differentially by age, but with little consideration of the relevant family dynamics.

In fact, the dynamics at work differ little whether the departing parent is going to war or to jail or into extended inpatient treatment. Faber and colleagues (2008) describe this as a reorganization of intra-familial boundaries and roles. Interviews with the families of active duty and military reservists reveal how the spouse and children left behind struggle to fill in for the absent soldier/caregiver more or less explicitly, taking on new responsibilities and, in so doing, at least temporarily redefining their interrelationships. These changes may be adaptive in the short run (even if unhealthy, as in the case of adultification and parentification), but can create barriers to the absent parent's reintegration upon his or her return.

The case of the enlisted soldier is unique among these three scenarios, however, in at least two ways. On the one hand, the military family's ability to anticipate and prepare for separation and reunion presumably works to the benefit of all.[13,14] The need to shift roles and responsibilities can be discussed in advance, plans for communication can be established, healthy goodbyes can be set in motion, and the timing of reunification is likely to be expectable. On the other hand, the soldier/parent lives in two very distinct worlds, his or her transition between these complicated by "the cultural burden of rank" (Horton, 2005, p. 260), that hierarchy unique to the armed forces that defines roles and demands obedience down an unambiguous chain of command in a manner quite different than the way most families work.

Like the incarcerated parent whose absence may be construed as abandonment, the military parent's legal relationship with his or her children can be compromised while deployed:

> After being away for months or years, service members may return home to find that the stay-at-home spouse has taken custody of the kids and won't give it back without a court order....Worse, due to the fact that mom or dad has been gone for a significant amount of time, a court may find that it is in the best interest of the children to remain where they are. (Neil, 2007)

Separation Due to a Parent's Illness or Hospitalization

The same dilemmas attributed to the children of incarcerated and deployed military parents apply to the children of those parents who are incapacitated or hospitalized due to illness (e.g., Maybery, Ling, Szakacs, & Reupert, 2005). In short, absence is absence is absence, both in the eyes of the law and in the eyes of the child.

The law often doesn't care why a parent is absent. If the absence exceeds the federal time limits for foster care (ASFA, 1997), the child must be moved toward permanency at the cost of the parent's opportunity for reunification. We saw this earlier with regard to incarcerated mothers (Satyanathan 2002). Hannett (2007) documents precisely the same dynamic at work when parents are hospitalized for drug rehabilitation: When a substance-abusing parent's "reasonable efforts" to achieve reunification exceed the period allowable for interim care, those very efforts can lead to termination.

Absence is absence is absence to the child, as well. How a child experiences and responds to a parent's absence due to incapacitating illness and/or hospitalization differs by duration of the separation (Nelson & While, 2002), developmental capacities (Diareme et al., 2007), and gender within the context of his or her larger family (Osborn, 2007) and social support system (e.g., Swick & Rauch, 2006), but little—if at all—as a function of the reason for the parent's absence. Thus, although we distinguish between the horrors associated with various cancers or HIV/AIDS (Antle et al., 2001), advanced diabetes, or multiple sclerosis (Steck et al., 2007), for example, the primitive me-here-now neediness within every child, regardless of age, resonates first and foremost with the *fact* of the parent's absence, not the "why" of it.[15,16]

Armsden and Lewis (1993) suggest that we should understand a child's experience of parental illness and associated unavailability across four dimensions: (a) as it impacts felt security, (b) the extent to which the parent's illness is personalized in the form of self-blame or as shared symptoms, (c) in terms of how the child understands his or her own associated vulnerability, and (d) in relation to the child's associated fantasies of rescue or loss or escape. Across studies, (Bibace & Walsch, 1979; Birenbaum, Yancey, Phillips, Chand, & Huster, 1999; Compas et al., 1994; Diareme et al., 2007; Osborn, 2007; Romer et al., 2002), these dimensions can be tracked as they play out by age groups in the context of a parent's debilitating illness or hospitalization. In short:

1. Unable to delay gratification and without the cognitive and linguistic means of tempering their responses, infants react to a parent's absence quickly and instinctively by crying and clinging, progressing into the grief of loss and associated interruptions of eating and sleeping routines. These reactions can occur even when the parent remains physically present but becomes emotionally unavailable, as can be the case with parental depression (Lagan, Knights, Barton, & Boyce, 2009).
2. In the toddler period, a parent's absence can exacerbate otherwise typical tantrums, magnifying oppositionality and impeding further development. This affect is amplified when a parent's incapacity and/or guilt hinder his or her firm, calm, and consistent responses.
3. Preschoolers are most likely to blame themselves for the loss, fantasizing an egocentric connection between their own wish or naughty behavior and the parent's illness or absence.[17] By the same token, children in this period may believe that a particular behavior, thought, or wish will "make Mommy all better." Regression occurs when recent developmental successes (e.g., toileting, sleeping alone, weaning) are lost in the face of a parent's continuing absence.
4. School-age children begin to be able to connect absence, illness, and death and thus fear that the parent may never return. This realization can spark renewed regression and/or acting out, with the additional cost to academic and social functioning.
5. Adolescents may be more deeply affected by parental illness than their 7- to 11-year-old peers, especially teenage girls when their mothers are ill (Quinn-Beers, 2001; Osborn, 2007; Romer et al., 2002). This

observation makes sense in light of teenagers' need to push off from a secure base into autonomy, a process that becomes complicated by guilt and anger and grief when that secure base is incapacitated or absent entirely. In some cases, a teenager will idealize the absent parent at the cost of her relationship with other caregivers, an experience that can push a parent who is already coping with an ill partner and doing double duty at home to the breaking point.

FAMILY LAW AND THE BEST INTERESTS OF THE SEPARATED CHILD

Relocation, incarceration, military deployment, and incapacity due to illness or hospitalization each represent their own unique dilemmas for the child and the family system, but together highlight questions about the child's well-being while a parent is absent.

Although our shared mandate is to assure that children have the opportunity to establish and maintain a healthy relationship with both of their parents (or, more broadly, with all of their caregivers), these dilemmas pose practical challenges and conflicting priorities for the family law professional. In the spirit of fulfilling this mandate, we might generalize the innovations that have arisen in these separate areas to apply across all of them. For example:

1. **Use transitional objects.** The developmental literature is replete with discussion of the value of transitional objects (see chapter 8) for children during temporary separations from parents. In the interests of at least reinforcing if not preserving parent–child relationships across extended separations, court orders, institutional policies, and caregivers must assure that children can receive age-appropriate transitional objects from absent parents. Even when an absent parent cannot communicate with a child directly via electronic media, a supply of emotionally salient objects must be provided and doled out across the span of absence as the child's need arises.

We must not make the mistake of assuming that transitional objects are important only to children. Assuring that the separated parent has tangible, visible, and/or audible representations of the absent child will similarly serve the relationship, motivating adult choices that may facilitate more frequent contact and earlier reunification.

2. Make contact predictable. Court orders, institutional policies, and caregiver practices must explicitly and uniformly anticipate reunification. Preseparation plans must explicitly anticipate when and how reunification will occur, whenever possible, and once settled these plans should be communicated to the child in an age-appropriate manner. In the case of relocation and incarceration, this means establishing a fixed and predictable schedule of contacts, acknowledging that, in the latter case, prison misbehavior is often punished by a loss of visitation rights, but that parent–child visitation should be held as sacrosanct, both for the sake of the child and in the knowledge that, in the long term, maintaining healthy family ties serves both the inmate and the community.

Smyth and Ferro (2002, p. 27) discuss innovative prisons which even provide for overnight, in-house contacts between prisoners and their families: "These visits may be in the form of overnight or special occasion visits that include special programming efforts, meals, arts and crafts, camping, etc. in a structured and well-supervised location at the prison."

In the case of active duty and reservist exercises and deployment, making the date of departure and deployment, the duration of absence, and the soldier's condition upon return (e.g., brief furlough vs. deactivation) predictable will better meet the needs of the parent, the child, and the family.

Predictability in the case of parental incapacity due to illness and hospitalization may be more challenging, particularly when the separation occurs as a result of sudden injury or onset of illness. Certainly we know that talking openly with children in a manner and at a level that they can understand serves their best interests (Diareme et al., 2007). When incapacity and/or hospitalization is related to chronic illness and is thus expectable even if it is not predictable, the process of the illness and associated interventions can still be made familiar and predictable to the child: "We all knew that Daddy would get sick sometime, but not when. Now that he's back in the hospital, we know what happens next. First..." Thus, although a mother with multiple sclerosis hopes for no future recurrences or her disease, she is well-advised to prepare with the family for the "what if?" so as to make the process of doctors' visits, medications, limited energy and mobility, and even hospitalization as mundane and predictable as possible.

3. Rely on technology whenever necessary. Although we don't yet know whether and how well real-time video exchange, instant messaging, texting, and similar (even yet-to-be-invented) surrogate means of contact suffice when face-to-face contact is impossible, it is better to fall back on technology than to needlessly prolong the absence. However, in the same way that face-to-face contact must be predictable, so too must digital communication be made predictable. Giving a child carte blanche to chat electronically with Dad, who lives across town, is confined to a hospital or a prison, or is posted to Afghanistan, at the very least risks undermining the authority of the continuing caregiver as well as distracting the child from homework, friendships, and clarinet lessons, as examples. By the same token, giving the absent parent carte blanche to reach the child risks inducing school refusal and needless anxiety over when the communication might occur and whether it might be missed.

4. Validate the absent adult's status as a parent. One of the issues that runs subtly through these literatures is that of the adult's identity in absentia. The parent who is incarcerated becomes "inmate number so-and-so." The hospitalized dad becomes a patient (or worse, a disease) and the active duty mom becomes a lieutenant. Even the dad left behind when Mom relocates can feel invalidated as a parent by virtue of the distance and loss of contact. In every case, as the individual's identity as a parent erodes, so too does the motivation to maintain contact and the willingness (if not the ability) to be sensitive and responsive to the child once reunited.

In every instance, in-person and on-line parent support groups can help to validate the individual's continuing role and the value that each has to offer his or her children. Coparent communication about the child must be maintained as well, validating the absent parent's value as a caregiver and co-decision maker. Tools such as www.ourfamilywizard.com can make this process easy regardless of geography or mobility. Together, these means of validation and inclusion can help the absent parent to maintain a healthy perspective on the child's needs and motivate that extra call or letter or video chat that can start an upward spiral of renewed parent–child affection.

5. Anticipate and minimize family barriers during separation, upon reunion, and beyond. One spouse takes over for the other. A child is prematurely promoted to become his younger sister's caregiver. Another becomes the remaining parent's confidant. Roles shift and alliances change in response to a parent's absence, only to be challenged upon his or her return. These barriers develop normally and necessarily in response to a prolonged absence but can be destructive to the child and a source of tremendous conflict upon reunion.

Family law professionals and the courts can help to minimize these destructive processes and the need for subsequent litigation in part through education. Families need to be taught about the developmental damage that can be associated with parentification and adultification. Just as divorcing parents are required in many states to complete a "child impact seminar" intended to help to keep the children out of the middle of the adult conflict, similar educational and support opportunities should exist for families separated as a result of relocation, military deployment, and hospitalization. The efficiencies afforded by the Internet can make a single such program simultaneously available to all parents everywhere at little or no cost.

A second answer calls for support. Adultification, parentification, and infantilization run rampant when caregivers don't have appropriate adult supports and turn to their children, instead. The prototypical mother who declares that her eldest son is "now the man of the family" in his father's absence must learn to rely on other adults. This, in turn, highlights the need for support for the parent who remains behind, the caregiver who is left to provide continuing care while a partner is imprisoned, at war, or hospitalized (e.g., Diareme et al., 2007; Faber et al., 2008). Whether such supports might serve in part to minimize the possibility that the parent left behind will alienate the child from the absent parent or otherwise monopolize the child's emotions at the cost of the child's relationship with the other parent is still unknown.

6. Enact legislation and institutional policy changes. A genuine commitment to our children's opportunity to establish and maintain a healthy relationship with each of their caregivers calls for changes in political and administrative policy in every venue in which parent–child relationships are threatened. This means, for example, responding to Satyanathan's (2002) call for changes to the federal legislation which bears on the opportunities for incarcerated parents to reunify with their children and succeed thereafter. This means building on the "family room" concept advanced by innovative hospitals, which allow children and spouses to stay in-hospital with an ill loved one for extended periods of time.[18]

7. Take a child-centered stance. Ultimately, we face the possibility that our strongest mandate—that of serving the child's best interests—will conflict with what has been called "the best interests of the family" or the mandate that children should have the opportunity to establish and maintain healthy relationships with all caregivers (see Orenstein, 2006). These are the sticky issues that family courts and their attendant professionals wade into time and again. How do we balance maintenance of a child's prior relationship with his incarcerated father with the knowledge that the man is in prison for having abused children? Should a child be encouraged or allowed to maintain contact with her hospitalized mother who is actively psychotic and who, even once properly medicated, remains at high risk of abrupt relapse? When and how should a child's continuing contact with a terminally ill parent be discontinued, if at all?

What of the parent who is absent so long without contact by choice, by medical necessity, by institutional mandate, and/or by court order, that he or she has become a stranger to his or her child in the interim? What of the father who was incarcerated before his 10-year-old daughter's birth or the woman in a coma who last knew her teenage son as a toddler? Rather than allow these relationships to end, we first carefully consider the potential costs and benefits of reunification.

SUMMARY

As different as the circumstances discussed in this chapter may be, the children who must learn to cope with prolonged separations share the same essential developmental needs. They need every reasonable opportunity to establish and maintain a secure attachment relationship with each of their caregivers, they need the means to understand and the tools with which to manage the period of their separation, and they need to be protected from the potentially destructive political mandates and shifts in family dynamics that can spontaneously emerge when parents live apart. It is our role as developmentally informed family law professionals to see that these dynamics are recognized and that these children's needs are met.

NOTES

1. I am not aware of case law or research relevant to the relocation of a nonresidential parent, although the associated child-centered considerations can be quite significant.

2. For other relevant resources, see: Carmody (2007); Duggan (2007); Haberman (2005); Kindregan (2002); Labrum (2004); Rotman, Tompkins, Linzer-Schwartz, and Samuels (2000); and Thompson (2004).

3. For a more general review of relevant case law, see Elrod (2006).

4. The New Jersey factors enumerated in *Baures v. Lewis*, [167 N.J. 91 (2001), the NJ Supreme Court (2001)] are: (1) reasons for the move; (2) reasons for the opposition; (3) past history of dealings between the parties as bears on the reasons for and against the move; (4) whether the child will receive comparable educational, health, and leisure opportunities; (5) any special needs or talents of the child that require accommodation and whether such accommodation is available in the new location; (6) whether a visitation and communication schedule can be developed that will allow the noncustodial parent to maintain a full and continuous relationship with the child; (7) the likelihood that the custodial parent will continue to foster the relationship of the child with the noncustodial parent; (8) the effect of the move on extended family relationships; (9) if the child is of age, and, if so, his or her preference; (10) whether the child is entering senior year in high school; (11) whether the noncustodial parent has the ability to relocate; and (12) any other factor bearing on the child's interest.

5. Among the factors identified by relevant sources that I have omitted or modified, I note particularly Austin's (2000b) reference to a history of child or spouse maltreatment such that "[r]elocation may be consistent with a need for fewer transition times for exchange of the child, less communication, and structured parenting time" (p. 201). I cannot condone this as relevant to relocation, but more generally support the idea that such history calls for these changes regardless of geography.

6. Heatherington & Kelly (2002) find that when a custodial parent moves more than 75 miles away, the likelihood that the noncustodial parent will drop out of the child's life rises significantly.

7. But see the discussion earlier regarding décalage and the choice to nurture a child's strengths versus his or her weaknesses in the interest of developmental synchrony.

8. Poehlmann (2005a) makes the excellent point that a parent's arrest is an excellent time to intervene proactively with these children in an effort to break this cycle. This calls for more than simply arranging for the placement of children whose parents are incarcerated, but screening for physical health and for socioemotional, cognitive, verbal, and academic developmental difficulties and responding accordingly.

9. Simmons (2000, p.4): "About 60 percent of children live with grandparents (usually maternal) after their mother's incarceration, 17 percent live with other relatives and a quarter live with non-relatives (often in foster care). In contrast, only half of incarcerated fathers were living with their youngest child prior to incarceration, and most of their children (nearly 90 percent) continued to live with their mothers after the incarceration."

10. I note *Hamele v. Hamele* (5 Conn. L. Rptr. 795 [Bridgeport Super. Ct. Dec. 31, 1991], 91 WL 288142, 1991) in which a 15-year-old refused to visit with his imprisoned father and the court declined to order him to do so.

11. Note, for example, denial of reunification in the case of infant A.H. (*Los Angeles Cty Department of Children and Family Services v. Robert S.*, B206036 no. CK56510): "At this juncture, Robert S[.] will remain incarcerated until sometime after/around January 2008. Given that [A. H.] is a newborn, such sentence precludes Robert S[.] from reunifying with his child within a designated 6-month reunification period."

12. The Virginia Joint Military Family Services Board (2001, p. 17) refers to the "strengths" associated with deployment and (p. 29) with relocation. This publication suggests that deployment, "fosters maturity...[is] growth inducing...encourages independence...encourages flexibility...builds skills for adjusting to separations and losses faced later in life...[and] strengthens family bonds." Children who relocate with military parents are credited as "culturally aware and knowledgeable in geography and social studies...independent, self-reliant and better 'team players'...[socially] sophisticated...politically aware...[and] better able to develop more portable achievements, skills and talents."

13. The United States Department of Defense sponsors a series of Web pages entitled, "Military Homefront" http://www.militaryhomefront.dod.mil/, which include concise pointers for families so as to help prepare children for a parent's deployment.

14. Faber et al (2008) highlights the greater challenges faced by families of reservists who are deployed, emphasizing that living off-base and maintaining civilian employment can increase the family stressors associated with military service.

15. The exception is evident in *somatic mirroring* (e.g., Iacoboni, 2008), a child's unconscious tendency to adopt physical complaints similar to those of the ill caregiver.

16. Although the nature of the parent's illness may be of little relevance, the severity of the illness may be relevant. Romer, Barkmann, Schulte-Markwort, Thomalla, and Riedesser (2002) found that the parent's perception of the severity of his or her own illness predicted the severity of the child's reaction more even than the objective (medical) severity of illness.

17. But a child's positive self-esteem may moderate this effect (Nelson & While, 2002), such that children with better self-esteem are less likely to blame themselves for a parent's illness.

18. Ronald McDonald House Charities (see http://www.rmhc.com/) provide comfortable living quarters for families of hospitalized children around the world. Comparable facilities for the children of hospitalized parents are much fewer and farther between.

12 Development and Parent–Child Reunification

Courts cannot, by order, create meaningful relationships between parents and their children; they can only create or maintain the circumstances that make meaningful relationships possible.

—P. Parkinson

"I'm looking for my family..."
"...why are you looking for them? They should be looking...for you!"
"They don't care. Forget 'em."
"You're right! They don't care, and if they did, they would have found me! Well, if they don't care, I don't care! I hope I never see them again!"
"Yeah! Forget about them! You're one of us now!"

—An American Tail

Social service agencies exercise the right of the state to protect children under the ancient concept of *parens patriae* as a last resort.[1] When abuse or neglect necessitates removing a child from his or her parent's care, the universal legal mandate[2] calls for "reasonable efforts" to be made toward prompt reunification in all but the most intractable cases of maltreatment (Bean, 2009). Failing such efforts, the courts can then go to the extreme of terminating parenting rights, the subject of the chapter to follow.

Dougherty (2004; see also Cordero, 2004) provides a concise and very practical summary of the policies and procedures that serve reunification and maximize the likelihood of its success.[3] She emphasizes removal policies that keep a child close to familiar people and places, that include safe, frequent and predictable parent–child contact throughout the period of separation, and that provide intensive, coordinated and child-centered services to all involved during separation, upon reunification and continuing thereafter.

This chapter considers the emotional purgatory of the child who will be or has been removed to foster care, a child who may not understand why he or she has been wrenched away from all things familiar and forced to live among strangers for an unknown and incomprehensible period. There can be no doubt that this process—itself the source of trauma so often—is necessary for children whose physical and emotional well-being is otherwise at stake. Given this reality, it is yet possible to make both removal and reunification a child-centered, developmentally and systemically informed process.

PREVALENCE AND DURATION OF FOSTER CARE

Casey Family Programs serves as a clearinghouse for foster and adoptive care information, resources, research, funding and services. According to the Casey Foundation,[4] in 2005, 513,000 children were in foster care, nearly half of whom were older than 10 and had reunification as their primary (agency determined) objective. Thirty-nine percent of all children in foster care remained so for less than one year, but 28% remained for more than three years.[5]

Wulczyn and Zimmerman (2005) provide an interesting summary of statistics relevant to social service removal, reunification, and termination of parental rights leading to adoption in the United States. In brief:

■ As of 2002, at least 37 states had provisions for concurrent reunification and termination/adoption planning.
■ Most children are returned from foster care to their birth parent(s).

- Post-foster care placement outcomes vary based on the child's age at placement and ethnicity. Infants are the most likely to be adopted among age groups and are routinely adopted more commonly than they are reunited with birth parents. Caucasian children are more likely to be reunited with birth parents across age groups while, across ages, African American children are more likely to be adopted than reunited with birth parents.
- The likelihood of reunification decreases as the duration of foster placement increases.
- Between 20 and 32% of children who exit foster care are returned to foster care within 10 years, the majority of recidivist placements occur within 1 year, and involve drug- and/or alcohol-involved birth parents (Brook & McDonald, 2009; Fuller, 2005).
- In general, the longer a child is in foster care the less likely he or she is to be returned to foster care subsequently. This observation can be misleading however, in that the longer a child remains in foster care the more likely he or she is to approach 18 years of age and thereby become ineligible for return regardless of need.

Conceptualizing Reunification

At the heart of both a child's removal from parental care and the factors which will dictate if and when and how the family is reunited is the concept of *parental fitness*: "[t]he legal standards for unfitness and best interests of the child are neither clearly defined nor exact. A court must balance competing interests (parents, children, and third parties) and examine various factors as it weighs the facts of an individual case in making its determination" (Wulczyn, 2004, p. 97).

As a starting point, parental fitness might reasonably be inferred by reference to the factors which define the Uniform Marriage and Divorce Act (UMDA, 1973; e.g., Melone & Karnes, 2008).[6] As modified to suit this context, these include:

1. The security of the existing attachment between the parent and the child
2. The parent's capacity to create and maintain a secure attachment with the child

3. The parent's capacity to provide the child with food, clothing, medical care or other remedial care, education, and opportunities for social growth
4. The permanence of the parent's existing or intended family unit and the physical environment in which they reside
5. The parent's mental and physical health to the extent that either or both limit his or her ability to fulfill these goals
6. The quality and appropriateness of proximal resources such as home, neighborhood, school, and community to the child's established and anticipated needs
7. The parent's existing and professed willingness and ability to facilitate and encourage the child's close and continuing relationship with his or her other caregivers.

Together, these factors might more generally be discussed as they constitute three interwoven, developmentally informed family systems concepts, each of which was introduced earlier and is applied here.

The Child's Attachment With the Absent Parent

Attachment security is psychology's best analogue to the UMDA's reference to "[t]he love, affection, and other emotional ties existing between the parties involved and the child." (For further discussion, see Barth, Crea, John, Thoburn, & Quinton, 2005; Cicchetti & Toth, 1992; Haight, Kagle, & Black, 2003; Harden, 2004; Lyons-Ruth, Connell, Zoll, & Stahl, 1987; Mennen & O'Keefe, 2005).

All other things being equal, reunification will be least conflicted, most time efficient, and most successful when the child has a secure attachment with the absent parent. However, because sensitive and responsive caregiving is both the necessary antecedent of attachment security and logically exclusive of maltreatment, the separated dyad is likely to either: (a) have been separated for reasons other than maltreatment (e.g., on the basis of false allegations of maltreatment, as a result of sociopolitical crisis,[7] or because of the parent's incarceration, hospitalization, or military deployment [see chapter 11]); or (b) have been separated for reasons of maltreatment and therefore is not likely to have had a secure attachment before the separation.

In the former case, when a secure dyad is separated, the separation itself can erode the quality of the relationship as a function of the duration of time apart (Bowlby, 1973; McWey & Mullis, 2004; Troutman, Ryan, & Cardi, 2000). When interim measures intended to maintain the quality of the relationship despite the separation are insufficient, when transitional objects are inadequate, when interim contacts via various media are infrequent or unpredictable, and/or when third-party influences undermine the quality of the attachment relationship (i.e., alienation, see chapter 16), what was once a secure attachment may soon cease to be. These security-eroding influences will be most corrosive most quickly with the least socially and emotionally mature children and in the most chaotic and conflicted families, the very children who are simultaneously the most vulnerable to concomitant behavioral and emotional difficulties (Bellamy, 2008; Fish & Chapman, 2004).

In the latter case, when an insecure dyad is separated, the same lack of caregiver sensitive/responsivity that is associated with insecure and disorganized attachments (Barnett, Butler, & Vondras, 1999; Cicchetti, Rogosch, & Toth, 2006) is also likely to be at the root of a parent's abusive and/or neglectful behavior (Egeland, Jacobvitz, & Sroufe, 1988) and must therefore be among the primary foci of interim intervention in the short-term interest of reunification[8] and the long-term interest of facilitating a secure parent–child attachment. This means that during the seaparation, the parent must have the opportunity to learn how to become more sensitive and responsive to the child's needs. Interventions such as Marvin's Circle of Security (Marvin, Cooper, Hoffman, & Powell, 2002) and others that utilize video feedback have great promise for application in this setting.

Unfortunately, the frank reality is that removal often serves as little more than an adult "time out," failing to change the underlying conditions that fuel the cycle of abuse, state intervention, removal, and ultimately termination:

> [I]n considering intervention strategies and social services that are intended to assist families at risk for maltreatment, the focus on early interactions and attachment is often missing. Most strategies address issues related to parental welfare and adaptation....Improvement of dysfunctional parent–child interaction is often nominally mentioned, but rarely systematically and intentionally addressed. (Tarabulsy et al., 2008, p. 325)

Worse still, inadequate, infrequent, and unpredictable interim contacts combined with alienating messages can actually make what was once an unhealthy relationship even worse, creating conditions ripe for visitation resistance and refusal, conditions that can condemn reunification efforts to fail even before they have begun.

The Absent Parent's Socioemotional Maturity

Sensitive/responsivity calls for certain minimal physical, behavioral, and developmental prerequisites[9] (see Bolton & Laner, 1981). A sensitive and responsive parent must have the sensory capacity to receive (typically to see and/or hear) the child's signals and the motor capacity and/or the assistive technologies to respond appropriately to those signals.[10] The parent has to be free of chemicals (e.g., drugs and alcohol), addictions (e.g., pornography or gambling), and psychopathologies (e.g., schizophrenia)[11] that regularly impede the ability to receive and sensitively respond to the child's signals. Further, the parent must have the socioemotional maturity to regularly choose to exercise these capacities in the child's best interests. As one researcher phrases it, what is necessary is "[the] ability to empathically understand and give priority to their child's needs" (Donald & Jureidini, 2004, p. 5).

Although this argument applies to parenting children of any age (and perhaps to engaging in any healthy relationship), it is most easily illustrated with regard to the care of an infant: At a minimum, a parent should be able to hear that her baby is crying and be able to promptly provide a bottle or a burp or a cuddle, unimpaired by substances and free of the competing and confusing demands of compulsions, hallucinations and delusions. These broadly constitute the UMDA's "mental and physical health" criteria.

But a parent must also have "[t]he capacity and disposition…to give the child love, affection, and guidance"—that is, the social and emotional wherewithal to choose to put aside other matters so as to respond to the baby's cry, to tolerate misinterpreting the child's needs, and to soothe the child all the while. This calls for the mature capacity to tolerate frustration, to delay gratification, to understand that the child has an interior life apart from one's own (theory of mind), and to regulate one's own needs.

The absence of these social and emotional capacities is often associated with the high rates of social service intervention, removal, and termination among teenage mothers, regardless of affluence, social support, and other otherwise moderating factors (Afifi, 2007; De Paul & Domenech, 2000; but see Kinard, 2003).[12]

The Extant Caregiver's Support for the Process

The UMDA recognizes this variable as, "[t]he willingness and ability of each of the parties to facilitate and encourage a close and continuing parent–child relationship between the child and the other parent or the child and the parents." Unfortunately, the legal–political reality often works against this goal.

The law's proper interest in minimizing the duration of the limbo that a child must endure while in temporary placement calls for simultaneous planning for *both* reunification and permanent out-of-home (adoption) placement. Interim (foster and kinship) caregivers thus often struggle with a systemically induced conflict of interest, a need to support reunification and a competing wish that reunification will fail so that out-of-home permanent placement (often adoption) can occur. This struggle understandably exposes children to lots of mixed messages, enough so that one savvy judge is known to advise his colleagues that "[i]f a foster parent is sabotaging or undermining reunification efforts, the judge can find that the foster placement is not in the best interests of the child and remove the child" (Johnson, n.d.).

This is the powerful dynamic of alienation, encountered earlier with regard to reunification following a parent's incarceration or military deployment and now evident as a critically important influence on parent–child reunification efforts, particularly as it appears in the context of contested custody litigation.

A DEVELOPMENTALLY INFORMED, SYSTEMIC MODEL OF REUNIFICATION

It is possible to piece together the disparate literatures concerned with attachment security (chapter 5), visitation resistance and refusal (chapter 10), relocation and involuntary separations (chapter 11), and reunification in the context of social service removal (the present chapter), so as to propose the necessary (even if not sufficient) components of an optimal parent–child reunification process:

1. Prevention must be the priority in every instance possible. It will always be more cost-effective and child-centered to intervene with at-risk families in an effort to avoid unnecessary separation than to remove a child to foster care and try to work toward reunification. We know a great deal about so-called, "family preservation programs" (Littel & Schuerman, 2002; see also: Bribitzer & Verdieck, 1988; Ensign, 1991; Feldman, 1990; Fraser, Pecora, & Haapala, 1991; Gershenson, 1991; Ratterman, Dodson, & Hardin, 1987; Schwartz, AuClaire, & Harris, 1991).[13] Unfortunately, we live in a squeaky-wheel society, a harsh reality that means that finite resources are seldom allocated before a problem erupts or, worse, before it reaches crisis proportions. As the federal government's General Accounting Office summarized in 1993:

> In 1981, the ratio of foster care expenditures to child welfare services appropriations was about 2 to 1; by 1992, this ratio was 8 to 1. Moreover, declining state revenues, compounded by burgeoning foster care caseloads and costs, have largely exhausted state moneys that could otherwise be used for family preservation services.

Tragically, by 2004, little had changed for the better. According to New Orleans Juvenile Court Judge Ernestine Gray (2004, p. 182), "[w]e must take steps to keep children from coming into the system. Both for the children and for society, it is far better to prevent the harm from happening than to have to repair the damage."

How do we go about prevention? Two central points resonate throughout this book: education and support. When schools and churches, synagogues and mosques, daycare centers and even grocery stores provide parents with materials and opportunities to learn about better parenting, children benefit. Sadly, proactive efforts focusing on parenting education, and child and family development routinely struggle to fund their programs, in part because limited social service budgets are being drained at the other end of the system, on children and parents already deeply entrenched in the sytem.

Education seldom succeeds without support. The second global emphasis of this book is on the flow of emotional resources within families. For parents to successfully fill their children's emotional gas tanks, they must be certain to fill their own. Adult supports in the form of counseling and psychotherapy, clerical and lay ministry, groups and clubs and chatrooms and parent support groups serve this purpose.

When a parent feels valued and validated by peers, the need to enlist children in destructive role reversals that open the door to abuse diminishes dramatically.

2. Preparation can help children and their families to manage separations when they must occur. Children who must be removed by state intervention; those separated from a caregiver by virtue of relocation, incarceration, imprisonment, or hospitalization; and those who are transitioning into permanence (Romaine, Turley, & Tuckey, 2007) will understand and manage the process best when a number of conditions are met. These include the following:

a) A simple, clear, and developmentally appropriate explanation for the separation must be offered consistently by all involved. This explanation should be scripted (Garber, 2008a), so as to minimize ambiguity, distortion, and contradiction. The script must anticipate and avoid the child's natural tendency to blame him- or herself for the situation, but at the same time must be careful not to blame a parent in a manner that might undermine the child's trust. Sometimes this means coaching the parent to offer the child a simple and clear statement about being apart so as to learn how to be a better family, reassuring the child that both will be fine and that their love for one another will never change.

b) Establishing means to minimize the erosion of the existing attachment relationship over time. Specifically:

■ Whenever possible, the duration of the intended separation should be established in advance so as to make reunification predictable and explained to the child in a manner that the child can understand. When the timing of reunification is uncertain (as when reunification is contingent upon a parent's efforts toward specific goals), a child can still be told that the present "experiment" will last until a specific date. On that date, the child will learn either when reunion will occur or how long the next "experiment" will last. When the period of separation is presented in understandable chunks of time in this way, the child is free not to worry, "Is today the day I'm going home?"

■ Maintaining the attachment requires establishing a schedule of frequent, healthy, and predictable interim contacts. The developmentally informed heuristic offered in chapter 8 applies here: In the ideal, a child should not be separated from an important caregiver for a number of consecutive nights in excess of twice the number of years in her age.

■ Whenever necessary, technology should be used to facilitate or supplement the schedule of interim parent–child contacts.

■ Whenever possible, transitional objects should be made available to both the parent and the child.

3. Social service and court involvement should automatically trigger child health, development, and achievement screening (Harden, 2004). Perhaps we can't proactively screen every child at ages 3, 5, 9, and 13 for major illnesses, toxic exposure, developmental differences, and learning disabilities, but we can and should screen every child who is brought into the system for any reason. The United States makes a superficial effort in this regard by requiring proof of immunizations for school enrolment and providing vision and hearing screening through the schools. But this is not enough.

The cost of early identification and remediation of these difficulties is a fraction of the long-term cost of allowing a child to remain untreated into adulthood. The events that bring children into the social service system and before family law professionals should spontaneously trigger thorough developmental screening and open doors to associated remedies.

4. Interventions should span the pendency of the *separation* (begun prior to and continued beyond permanency whenever possible) and include all relevant parties. Interim services and associated goals must look beyond the behavior that precipitated separation (e.g., relocation, parental drug abuse, violence, abuse and/or neglect) in order to more globally shore up parenting skills and facilitate secure relationships between the child and each of his or her caregivers, including interim (foster or kinship) providers, as appropriate. Specifically, interim interventions must:

a) Build caregivers' sensitive/responsivity. Many programs exist with which to implement this goal with teenage (Borkowski, Farris, & Weed, 2007; Deutscher, Fewell, & Gross, 2006; Letourneau, Weir, & Neufeld, 2008) and other high-risk parents (Cicchetti, Rogosch, & Toth, 2006; Suchman, DeCoste, Castiglioni, Legow, & Mayes, 2008).

b) Build caregivers' socioemotional maturity, including frustration tolerance, healthy anger expression and self-advocacy, delay of gratification, and theory of mind (Tarabulsy et al., 1998).

c) Build the quality of the specific dyad's interactions, using therapeutic visitation (Haight, Kagal, & Black, 2003) and video feedback (e.g.,Marvin et al., 2002). Worthy of note is the value of the Adult Attachment Interview in guiding work of this sort (Bick & Dozier, 2008).

5. The nature, frequency, and duration of services must be developmentally informed and systemically attuned. The child's developmental needs should dictate much more than the frequency of interim contacts with the absent caregiver. The entire package, from preseparation prophylaxis to the separation "script" to redefinition of roles within the interim and reconstituted family group, to consideration of alternate permanency outcomes, placement, and postplacement coping, needs to be tailored to the child's developmental capacity.

Social service and family law professionals who fail to recognize developmental décalage, who mistake an adultified or parentified child as mature, who don't grasp the limitations and qualitative differences associated with developmental stages, risk doing harm. As Badeau (2004), illustrates:

> Remember how far away summer vacation seemed at the beginning of a new school year when you were a child? Interventions for children and their families must respect and account for children's timetables. Too often, child welfare policies and practices take a "one-size-fits-all" approach. Instead, service delivery should look entirely different for infants, toddlers, school-age children and adolescents.

6. Family counseling should be available to the child's interim family group. Interim (foster and kinscare) caregivers must be assisted in understanding and responding to their charge's developmental needs, in appreciating their place in the child's transitional process, and in coping with the emotional/legal conflict of interest that can arise associated with concurrent placement planning (Chipungu & Bent-Goodley, 2004). At issue in particular is the establishment of healthy roles and boundaries and coping with the intense emotions associated with a child's entry, adjustment, and departure. Referral of interim caregivers to appropriate peer support groups will be one invaluable component of this process (Brown, 2008; Brown, Moraes, & Mayhew, 2005; see also foster parent resources in Appendix I).

7. These services must continue beyond permanency (e.g., Testa, 2004). This need is most obvious in the immediate postreunification (or postadoption or postguardianship) period, when the "honeymoon" ends and emotional and behavior problems begin to emerge. But post-permanency services continue to serve a critical (and cost-effective) need when a family crisis erupts, as when the antecedents of a prior separation trigger a child's fears of renewed loss, and at predictable developmental shifts. Adopted teens, for example, often face an identity crisis associated with an intense wish to reconnect **with** families of origin **that** can upset the entire family system.

SUMMARY

Our efforts to help parents and children manage their forced separations, to maintain the healthiest relationships possible while they remain apart, and to work toward reunification in the healthiest way possible serve not only the best interests of the children, but the best interests of the society, as well. This chapter has recommended a number of conditions and strategies intended to serve these goals, emphasizing prevention, education, and support in every instance possible. Recognizing our own limits and the frank reality that reunification cannot occur for some families, we turn now to a consideration of those circumstances that require the termination of a parent's rights.

NOTES

1. "[W]hile there is still reason to believe that positive, nurturing parent–child relationships exist, the *parens patriae* interest favors preservation, not severance, of natural familial bonds." *Santosky v. Kramer*, 455 U.S. 745 (1982).
2. The Adoption Assistance and Child Welfare Act of 1980 (Public Law 96-272; 671[a][15]). See also: the Adoption and Safe Families Act of 1997 (P.L. 105-89); the Foster Care Independence Act of 1999 (P.L. 106-169); the Promoting Safe and Stable Families Amendments of 2001 (P.L. 107-133); the Adoption Promotion Act of 2003 (P.L. 108-145); and the Keeping Children and Families Safe Act of 2003 (P.L. 108-36).

3. See: (a) Martens (2006) for an excellent review of relevant resources promoting successful reunification in the case of foster placement; (b) United States Department of Health and Human Services (2006) for an excellent review of foster, adoption, and reunification programs across the United States; and (c) the University of Arizona Web page that summarizes relevant federal laws and cases at http://www.law.arizona.edu/Depts/Clinics/CAC/fed.html
4. See http://www.aecf.org/
5. Retrieved February 22, 2009, from http://www.casey.org/MediaCenter/MediaKit/FactSheet.htm
6. For a discussion of the application of each criterion in a recent reunification matter, see *ROBERT HUNTER and LORIE HUNTER, Plaintiffs-Appellees, v. TAMMY JO HUNTER, Defendant-Appellant, and JEFFREY HUNTER, Defendant* No. 279862. Court of Appeals of Michigan. March 20, 2008; retrieved online February 15, 2009 from: http://www.plol.org/Pages/Secure/Document.aspx?d=FYKx4hLL1jbm3mEF Gj%2b3NQ%3d%3d&l=Cases&rp=4
7. Cross-cultural experience, separation due to war, political strife and migration are otherwise not considered here but have an important place in the literature. Among recent publications, see: Arnold (2006), Black (2006), Marte (2008), Rae-Espinoza (2007), and Schiff and Benbenishty (2006).
8. "[T]raumatic experiences, such as child maltreatment, can interfere with attachment and create a disturbed attachment….[A]busive parents tend to have had a childhood characterized by insecure, unstable, and/or pathological relations with their primary caregivers" (Ezzo, Evans, & McGovern-Kondik, 2004, p.31).
9. Relevant, but beyond the scope of this discussion, are: Condie and Condie (2008) and Watkins (1995).
10. In one fascinating study, teenage mothers were found to be neurologically less attentive and responsive to infant's needs than adult mothers: "[W]here self-report is used as a measure of maternal responsiveness, teen mothers are no different in responsiveness than adult mothers; however, where physiological and interactional measures of responsiveness are considered, teen mothers are less likely to show heightened or selective responses to infant cries or respond 'attentively' to the infant" (Giardino et al., 2008, p. 149).
11. In *In re Yves*, the appellate court asks, "Does the fact that a parent has a mental illness that is being successfully managed nevertheless provide a 'compelling reason' to deny reunification and instead adopt a permanency plan of long-term foster care?" It answers decisively that, "[The] Juvenile Judge's orders of long term and permanent foster care were clearly errone-

ous where evidence at relevant permanency plan hearings mandated by statute showed no likelihood of future neglect or abuse by the parent who concededly had been diagnosed previously as suffering from mental illness, but controlled it through medication and other treatment for the prior 2 years" (373 Md. 551 Nos. 24 & 50, September Term, 2002).

12. Kinard (2003) compares maternal abuse potential among three groups he defines as younger adolescents (up to 17 years of age), older adolescents (18–19), and adults (20–24), whereas the relevant socioemotional landmarks are not likely to be differentiated within this age range. As noted with regard to the "mature minor" concept in Chapter 14 (e.g., Cauffman & Steinberg, 2000a), mature socioemotional skills may not be attained until the early or mid-20s.

13. Noting that "current federal funding mechanisms for child welfare place a greater priority on supports to children while in foster care at the expense of building stronger families, and are contrary to the desired outcomes of child safety, permanency and well-being" (California Working Families, 2007); retrieved February 16, 2009, from: http://www.cwda.org/downloads/publications/cws/PreventingEntrance _Foster care.pdf

Development and the Termination of Parental Rights

The fundamental liberty interest of natural parents in the care, custody, and management of their child is protected by the Fourteenth Amendment, and does not evaporate simply because they have not been model parents or have lost temporary custody of their child to the State. A parental rights termination proceeding interferes with that fundamental liberty interest.

—*U.S. Supreme Court,* Santosky v. Kramer

The fact that appellant has a mental or emotional problem and is less than a perfect parent or that the children may be happier with their foster parents is not a legitimate reason to remove them from a natural parent competent to care for them in favor of a stranger.

—*Maryland Appellate Court,* In Re Yve S.

Terminating a parent's rights to a child is the family court's most extreme measure. It is the state's *parens patriae* prerogative taken to the nth degree. It is, in fact, the ultimate test of our commitment to the best interests of the child over and above our commitment to the integrity of the family and to the parent's right to raise his or her own offspring (see especially *Quilloin v. Walcott*, 434 U.S. 246 [1978]). This chapter examines termination proceedings from a developmental perspective, emphasizing the child's experience of this process and the means with which we might better meet children's needs when termination is necessary.

CRITERIA FOR THE TERMINATION OF PARENTAL RIGHTS

In *Santosky v. Kramer* (455 U.S. § 745 [1982]), the Supreme Court established clear and convincing evidence as the standard of proof in termination of parental rights (TPR) proceedings.[1] Every state and U.S. territory[2] uses this language to define TPR in one of two forms. The first requires the presence of one or more specific criteria, typically including:

- Severe or chronic abuse or neglect of the child
- Abuse or neglect of other children
- Abandonment of the child
- Long-term mental illness or comparable caregiving deficiency[3]
- Long-term alcohol-, drug-, or other addiction-related caregiving incapacity
- Failure to support or maintain contact with the child for a specific period[4]
- Involuntary termination of the rights of the parent to another child
- Felony conviction for a violent crime, especially against a family member
- Incarceration for a period that would be detrimental to the child

Alternately, TPR is defined without recourse to specific behaviors and conditions, but rather in terms of the impracticality of a safe reunification within a reasonable time (Ezzo et al., 2004). The Adoption and Safe Families Act (ASFA; Public Law 105-89) defines the time variable quite concretely as a separation of 15 out of the most recent 22 months, noting that some states allow exceptions if, for example, (a) the child has been in the care of a close relative, (b) the state's ongoing reasonable efforts toward reunification clearly contraindicate TPR, or (c) the state has failed to meet its "reasonable effort" criterion in this period.

The effect of TPR is to legally and finally sever the connection between a parent and a child, typically as a necessary precursor for the child's adoption into another home. TPR must be distinguished from *relinquishment* (a.k.a, "voluntary surrender"), the voluntary analogue (and in some states, one among the many preconditions) of TPR. In Wisconsin, for example, a parent can chose to relinquish all rights to a child within 72 hours of birth (Ann. Stat. § 48.415) so as to allow that child to be adopted.[5] Whereas TPR means a final and irreversible break between parent and child, relinquishment may not (Fravel, Grotevant, Boss, & McRoy, 1993; Grotevant, McRoy, Elde, & Frawel, 1994), thus laying the foundation for the concept of "open adoption" (Duxbury, 2007; McRoy, Grotevant, Ayers-Lopez, & Henney, 2007; Reamer & Siegal, 2007).

TPR must similarly be distinguished from guardianship (Brooks, 2001). A legal guardian is vested by the court with the responsibility of making substantial decisions in a child's life (sometimes limited to a particular realm, as when medical decision-making authority is assigned to a guardian). In the right circumstances, guardianship has the advantage over TPR and adoption of allowing the child and his or her biological relatives to maintain their respective roles and relationships, even maintaining frequent contact:

> Guardianship, unlike adoption, allows kin to retain their extended family identities as grandparents, aunts, and uncles. Children may retain rights of sibling visitation. Birth parents may still exercise a limited role in their children's upbringing as they hold onto certain residual rights and obligations, such as rights to visitation as well as obligation for child support. Birth parents may also petition the court to vacate the guardianship and return the children to parental custody if their circumstances change. (Testa, 2004, p. 121)

TIME AS A TPR VARIABLE

The court's decision to terminate a parent's rights is ultimately (but seldom explicitly) the result of a child-centered cost-benefit accounting; a calculus filled with immeasurable, unknowable *could-be* and *what-if* variables. Weighed out on the scales of justice are the real or inferred physical, social, emotional, moral, cognitive, academic, and occupational benefits of family continuity versus the real or inferred upheaval and trauma associated with the indeterminacy of foster or kinship care versus the fearful possibility of being returned to the care of an unfit parent,[6] all of this as a function of time.

True, we know that the child who enjoys the continuity, social and emotional congruity,[7] and familiarity of growing up in her birth home will be healthier than the child who is wrenched away from her birth family for an indeterminate period and thrust into the care of strangers, *all other things being equal.* But were all other things equal, the discussion of foster care, TPR, and adoption (and their alternatives) would never arise. What we don't know with any certainty is which among the infinite number of family-of-origin, interim-care-provider, and child-specific variables are most relevant, how to measure them, and what ratio of these variables tips the scales in favor of TPR.

Time is most certainly high on the list of relevant factors, but not only in the objective sense of calendar days and weeks and years. What matters is the child's subjective experience of time, keeping in mind that this changes with development (see chapter 8) and is likely to be strongly influenced by the conditions of separation (see chapter 11). On the one hand, the quality of a child's relationship with an absent caregiver is reasonably expected to erode over time. On the other hand, an absent parent's "reasonable efforts" to learn and grow and make the substantive changes necessary for reunification are reasonably expected to require time. We have previously discussed how this see-saw balancing act plays out when parents are incarcerated (Satyanathan, 2002), deployed with the military (Neil, 2007), or incapacitated or hospitalized due to illness (Hannett, 2007). In this chapter, we discuss what occurs when it fails.

Some states have rationalized this dilemma explicitly by recognizing the countervailing value of the foster parent bond.[8] To the extent that the quality of the parent–child attachment is poor to begin with and/ or erodes over time, these statutes allow that the court may consider the quality of the child's attachment to the interim (and prospective adoptive) caregiver in determining TPR. New Jersey law, for example, allows that:

> Courts may terminate parental rights if it can be shown through psychological evaluation or other expert testimony that the child has become psychologically bonded to his temporary caretaker, that he or she will suffer harm if removed from [the] temporary caretaker and that his/her caretaker would adopt the child should he/she be freed for adoption.[9]

In a similar manner, Connecticut allows that TPR proceedings must consider "the feelings and emotional ties of the child towards the parent and also towards others who have had custody or control of the child for at least a year and with whom the child has developed significant emotional ties."[10]

As a variable relevant to TPR, time must also be measured in terms of the child's age at the point of entry into the social services system. We know that although AFSA's standards have significantly reduced the duration of foster care and the number of children left languishing in legal/bureaucratic limbo, respect for parents' rights and the integrity of the family (not to mention systemic inefficiencies, e.g., Ratterman, 1991) can prolong the process at tremendous cost, measured in terms of social service dollars, community instability, and the child's social, emotional, and cognitive development.

Haugaard and Avery (2002, p. 142) summarize studies that converge on the conclusion that the duration of the removal-to-permanency process is related to the child's age upon entering the social services system, such that infants are likely to reach permanency most quickly[11] whereas 2- to 5-year-olds are commonly delayed in the process, possibly due to "stronger attachment to birth parents and prolonged attempts by social workers to reunify the child and birth family" (see also Stovall-McClough & Dozier, 2004). Across ages, five relevant factors—race, developmental differences, physical, and social and emotional disabilities—tend to further delay the permanency such that non-Caucasian, differently abled, and older children experience the greatest delays.

THE IMPACT AND MEANING OF TPR TO THE CHILD

A child's experience of TPR will vary as a function of developmental capacities at separation (often mistaken for age), how the parent–child relationship was maintained or neglected during the separation, and how the loss is explained. At one extreme, a child removed (or relinquished) at birth and immediately placed with foster/adoptive caregivers might have no sense of the loss until it becomes a matter of social consequence among peers in grade school or a question of identity and autonomy for the young teenager.

At the other extreme, an older child or adolescent whose fledgling identity is deeply rooted in his or family (no matter how dysfunctional) is likely to find removal, interim care, and out-of-home permanent placement traumatic.[12] The resulting rage, depression, anxiety, and acting out (e.g., running away, self-destructive behavior, promiscuous sexual behavior, substance abuse) can not only impede healthy development and disrupt family and community functioning, but may ultimately make the legally mandated transition untenable. The likelihood of such "adoption ruptures" increases with the child's age (Testa, 2004, p. 124). Implicit in this observation is the fact that even victims of abuse take comfort in the familiarity of their relationship with their abusers such that removal can spark a sometimes volcanic combination of relief and loss and fear and anger.[13]

Some children who are known to have suffered indescribable abuse and neglect, who have witnessed domestic violence, who have bounced between well-intended but limited foster care residences, and who continue to live with the constant uncertainty of whether Mom will arrive for the scheduled supervised visit and whether the court will let him go home, seem fine.

Don't fall for it. Each of these events, singly, is cause enough for a child to become angry or anxious, withdrawn or aggressive, or any of a hundred other profiles in pathology. All of these events combined are a certain recipe for profound insecurity, at the least.

Some of these children become chameleons. They deny or compartmentalize their pain in favor of fitting in to the immediate social environment the same way that the reptile changes his colors to fit in to the immediate physical environment. At a glance, this child may look fine. He's the 5-year-old who greets you by name, shakes your hand, and looks you in the eye, or the 10-year-old who says, "No thank you," he'd rather talk than play. This child has compromised his identity in favor of fitting in. Look beneath the surface. You're likely to discover that this child has secrets. He hoardes food, lights fires, abuses animals or harms himself. He steals or lies. He has an eating disorder, is failing school or is somaticizing his distress as bellyaches, headaches, or muscle pain. The incongruity between the harsh reality that this child has survived and his smiling, agreeable presentation should be clue enough. Referral for a mental health assessment will either make you look like a cynic or—far more likely—help you catch and begin to treat hidden distress.

Across age, the loss of a primary caregiver for any reason is likely to be recast in the child's thinking as a matter of personal failure, perhaps most powerfully when the loss occurs as a result of the child's own behavior. For example, children whose admission of abuse leads to removal easily and often blame themselves, a reality compounded exponentially by the perpetrator's selfish and destructive accusations of blame. "Guilt is a common response for victims of sexual abuse. They often feel that they share responsibility for the abuse and for what happens to the adult abuser" (Watson, 1994, p. 42). Psychotherapy can be critically important to help children to keep the experience of parental loss, relationships with interim caregivers, the prospect of termination, and the prospects for permanency in a healthy perspective.

Perhaps most critical to these considerations is the establishment of a single, child-centered, and consistent script explaining these events (Laufer, 2007). Ideally, social service workers, therapists, attorneys, court personnel, the parent saying goodbye, and the interim/permanent caregivers will all present the child with the same story. Developmentally appropriate children's books can serve as a common base upon which such a script can be built.[14]

PSYCHOTHERAPY, MENTORS, AND FOSTER CARE

The trauma and loss associated with family separation of any sort—as a result of relocation, incarceration, deployment, hospitalization, illness, or even the death of a parent—can have a crippling impact on development. Many children respond by regressing in the short run, falling back on previously successful (and now immature) developmental coping mechanisms. The obvious examples are legion: The 10-year-old who resumes bedwetting. The 12-year-old who resumes thumb-sucking. The 6-year-old who loses words and becomes mute. Regression in these cases can be a transitory and acute reaction, or it can become an entrenched and pathological state. (Read more in chapter 6.)

The longer-term outcomes associated with parental loss, removal, interim care, and permanent placement (not to mention the abuse, neglect, and abandonment that heralds these events) are sometimes planted like psychological landmines, silent and dormant for years to come. The child might grow into young adulthood with no obvious pain associated with these earlier events, only to find him- or herself unexpectedly walking through a minefield when related emotions are reignited. Therapists see this when the trauma associated with childhood sexual abuse is reawakened in an adolescent beginning to explore his or her own sexuality. In a like manner, a child's traumatic separation from a parent will sometimes reappear only when that person becomes a parent him- or herself.

The psychoanalytic literature refers to these landmines as *superego lacunae*. For present purposes, imagine that childhood trauma leaves one or more of the steps in the staircase of development loose or rotten or otherwise flawed. When that child walks back up the same staircase vicariously with his or her own child, the pair fall through, recreating the intergenerational cycle.

The literature on vulnerability and resilience (e.g., Garmezy, 1985; Maddi, 2002; Masten, 1999, 2002; Rutter, 2007; also see chapter 7) teaches us that children who experience trauma and loss have a greater likelihood of healthy outcomes if they have at least one stable attachment figure through it all. This is one strong argument for providing children who are at high risk for abuse and neglect, social service removal, interim care, and permanency planning the opportunity to engage in a supportive psychotherapy that spans the entire process. This therapy is often referred to as a "port in the storm" for the child.

In this age of managed health care and of cognitive-behavioral and "evidence-based" interventions (e.g., O'Donohue & Fisher, 2006), the psychotherapist's goal is efficiency. This is a very effective and practically desirable approach when the problem is well-defined. Many forms of anxiety, some forms of depression, and specific behavioral problems (e.g., bedwetting) can benefit quickly with lasting results.

However, research finds, time and again, across cultures and generations, modalities of service and presenting problems, that the effective component of any psychotherapy is the relationship itself.

It is a tragedy of our cost-conscious, efficiency-minded world that children who are enduring trauma seldom have the opportunity to establish and maintain a long-term psychotherapeutic relationship intended largely to anchor them through the process. This kind of "port in the storm" relationship can be the difference between dysfunction that leads to underachievement, under- or unemployment, failed intimate relationships, inappropriate parenting, and their associated costs on one hand and healthy outcomes on the other (Laursen & Birmingham, 2003).

Mentoring exists as an adjunct (and in some instances, as a viable and low-cost alternative) to psychotherapy (see Appendix IV). Research specifically finds that mentoring can provide a critical safety net to those children who are most at risk when removal, foster care, and permanency planning becomes necessary (Ahrens, DuBois, Richardson, Fan, & Lozano, 2008).

Mentoring (e.g., Big Brothers/Big Sisters) involves pairing a trained adult volunteer with an at-risk youth, *not* to provide psychotherapy and *not* to replace an existing or past caregiver, but to provide a consistent emotional anchor and a healthy role model. Mentoring has demonstrable effectiveness with youth at risk for gang activity (Sheehan, DiCara, LeBailly, & Kaufer-Christoffel, 1999) and teenage pregnancy (Black et al., 2006), with special needs populations (Britner, Balcazar, Blechman, Blinn-Pike, & Larose, 2006), with minority groups (Iglehart & Becerra, 2002), and perhaps most powerfully with children and teens in foster care (Greeson & Bowen, 2008) and those transitioning from long-term care into independent functioning (Mann-Feder & White, 2003). In one study of children in foster care:

> [Y]outh with histories of placement in foster care had worse adult out-comes compared with youth in the general population; however, [youth in foster care] with mentoring relationships during adolescence had more favorable outcomes in multiple domains of late adolescent/young adult functioning than non-mentored youth. Areas of improvement included educational attainment (borderline significance), suicidal risk, physical aggression, general health, and risk for having an [sexually transmitted infection]. (Aherns et al., 2008, p. e260)

"AGING OUT" OF FOSTER CARE AND EMANCIPATION

Between 20,000 and 25,000 teens reach age 18 or graduate from high school while in foster care each year and thereby "age out" of the system. As in so many matters that come before family law professionals, this determination is made without regard for a child's actual develop-mental capacities, except in those obvious and extreme cases of pro-found developmental disability (e.g., Jasper, 2008). As a result:

> A significant portion of youth exiting the foster care system face serious difficulty transitioning to life on their own. Many live on the streets,

lack the money to meet basic living expenses, fail to maintain regular employment, are involved with the criminal justice system, are unable to obtain health care, and experience early pregnancies. Although youth reported exposure to independent living training while in care, few reported concrete assistance. Multiple placements while in care and less education correlated with more difficult postdischarge functioning. (Reilly, 2003, p. 727)

The Child Welfare League of America[15] reports that between 12 and 36% of foster children who age out of care experience homelessness. As many as 30% of homeless people at any one time have a history of foster care removal.

This situation is hardly improved when states[16] allow minors to petition the court to be granted the rights and responsibilities of majority, a process known as emancipation. In California, for example, a minor may be emancipated under Family Code 7000-7002 if he or she is at least 14 years old, lives apart from parents or guardians, is financially self-sufficient, legally married, and/or on active military duty.

In 2005, a full 20% (more than 100,000) of children in foster care were 16 years of age or older. Of the 287,000 children who exited foster care in the same year, 9% (24,407) did so by becoming legally emancipated.[17] Ray (2008) summarizes outcome studies of emancipated youth:

> Emancipated adults are at a higher risk for substance abuse due to personal histories of abuse or tragedy, lack of access to health care, peer pressure, and general lack of direction....Early parenthood is another concern. In a 1990 survey, 40% of women reported having been pregnant at least one time in the 18–24 months since leaving foster care....Crime also factors in. In his study of emancipated youth, Mark Courtney found that twenty-five percent were incarcerated within a two-year period of leaving a foster care environment.

SUMMARY

When reunification efforts fail, family law professionals consider termination of a parent's rights as a last resort. Although termination may open the door for a child to establish healthy and secure relationships for the first time, it does so at a tremendous potential cost. Children are at very high risk to blame themselves for the separation in the first place and again when reunification fails. Thus, mental health, family law, child protective service, health care, and educational professionals must work hand-in-hand with the child and—when possible—the parent, to assure that termination is seen at least as much an opportunity as it is a crisis.

NOTES

1. Or, more stringently: "While the criteria for establishing the best interests of the child are not capable of specification, each case being largely dependent upon its own facts and circumstances, the proof necessary in order to deprive a person of his or her parental rights must be clear, cogent and convincing." (*Custory of Smith*, p. 39, 137 Wn. 2d 1, 39).
2. The United States Department of Health and Human Services provides a comprehensive compendium of TPR statutes at http://www.childwelf are.gov/systemwide/laws_policies/statutes/gro undterminall.pdf
3. Much has been written about the relationship between psychopathology and parenting capacity. I note Ezzo et al. (2004, p. 31): "[A]lthough most abusive parents exhibit deficits in a variety of areas of functioning, they rarely suffer from acute psychiatric disturbances" Bogacki & Weiss (2007). observe that parents with significant cognitive, developmental, and emotional differences may be the least able to defend themselves and may therefore be at highest risk of having their parenting rights terminated, even though many of these disabilities are very treatable. Lagan et al. (2009, p. 53) summarizes: "Often mothers with psychiatric illness struggle to meet the cognitive, emotional, and financial demands of drawn-out custody proceedings. For these mothers, there is a paucity of appropriate support available."
4. See, e.g., *Lassiter v. Department of Social Services*, 452 U.S. 18 (1981).
5. Many statutes allowing relinquishment of parental rights also allow for limited conditions under which relinquishment can be reversed. For example, according to New Mexico law (§ 32A-5-21), a minor child's relinquishment of her child can be reversed simply on the basis of her status as a minor, providing yet another instance in which the concept of the "mature minor" must be considered, as discussed in chapter 14.
6. Jonson-Reid (2003) documents foster care recidivism, noting that recidivism decreases as duration of and stability of foster care increases, when foster placement is with family members, and when in-home services were in place prior to placement.

7. Testa (2004) refers to the practice of "race matching," noting associated restrictions expressed in the 1994/1996 Multiethnic Placement Act (see Brooks, Barth, Bussiere, & Patterson, 1999), which prohibits federally funded agencies from making placement decisions on the basis of race, color, or national origin.

8. More broadly, the courts have begun to recognize the legitimacy of the child's experience of a nonbiological "psychological parent." For example: "One of the frequent consequences, for children, of the decline of the traditional nuclear family is the formation of close personal attachments between them and adults outside of their immediate families. Stepparents, foster parents, grandparents and other caretakers often form close bonds and, in effect, become psychological parents to children whose nuclear families are not intact....It would be shortsighted indeed, for this court not to recognize the realities and complexities of modern family life by holding today that a child has no rights, over the objection of a parent, to maintain a close extra-parental relationship which has formed in the absence of a nuclear family." (*Custody of Smith*, 1998, 137 Wn.2d 1, p. 36).

9. Retrieved February 21, 2009 from http://www.kidlaw.org/admin. asp?uri=2081&action=15&di=345&ext=pdf &view=yes

10. Retrieved February 21, 2009 from http://www.jud.state.ct.us/probate/termination.pdf

11. This observation is likely contaminated by voluntary relinquishments.

12. This outcome may be moderated when interim placement allows the child to remain in the same school and see the same friends.

13. "The consequences of a termination are profound. Children stand to lose a relationship with a parent who may be loved even if he or she has been neglectful or abusive. Children also risk losing contact with siblings and with extended family members." (from the Judicial Education Center's *Child Welfare Handbook* [available online]; retrieved February 21, 2009 from http://jec.unm.edu/resources/benchbooks/child_law/ch_22.htm#22-5-1).

14. Among recent examples see: Parr (2007) and Katz (2001).

15. Retrieved February 22, 2009 from http://www.cwla.org/programs/foster care/agingoutresources.htm

16. See http://www.jlc.org/factsheets/emancipationus/ for a comprehensive, state-by-state guide to relevant statutes and legislation.

17. Casey Family Foundation statistics accessed 02.22.2009 at: http://www.casey.org/MediaCenter/MediaKit/FactSheet.htm

Advanced Applications of Developmental Theory to Family Law Practice

"[T]he overwhelming majority of lawyers lack any knowledge about family systems and fail to recognize the ways in which their advocacy may inadvertently cause harm to children and families involved in child welfare proceedings. As a result, they may unintentionally create serious anti-therapeutic consequences for children and their families.

—*Susan L. Brooks*

Our interest in respecting the self-determination rights of minors is far more in evidence than our knowledge of minors' capacities to assume the roles that self-determination rights require.

—*T. Grisso and L. Vierling*

The simple reality is that standing on the shoulders of developmental theorists such as Piaget and Kohlberg, Bowlby and Ainsworth, Erikson and Sroufe and Rutter, we can still only see so far. But to try to build higher, to add yet more theory and data, risks falling from this precarious perch much as Dr. Seuss's overly ambitious *Yertle the Turtle* (1958) fell from his.

What remains is a handful of topics that pervade family law but which refuse to fit neatly into the structure and theory of the preceding chapters. This is due at least as much to the limits of my own development as a psychologist and family law professional, son and father, husband and human being, as it is to the imperfections of both social science research and the law itself. Thus, we conclude with a discussion of four disparate topics: the concept of the mature minor; the role of psychological assessment in family law practice; the complementary concepts of alignment and alienation; and the importance of recognizing one's own developmental limits in the course of serving the best interests of children.

14   What Is a "Mature Minor"?

[J]udges do not possess the ability to accurately assess a minor's competence.
                                                        —P. W. English and B. D. Sales

[O]ne pediatrician suggested that any child who could get to the doctor's Greenwich Village office by subway from the Bronx was, in her eyes, an adult.
                                                        —R. I. Simon and L. H. Gold

With few exceptions, having lived 6,570 days is sufficient to qualify one for the privileges and responsibilities of adulthood. Unlike the privilege of driving a car (but very much like the privilege of becoming a parent), there is no qualifying test. There are no cognitive, social, emotional, verbal, or physical prerequisites. One need only endure 18 years to achieve majority status.[1]

The few exceptions to this rule are matters that come before the courts. Majority status can be withheld, limited, or revoked when, for example, competence is in question (Grisso, 1986), when a guardian or conservator has been appointed (e.g., Jasper, 2008), and when the individual has been convicted of a felony.[2] On the flip side of this coin, majority status can be granted prior to attaining age 18 in most jurisdictions when a minor has been legally married, serves in the military, or is otherwise declared emancipated.

This chapter examines the concept of the "mature minor" under the law and how, if at all, this status might be defined. This discussion highlights both the longstanding disconnect between legal mandate and empirical knowledge and the pressing need for a marriage of the two. I recommend a model with which maturity might be defined, emphasizing the relevance of décalage to any such formulation.

MATURITY AS PROCESS OR AS END POINT?

The idea of an absolute sense of maturity or a threshold beyond which one achieves maturity is foreign to psychology. The social sciences do not think of maturity as an end point that can be reached. Rather, to the extent that the word is used at all, it is used in its relative sense to describe a process of growth, to indicate differences of growth between individuals (e.g., "Billy's thinking is more mature than Suzy's") or in the sense that I've used it here, to describe décalage within an individual (e.g., "Suzy is far more socially mature than she is physically mature"). For these reasons, there is no such thing as a "maturity test."

There are, however, many developmental screening instruments. These tend to be parent- or observer-report (e.g., pediatrician or teacher) questionnaires that check off successive behavioral landmarks so as to screen for developmental delay particularly among infants and toddlers. Leppert, O'Connor, and Rosier (2008, p. 395) review many of these, highlighting their value in the clinical setting as "the prelude to assessment, diagnosis, and therapeutic intervention."

There exist many fewer and far less well-known screening instruments for maturity among adolescents. Most notable among these is the Massachusetts Youth Screening Instrument (MAYSI-2; Grisso & Barnum, 2000; Vincent, Grisso, Terry & Banks, 2008), a reliable and valid means of screening the mental health needs of youth, 12 to 17 years of age, involved in the juvenile justice system.

Three related instruments are noteworthy in this context. The *Epstein-Dumas* Test of Adultness (EDTA)[3] purports to generate a maturity measurement, but lacks reliability, validity, and publication in peer reviewed media. Arlin's (1982) cognitive development screening tool has the advantages of validation and ease of administration, but has been used infrequently in the more than 25 years since its introduction. Most promising is the work of Cauffman and Steinberg (1996; 2000a,

2000b; Steinberg & Cauffman, 1996) to operationalize their "maturity of judgment" construct. Unfortunately, this impressive effort remains in development.

A BRIEF HISTORY OF THE "MATURE MINOR" STANDARD

Historically, the distinction regarding achievement of legal majority and the attendant capacity to make decisions in one's own best interests has been determined in many different ways. Under the British common law Rule of Sevens, for example, children under 7 years of age were seen as having no decision-making capacity. Between the ages of 7 and 13, the presumption of no decision-making capacity was rebuttable or could be disproven in court. Between the ages of 14 and 20, adult-like decision-making capacity was presumed but rebuttable, and from 21 on, the individual was granted unquestioned decision-making authority.

The Rule of Sevens was imported into United States law and debated as recently as 1987. At that time, the Tennessee Supreme Court recognized a minor's capacity to consent to medical treatment upon turning 14 years of age.[4] More recently, an Illinois Supreme Court ruling[5] allowed that a 17-year-old could refuse medical treatment by virtue of having established "clear and convincing evidence of maturity."

In both of these instances, and in many more like them, the court has exercised its prerogative to acknowledge the wishes of an individual who has not yet attained the age of majority but who appears to voice a well-reasoned opinion. This is the "mature minor." Whether states formally acknowledge this status or use this nomenclature, the effect is the same. A gray class of individuals has been created to stand ambiguously somewhere between black and white, between the minor who has no standing before the court and the adult who is presumed competent to be heard. To illustrate:

> Both the Tennessee Supreme Court and the Tennessee General Assembly have declined to adopt a per se rule that all persons under the age of eighteen lack the capacity to consent....The court recognized that "minors achieve varying degrees of maturity and responsibility (capacity)" and that "conditions in society have changed to the extent that maturity is now reached at earlier stages of growth than at the time the common law recognized the age of majority at 21 years." [6, 7]

More than a decade later, the indeterminate status of the "mature minor" remains a central controversy in both the psychological literature and in family law. It bears on questions of consent in research and medical treatment as examined in the empirical literature (English & Sales, 2005; Grisso & Vierling, 1978; Hickey, 2007; Marques-Lopez, 2006; Nelson, 2005[8] ; Pliner & Yates, 1992)[9] and as argued in the courts (e.g., *Hodgson v. Minnesota*, 1990; *Ohio v. Akron Center*, 1990). It arises with regard to the adjudication of minors as adults in criminal matters (Cauffman & Steinberg, 2000a, 2000b; Grisso, 1997; Steinberg & Scott, 2003)[10] and time and again with regard to abortion (Needle & Walker, 2008; Quinton, Major, & Richards, 2001).

Although the vast and provocative controversy regarding abortion among minors is well beyond the scope of this discussion, state-specific statutes and case law with regard to determination of "mature minor" status in this context is not only relevant, but instructive. Probably the most clearly defined authority was established in 2001 under Alabama law (§ 22-8-4), which states that "any minor who is age 14 or older, or has graduated from high school, or is married, or having been married is divorced or is pregnant may give effective consent to any legally authorized medical, dental, health or mental health services, and the consent of no other person shall be necessary." Nevertheless, an Alabama trial court ruled in 2005 that a 17-year-old required her parents' consent to obtain an abortion,[11] stating that,

> ...the minor was not sufficiently mature because...a mature minor would not have engaged in sexual activities if she wanted to keep her [college] scholarship or continue to be supported financially by her parents [and]...she has not had any work experience [and]...because she had not made any "serious decisions" in her life [and]...because she chose to engage in sexual intercourse in spite of seeing her friends who have become pregnant out of wedlock encounter hardships [and]...because she could wait several weeks and have an abortion without the necessity of a judicial bypass and without burdening this particular trial judge's conscience with granting a waiver of parental consent.

Upon appeal, the Alabama Court of Appeals ruled that:

> In direct contrast to the indicia of maturity the trial court relied on, the courts of this state have found academic performance, participation in extracurricular activities, plans for the future (including college), and

understanding the procedures and consequences of an abortion to indicate maturity.

CUSTODY AND THE MATURE MINOR

If we listen carefully, somewhere beneath the din of adults fighting their territorial and narcissistic custody battles, it's possible to hear the voice of the child. Questions as to whether, when, and how that voice should be solicited—and by whom, at what age, and to what degree that voice, once solicited, might become dispositive—remain the subject of considerable debate (Garber & Landerman, 2006).[12]

The Age of the Child

As early as 1875, a United States court denied a father custody because "thirteen-year-old Susan was of an age that was 'sufficient to enable her to make an intelligent and prudent choice'."[13] By 1899, the law allowed that "[w]hen an infant[14] has arrived at the age of discretion to choose for itself, the court will consult its wishes and preferences in the determination of the custody" (Hochheimer, 1895, p. 85).

Following in this tradition, the Uniform Marriage and Divorce Act (UMDA, 1973; cf., Melone & Karnes, 2008), now recognized by statute or case law in all fifty states, calls for consideration of "the wishes of the child as to his custodian." Nevertheless, if and how the child's voice is heard varies widely by jurisdiction, by individual jurist and investigator. An American Bar Association survey (2008a) finds that at least one state (New Mexico) has established that children as young as age 14 will be heard with regard to their postdivorce custodial preferences and that seven other states (California, Georgia, Hawaii, Nevada, Oklahoma, Pennsylvania, and South Carolina) ambiguously call for the courts to consider the wishes of a child of "sufficient maturity."[15] In practice, however:

> Judicial discretion often drives the form of child participation in custody determinations. Children can be asked to testify in court as to their wishes, they can be asked to speak with a judge in chambers (i.e., in camera), with or without the presence of attorneys, or a child's preference can be

filtered through a third party (e.g., a guardian ad litem or an evaluating mental health professional). (Crossman et al., 2002, p.8)

Crosby-Currie (1996) finds that more than 90% of family law professionals in the United States acknowledge differentially weighting children's custodial preference as a function of age in a manner reminiscent of the Rule of Sevens. That is, children under 8 years of age are seldom directly queried as to custodial preference. The preferences of children ages 8 through 11 may be solicited but are seldom given great weight, while the preferences of children age 14 and up are taken very seriously and, by age 16, may be dispositive in and of themselves.[16,17]

International Practices

These practices appear to vary only minimally among modern cultures. As examples, Israeli social workers base custody recommendations largely upon children's stated wishes without clear distinctions by age (Davidson-Arad & Cohen, 2004). The Finnish Child Custody and Right of Access Decree stipulates that the court may "ascertain the opinion of the child, if he is, on the basis of his age or other circumstances in the knowledge of the court, to be presumed to have attained such a degree of maturity that it is appropriate to take his opinion into account."[18]

The 1989 Children's Act of the United Kingdom calls for consideration of "the child's ascertainable wishes and feelings regarding the decision (considered in the light of the child's age and understanding)."[19] Nevertheless, three-quarters of jurists surveyed in the United Kingdom decline to elicit children's custodial wishes, regardless of age, due to concern over the (presumably) stressful social and emotional impact on the child (Douglas, Murch, Robinson, Scanlan, & Butler, 2001).

Of particular note is Britain's "Gillick Standard," the legal definition of "mature minor" for purposes of medical consent endorsed throughout the U.K. and New Zealand and adopted in Australia by the Australia Family Law Council (2004, pp. 38–39) to address minors' rights more broadly:

Australian law has recognised that parental rights and responsibilities decrease as children become more mature and able to make decisions (and take responsibility for those decisions) on their own behalf. A *Gillick* competent child, for the purposes of family law, is one whose capacities and maturity are such that parental authority over the child is displaced in relation to a particular issue. In other words, a court may find that whilst parental responsibility continues to vest in the parents, the child may make decisions in their own right that are inconsistent with the express wishes of the parents with respect to the child....It is also possible that the child is competent to make decisions in relation to certain issues, but not competent enough to make decisions in relation to other issues. For example, a particular child may have sufficient maturity to make a decision in relation to whether or not they attend a particular school, but not mature enough to make a decision in relation to living with a person other than his or her parents....*The child's age is not determinative of his or her relative maturity and hence capacity. The maturity and capacity of each child should be considered individually.* An important consideration is, however, the ability of the child or young person to understand the consequences of their decision, if it is acted upon. (emphasis added)

Surveys of Australian family law professionals, postdivorce parents, and their children reveal that, although jurists seldom choose to interview children with regard to custodial preferences (Parkinson & Cashmore, 2007), parents and children strongly believe that the child's opinion should be taken into account (Cashmore & Parkinson, 2008). When queried as to a minimum age at which this should occur, children generally suggested that age 7 was sufficient. By contrast, parents diverge widely on this topic, some recommending that children as young as 2 or 3 years of age should be heard, while others set the threshold as high as age 14. Many deferred to contextual variables (e.g., the presence of family violence) and to the child's "maturity" (Cashmore & Parkinson, 2008).

A majority of both parents and children interviewed in these studies expressed concerns that the child's opinion with regard to custody would have negative consequences for one or both of the child's parental relationships. In the extreme, a minority of parents judged that such negative consequences outweigh the child's potential benefit being heard. For example:

Ten parents (11.8%: seven fathers and three mothers), seven of whom were involved in contested matters...rejected the idea of their children being involved in the [custodial] process for two main reasons: first, the inappropriate pressure and burden of responsibility this places on children, and second, concern about the choice the child might make, especially under pressure or influence from the other parent. (Cashmore & Parkinson, 2008, p. 96)

Concerns of this nature may be universal (e.g., Gardner, 1999a; Warshak, 2003). Elsewhere, I have referred to this as a "'Sophie's Choice' in reverse, the kind of impossible dilemma which can traumatize a child who is already burdened with the powerful emotions which accompany any family's break-up" (Garber & Landerman, 2006).

Potential Consequences of Allowing Children a Voice in Custodial Placement

Crossman and colleagues (2002) identify several possible social and emotional outcomes weighing against hearing a child's voice with regard to his or her custodial placement. These include the child's resulting experience of guilt, betrayal, and anger; implicit questions regarding the child's motivation in stating a preference, including the possibilities of threat, coaching, and role reversal (e.g., the child's wish to care for the parent); and the critical matter of differentiating the child's stated wishes from his or her own best interests.

In fact, retrospective study of the social and emotional outcomes among children who have had a voice in their own custodial placement offers mixed impressions. For example, Rahabi (1999, abstract) observes that:

> The majority of participants who were not involved in their own custody determination lost contact with their non-custodial parent after the divorce. For participants who expressed their preference, it appears that the benefit of sharing a positive relationship with both parents in the future outweighs the conflicts and disappointments that they experienced during the custodial determination process.

Unfortunately, these reports fail to distinguish the long-term outcomes for children given a voice in their own custodial placement as a function of cognitive, social, or emotional maturity at the time the preference is elicited. The definitive study will examine the long-term outcomes for children who express a custody preference based on the child's developmental status, among many other relevant variables.[20,21]

THE MATURE MINOR FROM A DEVELOPMENTAL AND FAMILY SYSTEMS PERSPECTIVE

The possibility that the courts might accord minors certain privileges in the context of custody proceedings on the basis of maturity and, more generally, the extent to which age continues to be mistaken for maturity in such matters as emancipation and consent, highlight five important concerns:

1. **Chronological age cannot be sufficient to determine** maturity. Development proceeds at its own pace as a complex function of factors specific to the individual (e.g., temperament, intelligence, physical health), to the family (e.g., emotional support), and to the larger environment in which he or she grows (e.g., community, opportunity). As a result, any given developmental milestone will be attained across a range of ages within a group of healthy children. The fact that developmental theory often associates a particular developmental milestone with a particular age must be understood as no more than a convenience associated with statistical means and the exigencies of publication.

2. **Development is not a singular process.** Cognitive, socioemotional, physical, and verbal (as well as other) domains must be understood as separate but interactive developmental processes, normatively bootstrapping one upon the other upwards toward more sophisticated functioning. However, at any given time in any given individual, there are likely to be asynchronies between domains of development (décalage; see chapter 7), some of which may be functionally significant. In short, the chain of maturity is only as strong as its weakest link.

3. **Development in a single domain cannot be sufficient to determine** *maturity*. Local and state laws variously dictate the minimum height or weight necessary to legally enjoy certain amusement park rides. In this instance, the establishment of a physical criterion without regard to the simultaneous (but potentially asynchronous) cognitive, socioemotional, and verbal developments makes perfect sense.[22] By contrast, no such singular developmental criterion should determine something as emotionally powerful as the opportunity to choose between one or the other of one's own parents.

For example, it makes sense that attainment of Formal Operations might be used as a minimum cognitive threshold.[23] However, there is no necessary relationship between the ability to consider the hypothetical outcomes associated with one's choices and the socioemotional capacity to cope with those outcomes or the verbal capacity to express these complexities. In fact, the suggestion that cognitive development normatively precedes socioemotional development in mid- to late adolescence (the "maturity gap" that Galambos, Turner and Tilton-Weaver [2005] discuss; see chapter 7) speaks strongly against establishing exclusively cognitive criteria and in favor of establishing at least socioemotional criteria, as well.

4. **Development is not a unidirectional process.** Determination of one or a collection of necessary (even if not sufficient) developmental landmarks by which to adjudicate maturity and thereby grant a child standing in a custody proceeding ignores the phenomenon of regression. As discussed earlier (see chapter 6), the fact that individuals tend to retreat down the staircase of development under stress (such as that associated with family conflict and custody litigation) invites two types of errors with regard to any evaluation of maturity. In the first, we risk mistaking temporarily regressed functioning for global immaturity and thereby fail to credit the child for his or her genuine capacities. In the second, we risk crediting the child's genuine maturity, only to find that (potentially, in response to this determination) regression compromises the subsequent child's functioning (see chapter 6). These concerns call for assessment not only of contemporaneous functioning but of the history of functioning, as well.[24]

5. **The requisite developmental criteria must be measurable.** Replacing subjective judgments of maturity with reliable and valid measurements not only serves *Daubert* standards, but gives meaning to the idea of "clear and convincing evidence," as, for example, in New Hampshire's statute RSA 461-A:6, II, which states that "[i]f the court finds by clear and convincing evidence that a minor child is of sufficient maturity to make a sound judgment, the court may give substantial weight to the preference of the mature minor child as to the determination of parental rights and responsibilities."

A DEVELOPMENTALLY INFORMED MODEL OF THE "MATURE MINOR"

As family law professionals, we respect the wishes, needs, and rights of children. In doing so, we are careful to distinguish between what we understand a child *wants* and what the child *needs*. By serving the child's best interests we seek to understand, represent, and fulfill the child's needs, fully aware that, when the two are discrepant, we may find that serving the child's best interests is to act contrary to the child's wishes.[25]

In the course of seeking to understand and assert before the court a child's needs, we are particularly mindful of the developmental factors that bear on a child's ability to understand (a verbal and cognitive developmental factor) and to cope with (a matter of socioemotional development) the breadth, complexity, social and emotional impact, and likely short- and long-term consequences of the matter before the court. We are careful to recognize that a child's physical development and verbal fluency may have no necessary bearing on his or her cognitive and socioemotional maturity, careful not to infer developmental capacity in one domain on the basis of evidence of developmental capacities in others.

When striving to understand a child's needs in the context of custody litigation, in particular, we enlist qualified professionals and engage in child-centered procedures seeking to assess the child's experience of, feelings toward, and quality of relationships with the contesting parties and all others relevant to the two (or more) proposed custodial environments. We do so in a balanced manner, accounting for relevant ethnic, cultural, religious, and linguistic influences, careful to avoid leading questions (e.g., Garber, 2007b) and aware of the potential of concerned others' potential contamination of the child's presentation (e.g., Garber, 2004a; Gardner, 1999b; see chapter 16).

Understanding these many factors, we presume that the minor child is *not* competent to address the ultimate question of his or her own custodial placement and therefore take care not to put the child in a position to choose, unless and until he or she has consistently demonstrated:

1. **Formal operational thinking as evidenced by a history of real-life choices** obviously demonstrating both forethought with re-

gard to the likely consequences of his or her actions, and the impulse control and capacity to delay gratification necessary to act accordingly. This criterion does not call for evidence of *successful* decision making. Rather, the relevant consideration is the child's consistent use of these skills in guiding his or her choices.

A child's real-life incorporation of formal operational thinking cannot be adequately assessed only in interview. Challenging a child to think through "what-if" hypotheticals may be necessary, but cannot be sufficient. Sufficient data must include historical evidence that the child consistently and intentionally makes decisions with foresight and in consideration of likely outcomes. These data will most likely be found with regard to academic choices, athletic endeavors, peer relationships and peer group activities, substance use, sexual behaviors, money earning and spending practices, and how the child assigns priorities among these many competing factors.

2. **Evidence of the socioemotional capacities for responsibility, temperance and perspective** (Cauffman & Steinberg, 2000a; Steinberg & Cauffman, 1996; see chapter 5). The same process of behavioral deconstruction must find consistent evidence that the child:

a) Has a clear and healthy sense of self as apart from but in relation to others (autonomy); is able to distinguish between his or her own wishes and needs and those of relevant others, including parents, siblings, and peers (independence); and acts in the interest of his or her own long-term well-being.

b) Has adequate impulse control and respect for his or her own mortality and the physical well-being of others; this is contrary to the risk-taking and sensation-seeking behavior characteristic of many teenagers, suggesting instead an investment in the future; the goals associated with these choices must be realistic even if distant, unlikely, and frequently subject to change.

c) Spontaneously and regularly considers his or her choices as they may affect others from their points of view; this requires not only theory of mind, but a strong capacity for perspective taking and empathy; it is not enough for a child to be able to answer the question, "How do you think that made her feel?" What is necessary, instead, is evidence of spontaneous and consistent consideration of others' thoughts, feelings, and reactions without allowing these considerations to wholly determine the child's choices in and of themselves.

d) Evindence that the child engages in "jury-like deliberation" in an effort to balance these many factors without becoming crippled by associated anxiety or perseverating to the point of inaction.

This type of assessment may be foreign to many family law professionals and, indeed, may call for collaboration with child-centered, developmentally informed mental health professionals. Above and beyond the familiar interview-and-history process, this calls for deconstruction of a child's cognitive, social, and emotional experiences—itself a process that may tax the child's maturity. The child who is verbally able but interpersonally unwilling (e.g., becomes defensive) to engage in such a process despite the interviewer's open and neutral position may, by definition, be lacking in the requisite degree of maturity.

Discovery of a pattern of choices due to peer pressure, parentification, adultification, or infantilization and/or evidence of self-destructive and impulsive choices are contrary to a determination of maturity. Furthermore, evidence of serious psychopathology can be contrary to a determination of maturity to the extent that self-esteem is compromised (as, for example, is commonly associated with depression,), impulsivity is common (as is characteristic of ADHD and bipolar disorder), and/or overconcern for the negative ramifications of one's choices (as is typical of many anxiety disorders) is displayed.

I note that these criteria do not call for any necessary physical or verbal developmental achievements. The former is patently irrelevant to the concept of the mature minor. The latter—maturity of verbal comprehension and expression—is implicit in these criteria, acknowledging that any incidental limitation (accent, dialect, first language, multilingual status, hearing or speech impediment, or learning disability) must be accommodated so as to most accurately assess maturity.

SUMMARY

This chapter has discussed the complex considerations with which to determine if a child meets the status of a "mature minor," particularly with regard to a child's contribution to his or her own custodial status. Aware of the burdens associated with decision-making authority, the threshold must be set very high. The developmentally informed family law professional relies on interviews, history, and third-party report in search of specific cognitive, social and emotional criteria that, when consistently evident in a child's choices, may be sufficient for determination of maturity.

Are these criteria too demanding? It's natural to wonder, in fact, if *you and I* meet these criteria. I posit that the threshold beyond which a child's voice should be heard in family litigation should be quite high; that the child who is heard should be the exception, not the rule. Whether you and I pass muster is moot, given that we have attained the prerequisite 6,570-day mark under the law. However, the larger question about the family law professional's motivation, well-being and maturity is considered further in chapter 17.

NOTES

1. The age of majority differs to some extent across states and countries and sometimes by gender. Among U.S. territories, the age of majority is 14 in American Samoa, 19 in Nebraska and Alabama, and 21 in Mississippi, New York, and the District of Columbia. In Pakistan, males attain majority at 18 but females at 16. In El Salvador, males become adults at age 25, but females at 17. In a unique gender reversal, on the Isle of Man, males attain majority at age 14 and females at 18 (perhaps accounting for the British territory's name).

2. For example, felons may have compromised voting rights variously by state. See http://projectvote.org/fileadmin/ProjectVote/pdfs/felon_ voting_la ws_by_state_Sept_11_2008.pdf accessed 02.27.2009.

3. As advertised at the author's website http://howadultareyou.com/ (retreived February 27, 2009).

4. In *Cardwell v. Bechtol* 724 S.W. 2d 730 (Tennessee 1987) the court denied parents' malpractice claims for battery upon their child, allowing that the minor child's consent was sufficient.

5. *In re: E.G.*, Ill 2d 98, 549 N.E. 2d, 322 (1989).

6. Tennessee Supreme Court, *John Doe et al. v. Mama Taori's Premium Pizza, LLC, et al.* (2001, No. M1998-00992-COA-R9-CV).

7. The remainder of the Tennessee Court's decision is instructive, if unwieldy on the printed page: "[T]he General Assembly has enacted many statutes

reflecting its understanding that children mature at different rates and that they may have the same capacity as adults with regard to certain activities and decisions before they are eighteen years old. For example, children may engage in certain adult activities before they become eighteen. They may begin working part-time when they are fourteen; they may obtain a driver's license at sixteen; they may lease a safety deposit box; and they may marry if they are sixteen years old (or at a younger age if approved by a court). They may also make decisions regarding their healthcare such as executing a durable power of attorney for healthcare, consent to sterilization if they are married, and consent to medical treatment for drug abuse....The General Assembly has also decided that minors have the capacity to make decisions regarding sexual conduct and its effects. For example, they may consent to sexual conduct if they are over thirteen years old and if their partner is no more than four years older than they are; they may obtain contraceptive advice and supplies; they may consent to prenatal care; they may seek judicial consent for an abortion; and they may surrender a child for adoption....The General Assembly has determined that minors are incompetent with regard to relatively few activities. For example, minors cannot possess alcoholic beverages or beer or tobacco products. They cannot obtain handgun permits, and they cannot consent to 'female genital mutilation...'" (statutory references omitted).

8. Nelson (2005) concludes in relevant part: "These principles imply that the threshold for assent should be fixed at fourteen years of age and a dissent requirement should be adopted for all children in the context of non-beneficial research."

9. See Mehlman (undated) for a concise summary of case law including reference to HIV/AIDS-related matters.

10. Relevant Supreme Court cases include *Haley v. Ohio*, 332 U.S. 597, 598-601 (1948), *Gallegos v. Colorado*, 370 U.S., 49, 54-55 (1962), *Eddings v. Oklahoma*, 455 U.S., 104, 115 (1982) and *Thompson v. Oklahoma*, 487, U.S., 815, 835 (1988). The court states in the latter that "[i]nexperience, less education, and less intelligence make the teenager less able to evaluate the consequences of his or her conduct while at the same time he or she is much more motivated by mere emotion or peer pressure than an adult."

11. *In the Matter of Anonymous, a minor* (905 So.2d 845; 2040267), Court of Civil Appeals of Alabama, January 5, 2005.

12. For relevant law reviews, see, for example: House, 1998; Nemechek, 1998; and Sichel, 1991.

13. Crossman, Powell, Principe, and Ceci, 2002, citing *Ellis v. Jessup*, 74 Ky. 403, 11 Bush 402.

14. In the late nineteenth century, "infant" referred to "...the status of one who has not attained his majority, or full age of legal capacity, and is synonymous with minority and non-age" (Hochheimer, 1985, p.1).

15. I am aware that New Hampshire also recognizes the mature minor's standing under RSA 461-A:6, II. See *In the Matter of Richard L. Stapleford and Cheryl Stapleford* (Supreme Court of New Hampshire, 931 A.2d 1199 [2007]) for a unique application of this standard.

16. A post-hoc statistical analysis of 272 custody outcomes found that counselor recommendations were the best predictors of custodial decisions, but that, in lieu of counselor recommendations, children's preferences were the best predictors (Kunin, Ebbesen & Konecni, 1992).

17. In *Wisconsin v. Yoder*, (page 42, 406 U.S. 205, 246 [1972]), the United States Supreme Court comments that "[c]hildren far younger than the 14- and 15-year-olds...are regularly permitted to testify in custody and other proceedings. Indeed, the failure to call the affected child in a custody hearing is often reversible error. See, e. g., *Callicott v. Callicott*, 364 S. W. 2d 455 (Civ. App. Tex.) (reversible error for trial judge to refuse to hear testimony of eight-year-old in custody battle). Moreover, there is substantial agreement among child psychologists and sociologists that the moral and intellectual maturity of the 14-year-old approaches that of the adult."

18. Section 39(1); the entire act is available online at: http://74.125.47.132/search?q=cache:exQlDO8upYMJ:www.law.yale.edu/RCW/rcw/jurisdictions/euron/finland/Fin_Ch_Cust_Act_Eng.doc+Finnish+Child+Custody+and+Right+of+Access+Decree&hl=en&ct=clnk&cd=3&g l=us

19. See http://www.opsi.gov.uk/acts/acts1989/ukpga_19890041_en_1 for the full text.

20. These other variables would certainly include how and by whom the child's custodial preference is elicited, if and how the custodial outcome is attributed to/congruent with the child's preference, and how each parent responds to learning the child's expressed preference.

21. One might argue that angry, self-involved parents who contest custody are unlikely to have provided their children with the emotional security necessary to achieve a "mature minor" status. This creates a paradox in that the children most likely to qualify for "mature minor" status are also the children least likely to need to exercise the associated custodial discretion.

22. On the other hand, perhaps minimum socioemotional criteria should be adopted to assure that the experience isn't traumatic; or perhaps certain *maximum* cognitive developmental criteria should be established to preclude a full understanding of how fragile amusement park rides can be!

23. In fact, I would argue that achievement of Post–Formal Operations and the associated ability not simply to solve problems, but to anticipate them (e.g., Arlin, 1989) establishes a more conservative and valid cognitive threshold.

24. The *Diagnostic and Statistical Manual of Mental Disorders, Fourth Edition* (*DSM-IV*; American Psychiatric Association, 1994) calls for identification of a numeric (1–100) assessment of a child's global assessment of functioning (see Shaffer et al., 1983). Although devoid of developmental criteria, this scale is often used to compare a child's past and current functioning and might be useful at least with regard to the question of regression.

25. By extension, in jurisdictions and circumstances in which the child is represented before the court, the child's attorney proceeds in the knowledge that by representing the child's wishes, he or she may be arguing against the child's needs and therefore acting contrary to the child's best interests. See, for example, http://www.rollanet.org/~childlaw/galstd/mi-intro.htm (retreived February 27, 2009) for Michigan's discussion of these roles and their potential conflicts.

15

Psychological Assessment and Diagnosis in Family Law

How fair does a trial seem to the public where the defendant stands up and says, "Your Honor, I want to represent myself? I do not want this attorney. I want to defend myself." And the judge said, "Sit down, we have a psychological evaluation of you. You can't represent yourself."

—*Antonin Scalia,* Indiana versus Edwards

Never answer a question unless you know exactly who is asking, why it is being asked, and what will be done with the information.

—*Dilbert*

Psychological assessment is not a crystal ball that reveals the future of all who gaze upon it, nor is it the sword of Solomon, capable of divining where a child belongs. Unfortunately, it is all too often cast as both.[1]

Psychological assessment is the application of standardized methods for the purpose of eliciting responses that individually or in composite can be contrasted with those of one or more relevant normative samples. The similarity between a test-taker's responses and those of the comparison group(s) allows inferences about the participant's thinking, feeling, relating, and/or behavior. When test-taker and comparison group responses differ, statistical analyses help to define the relative importance or meaningfulness (reliability and validity) of these differences.

In this way, psychological assessment ("testing" or "evaluation") has established an important role in occupational/vocational selection (Toplis, Dulewicz, & Fletcher, 2005)—for example, among police force applicants (Cochrane, Tett, & Vandecreek, 2003; Rostow & Davis, 2004)[2]; in adult (Hersen, 2004), child, and adolescent (Maruish, 2004) clinical diagnosis and treatment; and in the diagnosis of neurological, attentional, and learning differences (Strauss, Sherman, & Spreen, 2006). Psychological tests, checklists, and inventories are similarly useful for assessing developmental status, especially in infancy and the toddler years (Bayley, 2006; Karabekiroglu & Aman, 2009), but less so across childhood and adolescence (Holmbeck et al., 2008), adulthood (Kliegel, Martin, & Jäger 2007), and the senior years (Henwood & Bartlett, 2008).

Psychological tests have established a strong foothold in family law matters, as well. Wading through the seemingly endless ambiguity and conflict that characterizes these matters, it's easy to reach for any tool that appears to provide black-and-white clarity. This appearance is only an illusion. Because family law litigation is ultimately concerned with the relationship or "fit" among specific individuals, these tests of individual functioning actually do little to help, but may do much to harm the process.

THE PROCESS OF PSYCHOLOGICAL ASSESSMENT

Valid uses of psychological testing share the essential quality of seeking to answer a question about an individual's functioning in a specific domain. The domain hardly matters, so long as psychologists have collected the requisite normative sample data against which the test-taker's responses can be compared. This is a relatively straightforward (although arduous) process if the question to be answered concerns, for example, rehabilitation and preparedness for the workforce (e.g., Kirsh & Cockburn, 2009), self-efficacy as it relates to (as examples) career choices (e.g., Rottinghaus, 2009), progress in correctional chemical dependency treatment (e.g., Sacks, McKendrick, Kressel, 2007), the quality and nature of depressive and anxiety symptoms (e.g., Watson et al., 2007), or pregnant and postpartum women's psychosocial risks (Bernazzani et al., 2005).[3]

To illustrate, if I'm concerned that Mr. Smith is a xenophobe, I can do one or more of four things: (a) I can observe Mr. Smith in interaction with strangers; (b) I can ask Mr. Smith whether he's afraid of strangers; (c) I can ask people who know Mr. Smith to report their experience of his attitudes about and behavior toward strangers; or (d) I can collect data from a group of known xenophobes, establish that these data distinguish them from a (control) group of "normal" (non-xenophobic) people and from (comparison) groups of agoraphobes and other anxiety disorders, assemble these distinguishing items in the form of a test, and then administer this test to Mr. Smith. The test might be a list of questions, or, if I discover that xenophobes reliably and uniquely mold Play-doh® into kumquats, I might ask Mr. Smith to make something with Play-doh®.

These four options correspond to the levels of inference described by Tippins and Wittman (2005), from (a) the most robust, direct observation to (b) direct report to (c) indirect report, to the fourth and weakest, (d) statistical inference. We fall back on statistical inference as a practical necessity because resources (time, effort, and money) often preclude sufficient direct observation, because individuals who know that they are being observed behave differently,[4] because people lie, and because character references usually come in equal and opposite numbers. None of this is sufficient reason, however, to overlook the weaknesses associated with statistical inference or to overstate the outcomes thus derived. In fact, psychologists are ethically bound to clarify the limitations associated with their methods,[5] in this case the relative probabilities associated with test-derived hypotheses.

Is Mr. Smith a xenophobe? With no opportunity to observe him in direct interaction with strangers, I ask him that directly and repeatedly over several interviews in several different ways. He says "No." I collect references that he provides to me, all of which say "No" (of course those provided by his estranged wife all say "Yes"). As a last resort, I ask him to make something out of Play-doh®. He looks confused, objects to the smell on his hands, but—eager to please the examiner—he proceeds to make a kumquat. Even though I know that 999 out of 1,000 xenophobes are kumquat molders, I don't know what percentage of kumquat molders are xenophobes. I have to allow that he may have had a kumquat for lunch or was once traumatized by a kumquat and produced the fruit for those reasons, rather than because he's a xenophobe. Thus, all that I can conclude is that, "although Mr. Smith and his references deny any evidence of xenophobia, this gentleman's behavior on the Play-doh® test is consistent with that of admitted xenophobes."

PSYCHOLOGICAL ASSESSMENT AND FAMILY LAW

Psychological assessment cannot be used in the same fashion to answer questions in family law, because of a problem with criterion validity (see chapter 2). Criterion validity describes the extent to which a test accurately screens test-takers for an established set of concurrent or expected future behaviors. We know, for example, what personality criteria are associated with successful astronauts (Musson, Sandal, & Helmreich, 2004) or air traffic controllers (Carretta & King, 2008) and can test for these attributes with some accuracy, thereby improving the likelihood that rookie air traffic controllers and astronauts will succeed in their respective jobs. These instruments have well established criterion validity. We do not know, however, what criteria are associated with successful husbands of Mary or parents of Timmy or guardians of Suzy. Because family law matters are about "fit," the relevant criteria for any such test will be unique to the individuals involved in every instance.

Brodzinsky (1993, p. 218) voices this concern from a different perspective:

> There is some question as to what constitutes appropriate criteria for assessing the validity of custody decision making instruments. Should data derived from these instruments be validated against judicial decision making, child outcome measures, parent outcome measures, relitigation data, or some other criteria assessing appropriateness of the custody/visitation decision? To date, there is no concensus [sic] on this issue among mental health professionals.

But don't we know generally what makes a good parent (or partner or guardian)?

No, we don't. For all of the research and statistics and books and journals and clinics and classes, the only variable that we consistently associate with "good" parenting within obvious limits of safety is sensitive/responsivity. You might recognize the phrase from our earlier discussion of attachment theory (see chapter 5). Sensitive-responsivity describes the caregiver's ability and willingness to accurately read and respond to his or her child's unique signals. Sensitive and responsive parenting is associated with a child's secure attachment, which in turn is associated with a host of positive and desirable developmental outcomes.

Unfortunately for those who would advocate for psychological testing in family law matters, sensitive/responsivity is not a generic quality that can be inferred from a Rorschach percept or a Minnesota Multiphasic Personality Inventory (MMPI) scale. It can be assessed within a particular caregiver–toddler relationship in the Strange Situation Paradigm (Ainsworth & Wittig, 1969) and later in development (albeit less reliably) by any of several attachment-related instruments (e.g., Shaver, Belsky, & Brennan, 2000; van IJzendoorn et al., 2004).[6] However, even these relatively robust developmental and research-based measures face a number of hurdles before they can become a routine part of family law matters, not the least of which is the fact that although they might allow inferences about an individual parent's sensitive/responsivity with a particular child, they are not necessarily of any value for comparing the parenting skills of two or more potential caregivers (Garber, 2009).

This means that even the most statistically sound, most reliable and valid, most *Daubert* -worthy assessment instrument has no necessary value to family law matters. It may have tremendous diagnostic value. It may be of critical importance in various clinical, academic, occupational/ vocational, and developmental settings. But, in the absence of objective criteria as to what constitutes a good-enough parent, spouse, or guardian, and in the absence of objective criteria with which to predict future abuse,[7] neglect, or alienation (or, for that matter, lottery winners and Nobel laureates), the use of such measures in family law is highly suspect, at the least, and more commonly risks doing harm (Archer, 2006; Bow, Gould, et al., 2006; Emery, Otto & O'Donoghue, 2005; Heilbrun, 1992). Roseby (1995, p. 98), for example, cautions that when psychological testing is introduced into custody evaluations, a "pathology hunt" ensues that "often holds the litigating, divorced family to a higher standard of mental health than intact and non-litigating divorcing families." Ten years later, little had changed:

> In point of fact, there is not much evidence that associates parenting skills with particular test signs. Much of evaluating psychologists' conclusions

and recommendations are based on clinical judgments and on extrapolation. (Craig, 2005, pp. 280–281)

These cautions are not new at all. Maccoby (2005, p. i) observed that,

> [S]tandard measures of parents' and children's intelligence, personality traits, and emotional states are wholly inappropriate for custody evaluations...even the measures and constructs that have been designed specifically to assess child custody arrangements for individual children have no proven validity as predictors of a child's well-being in the care of one or the other of two disputing parents.

Emery, Otto, and O'Donohue (2005, p. 8) similarly state:

> [A]ll measures that purport to assess constructs directly relevant to child custody determinations suffer from significant limitations. In fact, no study examining the properties of these measures has ever been published in a peer-reviewed journal—an essential criterion for science and, in theory, for the courts. In our view, the absence of scientific support should preclude the use of any of these forensic assessment instruments for any purpose other than research.

Even those who use these tests recognize their limitations in family law matters:

> [B]est practices dictate using data from psychological testing *only to generate hypotheses* about response sets (whether some party approaches test-taking openly and honestly or in a guarded, rigid, and prevaricating manner) and possible personality traits that can impair effective parenting. No personality test results should stand on their own as findings in the report. (Benjamin & Gollan, 2003, p. 53; emphasis added)

Despite this deluge of clear-headed criticism, the (mis-)application of borrowed clinical measures and reliance upon poorly constructed "forensic" measures is so common in family law as to be epidemic. Psych testing is, after all, big business. Psychological tests can seem to add an air of science to what is ultimately and irreducibly a question of emotions and relationships. For these reasons, the family law professional needs to know enough to understand the very limited value and huge potential damage that can be associated with the use of these instruments.

TYPES OF PSYCHOLOGICAL ASSESSMENT INSTRUMENTS

For the purposes of this brief overview, three types of tests are reviewed: Intelligence tests; projective or performance-based tests; and objective, structured tests.

Intelligence Tests

Otto, Edens, and Barcus (2000), summarizing prior surveys of custody evaluators' use of psychological tests, conclude that tests of adult intelligence are "occasionally employed."[8] In sharp contrast, Ackerman (2006, p. 142) recommends that, "[t]ests of cognitive functioning are an integral part of child custody evaluations...to determine if the parent is going to be able to academically support the children. To be able to do this, it is important for the parent's intelligence to be relatively equal to or higher than the children's intelligence."

In fact, tests of intellectual functioning in adults (e.g., Wechsler Adult Intelligence Scale, third revision [WAIS-III], or Stanford-Binet-fifth edition [SB5]) and in children (e.g., Weschsler Intelligence Scale for Children-fourth edition [WISC-IV], Wechsler Preschool and Primary Scale of Intelligence-third edition [WPPSI-III], McCarthy Scales of Children's Abilities [MSCA]) may help to define an individual's capacity to learn and his or her relative cognitive strengths and weaknesses. These results may have direct bearing on educational planning and curriculum accommodations. They may constitute a critically important step toward diagnosing a learning disability or sensory difference. But within obvious extremes,[9] intelligence tests have little or no relevance to matters of family law. As Otto and colleagues (2000, p. 334) state:

> [A]lthough it is generally accepted that the Wechsler scales provide valid estimates of intellectual ability, few would argue that the Wechsler scales validly inform an examiner's understanding of a father's relationship with his child or understanding and appreciation of his child's emotional adjustment (extremely low scores notwithstanding).

The proposition that IQ scores bear on a parent's ability to guide academic functioning confuses intelligence and achievement. In practice,

I commonly define intelligence as measuring how big the cup is and achievement as measuring how full the cup is. In the odd case where parents are contesting custody and both intend to home-school their children, achievement testing (e.g., the Wide Range Achievement Test–third edition [WRAT-3]) might be weakly relevant, so as to assure that the contending parents had mastered the curricula that must be taught but of arguably equal or greater relevance would be the quality of each parent's lesson plans, his/her experience as an educator, the child's history of achievement in their respective tutelage, compliance with state regulations, and a host of other (nonpsychometric) measures.

Projective or Performance-Based Measures

This refers to those minimally structured measures that seek to interpret a test-taker's responses to relatively ambiguous stimuli. These are sometimes referred to as "projective" instruments, in deference to the concept of projection originally associated with Freudian psychoanalytic theory. Projection refers to the extent to which our unique experience, needs, wishes, and fears shape how we see the world. The more ambiguous a stimulus, the more *who* we are influences *how* we see it. Thus, what one sees in a Rorschach inkblot is assumed to reflect that person's personality to some unknown degree. What one sees in card 16 of the Thematic Apperception Test (TAT)—an entirely blank rectangle of white cardboard—is assumed to reflect personality to an even greater degree because of the greater ambiguity (that is, the total absence) of structure.

The fictitious Play-doh® test used for illustration earlier in the chapter might qualify as a projective measure quite similar to the Rorschach Inkblot Test. In this task, the examiner would need to infer personality attributes from the test-taker's "projection" in the act of creating something from an amorphous ball of clay. The empirical data specific to kumquat makers gives the test a degree of reliability and validity that might make it useful for the purpose of diagnosing xenophobia, but the test still rests on the premises inherent in the idea of projection.

The use of projective measures in any setting remains a matter of longstanding controversy (Hunsley, Lee, & Wood, 2003). These arguments have little relevance here, however, because even blessed with robust psychometric properties, the criterion-validity problem endures. That is, there is no established link between any conclusion drawn from the Rorschach or the TAT (or the fictitious Play-doh® test) and the question of whether Mom or Dad is likely to be able to meet 5-year-old Ricky's needs.

The Rorschach Inkblot Test

The Rorschach is a personality assessment instrument comprised of 10 symmetrical inkblot images, some in color and some in black-on-white.[10] Test-takers are asked to explain what they "see" in these otherwise ambiguous images. Responses are thereafter interpreted in one of many ways (Wood, Nezworski, Lilienfeld, & Garb, 2003, the most common and most reliable and valid being Exner's Comprehensive System (2002).

The magic apparently associated with finding meaning in inkblots has helped to make the Rorschach into a celebrity of sorts. It is undoubtedly the most commonly referenced psychological test in the mass media and rivals the Freudian couch as a cultural icon associated with psychotherapy.

The Rorschach is no less a matter of discussion within psychology. Debate has raged nearly since the instrument's introduction regarding the value of inkblot responses (McGrath, 2008). This controversy may be nowhere as heated as it is among family law professionals (Erard, 2007; Evans & Schutz, 2008; Erickson, Lilienfeld, & Vitacco, 2007; Garb, 1999). At one extreme, Erickson and colleagues (2007, pp. 165–166) warn that "with the possible exception of detecting severe thought disorders in patients, there appears to be scant support for the use of the Rorschach test in family court evaluations." At the other extreme, Evans and Schutz (2008, p. 223) assert that "the Rorschach Inkblot Method (RIM) enjoys broad acceptance and usage in forensic psychological assessment, including Child Custody and Parenting Plan Evaluations." Because of or despite these positions, the Rorschach remains one of the most frequently researched (Erard, 2007) and commonly administered among psychological assessment instruments, especially in the context of contested custody proceedings (Otto, Edens, & Barcus, 2000).

Drawing Methods

Psychologists commonly use drawing tasks in the context of assessment, particularly with children and teens (Bekhit, Thomas, & Jolley, 2005;

Cashel, 2002) and often in the course of addressing family law matters. This is despite a complete absence of established reliability, validity, standardized administration, or interpretation methods (Lally, 2001; Motta, Little, & Tobin, 1993). These include Human Figure Drawings (Cox, 1993; Goodenough, 1926; Harris, 1963; Koppitz, 1968,1983), House-Tree-Person (Buck, 1948), and Kinetic Family Drawing (Handler, Campbell, & Martin, 2004) tasks.

These methods remain popular not only in clinical practice and as debriefing aids with trauma victims (Gross & Hayne, 1998; Stallard & Saltet, 2003), but also in the context of evaluation for the family courts (Hagan & Castagna, 2001; McCann, 2004). Used as a means of building rapport and for the purpose of opening up subjects for interview, drawings can be very helpful with children (Wakefield & Underwager, 1993), but do not in and of themselves meet *Duabert* criteria.

Bricklin's Instruments

Bricklin has published several custody-related assessment tools (1990a, 1990b; 1993; Bricklin & Elliot, 1991). These are appealing to the extent that they are relatively easy to administer and arguably *face valid* (that is, they look as if they assess what they purport to assess), but each of these lacks peer review, evidence of reliability, and substantive validity (Erickson, Lilienfeld, & Vitacco, 2007; Heinze & Grisso, 1996; Yanez & Williams, 2004; cf., Bricklin & Elliot, 2005).

Objective and Structured Measures

Relatively few psychological assessment instruments have been developed objectively, that is, exclusively on the basis of empirical evidence and without subjective interpretation. Objective and structured instruments compare an individual's pattern or constellation of responses with those of others in established diagnostic or functional categories and generalize on that basis. This means, among other things, that the individual items composing such instruments may have no obvious relationship (face validity) to the larger question, an attribute that frequently confuses and concerns uninformed consumers.

The Minnesota Multiphasic Personality Inventory, Second Edition (MMPI-2)

The MMPI in its various forms and editions is the single most widely administered, most highly respected, and arguably the most valuable instrument in the psychologist's arsenal (Ben-Porath, Graham, Hall, Hirschman, & Zaragoza, 1995; Bow, Flens, et al., 2006; Butcher, Graham, Ben-Porath, Tellegen, & Dahlstrom, 2001; Butcher & Williams, 2009; Pope, Butcher, & Seelen, 2000).[11] The MMPI-2 is a 567-item, true/false test that can take up to two hours to complete.[12] Despite its reputation as an endurance test, it is by far the preferred and most frequently administered instrument in the context of family law matters (Cashel, 2002; Emery, Otto, & O'Donahue, 2005). Otto and colleagues (2000) report between 70 and 92% of custody evaluators use the MMPI.

In addition to being an empirically derived, structured instrument, the MMPI has separate clinical and forensic normative scales. Unlike other instruments borrowed from clinical use and scored against clinical norms, this allows the MMPI-2 to account for the typical and expectable experiences of the population of family law litigants. Thus, whereas a high degree of defensiveness may be suggestive of pathology in a clinical sample, the same high degree of defensiveness is understood to be common to the point of normative among custody litigants (Wakefield & Underwager, 1993; cf., Bagby, Nicholson, Buis, Radovanovic, & Fidler, 1999). Graham (1988) is famously quoted as wondering if a custody litigant whose MMPI does *not* have a high defensiveness scale is perhaps not genuinely invested in winning his or her child's custody.

For all of its impressive psychometric qualities, for all of its genuine value in many other applications, and for all of its tremendous popularity in family law matters, the criterion validity problem applies here, as well. There is no MMPI profile associated with "good" parenting, that allows comparison between two adults' caregiving, or that speaks to whether a child should be removed from or returned to a specific adult (Posthuma, 2003). In practice, MMPI profiles cannot speak to family law matters *per se*. They can and do provide an empically sound profile of the test-taker's personality characteristics, but this profile must then be interpreted through some subjective (and usually unstated) filter for its relevance to the family law matter at hand.

Millon Clinical Multiaxial Inventory Third Edition (MCMI-III)

The MCMI-III is a 175-item, true/false, empirically derived instrument intended to diagnose psychopathology in adults. Despite concerns about construct validity (Erickson, Lilienfeld & Vitacco, 2007) and potential gender bias (Erard, 2007), the instrument has received broad acceptance in the forensic arena (Blood, 2008; Dyer, 2005; Halon, 2001; McCann et al., 2001).

DIAGNOSIS IN THE CONTEXT OF FAMILY LITIGATION

An essential but seldom recognized tension arises when mental health professionals enter into family law matters in nearly any role and especially to conduct psychological assessments. When the court orders Ms. Jones to participate in an anger management group or Mr. Smith to get parenting counseling, when a conscientious attorney refers her distressed client to therapy and when psychological testing becomes part of the process, the individuals involved typically (and often unknowingly) receive a *DSM-IV* or *ICD-10* diagnosis.

Psychologists are taught to apply diagnostic labels reflexively. Indeed, diagnosis is useful to the extent that it is valid and is used to guide the nature, direction, and duration of treatment (Kramer et al., 2008) and may be necessary, for third-party (insurance or managed health care) reimbursement.[13] However, when a litigant is found to have (or to once have had) a psychiatric diagnosis, the predators attack.

It is not at all unusual to discover that a divorcing mom has begun psychotherapy in a healthy and laudable effort to have a place to vent her upset away from the children, only then to have the fact of that therapy and the concomitant diagnosis held against her in court. No matter that seeking emotional support may be evidence of emotional maturity and may be of direct benefit to the children in her care. No matter that her diagnosis has no necessary bearing whatsoever on her parenting or coparenting capacity. Simply by virtue of being a diagnosis, the message is illness. In the hands of a determined litigator, an uninformed judge, or a naïve jury, any diagnosis means crazy and crazy is incompatible with parenting.

Tragically, this means that many parents choose—or are advised by counsel—to endure the tremendous emotional stresses associated with family court litigation unassisted, all to the detriment of their children. Although we are beginning to establish laws that protect children's therapies, mental health assessments, and diagnoses from this sort of intrusion and manipulation (e.g., *Berg v. Berg*, NH Supreme Court 2005-002[14]), litigants themselves seldom enjoy similar protections.

A FINAL WORD ON THE PLACE OF PSYCHOLOGICAL ASSESSMENT INSTRUMENTS IN FAMILY LAW

When we blindly allow psychological test data into the discussion of family law matters out of ignorance or intimidation, we risk failing our charge of serving a child's best interests. Several excellent volumes provide detailed analyses of common psychological tests and their place in the courtroom (Campbell & Lorandos, 2001; Goldstein, 2006). Using these and related materials, it is easy to criticize an instrument on the basis of its established reliability, error rate, and peer acceptance, three among the criteria established under *Daubert* (see chapter 2). It is just as easy, however, to find oneself confronted with a sheaf of published studies and pages of psychometric data, all seeming to support the dispositive value of the instrument at hand. Wading through this information is necessary, sometimes requiring consultation with an independent expert (Drogin & Barrett, 2007), but it is not sufficient.

Before a standardized psychological test can be brought to bear in a family law matter, it is also necessary to question the test's criterion validity. This captures the relevance standard under *Daubert*. By analogy, we know that we can measure shoe size quite reliably. The instruments with which we make this calculation are familiar standards, long ago accepted among relevant experts. But before we can accept the difference between a 10-EEE and a 7-narrow as relevant to custody, guardianship, or reunification matters, for example, we need to know the size of the child's foot. There is no necessary link between shoe size (no matter how accurately measured) and parenting capacity, just as there is no reliable and valid link between Rorschach percepts, IQ, or MMPI profiles and parenting, within obvious extremes. Just because a psychological test is statistically sound does not mean that it has a place in family law matters.

SUMMARY

There is much that we can reliably and validly measure about family law litigants, but little that is relevant to the questions that come before the family courts. It is less than helpful (and often simply harmful) to subject contesting parties and their children to assessments that are at best obliquely related to the question that stands before the court.

Family law matters are simply and irreducibly about the unique quality of relationships among contesting parties. Unless and until an empirically reliable, forensically validated method is established with which to measure the "fit" among individuals (e.g., an adult's ability to sensitively read and respond to his child's unique cues), we can do no more and no less than bring to this process a developmentally informed, systemic understanding, an objective, child-centered perspective and a conscientious commitment to serve the child's best interests.

NOTES

1. "Unfortunately few courts are aware how poorly informed most custody evaluators are, and assume they have great wisdom in this regard. Furthermore, the more judges are informed by these well-intentioned, but misguided experts, the more confused and ill-informed the judges become, as do most of the other players operating in the court system, e.g., mediators, law guardians, guardians ad litem, and attorneys" (Zorza, 2006, p. 5).
2. Noting the limits of the use of psychological testing in employment matters under the Americans with Disabilities Act (*Karraker v. Rent-a-Center, Inc.*, 411 F.3d 831 Fed. 7th Cir. [2005]).
3. The Buros Institute of Mental Measurement catalogues and critiques most psychological assessment instruments. See http://www.unl.edu/buros/bimm/index.html or *The Mental Measurement Yearbook* (Geisinger, Spies, Carlson, & Plake, 2007).
4. Known as the Heisenberg Effect.
5. The American Psychological Association's 2002 revised ethical standards, available at http://www.apa.org/ethics/code2002.html, state in substantial part: "9.06 Interpreting Assessment Results. When interpreting assessment results, including automated interpretations, psychologists take into account the purpose of the assessment as well as the various test factors, test-taking abilities, and other characteristics of the person being assessed, such as situational, personal, linguistic, and cultural differences, that might affect psychologists' judgments or reduce the accuracy of their interpretations. They indicate any significant limitations of their interpretations."
6. Many adult self-report attachment measures are reviewed at: http://psychology.ucdavis.edu/labs/Shaver/measures.htm
7. The prediction of dangerousness is a closely related subject deserving of whole volumes. We know that actuarial means of prediction are dramati-

cally more accurate than clinical (including psychometric) means of pre-diction (Hall, 2008; Quinsey, Harris, Rice, & Cormier, 2006; Norko & Baranoski, 2008). Nevertheless, Weiss (2000) makes the case for the rele-vance of MMPI data and Gray, Meloy, and Jumes, (2008) make the case for the use of Rorschach data. The case for IQ testing with regard to the punishment for violent behavior has been made in the psychological literature (e.g., Spain & Schmeden, 2005) and in the courts (*Penry v. Lynaugh*, US 492 U.S. 302, 1989. But the case for intelligence assessment as a predictor of violence is far less certain (e.g., Heilbrun, 1990).

8. Noting that intelligence tests may be of critical importance in criminal law matters, e.g., *Penry v. Lynaugh* (US 492 U.S. 302 [1989]) : "Penry, a retarded man with the mental age of barely seven years, was convicted of murder and sentenced to death. During the trial's proceedings, the jury was not instructed that it could consider the mitigating circumstances of Penry's mental retardation in imposing its sentence." See also *Abdul-Kabir v. Quarterman* (US 550 U.S. [2007]).

9. The caveat "within obvious extremes" applies to much of this discussion and refers to those circumstances that would likely be discerned by an attentive observer without the aid of psychometrics, e.g., when an individ-ual is mentally retarded, psychotic, or otherwise impaired in his or her ability to perceive and respond to the demands of day-to-day life. When these suspicions arise, testing may be very useful, for purposes of docu-menting the nature, severity, and relevance (if any) of the impairment.

10. In fact, my choice to describe the Rorschach Stimuli as "black on white" as opposed to "white on black" probably reveals something of my personality.

11. For one brief and relevant review of MMPI uses in forensic matters, see http://www.ipt-forensics.com/library/special_problems13.htm (accessed 03.01.2009).

12. Bow, Flens, et al. (2006) surveyed custody evaluators use of both the MMPI and the MCMI. They find serious and widespread nonstandardized administration problems (e.g., tests sent home, completed over the phone) that invalidate results.

13. Unfortunately, the most benign and often the most accurate diagnoses describing the acute and reactive distress associated with family law litigation may not be recognized as reimbursable by third-party payors. This varies by state and health care entity, but often includes *DSM-IV* diagnoses such as V61.20 (Parent–Child Relational Problem), V61.10 (Partner Relational Problem), and even the adjustment disorders (e.g., 309.0, Adjustment Disorder with Depressed Mood).

14. See http://www.courts.state.nh.us/supreme/opinions/2005/berg112.htm (retrieved March 1, 2009).

Alienation, Estrangement, and Alignment: The Tools and Weapons of Affiliation

Frustration over bitter custody battles should not tempt the legal system to blindly accept unproven theories such as PAS. Reliance on such simplified approaches to the complex problem of alleged abuse in the context of child custody disputes is likely to result in misdiagnosis and a failure to protect children.

—S. J. Dallam

There is, of course, no doubt that some parents, particularly mothers, are responsible for alienating their children from their fathers without good reason and thereby creating this sometimes insoluble problem.

—Lady Elizabeth Butler-Sloss, Chief Justice, United Kingdom

Today's Hester Prynne wears a red "A" not for adultery, but for alienation. Indeed, just as a woman's betrayal of her husband was deserving of public shaming in Nathaniel Hawthorne's portrayal of late-18th-century New England society, a parent's betrayal of a child's love for another parent is today's public outrage.

In the last 25 years, the concept of alienation has become a banner under which disenfranchised fathers march, a curse that angry parents hurl at their ex-partners, an exculpatory rationalization for sexual abuse allegations to some and an excuse for selfish indifference to others. It is the raison d'etre of a generation of family law professionals and the worst nightmare of most family courts, an allegation that amounts to abuse yet carries with it the aura of medical illness. For all of this controversy, for all of the millions of dollars invested in allegations and counterallegations, for all of the lives ruined or rescued in the interests of today's scarlet letter, alienation is seldom understood for what it is—a necessary and natural family-systems tool that is sometimes used as a weapon.

This penultimate chapter discusses alienation as an attachment phenomenon. It is a relationship dynamic that parents have used as long as families have existed to instill security and define who is in and who is out of the group.In self-serving hands, however, this same powerful dynamic can be used to harm children in the service of a caregiver's anger, fear, and neediness. In the process of serving a child's best interests, it is encumbent upon the family law professional to understand what is and what is not alienation, to recognize how and when it occurs, and to advise the court how best to help each child establish and maintain the healthiest relationship possible with each of his or her caregivers.

THE HISTORY OF ALIENATION IN FAMILY LAW

In the English Common Law tradition of chattel, a man owned his wife and his children no less than his horse or his plow. Thus, any individual whose actions cost a man consort with his wife might be sued for "alienation of affections." Although this tort was adopted by each of the original United States, late-19th-century legislation allowing women to own property[1] prompted some states to drop the provision, while other states simply made it "gender neutral." By 2007, only six states retained a spousal alienation-of-affections tort (Hawaii, Mississippi, New Mexico, North Carolina, South Dakota, and Utah). Oddly, it was Connecticut, a state that had legislatively abolished the tort in 1984, that explicitly linked alienation of affections to today's scarlet letter, identifying, "parental alienation" as "a unique and specific type of alienation of affections."[2]

The concept of parental alienation as it is commonly used today was first introduced in the social science literature in terms of the "pathological alignment" between a divorcing parent and his or her child (Wallerstein & Kelly, 1976, 1980).[3] With Gardner's 1985 suggestion that this dynamic might better be understood as a diagnosable syndrome deserving of inclusion in the DSM, Parental Alienation Syndrome (PAS) was born.[4,5]

According to Gardner, PAS is the result of one angry parent's "campaign of denigration" intending to "brainwash" or "program" a child in a cult-like manner such that:

> [C]hildren use extreme oppositional behavior to reject and denigrate a previously loved parent. Sometimes obscene language and cruelty are included. The children's perceptions and attitudes are black and white. The targeted or rejected parent is hated for unjustified or seemingly small or ridiculous reasons, or reasons that have nothing to do with reality. The child will often add his or her own untrue stories to contribute to the story created about the bad parent. Usually it appears that there is no remorse or guilt on the part of the child. (Andre, 2004)

Gardner's description of PAS ignited a firestorm of controversy that lasts to this day. Legitimate concerns include the contention that PAS: (a) does not fulfill the requirements that might otherwise constitute a diagnosable syndrome (Walker, Brantley, & Rigsbee, 2005; cf., Warshak, 2002; see also chapter 2); (b) has not met the reliability, validity, peer-publication, consensual acceptance, or (most importantly) falsifiability criteria of *Daubert* (Poliacoff, Greene, & Smith, 1999; Wood, 1994; Zirogiannis, 2001) and therefore has no place in court (Williams, 2001);[6] (c) lacks empirical evidence of its existence (American Psychological Association, 2005); (d) is sexist to the extent that it discriminates against mothers;[7] and (e) confuses cause and effect by failing to consider alternative and more likely explanations for a child's contact resistance (Garber, 1996, 2007a).

Kelly and Johnston (2001; cf., Johnston & Kelly, 2001) take the alienation concept out of the realm of diagnosable individual psychopathology and return it to its family systems origins. These authors recognize the multiple and simultaneous influences of each parent's words and actions, the child's developmental needs and vulnerabilities, the sibling dynamic, the tensions specific to the coparental conflict, the extended family alliances, and the child's experience of these many pressures.

Johnston (2003; Johnson & Johnston, 2004) presents the only scientific and empirical data on the subject presently available.[8] She concludes that most children who resist contact with one parent in favor of the other do so as a result of a mixture of many and varied factors. Among those who appeared aligned with one parent and rejecting of the other, the rejected parent's own lack of empathy, support, and parenting skills (i.e., sensitive/responsivity) proved to be equally or more important to explaining the schism than the words or actions of the aligned parent.

ALIENATION IN DEVELOPMENTAL PERSPECTIVE

Although PAS advocates generally acknowledge that contact resistance might be associated with age appropriate teenage rebellion, alienation has seldom otherwise been viewed through the lens of child and family development.

In a 2004 publication, I (Garber 2004a) suggested that (a) alienation is best understood as an attachment-related phenomenon and, as such, (b) that alienation is one among four necessary and natural dynamics which together constitute the "tools and weapons of affiliation." These two important points are elaborated here.

Alienation as a Contamination of the Child's Internal Working Model

Attachment theory teaches us that the quality of a child's relationship with a particular caregiver is a reflection of his or her accumulated experience of that caregiver's sensitive/responsivity (see chapter 5). Thus, the toddler's behavior toward his mother observed in the Strange Situation Paradigm (Ainsworth & Wittig, 1969) is not only a window on the security of that relationship in the present, but a précis of the child's longstanding history of his mother's care.

As that child's cognitive and language-comprehension skills develop, his internal model of mom's sensitive/responsivity begins to integrate not only his direct experience of her sensitive/responsivity, but indirect information about her, as well:

> The working models associated with secure or insecure attachments likely
> have their origins...not only in the child's direct representations of the

sensitivity of parental care, but in the secondary representations of their experience mediated through parental discourse. (Thompson, 2000, p. 150)

Once a child becomes developmentally capable of integrating third-party (incidental) information into his or her internal working models, four distinct possibilities arise, defined by the congruence of this information and the objective quality of the targeted caregiver's sensitive/responsivity.

1. Alignment can occur when a third-party message is congruent with the targeted caregiver's actual sensitive/responsivity. This is the healthy dynamic that contributes to a mutually supportive family system and allows the child to maintain the healthiest relationship that he or she can with each of his or her caregivers. For example, when Dad tells Sally that he has a super Mom, Dad's message effectively reinforces Sally's secure attachment to his objectively sensitive and responsive Mom.

2. Estrangement (Drozd & Oleson, 2004) can occur when a third-party message communicates insecurity about an objectively insensitive/unresponsive caregiver. In this case, the incidental message is congruent with the targeted caregiver's sensitive/responsivity, but both are negative. Estrangement is theoretically defensible (but not yet legally tested) when, for example, a parent must send a child for court-ordered contact with a caregiver who is known to be inappropriate (e.g., drug or alcohol abusing, neglectful or abusive). Thus, when Dad cautions Billy, "You can call me anytime if you get scared" because he knows that Mom is dangerous, he is justifiably undermining any degree to which the child might feel secure in her care.

3. Misalignment (Garber, 2007a) can occur when a third party encourages a child's security with a caregiver who is objectively insensitive/unresponsive. For example, I have seen addicts encourage their children to feel comfortable in the care of an adult who is known to be objectively insensitive/unresponsive simply to win the selfish freedom to indulge their need. Craving drugs, Mom tells Suzy, "Don't worry, you'll be fine. He won't hit you this time!"

4. Alienation can occur when a third party speaks or acts to or around a child in a manner that undermines the child's security in a caregiver who is objectively sensitive and responsive. Thus, when Dad exposes his kids to his anger about Mom's affair, he is effectively "poisoning the well." If Dad's words cause the child to (unjustifiably) resist Mom, alienation has occurred.

The Tools and Weapons of Affiliation

These four family-systems dynamics do no more and no less than communicate to the child who is "in" and who is "out" of the family system. They serve the primitive clan- or pack-based mentality by defining affiliation in the interests of adaptation and survival. Precisely as Bowlby described (1969, 1973), no matter the species, the offspring who are able to recognize which caregivers will provide safety and which will not are at an evolutionary advantage.

These tools of affiliation go unquestioned in healthy environments when, for example, a cautious father warns his 6-year-old to walk home on the opposite side of the street from their nasty neighbor (an instance of alienation or estrangement) or an embarrassed mother prompts her 9-year-old to "give grandma a kiss and a hug" (alignment or possibly misalignment). But, like any tools, these dynamics can be used as weapons, as when an angry and selfish dad rants to his 4-year-old about his (objectively loving and sensitive) mom (alienation) or an immature and selfish dad leaves his 10-year-old with a drunken friend (misalignment), because he "just needs a break."

One of the most important studies in the social sciences is known as The Robber's Cave Experiment (Sherif, Harvey, White, Hood, & Sherif, 1954, 1962).[9] The Robber's Cave illustrates the dynamics of affiliation at work among teenage boys. In brief:

A group of teens who don't know one another attend an overnight summer camp. Early on, the group is randomly divided into two teams. Each team is encouraged to establish an identity for itself. One becomes the "Eagles" and the other the "Rattlers." Alignment occurs as individuals build one another's mutual sense of belonging within their respective teams.

Competitive games are conducted, pitting the teams against each other. Rivalry develops, accompanied by jeers deriding the other team and cheers encouraging one's mates. Sherif (1970, p. 150) observes that "as intergroup conflict grew, its impact on the respective ingroups was undeniable. Ingroup solidarity increased, as members closed ranks." These are the complementary forces of alignment and alienation at work in tandem, building coherence within and boundaries between the two teams.

A crisis occurs which neither team can resolve on its own, but the two might resolve cooperatively. By working together, the crisis is resolved. The boundaries built by competition between the teams (alienation) diminish and a shared sense of mutual belonging (alignment) is rebuilt.

These essential dynamics and Sherif's research, in particular, have since become a cornerstone not only of social psychology, but of politics and international relations, as well. For example, Bishop and Cushing (2008, p. 283), cite Sherif when discussing American politics, stating, "It's the way teams coalesce, companies build identities and political parties maintain loyalty." And now we know what might have been obvious long ago, this is also how families are made and broken.

Speaking of alienation as a syndrome (as in Gardner's PAS) restricts us to the myopia associated with the medical model of illness, whereas speaking of alienation as an interpersonal dynamic allows us to understand the breadth of the problem far beyond divorce and contested custody matters. The former calls for fix-the-kid solutions (individual therapy, possibly even medication). The latter calls broadly for an understanding of the ways in which we encourage and inhibit children's secure attachment relationships and thereby facilitate their long-term well-being. The following sections elaborate on that understanding.

Divorce: The Tip of the Iceberg

With the exception of the article discussed above (Garber, 2004a), I am not aware of any published work that recognizes that parents can and do use alienation as a weapon against one another regardless of the legal status of their relationship. In fact, none of this is about divorce. It is about how children become caught in the middle of their caregivers' angry, self-serving, and immature conflicts. Divorce is simply an obvious and publicly visible landmark that brings these conflicts into focus before the courts. Without the benefit of such a lens, we have no means of even guessing how many children live this way every day. Astute pediatricians, school counselors, and child therapists recognize the problem. Unfortunately, far too many child-centered professionals do not, resulting in an unknowable number of misdiagnoses, unnecessary medications, and needlessly stigmatized and blamed children.[10] Given that commencing the divorce process requires a certain minimum effort—measured in terms of self-advocacy, literacy, money, and accumulated pain—it is reasonable to imagine that there may be 2 or 20 or 200 children caught in the middle of their parents' conflicts for every one whose parents stand before the bench.

Alienation and Children's Psychotherapy

When parents conflict, separate, and divorce, a psychotherapist can provide a child with a critically important "port in the storm." Unfortunately, the dynamics of alienation can extend to include children's therapists, not to mention teachers, coaches, best friends, grandparents, and neighbors.

I have discussed elsewhere the phenomenon of "therapist alienation" (Garber, 2004c), that dynamic which can occur when a naïve or ill-informed therapist accepts a parent's request to see his or her child without assuring that the child's other parent is aware and supportive of the process. If those two parents are married or otherwise share joint legal custody, state laws variously dictate the extent to which such a therapist must proactively respect the absent parent's rights.[11] However, above and beyond these legal limits and regardless of the legal status of the parents' relationship or their respective legal rights to the child, either parent can undermine the therapy by planting seeds of mistrust, at the least, and by explicitly threatening the child, at worst.

For example, the father who discovers after the fact that his 12-year-old son has been seeing Dr. Brilliant for many weeks reasonably feels left out of the loop. When this occurs in the larger context of coparental discord, separation, divorce, or a contested custody action (and the anxiety, anger, and fear usually associated with these actions), Dad reasonably fears that Dr. Brilliant is somehow Mom's secret ally and that together they are poisoning the son against him. A healthy, mature, and empowered Dad might shrug the news off in front of his son and then later, once he is alone, confront Mom and call Dr. Brilliant to learn more. A less healthy Dad simply erupts, "Your mother didn't tell me about him! Don't say another word to him!" In so doing, the secure, trusting, attachment-like relationship that is so critical to any psychotherapy can be undermined and the therapist—like the child—triangulated into the parents' conflict.

Alienation, Removal, Reunification, and Termination

Social service involvement in a family's life represents a special case deserving of a book (and a great deal of staff training) unto itself. The very fact of a social service agency's presence in a family risks undermining a child's security in that home, the more-or-less explicit message to the child being that Mom or Dad is an incompetent caregiver. This dynamic becomes one step worse when parents live apart and one uses social service involvement in the child's other home to his or her self-serving advantage: "I told you your mother is bad! Why do you think those ladies are asking all those questions?" Add to this those instances in which one parent makes a false report of abuse or neglect in order to implicitly enlist social services in his or her efforts to demean the child's other parent, and the effect is complete. What child can continue to feel safe with Mom when not only does Dad denigrate her, but the police and the state seem to mistrust her as well?

Unfortunately, all that social service agencies can do to minimize this manipulative and destructive dynamic is become educated. Within the limits of safety, service providers must go to extraordinary lengths to never undermine a parent's authority, question his or her competence, or become caught in the push–pull between conflicted homes either in the presence of or directly to a child of any age. When a child must be removed to foster care; when contact with a parent must be supervised, occur in a therapeutic milieu, or be terminated; when a parent must be hospitalized or incarcerated—whatever the complications, every effort must be made to script the events so that the child hears the same story from everyone, a story that emphasizes positives and love and respect and minimizes the child's self-blame, guilt, and loss of security, as much as possible.

Does this mean that we should lie to children? That we must try to build a child's sense of security in a caregiver who was unambiguously hurtful? No, of course not. To do so would be to engage in misalignment, a dynamic that creates confusion, mistrust, can contribute to a child's loss of self-worth and place him or her needlessly in danger.

Does this mean, instead, that we should warn children about the risks of contact with a parent who might reasonably be expected to be abusive or neglectful? As adults and as concerned professionals, our first responsibility is to assure a child's safety to the greatest degree possible so that he or she need never worry. Unfortunately, there will always be ambiguous circumstances in which a child must be prepared for reasonably anticipated but inescapable dangers. Take the case of Ms. Fearful, divorced from a man whom she knows to be neglectful but to whom the court has accorded unsupervised alternate-weekend visits. Days in advance of each contact, Ms. Fearful agonizes over whether to send the kids off for their weekend with Dad, worried that this will be the time that he allows them to be harmed. She knows that if she cancels the contact, she may incur contempt-of-court charges and related consequences, at least, outright accusations of alienating the kids, and even ex parte motions to change the custody arrangement, at most.

There is no simple or generic answer to these gut-wrenching dilemmas. Certainly, we must always value our children's safety above all else. Ms. Fearful's well-intended warning in advance of the kids' contact with Dad ("Call me if he starts yelling....Call 9-1-1 if you need to....—Make sure there's always an adult nearby....") may indeed be objectively defensible and will therefore constitute estrangement—but when the kids innocently repeat Mom's cautions to Dad? To my knowledge, no court has yet to acknowledge—never mind allow—this behavior.

Ms. Fearful's best alternative is to routinely teach her kids caution, preparedness, and self-defense, so that they have these skills available to them at all times, not just when they're off with Dad. Much as this general approach to parenting risks instilling cynicism, hypervigilance and even paranoia in young children, it may be preferable to teaching these skills as Dad's car is pulling in the driveway, a strategy that may create a self-fulfilling prophecy about Dad that undermines any opportunity that the kids may have to feel relatively secure with him.

Recognizing and Responding to Alienation

As is true in any matter of family law, alienation can only be understood as it exists in the relationships among people. Although some (generally PAS advocates) have suggested that alienation can be identified within the alienating parent (e.g., Gordon, Stoffey, & Bottinelli, 2008) and/or within the alienated child (Johnston, Walters, & Olesen, 2005), none of these contentions have yet been validated.

Instead, Lee and Oleson (2001, p. 282) recommend that identification of alienation requires that a specially trained mental health professional or team of professionals conduct a child-centered systemic evaluation, [12] specifying that:

> Evaluations should be neutral, comprehensive, and expeditious. Assessment should be done only by a court-ordered, neutral evaluator, who has clear authority and directives from the court. Even when the parents stipulate to the evaluation, their agreement should be formalized in a court order. Experts hired separately by each parent are very likely to polarize the case further....The failure to provide a complex, comprehensive evaluation with accompanying recommendations also can result in delay after the report is released, which can contribute to the crystallization and deepening of the child's alienation.

When alienation is identified, the courts must be involved in order to mandate and supervise the implementation and coordination of multiple, simultaneous remedies (Sullivan & Kelly, 2001), such remedies to include a uniquely determined constellation of education, individual, dyadic, and systemic therapies and structures (Freeman, Abel, Cowper-Smith, & Stein, 2004; Johnston, Walters, & Friedlander, 2001; Stahl, 1999) largely intended to minimize the child's exposure to the alienating message while simultaneously maximizing the child's positive, healthy experience of the targeted/alienated caregiver.[13] One example of such a model is provided later in this chapter.

Unfortunately, this is where professional consensus ends.

What we do know is that when alienation is severe, some professionals recommend that all parties participate in an intense immersion-like program (e.g., Deutsch, Sullivan, & Ward, 2008). Others support Gardner's (1998) recommendation for an abrupt change of custody (Turkat, 1994), based on an argument such as is offered by an *amicus curiae* brief in an Alabama Supreme Court matter:[14]

A concerted effort by one parent to interfere with the other parent's contact with the children is so inimical to the best interests of the children—the paramount concern in custody cases—as to, per se, raise a very strong probability that *the interfering parent is unfit to act as the primary (residential) parent or* custodial parent.

Finally, I note with regret that there are those relationships that have been so deeply undercut by alienation for so long, particularly when the impacted child reaches adolescence, that it may be necessary to advise the targeted parent to withdraw from the battle, but to always remain available in anticipation of the child's eventual return. Stahl (1999 p. 8) summarizes:

[I]in the most extreme examples, in which nothing seems to be working and the child appears to be at significant risk, it may be necessary to help the alienated parent [to] therapeutically disengage from the child until such time that the child can more adequately reestablish the relationship. From the perspective of the child, this may actually be a less damaging recommendation than a change of custody.

Following is a hypothetical constellation of services intended to remedy an 8-year-old boy's alienation from his father.

Relevant facts: Joe and Mary Smith divorced 5 years ago when their only child, Sam, was 3 years old. A contested custody battle resulted in joint legal custody, placing Sam in his Dad's care Wednesday evenings and alternate weekends from Friday after school until 6 p.m. Sunday. The custody battle also served to amplify and solidify the animosity between the parents.

When Sam began kindergarten at age 5, Mom complained that Wednesday-evening outings with Dad disrupted school on Thursday. The parents returned to court. A guardian ad litem investigated, supported Mom's contention, and the court eliminated the Wednesday overnight with Dad in favor of extending the alternate weekends through Monday mornings.

Mom remarried 2 years ago. Since then, Sam has been increasingly resistant to visits with Dad. During first grade he missed as many as half of his weekends, seeing his father only about once a month. Midway through second grade, Sam began to refuse any contact at all with his father. It's now been 9 months since father and son have seen each other except across a soccer field at Sam's Saturday games. Dad has overheard Mom and her new husband actively encouraging the child's resistance, demeaning him out loud. As a result, the parents are once again back in court.

After hearing arguments and reviewing a neutral mental health professional's family systems evaluation, the court acknowledges both that Mom and Step-dad are alienating Sam from his father and that father's drinking is part of the problem, as well. The court recongizes that Sam needs a healthy relationship with each of his caregivers unimpeded by the adults' self-serving conflict and therefore orders:

1. A parenting coordinator (PC) be hired to oversee this plan and to assist the three coparents to resolve their child-centered differences. The PC will have the privilege of receiving information from each of the subsidiary professionals at his or her discretion. The PC will deliver updates to the court every 3 months.
2. Dad will commence in individual psychotherapy and attend at least three AA meetings each week, without exception. Any evidence that he is consuming alcohol, inebriated, or otherwise impaired is sufficient cause for the PC to interrupt this plan pending further direction from the court.
3. Sam will commence individual psychotherapy. This therapy will be protected from the parents' and the court's intrusion in order to serve Sam's social and emotional needs. Both parents will actively support this therapy and will comply with the therapist's requests and recommendations.
4. A reunification therapist will be hired to facilitate the father–son relationship. This therapist will conduct initial interviews separately with each of the parents and with Sam and then will deliver a proposal as to how best to proceed, to be submitted to the PC for implementation.
5. A coparenting educator will meet with the three adults on a time-limited basis to (a) educate them about the effects of alienation, (b) facilitate respectful, child-centered communication, and (c) improve parenting consistency between the two homes.
6. A hearing will be conducted in 9 months, at which time the PC will report on the progress of these interventions and particularly on the status of the father–son contact. At this time the court will entertain motions defining proposed schedules of father–son contact based

on the relative success of these interventions, including Mom's and Dad's respective support of this process.

How many professionals does this include? A parenting coordinator. Dad's individual therapist. Dad's AA group. Sam's individual therapist. A father–son reunification facilitator. A coparenting educator. The lawyers, judge, and court personnel.

On the one hand, this is without question an expensive, time-consuming, and complicated proposal. It will require excellent communication and coordination among the professionals orchestrated by the parenting coordinator. On the other hand, the long-term cost to the child of allowing his separation from his father to grow or worse, the long-term cost of responding inadequately—of trying but failing while incurring pointless expenses, exacerbating tensions, and allowing the child to become just a little bit older in the process—is arguably far worse. I can't help but recall the idea that it does, indeed, take a village to raise a healthy child. Would we balk at a proposal calling for several physicians, nurses, technicians, and allied personnel to work together at even greater expense to perform surgery on the same child? Probably not. Why should the child's mental health be any less deserving?

SUMMARY

The concept of alienation has created an enormous amount of heat within the family courts, but very little light. We must be prepared to look beyond incendiary charges of alienation, to look beyond the debate as to whether alienation constitutes a "syndrome," to understand the family dynamics in which these allegations occur and the conditions under which each child seeks to maintain the healthiest relationship possible with each of his or her caregivers.

NOTES

1. In the U.K. the Married Women's Property Act (1882, 1893). Similar legislation was passed in the states, e.g., in New York (1848, 1860).
2. *Bouchard v. Sundberg*, 80 Conn. App. 180 (Conn. App. 11/18/2003).

3. In this regard, note the similarity between alienation and the compatible dynamics of infantilization, parentification, and adultification described elsewhere in this book.
4. A bibliography of Gardner's relevant work is available at http://www.rgardner.com/
5. "Parental Alienation Syndrome" is often discussed in the literature and on the Internet in concert with "Malicious Mother Syndrome" (a.k.a, "Divorce-Related Malicious Parent Syndrome"; see Turkat, 1995), sometimes equated with "Hostile Aggressive Parenting" and other times juxtaposed to "Maternal Alienation Syndrome" (Morris, 2004). None of these are recognized diagnoses, meet the criteria for being considered syndromes, or fulfill the requirements under *Daubert*.
6. Noting that Gardner claims that PAS has met *Frye* standards (or the comparable *Mohan* standard in Canada) in *Kilgore v. Boyd* (13th Circuit Court, Hillsborough County, FL, Case No. 94-7573, 733 So. 2d 546; Fla. 2d DCA 2000; Jan 30, 2001); *Bates v. Bates* (18th Judicial Circuit, Dupage County, IL, Case No. 99D958, Jan 17, 2002); and *Her Majesty the Queen vs. K.C. Superior Court of Justice* (Ontario, County of Durham, Central-East Region, Court File No. 9520/01. August, 9, 2002). Gardner further cites more than 50 cases through 2005 across 22 states, more than 20 cases across Canada, and additional cases spanning Europe. See http://www.rgardner.com/ retrieved March 9, 2009.
7. Gardner originally explained that angry mothers alienate children from fathers, but subsequently (2001) allowed that parents of either gender could and do alienate their children from the other. Nevertheless, Gardner reads to this author as if he returns to this "gender specificity" subsequently (2002).
8. By contrast, Gardner's self-published reports of nonrandom samples fail to test the null hypothesis; that is, he proceeds in a manner that can only confirm his hypothesis. Baker (2007) publishes compelling but unscientific anecdotal restrospective accounts which have been criticized as an "excellent example of pseudoscience" (Venzke, 2007).
9. This landmark study is discussed in detail at: http://www.age-of-the-sage.org/psychology/social/sherif_robbers_cave_experiment.html and http://psychclassics.yorku.ca/Sherif/ (each retrieved March 9, 2009).
10. Professionals who look *within* the child but fail to understand the dynamics that *surround* the child may be particularly prone to misdiagnose children who live in chaos and conflict with attention–deficit (hyperactivity) disorder (ADD or ADHD; Garber, 2001).
11. For example, see the New Hampshire Board of Mental Health Practice's interpretation of relevant laws at http://www.nh.gov/mhpb/joint_custody.html (retrieved March 9, 2009).

12. Contrary to the position taken in this book (see chapter 15), these authors recommend that "evaluators should strongly consider including cognitive and personality testing of the parents in their evaluation. Cognitive assessment can articulate the parent's intellectual strengths and weaknesses, style of thinking and problem solving, and the degree to which their cognitive functioning may be disrupted by underlying emotional factors. 'Objective' personality tests, such as the Minnesota Multiphasic Personality Inventory-2 and the Millon Clinical Multiaxial Inventory-III, may be less useful in this context, due to their face validity and the parent's need to create a positive impression. Projective assessment—such as the use of the Rorschach, Thematic Apperception Test, and projective drawings—may be more useful in accessing underlying psychological processes" (p. 293; citations omitted; cf., Lampel, 2002).

13. One innovative and promising process uses a one-way mirror to help a child (re-)develop a secure relationship with an an alienated parent from a safe distance (Weitzman, 2004).

14. *Tina S Wilson vs. Drew C Wilson*, DR-97-502272.03-C (emphasis in the original). Retrieved March 9, 2009, from www.ancpr.org

17 Development in the Mirror: On Becoming (and Remaining) a Family Law Professional

But where and how is the poor wretch to acquire the ideal qualification which he will need in this profession? The answer is in an analysis of himself, with which his preparation for his future activity begins.

—*Dr. Freud,* "Analysis Terminable and Interminable"

Be who you are and say what you feel, because those who mind don't matter and those who matter don't mind.

—*Dr. Seuss*

For many years, I have had the pleasure and the good fortune to be invited to speak to groups of professionals all around the country about child and family development in the context of family law. I find that there is no better way to broaden my thinking, validate my experience, and settle the storm of emotions that this work engenders than to talk shop with colleagues who share similar experiences. I routinely return home from these adventures travel-worn but professionally refreshed, eager to bring some new insight or practice tip back to the office.

By chance, I made a discovery several years ago at a conference-sponsored dinner: the "hot" salsa disappeared from the table much more quickly than the "mild" salsa. I noticed because I love spicy food.

So I asked the assembled group of conference organizers. Then I asked the entire group of attorneys, judges, guardians, mediators, and mental health professionals gathered the next day and I've asked nearly every group since. What I've discovered is that family law professionals crave spicy food.

This is in no way a scientific observation. Still, it seems to be a clue to who we are as a group. Although there are no broad and reliable demographics,[1] we do know that family law professionals come from diverse personal and professional backgrounds. We are trained as lawyers and psychologists, social workers and mediators, corporate executives and financial analysts. We each have a unique and compelling story about how and when and why we moved into family law. We all have horror stories and battle scars and complaints about the work. And perhaps we share a similar developmental course.

This final chapter asks you to look into the mirror, to understand your own development and the motivations, needs, wishes, and skills that bring you to this work. I offer these thoughts in the belief that the family law professional who neglects to subject him- or herself to at least the same level of scrutiny with which we view litigants and their children is at risk for tripping over his or her ego, falling into a deep pit of unrecognized bias, and otherwise allowing the children whom we serve to be at least partially obscured in the shadow of self. This work is exhausting and dangerous and seldom rewarding. Let this chapter be just the next step in your continuing development as a healthy human being and a skilled child-centered professional.

VOCATIONALLY INDUCED DÉCALAGE

For the sake of argument, let's assume that postbaccalaureate graduate training programs look at their annual pool of applicants as falling into three groups based on developmental status. One group is developmentally even-keeled. These potential students are without evidence of décalage (see chapter 7); that is, their physical, social, emotional, cognitive, and verbal development are all more or less equally mature.

A second group is developmentally asynchronous in a way that suits the program. These potential students manifest décalage congruent with the areas of growth most valued and valuable to the intended career.

A third group, by contrast, includes applicants with developmental asynchronies that are incongruent with the program.

To illustrate, I imagine that graduate training in civil engineering and religious ministry screen for different types of students. Both might accept applicants from group one, the developmentally even-keeled students. However, an applicant whose cognitive (analytical, sequential, mathematical) development far exceeds that of his or her social and emotional development would seem to be better suited to the engineering program, while an applicant with exceptional social, emotional, and spiritual development is likely to be a much better fit in the seminary.

Note that, once again, "fit" is at issue.

As it turns out, the schools each reject the incongruent (group three) applicants, accept the congruent (group two) applicants and half of the even-keeled (group one) applicants. Years pass. The members of each class endure rigorous graduate-level training, that enhances developmental capacities and builds specific skills important to their respective careers. Having spent years steeped in numbers and formulae, the students who entered engineering school already developmentally lopsided find themselves even more so upon graduation. The even-keeled students have endured the same immersion and are likely to graduate at least somewhat lopsided. But not all.

The graduating engineers who discover that building bridges doesn't fulfill them, like the graduating seminary students who find that pastoral care doesn't challenge them, face a dilemma. Some of each will quit and become corporate executives or lawyers or psychologists. Others will feel locked into their career choice and suffer and/or fail. Still others will stretch the boundaries of their work by creating a niche that meets their needs. The engineer will specialize in building beautiful and compassionate hospitals. The seminarian will trade in pastoral care for hermeneutics (analysis of the Bible).

The Development of the Lawyer

Most, but not all of this is speculation. Some of the relevant research is ongoing (e.g., Reeves, Hampton, Strohmer, & Leierer, 2008). A few small pieces of the puzzle are well established.

Daicoff (1999, 2004) provides a comprehensive and fascinating review of the development of law students and lawyers. She describes the typical lawyer as competitive, aggressive, achievement-motivated and invested in personal financial gain. She asserts that "lawyers overwhelmingly prefer thinking to feeling" (2004, p. 33), such that:

> An exclusive reliance on thinking may cause emotional distress to law students during law school and for years thereafter because it gets used in situations where consideration of extralegal matters is more appropriate. For example, lawyers' spouses often complain that the lawyers cannot turn off their "lawyer mode" at home, at times when they need to be more nonrational, subjective, or compassionate. In addition, an overreliance on thinking might contribute to an unbalanced approach to life and interpersonal difficulties with one's family and friends, which in turn leads to additional social isolation and thus more distress. (Daicoff, 2004, p. 144)

Shaub (2007) amplifies this final point, stating that:

> Lawyers tend toward social isolation when experiencing personal distress and have a significantly higher incidence of alcohol abuse and depression than the general population.[2]

Daicoff (2004) reviews research suggesting that lawyers share a characteristic level of moral development (see chapter 5).[3] She reports that "attorneys were disproportionately clustered at the fourth stage of moral development, unlike the usual distribution of the general population across Kohlberg's six moral stages" (2004, pp. 36–37)[4] and "law students' morality differed from the morality of college students, teachers and prison inmates in that it was consistently more 'conventional' and focused on maintaining social order and conformity" (1999, p. 66). This makes sense to the extent that lawyers work within the rigid and detailed rules that we know as law. A lawyer who sees injustice in the law is either disciplined or deified.

The Development of the Psychologist

It is ironic to discover that among all of the many aspects of human behavior, emotion, thinking, and development studied by psychologists, psychologists study themselves little at all.[5]

Graduate-school training in the clinical applications of psychology (Psy.D. programs more so than Ph.D. programs; social work, counseling, and comparable fields) emphasizes the development of emotion and relatedness. Donnan, Harlan, and Thompson (1969) characterize these as including capacities for unconditional positive regard, empathic understanding, congruence, and trust. "The psychotherapist's desired personality traits include inner stability and [a] high degree of self-knowledge leading to an understanding and accepting of his or her own self" (Vymetal, 2000, p. 165). As part of this process, psychologists are routinely encouraged (and sometimes required) to engage in their own personal psychotherapy both during training and periodically across the span of a career (Norcross, 2005).

We know nothing generally about the moral development of psychologists (and allied mental health providers) as a group, although the American Psychological Association's revised ethics statement (2002; see Standard 1.02) calls for what might be considered a very conventional compliance with authority.

We do know, at least anecdotally, that psychologists have as much difficulty taking off their work clothes as do lawyers and (presumably) many other professionals. For example, child psychologists reliably report that their adult partners complain about being "analyzed" and that their children are prone to scream, "Don't shrink me, Dad! I'm not one of your patients!"

FAMILY LAW IS FOR MISFITS

If it is fair to say that professionals with particularly strong social and emotional development are relatively well fitted to clinical mental health careers and those with particularly strong cognitive development are relatively well fitted to lawyering, then we might understand family law as one among many possible solutions for the "misfits."

The term "misfit" is generally heard as pejorative. I mean it with no negative connotation whatsoever. "Misfit" is used here simply to indicate an uncomfortable or untenable match between what might otherwise be complementary parts. By analogy, a shoe is a mis-fit if it doesn't suit the foot's dimensions. In both the earlier discussion of sensitive and responsive parenting and later when discussing psychological assessment in family law matters, "fit" and "misfit" are relevant concepts.

In this discussion, misfit refers to the relative match between an individual's development, needs, and interests and the functional requirements and opportunities inherent in a career. When a career is a misfit, its conditions are poorly suited to the individual's developmental needs, skills, and interests. We can measure career misfit demographically in terms of graduate school attrition and job (dis-)satisfaction, but we seldom know which aspect(s) of a career path (financial, interpersonal, opportunity for growth, etc.) fail to fit the individual's needs.

Studies typically find very high career satisfaction among psychologists. Norcross, Prochaska, and Farber (1993) report that as many as 89% of psychologists are satisfied with their work. He notes incidentally that when asked what career psychologists might chose in a next life, only 3% of respondents choose the law. Studies of attorneys typically find less satisfaction, or a greater percentage of misfit. Daicoff (2004) summarizes studies conducted in 1984, 1990, 1992, and 1995 as finding approximately 20 to 27% dissatisfaction with no corresponding suggestion of how many would rather be mental health providers.

Like the hypothetical engineer who feels that his work neglects his social and emotional needs or the seminarian whose work seems to lack the intellectual and analytical challenges that she enjoys, family law professionals as a group share a need for something more or different than our training otherwise provides. A serving of hot salsa on the side, so to speak. Daicoff (2004, p. 156-157) reports her experience that:

> [W]hen I have presented the lawyer personality research to practicing attorneys and then allowed them to identify whether they are thinkers or feelers, often the feelers indicate great job satisfaction. On additional questioning, anecdotally I have found that invariably they are practicing law in a niche specialty that is perfectly suited for a feeler. They are family law judges, guardians ad litem, government attorneys responsible for broad social policy relating to families, full-time mediators, and the like.

Regarding the emerging legal fields of therapeutic jurisprudence and preventive law (TJ/PL),[6] Daicoff speculates elsewhere (1999, pp. 828–829) that:

> For those lawyers with some or many atypical traits, incorporating TJ/PL principles into law practice may offer a uniquely satisfying and appropriate

way of practicing law....TJ/PL is particularly well suited for lawyers who are noncompetitive, nonmaterialistic, altruistic, or humanistic....They are likely to enjoy TJ/PL's emphasis on nonadvocacy, on the lawyer-client relationship, and on the role of the lawyer as planner, counselor, and negotiator. They do not mind foregoing the opportunity to represent the client aggressively in court in order to achieve a more cooperative, emotionally satisfying resolution of the client's problem.

There is no comparable literature with which to understand the mental health professionals who shift from the feeling emphasis of the psycho-therapist into the more analytical and adversarial practice of family law. The hypothesis I am recommending and my own personal experience is that clinical work alone is not enough for some.[7] Among these few, some leave the field entirely to become carpenters or poets or attorneys. For others, shifting into family law practice makes for a much better fit. But at what cost? Those of us who choose the hot salsa over the mild may enjoy the taste, but do so at the risk of being burned.

Compassion Fatigue, Vicarious Trauma, and Burnout

Wherever we come from, whatever hats we wear, however much family law might provide the spice that is otherwise missing from our professional lives, there is no debating that this work is intellectually demanding, interpersonally taxing, and emotionally exhausting. It requires empathy and unassailable boundaries, a clear sense of personal identity, and mature personal defenses but never defensiveness.[8] This work can be frustrating on the best of days:

> [T]here may be some built-up frustration on the part of the professionals working with the family, including the social worker, therapists, lawyers and the judge, at the parents' inability to understand or to alter poor parenting or lifestyle choices that endanger their children. (Judicial Education Center, 2009)

And on others it can be enraging. Unchecked, the family law professional risks losing perspective and neutrality, identifying with one litigant or a child victim to the detriment of all, not least of all him- or herself (Freedman, Rosenberg, Gettman, & Van Scoyk, 1993; Pickar, 2007). Given that the stakes in the matters before us are so high, it is not surprising that family law professionals face a very real threat of violence (Shavit, 2005a, 2005b).[9,10]

Family law professionals face the highest risks of licensing complaints and malpractice suits (Benjamin, Gollan, & Ally, 2007; Bow & Quinnell, 2001; Kirkland & Kirkland, 2001; Kirkland & Kirkland, 2006) within their respective guilds, except for those who are (accused of) sexually abusing their clients. As much as choosing to walk into this lion's den on a daily basis might speak to our developmental needs, it is simply and finally dangerous.

Least obvious but, I would argue, most prevalent among the dangers that we face in family law is that of compassion fatigue (see Appendix V for a brief bibliography).*Compassion fatigue*, also known as *secondary (or vicarious) traumatic stress disorder*, is the combination of helplessness, hopelessness, decreased energy, and depression-like symptoms that professionals who work with victims often acquire. It is the feeling that one's caring muscle has become atrophied. It is that disrespectful and even depersonalized ennui that can prompt a seasoned judge or guardian ad litem, mediator or evaluator to make a rash statement, to overlook an important detail, to begin to see case numbers and numbers of cases rather than names. These experiences, in turn, lead to anxiety and self-doubt and even self-loathing:

> Some individuals can tolerate the uncertainty of the legal process, while others find it overwhelming and maddening. For these individuals, litigation is a traumatic experience creating sleepless nights and agonizing days filled with obsessive thinking, panic attacks, and fear. Intrusive thoughts of the legal case can invade daily activities and disrupt evening dreams. It is as though time has stopped for everything else. (Cohen & Vesper, 2001, p.5) [11]

Family court attorneys (in any role) may be at particularly high risk for compassion fatigue (Rhode, 2006). Loners and isolative by nature, rational and logical/sequential to the exclusion of facing the weight of emotional experience, often lacking training about boundaries and generally averse to seeking therapy, attorneys often turn to substance abuse and even suicide as a result (Sells, 2002). In fact, these short-term and maladaptive coping strategies only compound the risk (Way, VanDeusen, Martin, Applegate, & Jandle, 2004).

Sinclair (2006) quotes one Canadian family law attorney:

> I love my work but lately I find it contaminating my personal life. I have nightmares about the horrible things I hear about from clients. My sex life has deteriorated, I'm irritable and distractible, I'm afraid for my kids and tend to overprotect them, and I don't trust anybody anymore. I don't know what is happening to me.

Family law judges, although often perceived as both literally and figuratively above it all, may be at particularly high risk for vicarious trauma (Chamberlain & Miller, 2008). In addition to the isolative tendencies associated with legal practice in general, judges seldom are able to consult with peers or let their guard down while off the bench.[12]

> Cases of horrible, sexual, predatory exploitation of children haunt me. I keep my balance and my job as a judge by profoundly guarding myself against being swept away by the gruesome evidence I have to confront. (Zimmerman, 2002, as quoted in Sinclair, 2006)

Jaffe and colleagues have studied judges' experiences of vicarious trauma. They refer to the "'torment' judges experience in dealing with cases of sexual abuse, child maltreatment, and domestic violence" (Jaffe, Crooks, Dunford-Jackson, & Town, 2003, p. 2). More generally:

> Judges have described how the nature of what they see and hear in the courtroom can shake their very faith in humanity. Along the way they describe depression, anxiety, sleep disturbances, hypervigilance, nightmares, and withdrawal from family and friends. The impact may be mild and short term or last for years and require mental health intervention. (Jaffe, Crooks, Dunford-Jackson, & Town, 2003, p. 10)

Lay therapists, court-appointed special advocate (CASA) workers, child protective services workers, assault advocates, and domestic violence shelter staff (across roles) are no less vulnerable:

> Throughout the course of their work, the sexual assault workers identified struggling with anger, personal safety, awareness of their own vulnerability to rape, particularly since they confronted it on a daily basis, and internalizing client's pain as key variables impacting their personal lives. (Carmody, 1997, p. 452)

Mental health professionals (who work in clinical roles) may have greater exposure but at least minimally lower risk of compassion fatigue by virtue of both the feelings orientation that leads most into the field and the relevant training along the way. Across guilds, psychotherapists are taught to recognize and respect boundaries (Gutheil & Brodsky, 2008) and are empowered to practice what they preach; that is, self-care and healthy emotional release.[13,14] In addition, some states require that mental health professionals maintain ongoing consultation with colleagues (if not periodic return to personal therapy) as a condition of licensure (Kaslow et al., 2007; Van Horne, 2004).[15]

Unrecognized and unrelieved, compassion fatigue is the first step down the slippery slope toward burnout. Worse, the real-world damage that can be done along the way can be catstrophic not only to one's career, family, and health, but also to those children and families caught in the wake of the professional's impairment.

THE DEVELOPMENT OF THE FAMILY LAW PROFESSIONAL

And so we end where we began, talking about development and fit. Much as the emotionally healthy toddler has a secure base to which she can return in times of stress, confident that Mom or Dad will be there to refuel her, much as a child with at least one constant emotional anchor has a chance of managing the horrors of intractable family conflict, neglect, and abuse, much as transitional objects can help a child tolerate parental separation, absence, and even termination, we must allow ourselves no less.

Development doesn't stop in late adolescence or early adulthood. It is a constant current running through our lives. As adults and professionals, as husbands and wives and parents ourselves, as adult children struggling with our elderly parents' care, we are growing and learning, taking steps up that continuing staircase of growth, sometimes awestruck by the vista from a new, higher level of development and other times forced backward when stress causes regression.

Psychology knows much less about these adult stages of development than about children's growth and change (cf., Kunz, 2007), but the basic dynamics never change. John Donne (1572–1631) was right: No man is an island.[16]

We are a socially and emotionally needy species. Some of us are prone, nonetheless, to believe that we can survive on theory and fact-patterns, logic and analysis. We fall victim to this misbelief as a defense against the chaos of the real world that surrounds us. We must recognize that we cannot help others from the lofty perch of intellect alone and, hiding in such an eyrie, we cannot even help ourselves.

The best prophylaxis (and, when necessary, the best remedy) for compassion fatigue, vicarious traumatization, and burnout, is healthy human connection. Rewarding and reciprocal relationships. As guardians ad litem, mediators, attorneys, judges, and on across the gamut of family law professions, we need our own secure bases, our own emotional anchors, and our own personal "port in the storm" no less than the children whom we are committed to assist. This means that we must never allow our work to become more important than our lives. We must give ourselves—and give others through our example—permission to set healthy limits, to respect healthy boundaries, and to care for ourselves.

In the workplace, across guilds, and independent of licensure requirements, this means making peer contact. It means making consultation and supervision and mentoring relationships a routine and respected part of our lives and the training of our successors (American Bar Association, 2001, 2003, 2008b; Lande, 2008; Weiss, 2004; Wasco & Campbell, 2002). We must practice what we preach, aware that we can help others toward health only when we, ourselves, are making healthy decisions in support of our own development every day:

> The key elements appear to be a search for balance between the bench and a home life as well as play and restful activities. An awareness of the importance of exercise and diet is essential to survival. Many judges stress the role of hobbies far removed from the bench, such as gardening and antique collecting. Some judges seek mentors and training opportunities that nourish their lifelong learning and support from colleagues. (Jaffe, 2003)

Or the same idea, as we might express it to a child:

> Don't underestimate the value of Doing Nothing, of just going along, listening to all the things you can't hear, and not bothering. (*Pooh's Little Instruction Book*, inspired by A.A. Milne)

SUMMARY

Behind the title, underneath the suit coat, beyond the five-syllable words and Latin phrases, we must never pretend that we are different than the people whom we seek to understand. No person should ever become a docket number. No child should ever become just another anonymous victim. Circumstance has seated us on one side of the desk and the anguished mother or angry father, the terrified son, and the confused daughter on the other; but these differences are small compared to what we share.

No matter our foibles or theirs, we share a commitment to the well-being of children. Thus, we do everything that we can to respect each child as a unique individual, to understand the snapshot of behavior that we capture as a single frame in the movie of his or her development, and as a dynamic part of a complex family system. We work to understand the *fit* between parent and child, and between parent and parent, always focused on facilitating a child's opportunity to be loved by and grow up in a healthy relationship with each of his caregivers.

This book can only be one part of our continuing commitment to understand ourselves and the children whom we serve. It is valuable if it has prompted you to ask questions and to consider new perspectives. But it cannot be enough.

Please return to these pages as to a gateway with each new forensic dilemma. Let the ideas and references, resources and recommendations launch you further toward greater understanding. Start a professional consultation group and talk in terms of development and systems—and "fit"—at least as much as you talk about motions and statutes. Invite me along and I'll offer what I can. I welcome your thoughts and ideas, questions, and experiences at http://www.healthyparent.com. And please don't forget the salsa!

NOTES

1. Kirkland and Sullivan (2008) surveyed a small (and potentially nonrepresentative) sample of parenting coordinators and found that 44% were psychologists, 19% master's-level social workers, 15% licensed counselors, 11% bachelor's-level providers, and a final 11% were attorneys. I note that legislative differences across states restricting the qualifications for various family law roles make it unlikely that this distribution is representative of the larger pool of professionals.
2. Weiss, writing for the *American Bar Association Journal*, reports that "[a] list of the best jobs for introverts ranks 'lawyer' the sixth-best job" (May

19, 2008); retrieved March 9, 2009 from: http://www.abajournal.com/ news/list_of_best_jobs_for_introverts_r anks_lawyer_sixth

3. Your quiet chuckle at the culturally endorsed oxymoron ("Lawyers don't have morals!") supports the point entirely. Although it's just a joke, it speaks to how we see attorneys and bears on understanding who enters law school. Only 19% of the public expresses confidence in lawyers. "Americans say that lawyers are greedy, manipulative, and corrupt" (American Bar Association, 2002b, p. 4). By contrast, Mills (2009) reports that 36% of survey respondents view the profession of psychology very favorably and an additional 46% report viewing it favorably.

4. Noting that Daicoff subsequently suggests that "ego strength" moderates rigid rule compliance.

5. Or perhaps there's no irony here. Although applicants to graduate study in psychology most frequently relate a wish to help others as motivating their career choice, privately many simply wish to escape from one side of the couch or the inkblot to the other. Norcross and Guy (2007, p. 8) refer to this as the "fantasy that psychotherapists' clinical skills would inoculate us from the inevitable stressors of living."

6. Daicoff uses "Preventive Law" to refer to "procedural justice, therapeutic jurisprudence, therapeutically oriented preventive law, problem-solving courts, restorative justice, collaborative law, transformative mediation, holistic lawyering, and creative problem solving" (204, p. 170).

7. True, much of contemporary psychotherapy is very cognitive and behavioral. It may be that many of the mental health professionals who gravitate toward this work are simply finding their niche. Still, the only element of any psychotherapy that has consistently been demonstrated to be effective is the quality of the relationship with the provider.

8. "Working in the domestic arena requires the development of 'thick skin' in practitioners in response to criticism as well as formal complaints" (Kirkland & Kirkland, 2006, p. 32).

9. See Dubin and Ning (2008) for relevant risk-management strategies.

10. The media abounds with relevant drama; see http://socialworknc.blogs pot.com/2008/02/wake-county-social-worker-assaulted.html or http:// www.usatoday.com/news/nation/200606-12-judge_x.htm   as   two examples.

11. Cohen and Vesper (2001) recommend that this experience be recognized in the *DSM* as "Forensic Stress Disorder."

12. A 2002a survey conducted by the American Bar Association found that 86% of judges never use the Judicial Division Web site, intended to be one of the judiciary's greatest means of peer consultation and mutual support.

13. "[T]herapist self-care is essential when working with patients who suffer from PTSD because this work can be functionally disruptive and psychologically destabilizing for the mental health professionals" (Farrar, 2002).

14. Adams and Riggs (2008) observe that therapists with a "self-sacrificing defense style" are at very high risk of vicarious traumatization and burnout: "Trainers and supervisors should not be surprised that graduate programs in applied psychology attract people who are highly motivated to help others and thus often willing to sacrifice of themselves in order to do so. However, current findings suggest that trainees with a self-sacrificing defense style characterized by reaction formation and pseudoaltruism may be particularly vulnerable to vicarious traumatization" (p. 31).

15. "Opportunities for collaboration, mentoring, and consultation reduce isolation and increase awareness. Colleagues can have a profound effect on the maintenance of professional values and standards. Supervision, training, and continuing education influence continued ethical behavior. In addition, emphasis on self-assessment and awareness of the risk of misconduct as a result of impairment is critical throughout the education and training of psychologists. Sustaining the value of consultation is essential to career-long adherence to standards of practice" (Van Horne, 2004, p. 176).

16. "All mankind is of one author, and is one volume; when one man dies, one chapter is not torn out of the book, but translated into a better language; and every chapter must be so translated....As therefore the bell that rings to a sermon, calls not upon the preacher only, but upon the congregation to come: so this bell calls us all: but how much more me, who am brought so near the door by this sickness....No man is an island, entire of itself...any man's death diminishes me, because I am involved in mankind; and therefore never send to know for whom the bell tolls; it tolls for thee" (Donne, Devotions Upon Emergent Occasions, *Meditation XVII*).

Appendices

I Learn More Now: Agencies, Organizations, and Experts

This listing by category is intended to be representative only. Readers are encouraged to start with these resources and build from there, seeking out case- and jurisdiction-specific resources from these starting points.

Inclusion in these listings is not an endorsement of either the quality or the nature of any particular service or service provider. Readers must always be alert to ascertain that resources and references brought to bear in any particular case are current, thorough, child-centered, and unbiased.

SELECT MENTAL HEALTH AND CHILD DEVELOPMENT–RELATED ORGANIZATIONS

American Academy of Child and Adolescent Psychiatry
Go to http://www.aacap.org/

American Academy of Pediatrics
Go to http://www.aap.org/ or contact at:
141 Northwest Point Blvd.
Elk Grove Village, IL 60007-1098
Phone: (847) 434-4000

American Education Research Association
Go to http://www.aera.net/

American Psychological Association
Go to http://apa.org/ or contact at:
750 First Street NE
Washington, DC 20002-4242
Phone (toll-free): (800) 374-2721

Association for Psychological Science
Go to http://www.psychologicalscience.org/

Center for Substance Abuse Treatment (CSAT)
Go to http://www.samhsa.gov/centers/csat2002/index.html
or contact at:
5600 Fishers Lane
Rockville, MD 20857
Phone (voice): (301) 443-5700
Phone (toll-free): (800) 662-HELP or (877) 767-8432
Phone (TDD): (800) 487-4889
Fax: (301) 443-8751
E-mail: info@samhsa.gov

Children of Alcoholics Foundation (COAF)
Go to http://www.coaf.org/ or contact at:
164 West 74th Street
New York, NY 10023
Phone: (212) 595-5810, ext. 7760
Phone (toll-free): 1-800-359-COAF (2623)
E-mail: coaf@phoenixhouse.org

Consortium of Social Science Associations
Go to http://www.cossa.org/index.shtml

Domestic Violence Resource Network (DVRN)
Go to http://www.bwjp.org/dv.html or contact at:
6400 Flank Drive
Suite 1300
Harrisburg, PA 17112
Phone (voice; toll-free): (800) 537-2238 or (800) 799-
SAFE (7233)

Phone (TTY; toll-free): (800) 553-2508 or (800) 787-3224
Fax: (717) 545-9456

Foundation for Child Development
Go to http://www.fcd-us.org/

International Society for the Study of Behavioural Development
Go to http://www.issbd.org/

International Society on Infant Studies
Go to http://www.isisweb.org/

Morris Center for Healing from Child Abuse
Go to http://www.ascasupport.org/ or contact at:
PO Box 14477
San Francisco, CA 94114
Phone: (415) 928-4576
E-mail: tmc_asca@dnai.com

National Association of School Psychologists
Go to http://www.nasponline.org/

National Association for the Education of Young Children
Go to http://www.naeyc.org/

National Center for Child Traumatic Stress
Go to http://nctsnet.org/ or contact at:
11150 W. Olympic Blvd.
Suite 650
Los Angeles, CA 90064
Phone: (310) 235-2633
Fax: (310) 235-2612

Prevent Child Abuse America (PCAA)
Go to http://www.preventchildabuse.org/ or contact at:
200 South Michigan Avenue
17th Floor
Chicago, IL 60604-2404
Phone: (312) 663-3520
Fax: (312) 939-8962
E-mail: mailbox@preventchildabuse.org

Society of Clinical Child and Adolescent Psychology
Go to http://sccap.tamu.edu/

Society for Developmental and Behavioral Pediatrics
Go to http://www.sdbp.org/

Society of Pediatric Psychology
Go to http://www.societyofpediatricpsychology.org/new.
shtml

Society for Prevention Research
Go to http://www.preventionresearch.org/

Society for Research on Adolescence
Go to http://www.s-r-a.org/

Society for Research in Child Development
Go to http://www.srcd.org

Zero to Three
Go to http://www.zerotothree.org/site/PageServer

SELECT FAMILY LAW–RELATED ORGANIZATIONS

American Bar Association's Center on Children and the
Law Go to http://www.abanet.org/child/home.html

American Judges Association Go to http://aja.ncsc.dni.us/

Association of Family and Conciliation Courts
Go to http://afccnet.org/

Australasian Therapeutic Jursiprudence Clearinghouse
Go to http://www.aija.org.au/index.php?option=com_
content&task=view&id= 206&Itemid=103

Center for Families, Children & the Courts (via University
of Baltimore School of Law) Go to http://law.ubalt.edu/
template.cfm?page=602

Center for Families, Children & the Courts Go to
www.courtinfo.ca.gov

Child Welfare League of America
Go to http://www.cwla.org/ or contact at:
2345 Crystal Drive
Suite 250 Arlington, VA 22202
Phone: 703/412-2400
Fax: 703/412-2401

International Academy of Collaborative Professionals Go
to http://www.collaborativepractice.com/

International Network on Therapeutic Jurisprudence Go
to http://www.law.arizona.edu/depts/upr-intj/

Juvenile Law Center Go to http://www.jlc.org or contact at:
The Philadelphia Building
4th Floor
1315 Walnut Street
Philadelphia, PA 19107
Phone (toll-free): (800) 875-8887
Fax: (215) 625-2808

National Center for Preventive Law
Go to http://www.preventivelawyer.org/main/default.asp or
contact at:
225 Cedar Street
San Diego, CA 92101
Phone: (619) 239-0391
Fax: (619) 525-7092

National Center for State Courts
Go to http://www.ncsconline.org/ or contact at:
300 Newport Avenue
Williamsburg, VA 23185-4147
Phone (toll-free): (800) 616-6164
Fax: (757) 564-2022
E-mail: webmaster@ncsc.org

National Center for Victims of Crime
Go to http://www.ncvc.org or contact at:
2000 M Street NW
Suite 480
Washington, DC 20036
Phone: (202) 467-8700
Fax: (202) 467-8701

SELECT PHYSICAL HEALTH AND ILLNESS–RELATED RESOURCES

Advisory Committee on Heritable Disorders and Genetic Diseases in Newborns and Children
Go to http://www.hrsa.gov/heritabledisorderscommittee/

American Academy of Family Physicians
Go to http://www.aafp.org/online/en/home.html
or contact at:
PO Box 11210
Shawnee Mission, KS 66207-1210
Phone: (913) 906-6000
Phone (toll-free): (800) 274-2237
Fax: 913-906-6075

American Academy of Pediatrics
Go to http://www.aap.org/ or contact at:
141 Northwest Point Blvd.
Elk Grove Village, IL 60007-1098
Phone: (847) 434-4000
Fax: (847) 434-8000

Canadian Paediatric Society
Go to http://www.cps.ca/english/index.htm or contact at:
2305 St. Laurent Blvd.
Ottawa, Ontario K1G 4J8
Phone: (613) 526-9397
Fax: (613) 526-3332

National Dissemination Center for Children with Disabilities (NICHCY)
Go to www.nichcy.org or contact at:
PO Box 1492
Washington, DC 20013-1492
Phone (voice/TTY): (202) 884-8200
Phone (voice/TTY; toll-free): (800) 695-0285
E-mail: nichcy@aed.org

National Institute on Deafness and Other Communication Disorders (NIDOCD)

Go to http://www.nidcd.nih.gov/ or contact at:
National Institutes of Health (NIH)
31 Center Drive
MSC 2320
Bethesda, MD 20892-2320
E-mail: nidcdinfo@nidcd.nih.gov

World Health Organization (WHO)
Go to: http://www.who.int/en/ or contact at:
Avenue Appia 20
1211 Geneva 27, Switzerland
Phone: +41-22-791-21-11
Fax: +41-22-791-31-11
E-mail: info@who.int

SELECT ORGANIZATIONS RELEVANT TO SPEECH, LANGUAGE, AND LEARNING DIFFERENCES

American Association on Intellectual and Developmental Disabilities (AAIDD)
Go to http://www.aamr.org/ or contact at:
444 North Capitol Street, NW
Suite 846
Washington, DC 20001-1512
Phone: 202/387-1968 Phone (toll-free): (800) 424-3688
Fax: (202) 387-2193

American Speech Language Hearing Association
Go to: http://www.asha.org/default.htm or contact at:
2200 Research Blvd.
Rockville, MD 20850-3289
Phone: (301) 296-5700

Council for Learning Disabilities (CLD)
Go to: www.cldinternational.org or contact at:
PO Box 4014
Leesburg, VA 20177
Phone: (571) 258-1010

Division for Learning Disabilities
Go to: www.dldcec.org or contact at:

Council for Exceptional Children
1110 N. Glebe Road
Suite 300
Arlington, VA 22201-5704
Phone: (703) 620-3660
Phone (toll-free): (888) CEC-SPED
E-mail: cec@cec.sped.org

International Dyslexia Association
Go to: www.interdys.org or contact at:
8600 LaSalle Road
Chester Building
Suite 382
Baltimore, MD 21286-2044
Phone: (410) 296-0232
Phone (toll-free): (800) 222-3123
E-mail: info@interdys.org

Learning Disabilities Association of America (LDA)
Go to www.ldaamerica.org or contact at:
4156 Library Road
Pittsburgh, PA 15234
Phone: (412) 341-1515
E-mail: info@ldaamerica.org

National Institute for Literacy
Go to www.nifl.gov/nifl/hotline.html or www.literacydirect
ory.org or contact at:
1775 I Street, NW
Suite 730 Washington, DC 20006-2401
Phone (voice; toll-free): (800) 228-8813
Phone (TTY; toll-free): (877) 576-7734

National Literacy Trust Go to http://www.literacytrust.org.
uk/index.html or contact at: 68 South Lambeth Road
London SW8 1RL
England, UK

ProLiteracy Worldwide
Go to www.proliteracy.org or www.newreaderspress.com/
index_h.html or contact at:

1320 Jamesville Avenue
Syracuse, NY 13210
Phone: (315) 422-9121
Phone (toll-free): (888) 528-2224
E-mail: info@proliteracy.org

SELECT ORGANIZATIONS RELEVANT TO CAREGIVERS AND CAREGIVING

AARP Grandparent Information Center (AARP GIC)
Go to http://www.aarp.org/families/grandparents/gic/ or contact at:
601 E Street NW
Washington, DC 20049
Phone: (202) 434-2296
Phone (toll-free): (888) 687-2277
Fax: (202) 434-6474
E-mail: gic@aarp.org

Annie E. Casey Foundation
Go to http://www.aecf.org/ or contact at:
701 St. Paul Street
Baltimore, MD 21202
Phone: (410) 547-6600
Fax: (410) 547-6624
E-mail: webmail@aecf.org

Child Welfare League of America
Go to http://www.cwla.org/ or contact at:
2345 Crystal Drive
Suite 250
Arlington, VA 22202
Phone: (703) 412-2400
Fax: (703) 412-2401

National Center for Youth Law
Go to http://www.youthlaw.org/ or contact at:
405 14th St., 15th Floor
Oakland, CA 94612
(510) 835-8098

National Center on Fathers and Families
Go to http://www.ncoff.gse.upenn.edu or contact at:
3700 Walnut Street
Box 58
Philadelphia, PA 19104-6216
Phone: (215) 573-5500
Fax: (215) 573-5508

National Center on Women and Family Law, Inc
Go to http://www.nwlc.org/ or contact at:
National Women's Law Center
11 Dupont Circle, NW # 800
Washington, DC 20036
Phone: (202) 588-5180
Fax: (202) 588-5185
E-Mail: Info@nwlc.org

National Family Preservation Network
Go to http://www.nfpn.org/ or contact at:
3971 North 1400 East
Buhl, ID 83316
Phone (toll-free): (888) 498-9047 (Mountain Time Zone)
E-mail: director@nfpn.org

National Resource Center for Family-Centered Practice
and Permanency Planning
Go to http://www.hunter.cuny.edu/socwork/nrcfcpp/ or
contact at:
Hunter College School of Social Work
129 East 79th Street
New York, NY 10075
Phone: (212) 452-7053
Fax: (212) 452-7475

SELECT ORGANIZATIONS RELEVANT TO FOSTER, ADOPTIVE, GUARDIAN AND KINSCARE FAMILIES

American Foster Care Resources, Inc. (AFCR)
Go to http://www.afcr.com or contact at:
PO Box 271
King George, VA 22485
Phone: (540) 775-7410 Fax: (540) 775-3271
E-mail: afcr@afcr.com

Casey Family Programs
Go to http://www.casey.org/Home/ or contact at:
1300 Dexter Avenue North
Floor 3
Seattle, WA 98109-3542
Phone: (206) 282-7300
Fax: (206) 282-3555

Concerned United Birthparents, Inc. (CUB)
Go to: http://www.cubirthparents.org or contact at:
PO Box 230457
Encinitas, CA 92023
Phone (toll-free): (800) 822-2777
Fax: (760) 929-1879
E-mail: info@CUBirthparents.org

Families for Russian and Ukrainian Adoption (FRUA)
Go to: http://www.frua.org/ or contact at:
PO Box 2944
Merrifield, VA 22116 Phone: (703) 560-6184
Fax: (413) 480-8257
E-mail: info@frua.org

Foster Family-based Treatment Association
Go to http://www.ffta.org or contact at:
294 Union Street
Hackensack, NJ 07601
Phone: (800) 414-3382 (FFTA)
Fax: (201) 489-6719
E-mail: ffta@ffta.org

Foundation for Grandparenting
Go to http://www.grandparenting.org/ or contact at:
108 Farnham Road
Ojai, CA 93023
E-mail: gpfound@grandparenting.org

Grandparents Rights Organization (GRO)
Go to: http://www.grandparentsrights.org or contact at:
100 West Long Lake Road
Suite 250
Bloomfield Hills, MI 48304 Phone: (248) 646-7177
Fax: (248) 646-9722
E-mail: RSVLaw@aol.com

GrandsPlace—Grandparents and Special Others Raising Children
Go to: http://www.grandsplace.com or contact at:
154 Cottage Road
Enfield, CT 06082
Phone: (860) 763-5789
Fax: (860) 763-1568
E-mail: kathy@grandsplace.com

International Adoption Alliance (IAA)
Go to: http://www.i-a-a.org/ or contact at:
PMB 154
2441-Q Old Fort Parkway
Murfreesboro, TN 37128
E-mail: interadopt@comcast.net

National Adoption Center (NAC)
Go to: http://www.adopt.org or contact at:
1500 Walnut Street
Suite 701 Philadelphia, PA 19102
Phone: (215)735-9988
Phone (toll-free): (800) TO-ADOPT
Fax: (215) 735-9410
E-mail: nac@adopt.org

National Adoption Information Clearinghouse
Go to www.naic.acf.hhs.gov or contact at:
330 C Street, SW
Washington, DC 20447
Phone (toll-free): (888) 251-0075

National Council for Single Adoptive Parents (NCSAP)
Go to: http://www.ncsap.org or contact at:
PO Box 567
Mount Hermon, CA 95041
Phone (toll-free): (888) 490-4600
E-mail: info@ncsap.com

National Foster Care Association
Go to http://nfpaonline.org/ or contact at:
2313 Tacoma Avenue S
Tacoma, WA 98402 Phone: (800) 557-5238
Fax: (253) 683-4249
E-mail: info@nfpaonline.org

(Find individual state associations at http://nfpaonline.org/reploc/)

Preserving Families, Serving Children's Needs, and Building Our Shared Future: A Proposal for a National Program of Continuing Parent Education

Parenting is at once the most demanding and the most important job that any adult will ever encounter, and yet there exists no requisite training, certification, or licensure. In that better informed parents are likely to have better social, emotional, and intellectual resources with which to raise healthier children, a national program of continuing parenting education (CPE) will be established.

The benefits of continuing education have been proven time and again across many professions. CPE will function in very much the same way, with the goal of allowing parents to remain current not only with the evolving fields of child and family development, education, and behavior management, but with the evolving needs of their growing children.

The benefits of healthier families and children are manifold and beyond any immediate cost accounting. It will always require less time, energy, and money to foresee and forestall a problem than it is to react once the problem has emerged. Thus, a curriculum in child and family development will be established and a nationwide network of parenting educators will be emplaced.

As motivation, and in the interests of funding this expansive effort, each family's federal tax deduction for dependent children will be made contingent upon annual completion of a certified CPE program, such that one 1.5-hour course will be necessary for each child credit. The costs of curriculum development, conduct, and improvement of the program will be paid from those additional funds collected from families who choose not to or otherwise fail to complete the course annually.

A research component will be built into this program so as to document the child and family impacts of CPE. Measures of participant parenting efficacy; family stability; child physical, academic, and social functioning will be tracked and compared to a random sampling of matched, non-CPE comparison children and families. Results will be published in the mass media, used to formulate the continuing CPE curriculum, and to justify the program's continuation.

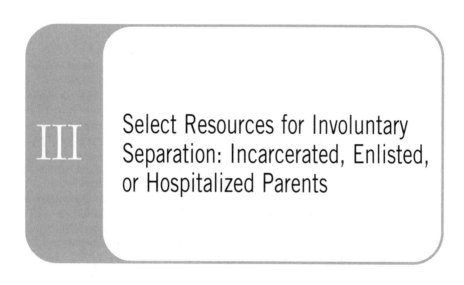

III

Select Resources for Involuntary Separation: Incarcerated, Enlisted, or Hospitalized Parents

PARENTAL INCARCERATION

Bakker, L. J., Morris, B. A., & Janus, L. M. (1978). Hidden victims of crime. *Social Work*, 23(2), 143–148.

Bates, R. (2001). *Improving outcomes for children and families of incarcerated parents.* Chicago: University of Illinois at Chicago, Jane Addams College of Social Work, Jane Addams Center for Social Policy and Research.

Baunach, P. (1985). *Mothers in prison.* New Brunswick, NJ: Transaction Books.

Bloom, B., & Steinhart, D. (1993). *Why punish the children? A reappraisal of the children of incarcerated mothers in America.* San Francisco: National Council on Crime and Delinquency.

Borgman, R. (1985). The influence of family visiting upon boys' behavior in a juvenile correctional institution. *Child Welfare, LXIV*(6), 629–638.

Carlson, B. E., & Cervera, N. (1991). Inmates and their families: Conjugal visits, family contact, and family functioning. *Criminal Justice and Behavior, 18*(3), 318–331.

Ferraro, K. J, Johnson, J. M., Jorgensen, S. R., & Bolton, F. G., Jr. (1983). Problems of prisoners' families: The hidden costs of imprisonment. *Journal of Family Issues, 4*(4), 575–591.

Hagan, J., & Coleman, J. P. (2001). Returning captives of the American war on drugs: Issues of community and family reentry. *Crime and Delinquency, 47*(3), 352–367.

Hairston, C. F. (1988). Family ties during imprisonment: Do they influence future criminal activity? *Federal Probation, LII*(1), 48–52.

Hairston, C. F. (1989). Men in prison: Family characteristics and parenting views. *Journal of Offender Counseling, Services and Rehabilitation, 14,* 3–30.

Hairston, C. F. (1991a). Family ties during imprisonment: Important to whom and for what? *Journal of Sociology and Social Welfare, XVIII*(1), 87–104.

Hairston, C. F. (1991b). Fathers in prison. *Journal of Sociology & Social Welfare, XVIII*(1), 31–40.

Hairston, C. F. (1991c). Mothers in jail: Parent-child separation and jail visitation. *Affilia, 6*(2), 9–27.

Hairston, C. F. (1992). Women in jail: Family needs and family supports. In *The state of corrections: Proceedings, ACA Annual Conference* (pp.179–184). Laurel, MD: American Correctional Association.

Hairston, C. F. (1995). Fathers in prison. In D. Johnston & K. Gables (Eds.), *Children of incarcerated parents* (pp. 31–40). Lexington, MA: Lexington Books.

Hairston, C. F. (1998). The forgotten parent: Understanding the forces that influence incarcerated fathers' relationships with their children. *Child Welfare, LXXVII*(5), 617–638.

Hairston, C. F. (2001). Fathers in prison: Responsible fatherhood and responsible public policies. *Marriage and Family Review, 32*(3–4), 111–135.

Hairston, C. F., Wills, S., & Wall, N. (1997). *Children, families, and correctional supervision: Current policies and new directions.* Chicago: University of Illinois at Chicago Press.

Hairston, C.F., & Addams, J. (2001). *Prisoners and families: Parenting during incarceration.* Paper presented at national policy conference, From Prison to Home: The Effect of Incarceration and Reentry on Children, Families, and Communities, University of Illinois at Chicago, January 30–31, 2002. Retrieved February 9, 2008, from http:// aspe.hhs.gov/HSP/prison2home02/Hairston.htm

Hungerford, G. P. (1993). *The children of inmate mothers: An exploratory study of children, caregivers and inmate mothers in Ohio.* Unpublished doctoral dissertation, Ohio State University, Columbus, OH.

Jeffries, J., Menghraj, S., & Hairston, C. F. (2001). *Serving incarcerated and ex-offender fathers and their families.* New York: Vera Institute of Justice.

Johnson, E. I., & Waldfogel, J. (2002). Children of incarcerated parents: Cumulative risk and children's living arrangements. Unpublished manuscript, Columbia University. Retrieved February 10, 2008, from http://www.jcpr.org/wpfiles/johnson_wald fogel.pdf

Johnson, E. I., & Waldfogel, J. (2003). Where children live when parents are incarcerated. *JCPR Policy Briefs, 2,* Northwestern University/University of Chicago.

Johnston, D. (2001, May). *Incarceration of women and effects on parenting.* Paper presented at Conference on the Effects of Incarceration on Children and Families, Northwestern University, Evanston, IL.

Koban, L. A. (1983). Parents in prison: A comparative analysis of the effects of incarceration on the families of men and women. *Research in Law, Deviance and Social Control, 5,* 171–183.

Koenig, C. (1985, January). *Life on the outside: A report on the experiences of the families of offenders from the perspective of the wives of offenders.* Canada, Pacific Region: Chilliwack Community Services and Correctional Service of Canada.

Lanier, C. S., Jr. (1991). Dimensions of father-child interaction in a New York state prison population. *Journal of Offender Rehabilitation, 16*(3/4), 27–42.

Lanier, C. S., Jr. (1993). Affective states of fathers in prison. *Justice Quarterly, 10*, 49–65.

Lynch, J. P., & Sabol, W. J. (2001, September). *Crime Policy Report: Vol. 3. Prisoner reentry in perspective.* Washington, DC: Urban Institute.

Martin, J. S. (2001). *Inside looking out: Jailed fathers' perceptions about separation from their children.* New York: LFB Scholarly Publishing.

Mumola, C. (2000, August). *Incarcerated parents and their children.* Washington, DC: U.S. Department of Justice.

Nurse, A. (2001). *Coming home to strangers: Newly paroled juvenile fathers and their children.* Paper presented at the Conference on the Effects of Incarceration on Children and Families, Northwestern University, Chicago, IL.

Poehlmann, J. (2005a). Children's family environments and intellectual outcomes during maternal incarceration. *Journal of Marriage and Family, 67*, 1275–1285.

Poehlmann, J. (2005b). Representations of attachment relationships in children of incarcerated mothers. *Child Development, 76*, 679–696.

Poehlmann, J. (2005c). Incarcerated mothers' contact with children, perceived family relationships and depressive symptoms. *Journal of Family Psychology, 19*(3), 350–357.

Poehlmann, J., Shafler, R., Maes, E., & Hanneman, A. (2008). Factors associated with young children's opportunities for maintaining family relationships during maternal incarceration. *Family Relations, 57*(3), 267–280.

Reed, D. F., & Reed, E. L. (1997). Children of incarcerated parents. *Social Justice, 24*(3), 152–169.

Schneller, D. P. (1976). *The prisoner's family: A study of the effects of imprisonment on the families of prisoners.* San Francisco: R&E Research Associates.

Sharp, S., & Marcus-Mendoza, S. (1998). *Gender differences in the impact of incarceration on children and spouses of drug offenders.* Paper presented at the annual meeting of the Academy of Criminal Justice Sciences, Albuquerque, NM.

Snyder-Joy, A., & Carlo, T. (1998). Parenting through prison walls: Incarcerated mothers and children's visitation programs. In S. Miller (Ed.,) *Crime, control and women: Feminist implications of criminal justice policy* (pp. 130–150). Thousand Oaks, CA: Sage.

Trzcinski, E., Satyanthan, D., & Ferro, L. (Eds.). (2002, March). *Michigan Family Impact Seminars: What about me? Children with incarcerated parents.* Detroit, MI: Wayne State University School of Social Work. Retrieved February 9, 2008, from http://fce.msu.edu/Family_Impact_Seminars/pdf/incarc.pdf

Wall, N. (1997). Policies affecting children whose parents are incarcerated. In *Dialogues on Child Welfare Issues Report.* Chicago: University of Illinois at Chicago Press.

ENLISTED PARENTS

Amen, D., Merves, E., Jellen, L., & Lee, R. (1988). Minimizing the impact of deployment separation on military children: Stages, current preventive efforts, and system recommendations. *Military Medicine, 153*, 441–446.

Boulding, E. (1950). Family adjustments to war separation and reunion. *Annals of the American Academy of Political and Social Science, 272*, 59–67.

Burrell, L. M. (2006). Moving military families: The impact of relocation on family well-being, employment, and commitment to the military. In C. A. Castro, A. B. Adler, & T. W. Britt (Eds.), *Military life: The psychology of serving in peace and combat* (Vol. 3; pp. 39–63). Westport, CT: Praeger Security International.

Duvall, E. (1945). Loneliness and the serviceman's wife. *Marriage and Family Living, 7,* 77–81.

Finkel, L. (2001). The effects of frequent geographic mobility on the social and emotional adjustment of military children and adolescents. *Dissertation Abstracts international: Section B: The Sciences & Engineering, 62,* 1573.

Finkel, L., Kelley, M., & Ashby, J. (2003). Geographic mobility, family, and maternal variables as related to the psychosocial adjustment of military children. *Military Medicine, 168,* 1019–1024.

Gibbs, D. A., Martin, S. L., Kupper, L. L., & Johnson, R. E. (2007). Child maltreatment in enlisted soldiers' families during combat-related deployments. *Journal of the American Medical Association, 298,* 528–535.

Graham-Weber, E. (2001). Impact of relocation on military adolescent school competence and behavior. *Dissertation Abstracts International: Section A: Humanities & Social Sciences, 62,* 1324.

Huebner, A. J., & Mancini, J. A. (2005). *Adjustments among adolescents in military families when a parent is deployed. Final report to the Military Family Research Institute and Department of Defense Quality of Life Office.* Blacksburg, VA: Department of Human Development, Virginia Polytechnic Institute and State University, http://www.unirel.vt.edu/news/Huebner_Mancini_teens_study.pdf

Jensen, P. S., Martin, D., & Watanabe, H. (1996). Children's response to separation during Operation Desert Storm. *Journal of the American Academy of Child and Adolescent Psychiatry, 35,* 433–441

Jensen, P., & Shaw, J. A. (1996). The effects of war and parental deployment upon children and adolescents. In R. J. Ursano & A. E. Norwood (Eds.), *Emotional aftermath of the Persian Gulf War: Veterans, families, communities, and nations* (pp. 83–109). Washington, DC: American Psychiatric Press.

Jensen, P., Lewis, R., & Xenakis, S. (1986). The military family in review: Context, risk, and prevention. *Journal of the American Academy of Child Psychiatry, 25,* 225–234.

Jensen, P., Martin, D., & Watanabe, H. (1996). Children's response to parental separation during Operation Desert Storm. *Journal of the American Academy of Child and Adolescent Psychiatry, 35,* 433–441.

Kelley, M. (1994a). Military-induced separation in relation to maternal adjustment and children's behaviors. *Military Psychology, 6,* 163–176.

Kelley, M. (1994b). The effects of military-induced separation on family factors and child behavior. *American Journal of Orthopsychiatry, 64,* 103–111.

Kelley, M. L., Hock, E., Smith, K. M., Jarvis, M. S., Bonney, J. F., & Gaffney, M. A. (2001). Internalizing and externalizing behavior of children with enlisted Navy mothers experiencing military-induced separation. *Journal of the American Academy of Child and Adolescent Psychiatry, 40,* 464–471.

Kelley, M., Simmer, P., & Harris, M. (1994). Effects of military-induced separation on the parenting stress and family functioning of deploying mothers. *Women in the Navy, 6,* 125–138.

LaGrone, D. (1978). The military family syndrome. *American Journal of Psychiatry, 135,* 1040–1043

Lamberg, L. (2004). When military parents are sent to war, children left behind need ample support. *Journal of the American Medical Association, 292,* 1541–1542.

Marchant, K., & Medway, F. (1987). Adjustment and achievement associated with mobility in military families. *Psychology in the Schools, 24,* 289–294.

McCarroll, J., Newby, J., Thayer, L., Ursano, R., Norwood, A., et al. (1999). Trends in child maltreatment in the U.S. Army, 1975–1997. *Child Abuse & Neglect, 23,* 855–861.

McCubbin, H., & Dahl, B. (1976). Prolonged family separation in the military: A longitudinal study. In H. McCubbin, B. Dahl, & E. Hunter (Eds.), *Families in the military system* (pp. 112–144). Beverly Hills, CA: Sage.

McKain, J. L. (1976). Alienation: A function of geographical mobility among families. In H. I. McCubbin, B. B. Dahl, & E. J. Hunter (Eds.), *Families in the military system* (pp. 69–91). Beverly Hills, CA: Sage.

Murray, J. (2002). Helping children cope with separation during war. *Journal for Specialists in Pediatric Nursing, 7,* 127–130.

Norwood, A. E., Fullerton, C. S., & Hagen, K. P. (1996). Those left behind: Military families. In R. J. Ursano & A. E. Norwood (Eds.), *Emotional aftermath of the Persian Gulf War: Veterans, families, communities, and nations* (pp. 163–197). Washington, DC: American Psychiatric Press

Peebles-Kleiger, M. J., & Kleiger, J. H. (1994). Re-integration stress for Desert Storm families: Wartime deployments and family trauma. *Journal of Traumatic Stress, 7,* 173–194.

Pincus, S. H., House, R., Christensen, J., & Adler, L. E. (2001). The emotional cycle of deployment: A military family perspective. *Journal of the Army Medical Department,* 615–623.

Rentz, E. D., Marshall, S. W., Loomis, D., Casteel, C., Martin, S. L., & Gibbs, D. A. (2007). Effect of deployment on the occurrence of child maltreatment in military and nonmilitary families. *American Journal of Epidemiology, 165,* 1199–1206.

Terr, L. (1992). Resolved: Military family life is hazardous to the mental health of children. *Journal of the American Academy of Child and Adolescent Psychiatry, 31,* 984–987.

Weber, E. G., & Weber, D. K. (2005). Geographic relocation frequency, resiliency, and military adolescent behavior. *Military Medicine, 170,* 638–642.

Wiens, T. W., & Boss, P. (2006). Maintaining family resiliency before, during, and after military separation. In C. A. Castro, A. B. Adler, & T. W. Britt (Eds.), *Military life: The psychology of serving in peace and combat* (Vol. 3; pp. 13–38). Westport, CT: Praeger Security International.

RESOURCES

The Military Child Education Coalition
Go to http://www.militarychild.org/ or contact at:

108 East FM 2410,
Suite D
PO Box 2519
Harker Heights, TX 76548-2519
Phone: (254) 953-1923 Fax: (254) 953-1925

Our Military Kids, Inc.
Go to http://www.ourmilitarykids.org/ or contact at:
6861 Elm Street
Suite 2-A
McLean, VA 22101
Monday–Friday, 9:00 a.m.–5:30 p.m. EST
Phone: (703) 734-6654
Phone (toll-free): (866) 691-6654 Fax: (703) 734-6503

National Military Family Association, Inc.
Go to http://www.nmfa.org/site/PageServer?pagename=homepage or contact at:
2500 North Van Dorn Street
Suite 102
Alexandria, VA 22302-1601
Phone: (703) 931-6632 (NMFA)
Phone (toll-free): (800) 260-0218 Fax: (703) 931-4600

Armed Forces Children's Education Fund, Inc.
Go to http://www.afcef.org/ or contact at:
PO Box 22524
Washington, DC 20026-4524
Phone: (858) 232-5719

The Military Homefront
Go to http://www.militaryhomefront.dod.mil/ or contact at:
Phone (toll-free): (800) 342-9647

U.S. Department of State Office of Children's Issues
Phone (toll-free): (888) 407-4747
Phone (from overseas): (202) 501-4444
E-Mail: AskCI@state.gov or AdoptionUSCA@state.gov

The Military Spouse
Go to http://www.milspouse.org/
Or subscribe at: AdoptionUSCA@state.gov

HOSPITALIZED PARENTS

Armistead, L., Klein, K., & Forehand, R. (1995). Parental physical illness and child
functioning. *Clinical Psychological Review, 15,* 409–422.

Armsden, G., & Lewis, F. M. (1993). The child's adaptation to parental medical illness: Theory and clinical implications. *Patient Education & Counseling, 22*, 153–165.

Bedway, A., & Smith, L. H. (1996). For kids only: Development of a program for children from families with a cancer patient. *Journal of Psychosocial Oncology, 14*, 19–28.

Birenbaum, L. K., Yancey, D. Z., Phillips, D. S., Chand, N., & Huster, G. (1999). School-age children's and adolescents' adjustment when a parent has cancer. *Oncology Nursing Forum, 26*, 1639–1645.

Compas, B. E., Worsham, N. L., Ey, S., & Howell, D. C. (1996). When mom or dad has cancer: II. Coping, cognitive appraisals, and psychological distress in children of cancer patients. *Health Psychology, 15*, 167–75.

Compas, B. E., Worsham, N. S., Grant, K. E., Mireault, G., Howell, D. C., Epping, J. E., & Malcarne, V. L. (1994). When mom or dad has cancer: Markers of psychological distress in cancer patients, spouses, and children. *Health Psycholology, 13*(6), 507–515.

Davey, M., Askew, J., & Godette, K. (2003). Parent and adolescent responses to non-terminal parental cancer: a retrospective multiple-case pilot study. *Family, Systems & Health, 21*, 245–258.

Dowdy, J. H., Kiev, C., Lathrop, D. L., & Winkle, M. (1997). Facilitating adjustment to catastrophic illness through involving children in age-appropriate education. *Journal of Rehabilitation, 63*, 22–25.

Downey, G., & Coyne, J. C. (1990). Children of depressed parents: an integrative review. *Psychological Bulletin, 108*, 50–76.

Drotar, D. (1994). Impact of parental health problems on children: concepts, methods and unanswered questions. *Journal of Pediatric Psychology, 19*, 525–536.

Edwards, B., & Clarke, V. (2004). The psychological impact of cancer diagnosis on families: The influence of family functioning and patients' illness characteristics on depression and anxiety. *Psycho-Oncology, 13*, 562–576.

Elizur, E., & Kaffman, M. (1983). Factors influencing the severity of childhood bereavement reactions. *American Journal of Orthopsychiatry, 53*, 668–76.

Faithful, J. (1997). HIV-positive and AIDS-infected women: Challenges and difficulties of mothering. *American Journal of Orthopsychiatry, 67*, 144–151.

Faulkner, R. A., & Davey, M. (2002). Children and adolescents of cancer patients: The impact of cancer on the family. *American Journal of Family Therapy, 30*, 63–72.

Goodman, S. H., & Gotlib, I. H. (1999). Risk for psychopathology in the children of depressed mothers: A developmental model for understanding mechanisms of transmission. *Psychological Review, 106*, 458–490.

Greening, K. (1992). The bear essentials' program: Helping children and their families cope when a parent has cancer. *Journal of Psychosocial Oncology, 10*, 47–61.

Hackl, K. L., Somlai, A. M., Kelly, J. A., & Kalichman, S. C. (1997). Women living with HIV/AIDS: The dual challenge of being a patient and caregiver. *Health & Social Work, 22*, 53–62.

Hoke, L. A. (2001). Psychosocial adjustment in children of mothers with breast cancer. *Psycho-Oncology, 10*, 361–369.

Howes, M. J., Hoke, L., Winterbottom, M., & Delafield, D. (1994). Psychosocial effects of breast cancer on the patient's children. *Journal of Psychosocial Oncology, 12*, 1–21.

Huizinga, G. A., Van der Graaf, W., Visser, A., Dijkstra, J. S., & Hoekstra-Weebers, J. (2003). Psychosocial consequences for children of a parent with cancer: A pilot study. *Cancer Nursing, 26,* 195–202.

Huizinga, G. A., Visser, A., Van der Graaf, W., Hoekstra, H. J., & Hoekstra-Weebers, J. E. H. M. (2005). The quality of communication between parents and adolescent children in the case of parental cancer. *Annals of Oncology, 16,* 1956–1961.

Issel, L. J., Ersek, M., & Lewis, F. M. (1990). How children cope with mother's breast cancer. *Oncology Nursing Forum, 17,* 5–13.

Lewis, F. M., Casey, S. M., Brandt, P. A., Shands, M. E., & Zahlis, E. H. (2006). The enhancing connections program: Pilot study of a cognitive-behavioral intervention for mothers and children affected by breast cancer. *Psycho-Oncology, 15,* 486–497.

Lewis, F. M., & Darby, E. L. (2003). Adolescent adjustment and maternal breast cancer: a test of the 'faucet hypothesis'. *Journal of Psychosocial Oncology, 21,* 81–104.

Lovejoy, M. C., Graczyk, P. A., O'Hare, E., & Neuman, G. (2000). Maternal depression and parenting behavior: A metaanalytic review. *Clinical Psychology Review, 20,* 561–592.

Niebuhr, V. N., Hughes, J. R., & Pollard, R. B. (1994). Parents with human immunodeficiency virus infection: Perceptions of their children's emotional needs. *Pediatrics, 93,* 421–426.

Rauch, P. K., & Muriel, A. C. (2005). *Raising an emotionally healthy child when a parent is sick.* Chicago: McGraw-Hill.

Rauch, P. K., Muriel, A. C., & Cassem, N. H. (2003). Parents with cancer: Who's looking after the children? *Journal of Clinical Oncology, 21,* 117s–121s.

Romer, G., Barkmann, C., Schulte-Markwort, M., Thomalla, G., & Riedesser, P. (2002). Children of somatically ill parents: A methodological review. *Clinical Child Psychology & Psychiatry, 7,* 17–38.

Siegel, K., Mesagno, F. P., Karus, D., Christ, G., Banks, K., & Moynihan, R. 1992). Psychosocial adjustment of children with a terminally ill parent. *Journal of the American Academy of Child & Adolescent Psychiatry, 31,* 327–333.

Sigal, J. J., Perry, C., Robbins, J. M., Gagne, M., & Nassif, E. (2003). Maternal preoccupation and parenting as predictors of emotional and behavioral problems in children of women with breast cancer. *Journal of Clinical Oncology, 21,* 1155–1160.

Visser, A., Huizinga, G. A., Hoekstra, H. J., Van der Graaf, W. T. A., Klip, E. C., Pras, E., et al. (2005). Emotional and behavioural functioning of children of a parent diagnosed with cancer: A cross-informant perspective. *Psycho-Oncology, 14,* 746–758.

Visser, A., Huizinga, G. A., van der Graaf, W., Hoekstra, H. J., & Hoekstra-Weebers, J. E. H. M. (2004). The impact of parental cancer on children and the family: A review of the literature. *Cancer Treatment Reviews, 30,* 683–694.

IV Mentoring Youth: Anchoring Kids Cast Adrift

SELECT REFERENCES

Ahrens, K. R., DuBois, D. L., Richardson, L. P., Fan, M. Y., & Lozano, P. (2008). Youth in foster care with adult mentors during adolescence have improved adult outcomes. *Pediatrics, 121*(2), e246–e252. DOI:10.1542/peds.2007-0508.

Britner, P. A., Balcazar, F. E., Blechman, E. A., Blinn-Pike, L., & Larose, S. (2006). Mentoring special youth populations. *Journal of Community Psychology, 34*(6), 747–763.

Courtney, M., & Dworsky, A. (2005). *Midwest evaluation of adult functioning of former foster youth: Outcomes at age 19.* Chicago: Chapin Hall Center for Children.

Courtney, M. E., Piliavin, I., Grogan-Kaylor, A., & Nesmith, A. (2001). Foster youth transitions to adulthood: A longitudinal view of youth leaving care. *Child Welfare, 80*(6), 685–717.

DuBois, D. L., Holloway, B. E., Valentine, J. C., & Cooper, H. (2002). Effectiveness of mentoring programs for youth: A meta-analytic review. *American Journal of Community Psychology, 30,* 157–197.

Dworsky, A. (2005). The economic self-sufficiency of Wisconsin's former foster youth. *Children and Youth Services Review, 27*(10), 1085–1118.

Geenen, S., & Powers, L. E. (2007). "Tomorrow is another problem": The experiences of youth in foster care during their transition to adulthood. *Children and Youth Services Review, 29,* 1085–1101.

Georgiades, S. D. (2005). Emancipated young adults' perspectives on independent living programs. *Families in Society, 86*(4), 503–510.

Greeson, J. K. P.; Bowen, N. K. (2008, October). "She holds my hand": The experiences of foster youth with their natural mentors. *Children and Youth Services Review, 30*(10), 1178–1188.

Iglehart, A. P., & Becerra, R. M. (2002). Hispanic and African American youth: Life after foster care emancipation. *Journal of Ethnic and Cultural Diversity in Social Work, 11*(1/2), 79–107.

Laursen, E. K., & Birmingham, S. M. (2003). Caring relationships as a protective factor for at-risk youth: An ethnographic study. *Families in Society, 84*(2), 240–246.

Mann-Feder, V. R., & White, T. (2003). Facilitating the transition from placement to independent living: Reactions from a program of research. *International Journal of Child & Family Welfare, 4*, 198–204.

McLearn, K.T., Colasanto, D., & Schoen, C. (1998). Mentoring matters: A national survey of adults mentoring young people. In J. B. Grossman (Ed.), *Contemporary issues in mentoring* (pp. 67–83). Philadelphia: Public/ Private Ventures.

Miller, C. (2006). *Mentoring teens: A resource guide.* North Charlestown, SC: Booksurge.

Osterling, K. L., & Hines, A. M. (2006). Mentoring adolescent foster youth: Promoting resilience during developmental transitions. *Child and Family Social Work, 11*, 242–253.

Philip, K., & Hendry, L. B. (2000). Making sense of mentoring or mentoring making sense? Reflections on the mentoring process by adult mentors with young people. *Journal of Community & Applied Social Psychology, 10*, 211–223.

Reilly, T. (2003). Transition from care: Status and outcomes of youth who age out of foster care. *Child Welfare, 82*(6), 727–746

Rhodes, J. (2004). *Stand by me: The risks and rewards of mentoring today's youth.* Boston: Harvard University Press.

Schulz, S. (1995). The benefits of mentoring. In M.W. Galbraith & N.H. Cohen (Eds), *Mentoring: New strategies and challenges, new directions for adult and continuing education* (vol. 66, 57–67). San Francisco: Jossey-Bass.

Spencer, R. (2006). Understanding the mentoring processes between adolescents and adults. *Youth & Society, 37*(3), 287–315.

SELECT RESOURCES

Big Brothers Big Sisters National Office
Go to http://www.bbbs.org or contact at:
230 North 13th Street
Philadelphia, PA 19107
Phone: (215) 567-7000 Fax: (215) 567-0394

MENTOR/National Mentoring Partnership
Go to http://www.mentoring.org/ or contact at:
1600 Duke Street, Suite 300
Alexandria, VA 22314
Phone: (703) 224-2200

V

On Compassion, Fatigue, Burnout, and Vicarious Traumatization

SELECT REFERENCES

Adams, R. E., Figley, C. R., & Boscarino, J. A. (2008). The Compassion Fatigue Scale: Its use with social workers following urban disaster. *Research on Social Work Practice, 18*(3), 238–250.

Baird, S., & Jenkins, S. R. (2003). Secondary traumatic stress and burnout in sexual assault and domestic violence staff. *Violence and Victims, 18*(1), 71–86.

Beevar, D. S. (2003). The impact on the family therapist of a focus on death, dying, and bereavement. *Journal of Marital and Family Therapy, 29*(4), 469–477.

Bertolino, B., & Thompson, K. (1999). *The residential youth care worker in action.* Binghampton, NY: Hawthorne Press.

Catherall, D. R. (1999). Coping with secondary traumatic stress: The importance of the therapist's professional peer group. In B. H. Stamm (Ed.), *Secondary traumatic stress: Self-care issues for clinicians, researchers, and educators* (2nd ed., pp. 80–92). Baltimore, MD: Sidran Press.

Eastwood, C. D., & Ecklund, K. (2008). Compassion fatigue risk and self-care practices among residential treatment center childcare workers. *Residential Treatment for Children & Youth, 25*(2), 103–122.

Figley, C. R. (1995a). Compassion fatigue as secondary traumatic stress disorder: An overview. In C. R. Figley (Ed.), *Compassion fatigue: Coping with secondary traumatic stress disorder in those who treat the traumatized* (pp. 1–20). New York: Brunner-Routledge.

Figley, C. R. (1995b). Epilogue: The transmission of trauma. In C. R. Figley (Ed.), *Compassion fatigue: Coping with secondary traumatic stress disorder in those who treat the traumatized* (pp. 249–254). New York: Brunner-Routledge.

Figley, C. R. (1998a). Introduction. In C. R. Figley (Ed.), *Burnout in families: The systemic costs of caring* (pp. 1–13). Boca Raton, FL: CRC Press.

Figley, C. R. (1998b). Burnout as systemic traumatic stress. In C. R. Figley (Ed.), *Burnout in families: The systemic costs of caring* (pp. 15–28). Boca Raton, FL: CRC Press.

Figley, C. R. (1999). Compassion fatigue: Toward a new understanding of the costs of caring. In B. H. Stamm (Ed.), *Secondary traumatic stress: Self-care issues for clinicians, researchers, and educators* (2nd ed., pp. 3–28). Baltimore, MD: Sidran Press.

Figley, C. R. (2002a). Introduction. In C. R. Figley (Ed.), *Treating compassion fatigue* (pp. 1–14). New York: Brunner-Routledge.

Figley, C. R. (2002b). Compassion fatigue: Psychotherapist's chronic lack of self care. *Journal of Clinical Psychology In Session: Psychotherapy in Practice, 58*(11), 1433–1441.

Harris, D. J., Kirschner, C. L., Rozek, K. K., & Weiner, N. A. (2001). Violence in the judicial workplace: One state's experience. *Annals of the American Academy of Political and Social Science, 576,* 38–53.

Inbar, J., & Ganor, M. (2003). Trauma and compassion fatigue: Helping the helpers. *Journal of Jewish Communal Service, 79*(2), 109–111.

Johnson, M., & Stone, G. L. (1987). Social workers and burnout: A psychological description. In D. F. Gillespie (Ed.), *Burnout among social workers* (pp. 67–80). New York: Haworth Press.

Joinson, C. (1992). Coping with compassion fatigue. *Nursing, 22,* 116–122.

Kanter, J. (2007). Compassion fatigue and secondary traumatization: A second look. *Clinical Social Work Journal, 35*(4), 289–293.

Maslach, C. (1982). Understanding burnout: Definitional issues in analyzing a complex phenomenon. In W. S. Paine (Ed.), *Job stress and burnout: Research, theory and intervention perspectives* (pp. 29–40). Beverly Hills, CA: Sage.

Maslach, C., Jackson, S. E., & Leiter, M. P. (1997). Maslach Burnout Inventory. In C.P. Zalaquett & R.J. Wood (Eds.), *Evaluating stress* (pp. 191–218). San Francisco, CA: Jossey-Bass.

Maslach, C., & Leiter, M. P. (1997). *The truth about burnout.* San Francisco: Jossey-Bass.

McCann, L., & Pearlman, L. A. (1990). Vicarious traumatization: A framework for understanding the psychological effects of working with victims. *Journal of Traumatic Stress, 3,* 131–149.

O'Halloran, M. S., & O'Halloran, T. (2001). Secondary traumatic stress in the classroom: Ameliorating stress in graduate students. *Teaching of Psychology, 28*(2), 92–97.

Pearlman, L. A., & Mac Ian, P. S. (1995). Vicarious traumatization: An empirical study of the effects of trauma work on trauma therapists. *Professional Psychology: Research and Practice, 25,* 558–563.

Pines, A., & Aronson, E. (1988). *Career burnout: Causes and cures.* New York: Free Press.

Rasmussen, B. (2005). An intersubjective perspective on vicarious trauma and its impact on the clinical process. *Journal of Social Work Practice, 19,* 19–30.

Roberts, S. B., Ellers, K. L., & Wilson, J. C. (2008). Compassion fatigue. In S. B. Roberts & W. W. C. Ashley, Sr. (Eds.), *Disaster spiritual care: Practical clergy responses to community, regional and national tragedy* (pp. 209–226). Woodstock, VT: SkyLight Paths Publishing.

Rothschild, B., & Rand, M. L. (2006). *Help for the helper: The psychophysiology of compassion fatigue and vicarious trauma.* New York: Norton.

Salston, M., & Figley, C. R. (2003). Secondary traumatic stress effects of working with survivors of criminal victimization. *Journal of Traumatic Stress, 16,* 167–174.

Trippany, R. L., White Kress, V. E., & Wilcoxon, S. A. (2004). Preventing vicarious trauma: What counselors should know when working with trauma survivors. *Journal of Counseling and Development, 82,* 31–37.

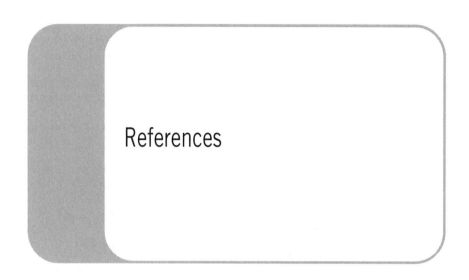

References

Aaronson, J. (2007). *Overnight placement for infants and toddlers: Attachment-oriented guidance for professionals counseling high conflict separated parents.* Retrieved March 1, 2009, from http://divorce-conflict-solutions.com/papers/Overnight_Placement.doc

Abikoff, H. B., Vitiello, B., Riddle, M. A., Cunningham, C., Greenhill, L. L., Swanson, J. M., et al. (2007). Methylphenidate effects on functional outcome in preschoolers with attention-deficit/ hyperactivity disorder: Results from the National Institute of Mental Preschoolers with Attention Deficit/Hyperactivity Disorder Treatment Study (PATS). *Journal of Child Adolescent Psychopharmacology, 17*, 581–592.

Achenbach, T. M., & Edelbrock, C. S. (1979). The Child Behavior Profile: II. Boys aged 12–16 and girls aged 6–11 and 12–16. *Journal of Consulting and Clinical Psychology, 47*, 223–233.

Ackerman, M. (2005). The Ackerman-Schoendorf Scales for Parent Evaluation of Custody (ASPECT): A review of research and update. *Journal of Child Custody, 2*(1/2), 179–193.

Ackerman, M. (2006). *Clinician's guide to child custody evaluations, 2006 edition.* Hoboken, NJ: John Wiley.

Adams, S. A., & Riggs, S. A. (2008). An exploratory study of vicarious trauma among therapist trainees. *Training and Education in Professional Psychology, 2*, 26–34.

Afifi, T. O. (2007). Child abuse and adolescent parenting: Developing a theoretical model from an ecological perspective. *Journal of Aggression, Maltreatment & Trauma, 14*(3), 89–105.

Ahrens, K. R., DuBois, D. L., Richardson, L. P., Fan, M. Y., & Lozano, P. (2008). Youth in foster care with adult mentors during adolescence have improved adult outcomes. *Pediatrics, 121*(2), e246–e252. DOI:10.1542/peds.2007-0508.

325

Ainsworth, M., & Wittig, B. (1969). Attachment and exploratory behavior of one-year-olds in a strange situation. In B. Foss (Ed.), *Determinants of infant behavior: Vol. 4* (pp. 111–136). London: Methuen.

Ainsworth, M. D. S., & Bell, S. M. (1970). Attachment, exploration, and separation: Illustrated by the behavior of one-year-olds in a strange situation. *Child Development, 41,* 49–67.

Ainsworth, M. D. S., Bell, S. M. V., & Stayton, D. J. (1971). Individual differences in strange-situation behavior of one-year-olds. In H. R. Schaffer (Ed.), *The origins of human social relations.* London: Academic Press.

Alexander, F., & Strang, R. (1953). From adolescence to adulthood. In J. M. Seidman, (Ed.), *The adolescent: A book of readings* (pp. 754–768). Fort Worth, TX: Dryden Press.

Almeida, D. M., & Galambos, N. L. (1991). Examining father involvement and father–adolescent relations. *Journal of Research on Adolescence, 1,* 155–172.

Altobelli, T. (2005). Rethinking contact arrangements involving young children. *Australian Journal of Family Law, 19,* 29–43.

Altobelli, T. (2008). *Hot topics in kids' matters. New South Wales Young Lawyers Family Law Seminar,* Sydney, Australia. Retrieved January 30, 2009, from http://www.famil lawwebguide.com.au/attachment.php?id=1097&keep_s ession=710713419

Amato, P. (2001). Children of divorce in the 1990s: An update of the Amato and Keith (1991) meta-analysis. *Journal of Family Psychology, 15*(3), 355–370.

Ambert, A. (2001). *The effects of children on parents* (2nd ed.). New York: Haworth Press.

American Academy of Child and Adolescent Psychiatry. (1999). *Practice parameters for the assessment and treatment of children, adolescents, and adults with mental retardation and comorbid mental disorders.* Retrieved December 30, 2008, from http://www.aacap.org/galleries/PracticeParameters/Mr.pdf

American Academy of Pediatrics. (2000). *Premature babies: Special health issues.* Retrieved November 8, 2008, from http://www.medem.com/MedLB/article_detail lb.cfm?article_ID=ZZZ27U H3R7C&sub_cat=26

American Academy of Pediatrics. (2005). Policy statement: Breastfeeding and the use of human milk. *Pediatrics, 115*(2), 496–506. Retrieved February 2, 2009, from http://aappolicy.aappublications.org/cgi/reprint/pediatrics;115/2 /496.pdf

American Bar Association. (2001). *Model standards of practice for family and divorce mediation.* Retrieved March 14, 2009, from http://www.abanet.org/family/reports/mediation.pdf

American Bar Association. (2002a). *ABA Judicial Division Judges Network survey report.* Retrieved March 15, 2009, from http://www.abanet.org/jd/judicialoutreachnetwork/pdf/surveyreport august2002.pdf

American Bar Association. (2002b). *Public perceptions of lawyers: Consumer research findings.* Retrieved March 12, 2009, from http://www.abanet.org/litigation/lawyers/publicperceptions.pdf

American Bar Association. (2003). *Teach your students well: Incorporating domestic violence into law school curricula.* Retrieved March 14 2009, from http://www.abanet.org/domviol/teach_students.pdf

American Bar Association. (2008a). Family law in the fifty states: Case digests. *Family Law Quarterly, 41,* 710.

American Bar Association. (2008b). *Improving civil mediation: Recommended considerations for civil mediators in private practice.* Retrieved March 15, 2009, from http:// meetings.abanet.org/webupload/commupload/DR020600/sitesofi nterest_files/medi atorspamphletweb.pdf

American Psychiatric Association. (1994). *Diagnostic and statistical manual of mental disorders* (4th ed.). Washington, DC: American Psychiatric Association.

American Psychological Association. (1994). Guidelines for child custody evaluations in divorce proceedings. *American Psychologist, 49*(7), 677–680.

American Psychological Association. (2002). *Ethical principles of psychologists and code of conduct.* Retrieved November 8, 2008, from http://www.apa.org/ethics/ code2002.html

American Psychological Association. (2005). *Statement on parental alienation syndrome.* Retrieved March 9, 2009, from http://www.apa.org/releases/passyndrome.html

American Psychological Association. (2009). *Guidelines for child custody evaluations in family law proceedings.* Retrieved April 11, 2009, from http://www.apa.org/practice/ guidelines-evaluation-child-custody-family-law.pdf

Andre, K. (2004, winter). The parental alienation syndrome. *Annals of Psychotherapy.* Retrieved March 8, 2009, from http://parentalalienationsolutions.com/PDF/parental AlienationSynd rome.pdf

Andreasen, N. C., Calage, C. A., & O'Leary, D. S. (2008). Theory of mind and schizophrenia: A positron emission tomography study of medication-free patients. *Schizophrenia Bulletin, 34*(4), 708–719.

Anthony, E., & Cohler, B. (Eds.). (1987). *The invulnerable child.* New York: Guilford.

Antle, B. J., Wells, L. M., Goldie, R. S., DeMatteo, D., & King, S. M. (2001). Challenges of parenting for families living with HIV/AIDS. *Social Work, 46*(2), 159–169.

Archer, J. (2008). Theories of grief: Past, present, and future perspectives. In M. S. Stroebe, R. O. Hansson, H. Schut, W. Stroebe, & E. Van den Blink (Eds.), *Handbook of bereavement research and practice: Advances in theory and intervention* (pp. 45–65). Washington, DC: American Psychological Association.

Archer, R. P. (Ed.). (2006). *Forensic uses of clinical assessment instruments.* Mahwah, NJ: Lawrence Erlbaum.

Ari, M., Bal, S., Tugrul, B., Uzmen, S., & Ydogan, S. A. (2000). Helping six-year-old kindergarten children to acquire the concept of conservation through training. *Hacettepe Üniversitesi E?itim Fakültesi Dergisi, 18,* 17–25.

Arlin, P. K. (1975). Cognitive development in adulthood: A fifth stage? *Developmental Psychology 11,* 602–606.

Arlin, P. K. (1982). A multitrait-multimethod validity study of a test of formal reasoning. *Educational and Psychological Measurement, 42,* 1077–1088.

Arlin, P. K. (1989). Problem solving and problem finding in young artists and young scientists. In M. L. Commons, J. D. Sinnot, F. A. Richards, & C.Armon (Eds.), *Adult development: Vol. 1: Comparisons and applications of developmental models.* New York: Praeger Press.

Armsden, G. C., & Lewis, F. M. (1993). The child's adaptation to parental medical illness: Theory and clinical implications. *Patient Education & Counseling, 22,* 153–165.

Arnett, J. J. (2000). Emerging adulthood: A theory of development from the late teens through the twenties. *American Psychologist, 55,* 469–480.

Arnold, E. (2006). Separation and loss through immigration of African Caribbean women to the UK. *Attachment & Human Development, 8*(2), 159–174.

Artis, J. E. (2004). Judging the best interests of the child: Judges accounts of the Tender Years Doctrine. *Law and Society Review, 38*(4), 769–806.

Asberg, K. K., Bowers, C., Renk, K., & McKinney, C. (2008). A structural equation modeling approach to the study of stress and psychological adjustment in emerging adults. *Child Psychiatry & Human Development, 39*(4), 481–501.

Association of Family and Conciliation Courts. (2006). Guidelines for parenting coordination. *Family Court Review, 44,* 164–181.

Aunos, M., & Feldman, M. B. (2007). Parenting by people with intellectual disabilities. In I. Brown & M. Percy (Eds.), *A comprehensive guide to intellectual and developmental disabilities.* Baltimore, MD: Paul H. Brookes Publishing.

Austin, W. G. (2000a). A forensic psychology model of risk assessment for child custody relocation law. *Family and Conciliation Courts Review, 38,* 192–204.

Austin, W. G. (2000b). Relocation law and the threshold of harm: Integrating legal and behavioral perspectives. *Family Law Quarterly, 34,* 63–82.

Austin, W. G. (2000c). Risk reduction interventions in the child custody relocation case. *Journal of Divorce and Remarriage, 33,* 65–73.

Austin, W. G. (2005). The child and family investigator's evaluation of the relocation case. In R. M. Smith (Ed.), *The role of the child and family investigator and the child's legal representative in Colorado* (pp. C9-1–C9-28). Denver, CO: Colorado Bar Association.

Austin, W. G. (2008a). Relocation, research, and forensic evaluation: Part I: Effects of residential mobility on children of divorce. *Family Court Review, 46*(1), 137–150.

Austin, W. G. (2008b). Relocation, research, and forensic evaluation: Part II: Research in support of the relocation risk assessment model. *Family Court Review, 46*(2), 347–365.

Australia Family Law Council. (2004). *Pathways for children: A review of children's representation in family law.* Retrieved January 24, 2009, from http://agsearch.ag. gov.au/search/agd;jsessionid=94076E4FD7061D3504B01870A29542EC?query=% 22mature+minor%22&new=1

Awad, G. A., & Parry, R. (1980). Access following marital separation. *Canadian Journal of Psychiatry, 25,* 357–364.

Babb, B. (1997). An interdisciplinary approach to family law jurisprudence: Application of an ecological and therapeutic perspective. *Indiana Law Journal, 72,* 775–808.

Badeau, S. H. (2004). Five commentaries: Looking to the future. *Future of Children, 14*(1),175–189.

Bagby, R. M., Nicholson, R. A., Buis, T., Radovanovic, H., & Fidler, B. J. (1999). Defensive responding on the MMPI-2 in family custody and access evaluations. *Psychological Assessment, 11,* 24–28.

Baillargeon, R. (1987). Object permanence in 3 1/2 and 4 1/2 month old infants. *Developmental Psychology, 23,* 655–664.

Baillieu, N., & Potterton J. (2008).The extent of delay of language, motor, and cognitive development in HIV-positive infants. *Journal of Neurology and Physical Therapy, 32*(3), 118–121.

Baird, A. A. (2008). Adolescent moral reasoning: The integration of emotion and cognition. In W. Sinnott-Armstrong (Ed.), *Moral psychology: Vol 3: The neuroscience of morality: Emotion, brain disorders, and development* (pp. 323–342). Cambridge, MA: MIT Press.

Baker, A. J. L. (2007). *Adult children of parental alienation syndrome: Breaking the ties that bind*. New York: W.W. Norton.

Bakersman-Kranenburg, M. J., Breddels-van Baardewijk, P., Juffer, F., Velderman, M. K., & van IJzendoorn, M. H. (2008). Insecure mothers with temperamentally reactive infants: A chance for intervention. In F. Juffer, M. J. Bakersman-Kranenburg, & M. H. van IJzendoorn (Eds.), *Promoting positive parenting: An attachment-based intervention.* (pp. 75–90). New York: Taylor & Francis Group/Lawrence Erlbaum.

Barnett, D., Butler, C., & Vondra, J. (1999). Atypical attachment in infancy and early childhood among children at developmental risk. VII. Atypical patterns of early attachment: Discussion and future directions. *Monograph of the Society for Research in Child Development, 64*(3), 172–209.

Baron-Cohen, S., Leslie, A. M., & Frith, U. (1985). Does the autistic child have a "theory of mind"? *Cognition, 21,* 37–46.

Barone, N. M., Weitz, E. I., & Witt, P. H. (2005). Psychological bonding evaluations in termination of parental rights cases. *Journal of Psychiatry & Law, 33,* 387–412.

Barth, R. P., Crea, T. M., John, K., Thoburn, J., & Quinton, D. (2005). Beyond attachment theory and therapy: Towards sensitive and evidence-based interventions with foster and adoptive families in distress. *Child & Family Social Work, 10*(4), 257–268.

Bartlett, K. (2002). U.S. custody law and trends in the context of the ALI principles of the Law of Family Dissolution. *Virginia Journal of Social Policy and the Law, 10,* 5–53.

Baute, P. (2008). *The role of the psychologist or other scientists in expert witnesses. Falsifiability: A paradigm shift in what is admissible.* Retrieved November 9, 2008, from http://www.paschalbaute.com/index.cfm?fuseaction=articles.roleofpysch

Bayley, N. (2006). *Bayley Scales of Infant and Toddler Development technical manual* (3rd ed.). San Antonio, TX: Psychological Corporation.

Bean, K. S. (2009). Aggravated circumstances, reasonable efforts, and ASFA. *Boston College Third World Law Journal.* Posted December 7, 2008. Retrieved February 15, 2009, from http://papers.ssrn.com/sol3/papers.cfm?abstract_id=1312042

Beaudry, M., Simard, M., Drapeau, S., & Charbonneau, C. (2000). What happens to the sibling subsystem following parental divorce? In C. Violato, E. Oddone-Paolucci, & M. Genuis (Eds.), *The changing family and child development* (pp. 105–116). Aldershot, England: Ashgate.

Behen, M. E., Helder, E., Rothermel, R., Solomon, K., & Chugani, H. T. (2008). Incidence of specific absolute neurocognitive impairment in globally intact children with histories of early severe deprivation. *Child Neuropsychology, 14*(5), 453–469.

Bekhit, N. S., Thomas, G. V., & Jolley, R. P. (2005). The use of drawing for psychological assessment in Britain: Survey findings. *Psychology and Psychotherapy: Theory, Research and Practice, 78*(2), 205–217.

Bell, S. M. (1970). The development of the concept of the object as related to infant-mother attachment. *Child Development, 41,* 291–311.

Bellamy, J. L. (2008). Behavioral problems following reunification of children in long-term foster care. *Children and Youth Services Review, 30*(2), 216–228.

Belmonte, M. K., Allen, G., Beckel-Mitchener, A., Boulanger, L. M., Carper, R. A., & Webb, S. J. (2004). Autism and abnormal development of brain connectivity. *Journal of Neuroscience, 24*(42), 9228–9231.

Belsky, J. (1984). The determinants of parenting. *Child Development, 55*, 83–96.

Benjamin, G. A. H., & Gollan, J. K. (2003). *Family evaluation in custody litigation: Reducing risks of ethical infractions and malpractice.* Washington, DC: American Psychological Association.

Benjamin, G.A.H., Gollan, J., & Ally, G. A. (2007). Family evaluation in custody litigation: Reducing risks of ethical infractions and malpractice. Journal of Forensic Psychology Practice, 7, 101–111.

Bennett, D. S., Bendersky, M., & Lewis, M. (2008). Children's cognitive ability from 4 to 9 years old as a function of prenatal cocaine exposure, environmental risk, and maternal verbal intelligence. *Developmental Psychology, 44*(4), 919–928.

Bénony, C., Golse, B., Larome, A., & Bénony, H. (2004). Amyotrophie spinale infantile de type II et compétences langagiéres. À propos de Julie, 27 mois. (Type II Spinal Muscular Atrophy and language skills). *Annales Médico-Psychologiques, 162*(2), 134–139.

Ben-Porath, Y. S., Graham, J. R., Hall, G. C. N., Hirschman, R. D., & Zaragoza, M. S. (Eds.). (1995). *Forensic applications of the MMPI-2.* Thousand Oaks, CA: Sage.

Berger, M. A. (2000). The Supreme Court's trilogy on the admissibility of expert evidence. In *Reference manual on scientific evidence* (2nd ed., pp. 9–38). Washington, DC: Federal Judicial Center.

Berk, L. E., Mann, T. D., & Ogan, A. T. (2006). Make-believe play: Wellspring for the development of self-regulation. In D. G. Singer, R. Golinkoff, & K. Hirsh-Pasek (Eds.), *Play = learning: How play motivates and enhances children's cognitive and social-emotional growth* (pp. 74 –100). New York: Oxford University Press. Retrieved January 4, 2009, from http://udel.edu/~roberta/play/BerkMannOgan.pdf

Berk, S. B. (2004). Sensitive period effects on the acquisition of language: A study of language development (January 1, 2003). *ETD Collection for University of Connecticut.* Paper AAI3118939. Retrieved June 13, 2009, from http://digitalcommons.uconn.edu/dissertations/AAI3118939

Bernabei, P., Cerquiglini, A., Cortesi, F., & D'Ardia, C. (2007). Regression versus no regression in the autistic disorder: Developmental trajectories. *Journal of Autism and Developmental Disorders, 37*(3), 580–588.

Bernazzani, O., Marks, M. N., Bifulco, A., Siddle, K., Asten, P., & Conroy, S. (2005). Assessing psychosocial risk in pregnant/postpartum women using the Contextual Assessment of Maternity Experience (CAME): Recent life adversity, social support and maternal feelings. *Social Psychiatry and Psychiatric Epidemiology, 40*(6), 497–508.

Bernstein, D. (2002). Disinterested in *Daubert*: State courts lag behind in opposing "junk" science. *Washington Legal Foundation, 12*(14). Retrieved November 10, 2008, from http://www.wlf.org/upload/6-21-02Bernstein.pdf

Bernthal, J. E., Bankson, N. W., & Flipsen, P. (2008). *Articulation and phonological disorders.* New York: Allyn & Bacon.

Beyers, W., & Goossens, L. (2008). Dynamics of perceived parenting and identity formation in late adolescence. *Journal of Adolescence, 31*(2), 165–184.

Bibace, R., & Walsh, M. E. (1979). The development of conceptions of illness. In G. Stone, N. Adler, & F. Cohen (Eds.), *Health psychology*. San Francisco: Jossey-Bass.

Bick, J., & Dozier, M. (2008). The role of parent state of mind in an intervention for foster parents. In H. Steele & M. Steele (Eds.), *The Adult Attachment Interview in clinical context*. New York: Guilford

Biehl, M. C., Natsuaki, M. N., & Ge, X. J. (2007). The influence of pubertal timing on alcohol use and heavy drinking trajectories. *Journal of Youth and Adolescence, 36,* 153–167.

Binkard, B. (1987). *Brothers & sisters talk with PACER*. Minneapolis, MN: Parent Advocacy Coalition for Educational Rights (PACER) Center. (Available from PACER Center, Inc., 4826 Chicago Ave., South, Minneapolis, MN 55417.)

Birditt, K. S., Fingerman, K. L., Lefkowitz, E. S., & Dush, C. M. K. (2008). Parents perceived as peers: Filial maturity in adulthood. *Journal of Adult Development, 15*(1), 1–12.

Birenbaum, L. K., Yancey, D. Z., Phillips, D. S., Chand, N., & Huster, G. (1999). School-age children's and adolescents' adjustment when a parent has cancer. *Oncology Nursing Forum 26,* 1639–1645.

Biringen, Z., Greve, J., Howard, W., Leith, D., Tanner, L., Moore, S., et al. (2002). Commentary on Warshak's "Blanket restrictions: Over-night contact between parents and young children." *Family Court Review, 40,* 204–207.

Birnbaum, R., & Alaggia, R. (2006). Supervised visitation: A call for a second generation of research. *Family Court Review, 44*(1), 119–134.

Bishop, B. & Cushing, R. G. (2008). *The big sort: Why the clustering of like-minded America is tearing us apart*. New York: Houghton Mifflin Harcourt.

Bishop, D. V. M., & Leonard, L. B. (2000). Speech and language impairments in children: Causes, characteristics, intervention and outcome. New York: Psychology Press.

Bishop, J. A., & Inderbitzen, H. M. (1995). Peer acceptance and friendship: An investigation of their relation to self-esteem. *Journal of Early Adolescence, 15,* 476–489.

Bishop, S., Gahagan, S., & Lord, C. (2007). Re-examining the core features of autism: A comparison of autism spectrum disorder and fetal alcohol spectrum disorder. *Journal of Child Psychology and Psychiatry, 48*(11), 1111–1121.

Black, A. E. (2006). The separation and reunification of recently immigrated Mexican families. *Dissertation Abstracts International: Section B: The Sciences and Engineering, 66* (11-B).

Black, M. M., Bentley, M. E., Papas, M. A., Oberlander, S., Teti, L. O., McNary, S., et al. (2006). Delaying second births among adolescent mothers: A randomized, controlled trial of a home-based mentoring program. *Pediatrics, 118,* e1087–e1099.

Blenkner, M. (1965). Social work and family relationships in later life with some thought on filial maturity. In E. Shanas & G. Streib (Eds.), *Social structure and the family: Generational relations*. Englewood Cliffs, NJ: Prentice Hall.

Blood, L. (2008). The use of the MCMI-III in completing parenting capacity assessments. *Journal of Forensic Psychology Practice, 8*(1), 24–38.

Boden, J. M., Horwood, L. J., & Fergusson, D. M. (2007). Exposure to childhood sexual and physical abuse and subsequent educational achievement outcomes. *Child Abuse & Neglect, 31*(10), 1101–1114.

Bogacki, D. F., & Weiss, K. J. (2007). Termination of parental rights: Focus on defendants. *Journal of Psychiatry & Law, 35*(1), 25–45.

Bolton, F., & Laner, R. (1981). Maternal maturity and maltreatment. *Journal of Family Issues, 2*, 485–508.

Bone, J. M., & Walsh, M. R. (1999). Parental alienation syndrome: How to detect it and what to do about it. *Florida Bar Journal, 73*, 44–48. Retrieved November 17, 2008, from www.fact.on.ca/Info/pas/walsh99.htm

Borke, H. (1975). Piaget's mountain revisited: Changes in the egocentric landscape. *Developmental Psychology, 11*, 240–244.

Borke, J., Lamm, B., Eickhorst, A., & Keller, H. (2007). Father–infant interaction, paternal ideas about early child care, and their consequences for the development of children's self-recognition. *Journal of Genetic Psychology, 168*(4), 365–379.

Borkowski, J. G., Farris, J. R., & Weed, K. (2007). Toward resilience: Designing effective prevention programs. In J. G. Borkowski, J. R. Farris, T. L. Whitman, S. S. Carothers, K. Weed, & D. A. Keogh (Eds.), *Risk and resilience: Adolescent mothers and their children grow up* (pp. 259–278). Mahwah, NJ: Lawrence Erlbaum.

Bornstein, M. H., Gini, M., Suwalsky, J., Putnick, D. L., & Haynes, O. M. (2006). Emotional availability in mother-child dyads: Short-term stability and continuity from variable-centered and person-centered perspectives. *Merrill-Palmer Quarterly, 52*, 547–571.

Bornstein, M. H., Leach, D. B., & Haynes, O. M. (2004). Vocabulary competence in first- and secondborn siblings of the same chronological age. *Journal of Child Language, 31*(4), 855–873.

Bornstein, M. H., Putnick, D. L., Heslington, M., Gini, Suwalsky, J. T. D., Venuti, P., et al. (2008). Mother–child emotional availability in ecological perspective: Three countries, two regions, two genders. *Developmental Psychology, 44*(3), 666–680.

Boss, P. (2002). *Family stress management.* Newbury Park, CA: Sage.

Boss, P., & Greenberg, J. (1984). Family boundary ambiguity: A new variable in family stress theory. *Family Process, 23*, 535–546.

Bow, J. N., Flens, J. R., Gould, J. W., & Greenhut, D. (2006). An analysis of administration, scoring, and interpretation of the MMPI-2 and MCMI-II/III in child custody evaluations. *Journal of Child Custody, 2*(4), 1–22.

Bow, J. N., Gould, J. W., Flens, J. R., & Greenhut, D. (2006). Testing in child custody evaluations: Selection, usage, and *Daubert* admissibility: A survey of psychologists. *Journal of Forensic Psychology Practice, 6*, 17–38.

Bow, J. N., & Quinnell, F. A. (2001). Psychologists' current practices and procedures in child custody evaluations 5 years after American Psychological Association guidelines. *Professional Psychology: Research and Practice, 32*, 261–268.

Bowen, C. (1998). *Typical speech development: the gradual acquisition of the speech sound system.* Retrieved November 30, 2008, from http://www.speech-language-therapy.com/acquisition.html

Bowlby, J. (1958). The nature of the child's tie to his mother. *International Journal of Psychoanalysis, 39*, 350–373.

Bowlby, J. (1969). *Attachment and loss: Vol. 1. Attachment.* New York: Basic Books.

Bowlby, J. (1973). *Attachment and loss: Vol. 2. Separation.* New York: Basic Books.

Bradbrook, A. J. (1971). The role of judicial discretion in child custody adjudication in Toronto. *University of Toronto Law Journal, 21,* 402–408.

Bradmetz, J., & Schneider, R. (1999). Is Little Red Riding Hood afraid of her grandmother? Cognitive vs emotional response to a false belief. *British Journal of Developmental Psychology, 17,* 501–574.

Braver, S. L., Ellman, I. M., & Fabricius, W. V. (2003). Relocation of children after divorce and children's best interests: New evidence and legal considerations. *Journal of Family Psychology, 17,* 206–219.

Brazelton, T. B., & Cramer, B. G. (1991). *The earliest relationships.* London: Karnak Books.

Breckler, S. (2007). The sanctity of peer review. *Monitor on Psychology, 32*(8), 26.

Bretherington, I. (1985). Attachment theory: Retrospect and prospect. *Monographs of the Society for Research in Child Development, 50* (1–2, Serial No. 209), 3–35.

Bribitzer, M. P., & Verdieck, M. J. (1988). Home-based, family-centered intervention: Evaluation of a foster care prevention program. *Child Welfare, 67*(3), 255–66.

Bricklin, B. (1990a). *Bricklin Perceptual Scales manual.* Furlong, PA: Village Publishing.

Bricklin, B. (1990b). *Parent Awareness of Skills Survey manual.* Furlong, PA: Village Publishing.

Bricklin, B. (1993). *Tests manuals supplement #9.* Furlong, PA: Village Publishing.

Bricklin, B., & Elliot, G. (1991). *Parent Perception of Child Profile.* Furlong, PA: Village Publishing.

Bricklin, B. & Elliot, G. (2005). Empirically assisted assessment of family systems. In L. Gunsberg, & P. Hymowitz (Eds.), *A handbook of divorce and custody: Forensic, developmental, and clinical perspectives* (pp. 201–219). New York: The Analytic Press/ Taylor & Francis Group.

Bricklin, B., & Halbert, M. H. (2004a). Can child custody data be generated scientifically? Part I. *American Journal of Family Therapy, 32*(2), 119–138.

Briggs, J. L. (2008). Autonomy and aggression in the three-year-old: The Utku Eskimo case. In R. A. LeVine & R. New (Eds.), *Anthropology and child development: A cross-cultural reader* (pp. 187–197). Malden, MA: Blackwell.

Bringuier, J. (1980). *Conversations with Piaget.* Chicago: University of Chicago Press.

British Children's Act. (1989). *An Act of the British Parliament.* Retrieved April 24, 2008, from http://www.opsi.gov.uk/acts/acts1989/plain/ukpga_19890041_en

Britner, P. A., Balcazar, F. E., Blechman, E. A., Blinn-Pike, L., & Larose, S. (2006). Mentoring special youth populations. *Journal of Community Psychology, 34*(6), 747–763.

Broberg, A. G. (2000). A review of interventions in the parent–child relationship informed by attachment theory. *Acta Paediatrica Supplement, 434,* 37–42.

Broberg, A., Wessels, H., Lamb, M., & Hwang, P. (1997). Effects of day care on the cognitive abilities in 8-year-olds. *Developmental Psychology, 33,* 62–69.

Brodzinsky, D. M. (1993). On the use and misuse of psychological testing in child custody evaluations. *Professional Psychology: Research & Practice, 24,* 213–219.

Bronson, M. B. (2001). *Self-regulation in early childhood: Nature and nurture.* New York: Guilford.

Bronte-Tinkew, J., Carrano, J., Horowitz, A., & Kinukawa, A. (2008). Involvement among resident fathers and links to infant cognitive outcomes. *Journal of Family Issues, 29*(9), 1211–1244.

Bronte-Tinkew, J., & Moore, K. (2006). The father–child relationship, parenting styles, and youth risk behaviors. *Journal of Family Issues, 27*(6), 850–881.

Brook, J., & McDonald, T. (2009). The impact of parental substance abuse on the stability of family reunifications from foster care. *Children and Youth Services Review, 31*(2), 193–198.

Brooks, D., Barth, R. P., Bussiere, A., & Patterson, G. (1999). Adoption and race: Implementing the Multiethnic Placement Act and the Interethnic Adoption Provisions. *Social Work, 22*, 167–178.

Brooks, S. L. (2001). The case for adoption alternatives. *Family Court* Review, *39* (1), 43–57.

Brooks, S. L., & Roberts, D. E. (2002). Social justice and family court reform. *Family Court Review, 40*, 453–457.

Brown, J., Moraes, S., & Mayhew, J. (2005). Service needs of foster families with children who have disabilities. *Journal of Child and Family Studies, 14*, 417–429.

Brown, J. D. (2008). Foster parents' perceptions of factors needed for successful foster placements. *Journal of Child and Family Studies 17*(4), 538–554.

Buck, J. N. (1948). The H-T-P technique: A qualitative and quantitative scoring manual. *Journal of Clinical Psychology, 4*(4), 317–396.

Buehler, C., Lange, G., & Franck, K. L. (2007). Adolescents' cognitive and emotional responses to marital hostility. *Child Development, 78*, 775–789.

Bugental, D. B. (2003). *Thriving in the face of childhood adversity.* New York: Psychology Press.

Buggey, T. (2005). *Video self-modeling applications with students with autism spectrum disorder in a small private school setting.* Unpublished manuscript, The University of Memphis, Memphis, TN.

Burack, J. A., Charman, T., Yirmiya, N., & Zelazo, P. R. (2001). *The development of autism: Perspectives from theory and research.* Mahwah, NJ: Lawrence Erlbaum.

Burkett, L. P. (1991). Parenting behaviors of women who were sexually abused as children in their families of origin. *Family Process, 30*, 421–434.

Burton, L. (2007). Childhood adultification in economically disadvantaged families: A conceptual model. *Family Relations, 56*(4), 329–345.

Busby, J., & Suddendorf, T. (2005). Recalling yesterday and predicting tomorrow. *Cognitive Development, 20*, 362–372.

Bush, J. E., & Ehrenberg, M. F. (2003). Young persons' perspectives on the influence of family transitions on sibling relationships: A qualitative exploration. *Journal of Divorce & Remarriage, 39*, 1–36.

Butcher, J. N., Graham, J. R., Ben-Porath, Y. S., Tellegen, A., & Dahlstrom, W. G. (2001). *The Minnesota Multiphasic Personality Inventory-2 manual for administration* (rev. ed.). Minneapolis, MN: University of Minnesota Press.

Butcher, J. N. & Williams, C. L. (2009). Personality assessment with the MMPI-2: Historical roots, international adaptations, and current challenges. *Applied Psychology: Health and Well-Being, 1*, 105–135.

Butzer, B., & Campbell, L. (2008). Adult attachment, sexual satisfaction, and relationship satisfaction: A study of married couples. *Personal Relationships, 15*(1), 141–154

Byng-Hall, J. (2008) The significance of children fulfilling parental roles: Implications for family therapy. *Journal of Family Therapy, 30,* 147–162.

Caldera, Y. (2004, spring). Paternal involvement and infant–father attachment: AQ-set study. *Fathering.* Retrieved May 25, 2008, from: http://findarticles.com/p/articles/mi_m0PAV/is_2_2/ai_n6121483/print

California Working Families. (2007). *Recommendations on preventing entrance into foster care.* Retrieved February 16, 2009, from http://www.cwda.org/downloads/publica tions/cws/PreventingEntrance_Fostercare.pdf

Cameron, L. (2008). The Maine effect, or how I finally embraced the social model of disability. *Intellectual and Developmental Disabilities, 46*(1), 54–57.

Campbell, T. W., & Lorandos, D. (2001). *Cross-examining experts in the behavioral sciences.* St. Paul, MN: West Group.

Capron, C., & Duyme, M. (1989). Assessment of the effects of socio-economic status on IQ in a full cross-fostering study. *Nature, 340,* 552–554.

Carlson, M. J., & McLanahan, S. S. (2004). Early father involvement in fragile families. In R. D. Day & M. E. Lamb (Eds.), *Conceptualizing and measuring father involvement* (pp. 241–271). Mahwah, NJ: Lawrence Erlbaum.

Carmody, M. (1997). Submerged voices: Coordinators of sexual assault services speak of their experiences. *Affiliated Journal of Women and Social Work, 12*(4), 452–462.

Carmody, T. (2007). Child relocation: An intractable international family law problem. *Family Court Review, 45*(2), 214–246.

Carretta, T. R., & King, R. E. (2008). Improved military air traffic controller selection methods as measured by subsequent training performance. *Aviation, Space, and Environmental Medicine, 79*(1), 36–43.

Cashel, M. L. (2002). Child and adolescent psychological assessment: Current clinical practices and the impact of managed care. *Professional Psychology: Research & Practice, 33,* 446–453.

Cashmore, J., & Parkinson, P. (2008). Children's and parents' perceptions on children's participation in decision making after parental separation and divorce. *Family Court Review, 46*(1), 91–104.

Cashmore, J., Parkinson, P., & Taylor, A. (2008). Overnight stays and children's relationships with resident and nonresident parents after divorce. *Journal of Family Issues, 29*(6), 707–733.

Cassidy, J., & Shaver, P. R. (1999). *Handbook of attachment: Theory, research and clinical applications.* New York: Guilford.

Castro, D. M., Jones, R. A., & Mirsalimi, H. (2004). Parentification and the imposter phenomenon: An empirical investigation. *American Journal of Family Therapy, 32,* 205–216.

Cauffman, E., & Steinberg, L. (2000a). (Im)maturity of judgment in adolescence: Why adolescents may be less culpable than adults. *Behavioral Sciences and the Law, 18,* 741–760.

Cauffman, E., & Steinberg, L. (2000b). Researching adolescent's decision making relevant to culpability. In T. Grisso & R. Schwartz (Eds.), *Youth on trial.* Chicago: University of Chicago Press.

Caughy, M. O., DiPietro, J., & Strobino, D. M. (1994). Day-care participation as a protective factor in the cognitive development of low-income children. *Child Development, 65* [Special Issue: Children and poverty], 457–471.

Chamberlain, J., & Miller, M. K. (2008). Stress in the courtroom: Call for research. *Psychiatry, Psychology and Law, 15*(2), 237–250.

Chase, N. (1999). Parentification: An overview of theory, research and societal issues. In N. Chase (Ed.), *Burdened children: Theory, research and treatment of parentification.* Thousand Oaks, CA: Sage.

Cheng, E. K., & Yoon, A. (2005). *Does Frye or Daubert matter? A study of scientific admissibility standards.* Brooklyn Law School, Legal Studies Paper No. 22. Retrieved June 13, 2009, from http://ssrn.com/abstract=609581

Chiodo, L.M., Covington, C., Sokol, R. J., Hannigan, J. H., Jannise, J., Ager, J., et al. (2007). Blood lead levels and specific attention effects in young children. *Neurotoxicology and Teratology, 29*(5), 538–546.

Chipungu, S., & Bent-Goodley, T. (2004). Challenges of contemporary foster care. *Future of Children, 14*(1), 75–93.

Chowdhury, A., & Choudhury, R. (1993). Exploring research strategies for identifying invulnerable children: An Indian context. *Early Child Development & Care, 93,* 87–100.

Christopoulos, P., Deligeoroglou, E., Laggari, V., Christogiorgos, S., & Creatsas, G. (2008). Psychological and behavioural aspects of patients with Turner Syndrome from childhood to adulthood: A review of the clinical literature. *Journal of Psychosomatic Obstetrics & Gynecology, 29*(1), 45–51.

Cicchetti, D., & Garmezy, N. (1993). Prospects and promises in the study of resilience. *Development and Psychopathology, 5,* 497–502.

Cicchetti, D., & Toth, S. L. (1992). The role of developmental theory in prevention and intervention. *Development and Psychopathology, 4,* 489–493.

Cicchetti, D., Rogosch, F. A., & Toth, S. L. (2006). Fostering secure attachment in infants in maltreating families through preventive interventions. *Development and Psychopathology, 18,* 623–649

Clark, C. A. C., Woodward, L. J., Horwood, L. J., & Moor, S. (2008). Development of emotional and behavioral regulation in children born extremely preterm and very preterm: Biological and social influences. *Child Development, 79*(5), 1444–1462.

Clarke-Stewart, K. A. (1980). The father's contribution to children's cognitive and social development in early childhood. In F. A. Pedersen (Ed.), *The father-infant relationship: Observational studies in a family setting* (pp.111–146). New York: Praeger.

Clarke-Stewart, K. A., & Hayward, C. (1996). Advantages of father custody and contact for the psychological well-being of school-age children. *Journal of Applied Developmental Psychology, 17,* 239–270.

Clayton, V. (1982). Wisdom and intelligence: The nature and function of knowledge in the later years. *International Journal of Aging and Human Development, 15*(4), 315–321.

Cochrane, R. E., Tett, R. P., & Vandecreek, L. (2003). Psychological testing and the selection of police officers: A national survey. *Criminal Justice and Behavior, 30*(5), 511–537.

Cohen, L. J., & Vesper, J. H. (2001). Forensic stress disorder. *Law and Psychology Review, 25*,1–27.

Cohen, N. J. (2001). *Language impairment and psychopathology in infants, children, and adolescents.* Thousand Oaks, CA: Sage.

Colvert, E., Rutter, M., Kreppner, J., Beckett, C., Castle, J., Groothues, C., et al. (2008). Do theory of mind and executive function deficits underlie the adverse outcomes associated with profound early deprivation?: Findings from the English and Romanian adoptees study. *Journal of Abnormal Child Psychology, 36*(7), 1057–1068.

Compas, B. E., Worsham, N. L., Epping-Jordan, J. E., et al. (1994). When mom or dad has cancer: Markers of psychological distress in cancer patients, spouses, and children. *Health Psychology, 13*(6), 507–515.

Condie, L. (2003). Parenting evaluations for the court. Care and protection matters. *Perspectives in Law & Psychology, 18*, 327–383.

Condie, L. O., & Condie, D. (2008). Parents with brain impairment: Care and protection matters. In H. V. Hall (Ed.), *Forensic psychology and neuropsychology for criminal and civil cases* (pp. 131–167). Boca Raton, FL: CRC Press.

Conners, C. K., Sitarenios, G., Parker, J. D., & Epstein, J. N. (1998). Revision and restandardization of the Conners Teacher Rating Scale (CTRS-R): Factor structure, reliability, and criterion validity. *Journal of Abnormal Child Psychology, 26*(4), 279–291.

Cook, W. L. (2000). Understanding attachment security in family context. *Journal of Personality and Social Psychology, 78*(2), 285–294.

Coplan, J., Contello, K. A., Cunningham, C. K., Weiner, L. B., Dye, T. D., Roberge, L., et al. (1998). Early language development in children exposed to or infected with human immunodeficiency virus. *Pediatrics, 102*, e8–e19.

Cordero, A. (2004). When family reunification works: Data-mining foster care records. *Families in Society, 85*(A), 571–580.

Costa, R. D. (2003). Now I lay me down to sleep: A look at overnight visitation rights available to incarcerated mothers. *New England Journal on Criminal & Civil Confinement, 29*(1), 67–98.

Cox, J. (2005). Postnatal depression in fathers. *Lancet, 366*(9490), 982.

Cox, M. (1993). *Children's drawings of the human figure.* Hove, UK: Erlbaum.

Craig, R. J. (205). *Personality-guided forensic psychology.* Washington, DC: American Psychological Association.

Cronbach, L. J., & Meehl, P. E. (1955). Construct validity in psychological tests. *Psychological Bulletin, 52*, 281–302. Retrieved June 13, 2009, from http://psychclassics.yorku.ca/Cronbach/construct.htm

Crook, W. P., & Oehme, K. (2007). Characteristics of supervised visitation programs serving child maltreatment and other cases. *Brief Treatment and Crisis Intervention, 7*(4), 291–304.

Crosby-Currie, C. (1996). Children's involvement in contested custody cases: Practices and experiences of legal and mental health professionals. *Law & Human Behavior, 20*, 289–311.

Cross, T. L., Gust-Brey, K., & Ball, P. B. (2002). A psychological autopsy of the suicide of an academically gifted student: Researchers' and parents' perspectives. *Gifted Child Quarterly, 46*, 247–264.

Crossman, A., Powell, M. B., Principe, G., & Ceci, S. (2002). Child testimony in custody cases: A review. *Journal of Forensic Psychology Practice, 2* (1), 1–32.

Cummings, E. M., & Davies, P. T. (1994). *Children and marital conflict: The impact of family dispute and resolution.* New York: Guilford.

Daicoff, S. (1999). Making law therapeutic for lawyers: Therapeutic jurisprudence, preventive law, and the psychology of lawyers. *Psychology, Public Policy, & Law,*

Daicoff, S. S. (2004). *Lawyer, know thyself: A psychological analysis of personality strengths and weaknesses.* Washington, DC: American Psychological Association.

Dalenberg, M. (2006). Recovered memory and the *Daubert* criteria: recovered memory as professionally tested, peer reviewed, and accepted in the relevant scientific community. *Trauma Violence Abuse, 7*(4), 274–310.

Dallam, S. J. (1999). The parental alienation syndrome: Is it scientific? In E. St. Charles & L. Crook (Eds.), *Expodse: The failure of family courts to protect children from abuse in custody disputes.* Los Gatos, CA: Our Children Charitable Foundation. Retrieved March 9, 2009, from http://www.leadershipcouncil.org/1/res/dallam/3.html

Dauber, S. L., & Benbow, C. P. (1990). Aspects of personality and peer relations of extremely talented adolescents. *Gifted Child Quarterly, 34,* 10–15.

Daubert v. Merrell Dow Pharmaceuticals, Inc., 509 U.S. 579, 113 S. Ct. 2795 (1993).

Davidson-Arad, B., & Cohen, O. (2004). Custody recommendations of Israeli social workers: Child's expected quality of life and child's preference. *Journal of Child Custody, 1*(4), 9–26.

Day, R. D., & Lamb, M. E. (2004). Conceptualizing and measuring father involvement: Pathways, problems and progress. In R. D. Day & M. E. Lamb (Eds.), *Conceptualizing and measuring father involvement* (pp. 1–16). Mahwah, NJ: Lawrence Erlbaum.

de Klerk, V. (2005). Slang and swearing as markers of inclusion and exclusion in adolescence. In A. Williams & C. Thurlow (Eds.), *Talking adolescence: Perspectives on communication in the teenage years* (pp. 111–127). New York: Peter Lang.

De Paul, J., & Domenech, L. (2000). Childhood history of abuse and child abuse potential in adolescent mothers: A longitudinal study. *Child Abuse & Neglect, 24,* 701–713.

Deason, D., & Randolph, D. (1998). A systematic look at the self: The relationship between family organization, interpersonal attachment and identity. *Journal of Social Behavior and Personality, 13*(3), 465–479.

Dember, C., & Fliman, V. (2005). Tailoring parental visitation orders to the developmental needs of children. In L. Gunsberg & P. Hymowitz (Eds), *A handbook of divorce and custody: Forensic, developmental, and clinical perspectives.* New York: Analytic Press.

Desmarais, C., Sylvestre, A., Meyer, F., Bairati, I., & Rouleau, N. (2008). Systematic review of the literature on characteristics of late-talking toddlers. *International Journal of Language & Communication Disorders, 43*(4), 361–389.

Deutsch, R. (2009). President's message. *AFCC News, 28*(1), 3.

Deutsch, R., Sullivan, M., & Ward, P. (2008). Overcoming barriers: bringing families together at common ground center. *AFCC News, 27*(4), 8. Retrieved March 9, 2009, from http://www.cgcvt.org/programs/obfc.shtml

Deutscher, B., Fewell, R. R., & Gross, M. (2006). Enhancing the interactions of teenage mothers and their at-risk children: Effectiveness of a maternal-focused intervention. *Topics in Early Childhood Special Education, 26,* 194–205.

Diareme, S., Tsiantis, J., Romer, G., Tsalamanios, E., Anasontzi, S., & Paliokosta, H. (2007). Mental health support for children of somatically ill parents: A review of theory and intervention concepts. *Family Systems & Health, 25*(1), 98–118.

DiCaccavo, A. (2006). Working with parentification: Implications for clients and counselling psychologists. *Psychology and Psychotherapy: Theory, Research and Practice, 79*, 469–478.

Dickinson, D. K., & Neuman, S. B. (2006). *Handbook of early literacy research, Volume 2.* New York: Guilford.

Diekema, D. S. (2005). Responding to parental refusals of immunization of children. *Pediatrics, 115*(5), 1428–1431.

Dishion, T. J., Poulin, F., & Medici-Skaggs, N. (2000). The ecology of early autonomy in adolescence: Biological and social influences. In K. A. Kerns, J. Contreras, & A. M. Neal-Barnett (Eds.), *Family and peers: Linking two social worlds* (pp. 27–45). Westport, CT: Praeger.

Dixon, J. W. (2002). *Battered woman syndrome.* Retrieved November 17, 2008, from http://www.expertlaw.com/library/domestic_violence/battered_women .html

Dockrell, J., Campbell, R., & Neilson, I. (1980). Conservation accidents revisited. *International Journal of Behavioral Development. 3*(4), 423–439.

Donald, T., & Jureidini, J. (2004). Parenting capacity. *Child Abuse Review, 13*, 5–17.

Donleavy, G. D. (2008). No man's land: Exploring the space between Gilligan and Kohlberg. *Journal of Business Ethics, 80*(4), 807–822.

Donnan, H. H., Harlan, G. E., & Thompson, S. A. (1969). Counselor personality and level of functioning as perceived by counselees. *Journal of Counseling Psychology, 16*(6), 482–485.

Dougherty, S. (2004). *Promising practices in reunification.* The National Resource Center for Foster Care & Permanency Planning, Hunter College School of Social Work. Retrieved January 27, 2009, from http://www.hunter.cuny.edu/socwork/nrcfcpp/downloads/promising-practices-in-reunification.pdf

Douglas, G., Murch, M., Robinson, M., Scanlan, L., & Butler, I. (2001). Children's perspectives and experience of the divorce process. *Family Law, 31*, 373–377.

Drogin, E. Y. & Barrett, C. L. (2007). Off the witness stand: The forensic psychologist as consultant. In A. M. Goldstein (Ed.), *Forensic psychology: Emerging topics and expanding roles* (pp. 465–488). Hoboken, NJ: John Wiley.

Droit-Volet, S. (2008). A further investigation of the filled-duration illusion with a comparison between children and adults. *Journal of Experimental Psychology: Animal Behavior Processes, 34*(3), 400–414.

Droit-Volet, S., & Meck, W. H. (2008). How emotions colour our time perception. *Trends in Cognitive Sciences, 12*, 504–513.

Drozd, L. M., & Olesen, N. W. (2004). Is it abuse, alienation, and/or estrangement? A decision tree. *Journal of Child Custody, 1*(3), 65–106.

Drummet, A. R., Coleman, M., & Cable, S. (2003). Military families under stress: Implications for family life education. *Family Relations, 52*, 279–287.

Drummond, J., Letourneau, N., Weir, A., & Neufeld, S. (2008). Effectiveness of teaching an early parenting approach within community-based support services for adolescent mothers. *Research in Nursing and Health, 31*(1), 12–22.

Dubin, W. R., & Ning, A. (2008). Violence toward mental health professionals. In R. I. Simon & K. Tardiff (Eds.), *Textbook of violence assessment and management* (pp. 461–481). Arlington, VA: American Psychiatric Press.

Duggan, W. D. (2007). Rock-paper-scissors: Playing the odds with the law of child relocation. *Family Court Review, 45*(2), 193–213.

Duncan, G. J., Brooks-Gunn, J., & Klebanov, P. K. (1994). Economic deprivation and early childhood development. *Child Development 65*(2), 296–318.

Duncan, K. L. (1996), Lies, damned lies and statistics? Psychological syndrome evidence in the courtroom after *Daubert. Indiana Law Journal, 71*, 753–771.

Dunlop, A.-W., Knott, F., & MacKay, T. (2008). Developing social interaction and understanding in high-functioning individuals with autism spectrum disorder. In E. McGregor, M. Núñez, K. Cebula, & J. C. Gómez (Eds.), *Autism: An integrated view from neurocognitive, clinical, and intervention research* (pp. 260–280). Malden, MA: Blackwell.

Duthie, J. K., Nippold, M. A., Billow, J. L., & Mansfield, T. C. (2008). Mental imagery of concrete proverbs: A developmental study of children, adolescents, and adults. *Applied Psycholinguistics, 29*(1), 151–173.

Duxbury, M. (2007). *Making room in our hearts: Keeping family ties through open adoption.* New York: Routledge/Taylor & Francis Group.

Dyer, F. J. (2004). Termination of parental rights in light of attachment theory: The case of Kaylee. *Psychology, Public Policy and the Law, 10*(1-2), 5–30.

Dyer, F. J. (2005). Forensic application of the MCMI-III™ in light of current controversies. In R. J. Craig (Ed.), *New directions in interpreting the Millon™ Clinical Multiaxial Inventory-III (MCMI-III™)* (pp. 201–223). Hoboken, NJ: John Wiley.

Egeland, B., Jacobvitz, D., & Sroufe, A. (1988). Breaking the cycle of abuse. *Child Development, 59*, 1080–1088.

Egeland, M., & Erickson, F. (1999). Attachment theory and research. *Zero to Three Journal.* Retrieved from http://www.zerotothree.org/vol20-2.html

Einfeld, S. L., & Tonge, B. J. (1996). Population prevalence of psychopathology in children and adolescents with intellectual disability: II epidemiological findings. *Journal of Intellectual Disability Research, 40*(2), 99–109.

Eisen, M., Quas, J. A., & Goodman, G. S. (2002). *Memory and suggestibility in the forensic interview.* New York: Lawrence Erlbaum.

Eisenberg, N., & Strayer, J. (1990). *Empathy and its development.* Cambridge, MA: Cambridge University Press Archive.

Eisenberg, N., Fabes, R.A., Guthrie, I.K., & Reiser, M. (2000). Dispositional emotionality and regulation: Their role in predicting quality of social functioning. *Journal of Personality and Social Psychology, 78*(1), 136–57.

Ellis, E. M. (2000). Evaluation of sexual abuse allegations in child custody cases. In *Divorce wars: Interventions with families in conflict* (pp. 267–294). Washington, D C: American Psychological Association

Ellman, I. M. (2004). Should visitation denial affect the obligation to pay support? *Arizona State Law Journal, 36*, 661.

Elrod, L. D. (2006). A move in the right direction? Best interests of the child emerging as the standard for relocation cases. *Journal of Child Custody, 3*(3/4), 29–61.

Emery, R., Otto, R., & O'Donohue, W. (2005). A critical assessment of child custody evaluations—limited science and a flawed system. *Psychological Science, 6*(1), 1–29.

Emery, R. E. (1999). *Marriage, divorce, and children's adjustment* (2nd ed.). Thousand Oaks, CA: Sage.

Emery, R. E., & Forehand, R. (1996). Parental divorce and children's well-being: A focus on resilience. In R. J. Haggerty & L. R. Sherrod (Eds.), *Stress, risk, and resilience in children and adolescents: Processes, mechanisms, and interventions* (pp. 64–99). New York: Cambridge University Press.

English, P. W., & Sales, B. D. (2005). *More than the law: Social and behavioral knowledge in legal decision-making.* Washington, DC: American Psychological Association.

Enos, S. (2001). *Mothering from the inside: Parenting in a women's prison.* Albany, NY: State University of New York Press.

Ensign, K. (1991). *Prevention services in child welfare: An exploratory paper on the evaluation of family preservation and family support programs.* Washington, DC: U.S. Department of Health and Human Services, Office of Assistant Secretary for Planning and Evaluation.

Erard, R. E. (2007). Picking cherries with blinders on: A comment on Erickson et al. (2007) 'Regarding the use of tests in family court.' *Family Court Review, 45*(2), 175–184.

Erath, S. A., Flanagan, K. S., & Bierman, K. L. (2008). Early adolescent school adjustment: Associations with friendship and peer victimization. *Social Development, 17*(4), 853–870.

Erickson, S. K., Lilienfeld, S. O., & Vitacco, M. J. (2007, April). A critical examination of the suitability and limitations of psychological tests in family court. *Family Court Review, 45,* 153–170.

Erikson, E. H. (1950). *Childhood and society.* New York: Norton.

Erikson, E. H. (1959). *Identity and the life cycle.* New York: International Universities Press.

Erikson, E. H. (1968). *Identity, youth and crisis.* New York: Norton.

Espy, K. A., Molfese, V. J., & DiLalla, L. F. (2001). Effects of environment on intelligence in children: Growth curve modeling of longitudinal data. *Merrill Palmer Quarterly, 47,* 42–72.

Estes, A. M., Dawson, G., Sterling, L., & Munson, J. (2007). Level of intellectual functioning predicts patterns of associated symptoms in school-age children with autism spectrum disorder. *American Journal on Mental Retardation, 112*(6), 439–449.

European Union. (2005). *Charter of fundamental rights of the European Union.* Retrieved July 20, 2009, from
http://ec.europa.eu/justice_home/unit/charte/index_en.html

Evans, F. B., & Schutz, B. M. (2008). The Rorschach in child custody and parenting plan evaluations: A new conceptualization. In C. B. Gacono, F. B. Evans, N. Kaser-Boyd, & L. A. Gacono (Eds.), *The handbook of forensic Rorschach assessment* (pp. 233–254). New York: Routledge/Taylor & Francis Group.

Exner, J. (2002). *The Rorschach: Basic foundations and principles of interpretation* (4th ed.). Hoboken, NJ: Wiley.

Ezzo, F. R., Evans, T. M., & McGovern-Kondik, M. (2004). Termination of parental rights: Integration of theory, practice, and demographics. *American Journal of Forensic Psychology, 22,* 29–42.

Faber, A. J., Willerton, E., Clymer, S. R., MacDermid, S. M., & Weiss, H. M. (2008). Ambiguous absence, ambiguous presence: A qualitative study of military reserve families in wartime. *Journal of Family Psychology, 22*(2), 222–230.

Fabricius, W. V., & Braver, S. L. (2006). Relocation, parent conflict, and domestic violence: Independent risk factors for children of divorce. *Journal of Child Custody: Research, Issues, and Practices, 3,* 7–27.

Farmer, M. (2006). Language and the development of social and emotional understanding. In J. Clegg & J. Ginsborg (Eds.), *Language and social disadvantage: Theory into practice.* Chichester, UK: Wiley.

Farrar, A. R. (2002). *Vicarious traumatization of the mental health professional.* Retrieved March 14, 2009, from http://www.apa.org/apags/profdev/victrauma.html

Feiring, C., Simon, V. A., & Cleland, C. M. (2009). Childhood sexual abuse, stigmatization, internalizing symptoms, and the development of sexual difficulties and dating aggression. *Journal of Consulting and Clinical Psychology, 77*(1), 127–137.

Feldman, D. (1993). Child prodigies: A distinctive form of giftedness. *Gifted Child Quarterly, 37,* 188–193.

Feldman, D. A. (2004). Piaget's stages: The unfinished symphony of cognitive development. *New Ideas in Psychology, 22,* 175–231.

Feldman, L. (1990). *Evaluating the impact of family preservation services in New Jersey.* Trenton, NJ: New Jersey Division of Youth and Family Services, Bureau of Research, Evaluation and Quality Assurance.

Feldman, R. (2007). Parent–infant synchrony and the construction of shared timing: Physiological precursors, developmental outcomes, and risk conditions. *Journal of Child Psychology and Psychiatry, 48*(3–4), 329–354.

Fergusson, D. M., Boden, J. M., & Horwood, L. J. (2008). Exposure to childhood sexual and physical abuse and adjustment in early adulthood. *Child Abuse & Neglect. 32*(6), 607–619.

Ferraris, A. (2005). Sibling visitation as a fundamental right. *New England Law Review, 39,* 715.

Fields, L. F., Mussetter, B. W., & Powers, G. T. (1997). Children denied two parents: An analysis of access denial. *Journal of Divorce and Remarriage, 27*(1–2), 49–62.

Fingelkurts, A. A., & Fingelkurts, A. A. (2002) Exploring giftedness. In S. P. Shohov (Ed.), *Advances in psychology research* (Vol. 9, pp. 137–155). Hauppauge, NY: Nova Science.

Finkenauer, C., Engels, R. C. M. E., & Meeus, W. (2002). Keeping secrets from parents: Advantages and disadvantages of secrecy in adolescence. *Journal of Youth & Adolescence, 31,* 123–136.

Fish, B., & Chapman, B. 2004. Mental health risks to infants and toddlers in foster care. *Clinical Social Work Journal, 32,* 2, 121–140.

Flannery, M. (2004). Is "bird nesting" in the best interest of children? *Southern Methodist University Law Review, 57,* 295–352.

Flens, J. R., & Drozd, L. (Eds.). (2005). *Psychological testing in child custody evaluations.* New York: Haworth Press.

Flouri, E., & Buchanan, A. (2004). Early father's and mother's involvement and child's later educational outcomes. *British Journal of Educational Psychology, 74,* 141–153.

Flouri, E. (2008). Temperament influences on parenting and child psychopathology: Socio-economic disadvantage as moderator. *Child Psychiatry & Human Development, 39*(4), 369–379.

Foley, D. L., Rowe, R., Maes, H., Silberg, J., Eaves, L., & Pickles, A. (2008). The relationship between separation anxiety and impairment. *Journal of Anxiety Disorders, 22*(4), 635–641.

Fonagy, P., Steele, H., & Steele, M. (1991). Maternal representations of attachment during pregnancy predict the organization of infant-mother attachment at one year of age. *Child Development, 62*, 891–905.

Ford, D. Y. (2008). Intelligence testing and cultural diversity: The need for alternative instruments, policies, and procedures. In J. L. VanTassel-Baska (Ed.), *Alternative assessments with gifted and talented students. The critical issues in equity and excellence in gifted education series* (pp. 107–128). Waco, TX: Prufrock Press.

Fosco, G., & Grych, J. (2008). Emotional, cognitive and family systems mediators of children's adjustment to interparental conflict. *Journal of Family Psychology, 22*(6), 843–854.

Fraley, R. C., & Spieker, S. J. (2003). Are infant attachment patterns continuously or categorically distributed? A taxometric analysis of Strange Situation behavior. *Developmental Psychology, 39*, 387–404.

Fraser, M. W., Pecora, P. J., & Haapala, D. A. (1991). *Families in crisis: The impact of intensive family preservation services.* New York: Aldine de Gruyter.

Fravel, D. L., Grotevant, H. D., Boss, P. G., & McRoy, R. G. (1993). Boundary ambiguity across levels of openness in adoption. In M. Crosbie-Burnett (Ed.), *Proceedings of the Theory of Constriction and Methodology Workshop of the National Council on Family Relations.*

Freedman, M. R., Rosenberg, S. J., Gettman, D., & Van Scoyk., S. (1993). Evaluating countertransference in child custody evaluations. *American Journal of Forensic Psychology, 11*(3), 61–73.

Freeman, R., & Freeman, G. (2003). *Managing contact difficulties: A child-centred approach.* Ottawa: Department of Justice (Canada). 2003-FCY-5E.

Freeman, R., Abel, D., Cowper-Smith, M., & Stein, L. (2004). Reconnecting children with absent parents: A model for intervention. *Family Court Review, 42*(3), 439–459.

Friend of the Court Bureau. (2001). *Michigan custody guidelines.* Lansing, MI: State Court Administrative Office. Retrieved September 4, 2007, from http://courts.michigan.gov/scao/resources/publications/manuals/fo cb/custodyguideline.pdf

Freud, S. (1961). Civilization and its discontents (reissue ed. July 1989). New York: W. W. Norton.

Freud, S. (1964). Analysis terminable and interminable. In J. Strachey (Ed. & trans), *The standard edition of complete psychological works of Sigmund Freud* (Vol. 23, pp. 209–253). London: Hogarth Press and Institute for Psychoanalysis. (Original work published 1937)

Fromm-Reichmann, F. (1948) Notes on the development of treatment of schizophrenics by psychoanalytical psychotherapy. *Psychiatry: Interpersonal & Biological Processes, 11*, 263–273.

Frye v. United States, 293 F. 1013 (D. C. Cir. 1923).

Fu, G. & Wang, L. (2005). The moral understanding and evaluation of lying or truth telling of primary school children under the circumstances of individual benefit or collective benefit. *Psychological Science (China)*, 28(4), 859–862.

Fulgini, A. J. (1998). Authority, autonomy, and parent-adolescent conflict and cohesion: A study of adolescents from Mexican, Chinese, Filipino, and European backgrounds. *Developmental Psychology*, 34, 782–792.

Fuller, T. (2005). Child safety at reunification: A case-control study of maltreatment recurrence following return home from substitute care. *Children and Youth Services Review*, 27, 1293–1306.

Galambos, N. L., Turner, P. K., & Tilton-Weaver, L. C. (2005). Chronological and subjective age in emerging adulthood: The crossover effect. *Journal of Adolescent Research*, 20, 538–556.

Galambos, N. L., Magill-Evans, J., & Darrah, J. (2008). Psychosocial maturity in the transition to adulthood for people with and without motor disabilities. *Rehabilitation Psychology*, 53(4), 498–504.

Gallucci, N. T. (1988). The emotional adjustment of gifted children. *Gifted Child Quarterly*, 32(2), 273–276.

Garb, H. N. (1999). Call for a moratorium on the use of the Rorschach Inkblot test in clinical and forensic settings. *Assessment*, 6, 313–317.

Garbarino, J. (2008). *Children and the dark side of human experience: Confronting global realities and rethinking child development*. New York: Springer Science / Business Media.

Garber, B. D. (1996). Alternatives to alienation: Acknowledging the broader scope of children's emotional difficulties during parental separation and divorce. *New Hampshire Bar Journal*, 37(1), 51.

Garber, B. D. (2001, February 9). ADHD or not ADHD: Custody and visitation considerations. *New Hampshire Bar News*. Retrieved June 2, 2009, from http://www.nhbar.org/publications/archives/display-news-issue.asp?id=83

Garber, B. D. (2004a). Parental alienation in light of attachment theory: Consideration of the broader implications for child development, clinical practice and forensic process. *Journal of Child Custody*, 1(4), 49–76.

Garber, B. D. (2004b). Directed co-parenting intervention: Conducting child centered interventions in parallel with highly conflicted co-parents. *Professional Psychology: Research and Practice*, 35(1), 55–64.

Garber, B. D. (2004c). Therapist alienation: Foreseeing and forestalling dynamics undermining therapies with children. *Professional Psychology: Research and Practice*, 35(4) 357–363.

Garber, B. D. (2006). *Uncoupled: Co-parenting interventions in the best interests of the children*. Invited presentation, Cambridge Health Alliance/Harvard Medical School, Cambridge, MA.

Garber, B. D. (2007a). Conceptualizing visitation resistance and refusal in the context of parental conflict, separation and divorce. *Family Court Review*, 4(1), 588–599.

Garber, B. D. (2007b). Developing a structured interview tool for children embroiled in family litigation and forensic mental health services: Query Grid. *Journal of Forensic Psychology Practice*, 7(1), 1–18.

Garber, B. D. (2008a). *Keeping kids out of the middle*. Deerfield Beach, FL: Health Communications.

Garber, B. D. (2008b). *One size can never fit all*. Minneapolis, MN: Minnesota Association of Conflict Resolution Specialists.

Garber, B. D. (2009). Attachment methodology in custody evaluation: Four hurdles standing between developmental theory and forensic application. *Journal of Child Custody*. 6(1&2), 38–61.

Garber, B. D., & Landerman, L. (2006, Summer). How should the child's voice be heard when parental rights and responsibilities are contested? *New Hampshire Bar Journal*. Retrieved June 13, 2009 from http://www.healthyparent.com/voice%20article.jpg

Gardner, R. (2001). The empowerment of children in the development of parent alienation syndrome. *American Journal of Forensic Psychology, 20*(2), 5-29

Gardner, R. A. (1985). Recent trends in divorce and custody litigation. *Academy Forum, 29*(2), 3–7.

Gardner, R.A. (1998). *The parental alienation syndrome* (2nd ed.). Cresskill, NJ: Creative Therapeutics.

Gardner, R. A. (1999a). Guidelines for assessing parental preference in child-custody disputes. *Journal of Divorce & Remarriage, 30* (1/2), 1–9.

Gardner, R. A. (1999b). Differentiating between parental alienation syndrome and bona fide abuse-neglect. *American Journal of Family Therapy, 27*, 97–107.

Gardner, R. A. (2002). The denial of parental alienation syndrome (PAS) also harms women. *American Journal of Family Therapy, 30*(3), 191–202.

Garmezy, N. (1985). Stress-resistant children: The search for protective factors. In M. W. Fraser (Ed.), *Risk and resilience in childhood*. Washington, DC: NASW Press.

Garrity, C. B. & Baris, M. A. (1994). *Caught in the middle*. Lanham, MD: Lexington Books.

Ge, X., Conger, R., & Elder, G., Jr. (1996). Coming of age too early: Pubertal influences on girls' vulnerability to psychological distress. *Child Development, 67*, 3386–3400.

Ge, X., Conger, R., & Elder, G. Jr. (2001). The relation between puberty and psychological distress in adolescent boys. *Journal of Research on Adolescence, 11*, 49–70.

Geisinger, K. F., Spies, R. A., Carlson, J. F., & Plake, B. S. (Eds.). (2007). *The seventeenth mental measurements yearbook*. Lincoln, NE: Buros Institute of Mental Measurements.

General Accounting Office. (1993, June). *Foster care services to prevent out-of-home placements are limited by funding barriers*. Report to the Chairman, Subcommittee on Oversight of Government Management, Committee on Governmental Affairs, U.S. Senate. Retrieved February 16, 2009, from http://archive.gao.gov/t2pbat5/149537.pdf

General Electric Co. v. Joiner, 522 U.S. 136, 118 S. Ct. 512 (1997).

George, C., Kaplan, N., & Main, M. (1996). Adult attachment inventory interview protocol. In T. Ward, D. Polaschek, & A. R. Beech (Eds.), *Theories of sexual offending*. Chichesster, UK: John Wiley.

Gershenson, C. (1991). *The effectiveness of intensive family preservation services: A summary of current research*. Washington, DC: Center for the Study of Social Policy.

Gest, S. D., Sesma, A., Masten, A. S., & Tellegen, A. (2006). Childhood peer reputation as a predictor of competence and symptoms 10 years later. *Journal of Abnormal Child Psychology, 34,* 509–526.

Giardino, J., Gonzalez, A., Steiner, M., & Fleming, A. S. (2008). Effects of motherhood on physiological and subjective responses to infant cries in teenage mothers: A comparison with non-mothers and adult. *Hormones and Behavior, 53*(1), 149–158.

Gillberg C., & Heijbel, H. (1998). MMR and autism. *Autism, 2,* 423–424.

Gilmour, J., & Skuse, D. (1999). A case comparison study of the characteristics of children with short stature syndrome induced by stress and a series of unaffected 'stressed' children. *Journal of Child Psychology and Psychiatry, 40,* 969–978.

Glendon, M. A. (1986). Fixed rules and discretion in contemporary family law and succession law. *Tulane Law Review, 60,* 1165–1197.

Gluckman, P., & Hanson, M. (2006). Evolution, development and timing of puberty. *Trends in Endocrinology & Metabolism, 17*(1), 7–12.

Goldstein, A. M. (2006). *Forensic psychology: Emerging topics and expanding roles.* New York: John Wiley.

Goodenough, F. L. (1926). *The measurement of intelligence by drawings.* New York: World Books.

Goodheart, C. D., Kazdin, A. E., & Sternberg, R. J. (Eds.). (2006). *Evidence-based psychotherapy: Where practice and research meet.* Washington, DC: American Psychological Association.

Gordon, R. M., Stoffey, R., & Bottinelli, J. (2008). MMPI-2 findings of primitive defenses in alienating patients. *American Journal of Family Therapy, 36*(3), 211–228.

Gottfried, A. W., Gottfried, A. E., Bathurst, K., & Guerin, D. W. (1994). *Gifted IQ: Early developmental aspects. The Fullerton longitudinal study.* New York: Plenum.

Gottfried, S. (2002). Virtual visitation: The wave of the future in communication between children and non-custodial parents in relocation cases. *Family Law Quarterly, 36,* 475.

Gould, J. W., & Martindale, D. A. (2008). Custody evaluation reports: The case for references to the peer-reviewed professional literature. *Journal of Child Custody, 5*(3), 217–227.

Graber, J. A., Lewinson, P. M., Seeley, J. R., & Brooks-Gunn, J. (1997). Is psychopathology associated with the timing of pubertal development? *Journal of the American Academy of Adolescent and Child Psychiatry, 36,* 1768–1776.

Graham, J. R. (1988, August). *Establishing validity of the revised form of the MMPI.* Symposium presentation at the 96th Annual Convention of the American Psychological Association, Atlanta, GA.

Grant, P. A., & Klee, S. (2005). Representation of the child to the court: The law guardian and guardian ad litem. In L. Gunsberg & P. Hymowitz (Eds.), *A handbook of divorce and custody: Forensic, developmental, and clinical perspectives* (pp. 21–29). New York: The Analytic Press/Taylor & Francis Group.

Gray, B. T., Meloy, J. R., & Jumes, M. T. (2008). Dangerousness risk assessment. In C. B. Gacono, F. B. Evans, N. Kaser-Boyd, & L. Gacono (Eds.), *The handbook of forensic Rorschach assessment. The LEA series in personality and clinical psychology* (pp. 175–194). New York: Routledge/Taylor & Francis Group.

Gray, E. (2004). Five commentaries: Looking to the future: Commentary 4. *Future of Children, 14*(1), 182–183.

Greenberg, L. R., Gould, J. W., Schnider, R., Gould-Saltman, D. J., & Martindale, D. (2003). Effective intervention with high-conflict families: How judges can promote and recognize competent treatment in family court. *Journal of the Center for Families, Children & the Courts, 4*, 49–66.

Greenspan, S. I. (1981). *Psychopathology and adaptation in infancy and early childhood. Principles of clinical diagnosis and preventive intervention.* New York: International Universities Press.

Greeson, J. K. P., & Bowen, N. K. (2008). "She holds my hand": The experiences of foster youth with their natural mentors. *Children and Youth Services Review, 30*(10), 1178–1188.

Grigorenko, E., & Sternberg, R. J. (2001). *Family environment and intellectual functioning: A life-span perspective.* New York: Lawrence Erlbaum.

Grisso, T. (1986). *Evaluating competencies: Forensic assessments and instruments.* New York: Plenum.

Grisso, T. (1997). The competence of adolescents as trial defendants. *Psychology, Public Policy, & Law, 3*, 3–32

Grisso, T. (2003). *Evaluating competencies: Forensic assessments and instruments* (2nd ed.). New York: Kluwer Academic/Plenum.

Grisso, T., & Barnum, R. (2000). *Massachusetts Youth Screening Instrument-2 (MAYSI-2): User's manual and technical report.* Worchester, MA: University of Massachusetts Medical School. Retrieved February 27, 2009, from http://www.maysiware.com/MAYSI2.htm

Grisso, T., Steinberg, L., Woodland, J., Cauffman, E., Scott, E., Graham, S., Lexcen, P., Reppucci, N. D., & Schwartz, R. (203). Juveniles's competency: A comparison of adolescents' and adults' capacities as trial defendants. *Law and Human Behavior, 27*, 333–363.

Grisso, T., & Vierling, L. (1978). Minors' consent to treatment: A developmental perspective. *Professional Psychology, 9*, 412–427.

Grob, S. A. (1993). Sibling visitation: A child's right. *Colorado Lawyer, 22*, 283.

Grodzinsky, Y. & Amunts, K. (2006). *Broca's region.* New York: Oxford University Press.

Gross, J., & Hayne, H. (1998). Drawing facilitates children's verbal reports of emotionally laden events. *Journal of Experimental Psychology: Applied, 4*, 163–179.

Grossman, K. E., Grossman, K., & Waters, E. (Eds.). (2005). *Attachment from infancy to adulthood: The major longitudinal studies.* New York: Guilford.

Grossman, N. S., & Okun, B. F. (2006).The need for a systems understanding of the legal system. *Family Psychologist, 22*(4), 26–27.

Grossman, N. S., &, Okun, B. F. (2007). A systems understanding of the legal system—further discussions. *Family Psychologist, 23*(1), 26–27.

Grotevant, H. D., McRoy, R. G., Elde, C. L., & Frawel, D. L. (1994) Adoptive family system dynamics: Variation by level of openness in the adoption. *Family Process, 33*, 125–146.

Grych, J. H., & Fincham, F. D. (2001). *Interparental conflict and child development: Theory, research, and applications.* Boston: Cambridge University Press.

Guidubaldi, J., & Duckworth, J. (2001). Divorce and children's cognitive ability. In E. L. Grigorenko & R. J. Sternberg (Eds.), *Family environment and intellectual functioning.* Mahwah, NJ: Lawrence Erlbaum.

Gutheil, T. G., & Brodsky, A. (2008). *Preventing boundary violations in clinical practice.* New York, NY: Guilford.

Haberman, P. S. (2005). Before death, we must part: Relocation and protection for domestic violence victims in volatile divorce and custody situations. *Family Court Review, 43*(1), 149–163.

Hadjistavropolus, T., & Bieling, P. J. (2000). When reviews attack: Ethics, free speech, and the peer review process. *Canadian Psychology, 41,* 152–159.

Hagan, M. A., & Castagna, N. (2001). The real numbers: Psychological testing in custody evaluations. *Professional Psychology: Research and Practice, 32,* 269–271.

Haier, R. J., & Denham, S. A. (1976). A summary profile of the nonintellectual correlates of mathematical precocity. In D. P. Keating (Ed.), *Intellectual talent: Research and development* (pp. 225–241). Baltimore, MD: Johns Hopkins University Press.

Haight, W. L., Kagle, J. D., & Black, J. E. (2003). Understanding and supporting parent-child relationships during foster care visits: Attachment theory and research. *Social Work, 48,* 195–207.

Hairston, C. F. (2002, April). The importance of families in prisoners' community reentry. *ICCA Journal on Community Corrections,* pp. 11–14

Hairston, C. F., & Addams, J. (2001). *Prisoners and families: Parenting during incarceration.* Commissioned paper, "From Prison to Home" Project, University of Illinois at Chicago. Retrieved February 9, 2008, from http://aspe.hhs.gov/HSP/prison2home02/Hairston.htm

Hall, H. V. (2008). Violence prediction and risk analysis. In H. V. Hall (Ed.), *Forensic psychology and neuropsychology for criminal and civil cases* (pp. 207–235). Boca Raton, FL: CRC Press.

Halon, R. L. (2001). The Millon Clinical Multiaxial Inventory-III: The normal quartet in child custody cases. *American Journal of Forensic Psychology, 19,* 57–75.

Hamer, R. (1990, November). What can my baby see? *Parent's Press, 11*(2). Retrieved December 20, 2008, from http://www.ski.org/Vision/babyvision.pdf

Handler, L., Campbell, A., & Martin, B. (2004). Use of graphic techniques in personality assessment: Reliability, validity, and clinical utility. In M. Hilsenroth & D. Segal (Eds.), *Comprehensive handbook of psychological assessment: Vol. 2. Objective and projective assessment of personality and psychopathology* (pp. 387–404). New York: John Wiley.

Hannett, M.J. (2007). Lessening the sting of ASFA: The rehabilitation-relapse dilemma brought about by drug addiction and termination of parental rights. *Family Court Review, 45*(3), 524–537.

Harden, B. (2004). Safety and stability for foster children: A developmental perspective. *Future of Children, 14*(1), 1–9.

Harris, A. (2005, August 10). Court orders $60,000 bond to ensure visitation. *New York Law Journal.* Retrieved January 11, 2008, from http://www.law.com/jsp/article.jsp?id=1123578313007

Harris, D. B. (1963). *Children's drawings as measures of intellectual maturity: A revision and extension of the Goodenough Draw-a-Man test.* New York: Harcourt, Brace and World.

Harris, M. (1992). *Language experience and early language development. From input to uptake.* Mahwah, NJ: Lawrence Erlbaum.

Hartson, J., & Payne, B. (2007). *Creating effective parenting plans: A developmental approach for lawyers and divorce professionals.* New York: American Bar Association.

Haugaard, J. J., & Avery, R. J. (2002). Termination of parental rights to free children for adoption: Conflicts between parents, children, and the state. In B. L. Bottoms, M. B. Kovera, & B. D. McAuliff (Eds.), *Children, social science, and the law* (pp. 131–152). New York: Cambridge University Press.

Heatherington, M., & Kelly, J. (2002). *For better or for worse: Divorce reconsidered.* New York: W. W. Norton.

Heilbrun, A. B. (1990). The measurement of criminal dangerousness as a personality construct Further validation of a research index. *Journal of Personality Assessment, 54,* 141–148.

Heilbrun, K. (1992). The role of psychological testing in forensic assessment. *Law and Human Behavior, 16,* 257–272.

Heinze, M. C., & Grisso, T. (1996). Review of instruments assessing parenting competencies used in child custody evaluations. *Behavioral Sciences & the Law, 14,* 293–313.

Henwood, T. R., & Bartlett, H. P. (2008). Measuring the impact of increased exercise on quality of life in older adults: The UQQoL, a new instrument. *European Journal of Ageing, 5*(3), 241–252.

Herer, Y., & Mayseless, O. (2000). Emotional and social adjustment of adolescents who show role-reversal in the family. *Megamot, 3,* 413–441.

Hernandez v. New York, 500 U.S. 352 (1991). United State Supreme Court ruling. Retrieved November 30, 2008, from http://caselaw.lp.findlaw.com/cgi-bin/getcase.pl?court=us&vol=500&invol=352

Hersen, M. (Ed.). (2004). *Comprehensive handbook of psychological assessment: Vol. 1.* Hoboken, NJ: John Wiley.

Hesse, E. (1999). The Adult attachment interview: Historical and current perspectives. In J. Cassidy & P. R. Shaver (Eds.), *Handbook of attachment: Theory, research, and clinical applications* (395–433). New York: Guilford.

Hickey, K. (2007). Minors' rights in medical decision making. *JONA's Healthcare Law, Ethics, and Regulation, 9*(3), 2007, 100–107.

Hill, J., & Nathan, R. (2008). Childhood antecedents of serious violence in adult male offenders. *Aggressive Behavior, 34*(3), 329–338.

Hinds, R. W., & Bradshaw, R. (2005). Gender bias in lawyers' affidavits to the Family Court of Australia. *Family Court Review, 43*(3), 445–453.

Hochheimer, L. (1895). *A treatise on the law relating to the custody of infants.* Baltimore: J. Murphy.

Hodapp, R. M., & Krasner, D. V. (1994). Families of children with disabilities: Findings from a national sample of eighth-grade students. *Exceptionality, 5* (2), 71–81. Retrieved January 2, 2009, from http://www.informaworld.com/10.1207/s15327035ex0502_2

Hodges, W. F. (1991). *Interventions for children of divorce: Custody, access, and psychotherapy* (2nd ed.). New York: Wiley.

Hollander, E., & Anagnostou, E. (Eds.). (2007). *Clinical manual for the treatment of autism. Treatment of autism with selective serotonin reuptake inhibitors and other antidepressants* (pp. 81–97). Washington, DC: American Psychiatric Press.

Holmbeck, G. N., Thill, A. W., Bachanas, P., Garber, J., Miller, K. B., Abad, M., et al. (2008). Evidence-based assessment in pediatric psychology: Measures of psychosocial adjustment and psychopathology. *Journal of Pediatric Psychology, 33*(9), 958–980.

Homer, B. D., & Hayward, E. O. (2008). Cognitive and representational development in children. In K. B. Cartwright (Ed), *Literacy processes: Cognitive flexibility in learning and teaching* (pp. 19–41). New York: Guilford.

Hooper, L. M. (2007). Expanding the discussion regarding parentification and its varied outcomes: Implications for mental health research and practice. *Journal of Mental Health Counseling, 29,* 322–337.

Hooper, S. R., Roberts, J. E., Zeisel, S. A., & Poe, M. (2003). Core language predictors of behavioral functioning in early elementary school children: Concurrent and longitudinal findings. *Behavior Disorders, 29*(1), 10–24.

Hora, P. F., & Schma, W. G. (1998). Therapeutic jurisprudence. *Judicature, 82,* 8–12

Horn, S. S. (2003). Adolescents' reasoning about exclusion from social groups. *Developmental Psychology, 39*(1), 71–84.

Horton, D. (2005). Consultation with military children and schools: A proposed model. *Consulting Psychology Journal: Practice and Research, 57*(4), 259–265.

Hosek, S. G., Harper, G. W., & Domanico, R. 2005. Predictors of medication adherence among HIV-infected youth. *Psychological Health Medicine, 10,* 166–179.

Hoult, J. (2006). The evidentiary admissibility of parental alienation syndrome: Science, law, and policy. *Children's Legal Rights Journal, 26*(1), 1–61. Retrieved June 13, 2009, from http://www.leadershipcouncil.org/docs/Hoult.pdf

House, B. L. (1998). Comment: Considering the child's preference in determining custody: Is it really in the child's best interest? *Journal of Juvenile Law, 19,* 176.

Hughes, J. R. (2008). A review of recent reports on autism: 1000 studies published in 2007. *Epilepsy & Behavior, 13*(3), 425–437.

Hulett, L. (2004. October). *Going beyond supervised contact: Developing a more holistic service model which facilitates child focused parenting.* Workshop session at Pursuing Excellence in Family Services: Family Services Australia 2004 National Conference, Sydney. Retrieved February 7, 2009, from http://pandora.nla.gov.au/pan/43308/2005 0923-0000/www.fsa.org.au/content-sections/files/Lyn%20Hulett_2004_ncp.pdf

Hünefeldt, T., Lucidi, A., Furia, A., & Rossi-Arnaud, C. (2008). Age differences in the interrogative suggestibility of children's memory: Do shift scores peak around 5–6 years of age? *Personality and Individual Differences, 45*(6), 521–526.

Hunsley, J., Lee, C. M., & Wood, J. M. (2003). Controversial and questionable assessment techniques. In S. O. Lilienfeld, S. Lynn, & J. Lohr (Eds.), *Science and pseudoscience in clinical psychology* (pp. 39–76). New York: Guilford.

Iacoboni, M. (2008). *Mirroring people.* New York: MacMillan.

Iglehart, A. P., & Becerra, R. M. (2002). Hispanic and African American youth: Life after foster care emancipation. *Journal of Ethnic and Cultural Diversity in Social Work, 11*(1/2), 79–107.

Ikeuchi, H., & Fujihara, T. (2004). Social psychological determinants of appearance-disappearance of transitional objects: Focusing on nursing environment and marital stress. *Japanese Journal of Social Psychology, 19*(3), 184–194.

Irwin, J. A., Carter, A. S., & Briggs-Gowan, M. J. (2002), The social-emotional development of "late-talking" toddlers. *Journal of the American Academy of Child & Adolescent Psychiatry, 41*, 1324–1332

Jackson, E., Campos, J. J., & Fischer, K. W. (1978). The question of decalage between object permanence and person permanence. *Developmental Psychology, 14*, 1–10.

Jackson, S. M., & Peterson, J. S. (2003). Depressive disorder in highly gifted adolescents. *Journal of Secondary Gifted Education, 14*, 175–186.

Jaffe, P. (2003). Domestic and family violence: Vicarious trauma and judges. *Recorder, 12*(5), 9–10. Retrieved March 15, 2009, from http://www.tmcec.com/tmcec/Resources/The_Recorder

Jahromi, L. B., & Stifter, C. A. (2008). Individual differences in preschoolers' self-regulation and theory of mind. *Merrill-Palmer Quarterly, 54*, 125–150.

James, B., & Gibson, C. (1991), Supervising visits between parent and child. *Family & Conciliation Courts Review, 29*, 73–84.

Jarosewich, T., Pfeiffer, S. I., & Morris, J. (2002). Identifying gifted students using teacher rating scales: A review of existing instruments. *Journal of Psychoeducational Assessment, 20*, 322–336.

Jasper, M. C. (2008). *Guardianship, conservatorship and the law.* New York: Oxford University Press.

Johnson, D. F. (2007, August). Rights and responsibilities of foster parents in the courtroom. *Judge's Page Newsletter*, 19–20. Retrieved February 15, 2009, from http://www.nationalcasa.org/JudgesPage/Article/rights_and_responsibilities.htm   OR http://www.nationalcasa.org/download/Judges_Page/0708_the_role_of_foster_parents_in_the_dependency_court_issue_0119.pdf

Johnson, E., & Johnston, J. (2004). *Research on high conflict parents and alienated children.* Workshop 9, Association of Family and Conciliation Courts annual conference, San Antonio, TX.

Johnston, C., & Lee, C. M. (2005). Children's attributions for their own versus others' behavior: Influence of actor versus observer differences. *Journal of Applied Developmental Psychology, 26*, 314–328.

Johnston, J. (1995). Research update: Children's adjustment in sole custody compared to joint custody families and principles for custody decision making. *Family and Conciliation Courts Review, 33*, 415–422.

Johnston, J. (2003). Parental alignments and rejection: An empirical study of alienation in children of divorce. *Journal of the American Academy of Psychiatry and the Law, 31*, 158–170.

Johnston, J., & Kelly, J. B. (2001). Rejoinder to Gardner's "Commentary on Kelly and Johnston's 'The alienated child: A reformulation of parental alienation syndrome.'" *Family Court Review, 42*, 622–628.

Johnston, J. R. (1993). Children of divorce who refuse visitation. In C. E. Depner & J. H. Bray (Eds.), *Nonresidential parenting: New vistas in family living* (pp. 109–135). San Francisco: Sage.

Johnston, J. R. (2003). Parental alignments and rejection: An empirical study of alienation in children of divorce. *Journal of the American Academy of Psychiatry and the Law, 3*(2), 158–170.

Johnston, J. R., & Roseby, V. (1997). *In the name of the child: A developmental approach to understanding and helping children of conflicted and violent divorce.* New York: Free Press.

Johnston, J. R., Walters, M. G., & Friedlander, S. (2001). Therapeutic work with alienated children and their families. *Family Court Review, 39*(3), 316–333.

Johnston, J. R., Walters, M. G., & Olesen, N. W. (2005). The psychological functioning of alienated children in custody disputing families: An exploratory study. *American Journal of Forensic Psychology, 23*(3), 39–64.

Jonson-Reid, M. (2003). Foster care and future risk of maltreatment. *Children and Youth Services Review, 25,* 271–294.

Judicial Education Center. (2009). *Child welfare handbook.* Retrieved February 21, 2009, from http://jec.unm.edu/resources/benchbooks/child_law/ch_22.htm#22-5-1

Junaid, K.A., & Fellowes, S. (2006). Gender differences in the attainment of motor skills on the Movement Assessment Battery for Children. *Physical and Occupational Therapy in Pediatrics, 26*(1–2), 5–11.

Jurkovic, G. J. (1998). Destructive parentification in families: Causes and consequences. In L. L'Abate (Ed.), *Handbook of family psychopathology* (pp. 237–255). New York: Guilford.

Jurkovic, G. J., Thirkield, A., & Morrell, R. (2001). Parentification of adult children of divorce—a multidimentional analysis. *Journal of Youth & Adolescence, 30*(2), 245–257.

Kaland, N., Callesen, K., Moller-Nielsen, A., Mortensen, E. L., & Smith, L. (2008). Performance of children and adolescents with Asperger syndrome or high-functioning autism on advanced theory of mind tasks. *Journal of Autism and Developmental Disorders, 38*(6), 1112–1123.

Kaplan, L., Hennon, C. B., & Ade-Ridder, L. (2000). Splitting custody of children between parents: Impact on the sibling system. *Families in Society, 74*(3), 131–144.

Kaplowitz, P., & Oberfield, S. (1999). Reexamination of the age limit for defining when puberty is precocious in girls in the United States: Implications for evaluation and treatment. Drug and Therapeutics and Executive Committees of the Lawson Wilkins Pediatric Endocrine Society. *Pediatrics, 104,* 936–941.

Karabekiroglu, K., & Aman, M. G. (2009). Validity of the Aberrant Behavior Checklist in a clinical sample of toddlers. *Child Psychiatry & Human Development, 40*(1), 99–110.

Karlsson, A., Arman, M., & Wikblad, K. (2008). Teenagers with type 1 diabetes—A phenomenological study of the transition towards autonomy in self-management. *International Journal of Nursing Studies, 45*(4), 562–570.

Kaslow, N. J., Rubin, N. J., Forrest, L., Elman, N. S., Van Horne, B. A., Jacobs, S. C., et al. (2007c). Recognizing, assessing, and intervening with problems of professional competence. *Professional Psychology: Research and Practice, 38,* 479–492.

Katz, K. (2001). *Over the moon: An adoption tale.* New York: Henry Holt.

Kaye, D. H. (2005). On "falsification" and "falsifiability": The first *Daubert* factor and the philosophy of science. *Jurimetrics Journal, 45,* 473–481.

Kelly, J. B. (1988). Longer-term adjustment in children of divorce: Converging findings and implications for practice. *Journal of Family Psychology, 2,* 119–140.

Kelly, J. B., & Johnston, J. R. (2001). The alienated child: A reformulation of parental alienation syndrome. *Family Court Review, 39*(3), 249–263.

Kelly, J. B., & Lamb, M. E. (2000). Using child development research to make appropriate custody and access decisions for young children. *Family Court Review, 38*(3), 297–311.

Kelly, J. B., & Lamb, M. E. (2001). Using the empirical literature to guide the development of parenting plans for young children. *Family Court Review, 39*(4), 365–371.

Kelly, R. F., & Ward, S. L. (2002). Allocating custodial responsibilities at divorce: Social science research and the American Law Institute's approximation rule. *Family Court Review, 40,* 350.

Kenyon, D. B., & Koerner, S. S. (2008). Post-divorce maternal disclosure and the father-adolescent relationship: Adolescent emotional autonomy and inter-reactivity as moderators. *Journal of Child and Family Studies, 17*(6), 791–808.

Kern, S., & Gayraud, F. (2007). Influence of preterm birth on early lexical and grammatical acquisition. *First Language, 27*(2), 159–173.

Kinard, E. M. (2003). Adolescent child bearers in later life—Maltreatment of their school age children. *Journal of Family Issues, 24,* 687–706.

Kindregan, C. P., Jr. (2002). Family interests in competition: Relocation and visitation. *Suffolk University Law Review, 3*(31).

Kirkland, K., & Kirkland, K. L. (2001). Frequency of child custody evaluation complaints and related disciplinary action: A survey of the Association of State and Provincial Psychology Boards. *Professional Psychology: Research and Practice, 32,* 171–174.

Kirkland, K., & Kirkland, K. E. (2006). Risk management and aspirational ethics for parenting coordinators. *Journal of Child Custody, 3*(2), 23–43.

Kirkland, K., McMillan, E. L., & Kirkland, K. L. (2005). Use of collateral sources in child custody evaluations. *Journal of Child Custody, 2*(4), 95–109.

Kirkland, K., & Sullivan, K. (2008). Parenting coordination (PC) practice: A survey of experienced professionals. *Family Court Review, 46*(4), 622–636.

Kirsh, B., & Cockburn, L. (2009). The Canadian Occupational Performance Measure: A tool for recovery-based practice. *Psychiatric Rehabilitation Journal, 32*(3), 171–176.

Klaus, M. H., & Kennell, J. H. (1976). *Maternal-infant bonding. The impact of early separation or loss on family development.* St. Louis, MO: Mosby.

Kliegel, M., Martin, M., & Jäger, T. (2007). Development and validation of the Cognitive Telephone Screening Instrument (COGTEL) for the assessment of cognitive function across adulthood. *Journal of Psychology: Interdisciplinary and Applied, 141*(2), 147–170.

Kligler, B., & Lee, R. A. (2004). *Integrative medicine: Principles for practice.* New York: McGraw-Hill.

Kohlberg, L. (2008). The development of children's orientations toward a moral order: I. Sequence in the development of moral thought. *Human Development, 51*(1), 8–20.

Kopp, C. B. (1982). Antecedents of self-regulation: A developmental perspective. *Developmental Psychology, 18,* 199–214.

Kopp, C. B. (1991). Young children's progression to self-regulation. In M. Bullock (Ed.), *Contributions to human development: Vol. 22. The development of intentional action: Cognitive, motivational, and interactive processes* (pp. 38–54). Basel, Switzerland: Karger.

Koppitz, E. M. (1968). *Psychological evaluation of children's human figure drawings.* London: Grune & Stratton.

Koppitz, E. M. (1983). Projective drawings with children and adolescents. *School Psychology Review, 12,* 421–427.

Kotulak, R. (2008). The effect of violence and stress in kids' brains. In M. H. Immordino-Yang (Ed.), *The Jossey-Bass reader on the brain and learning* (pp. 216–225). San Francisco: Jossey-Bass.

Kovacs, M. (1992). *Children's Depression Inventory (CDI) manual.* North Tonawanda, NY: Multi-Health Systems.

Kramer, M. S., Aboud, F., Mironova, E., Vanilovich, I., Platt, R. W., Matush, L., et al. (2008). Breastfeeding and child cognitive development: New evidence from a large randomized trial. *Archives of General Psychiatry, 65*(5), 578–584.

Kramer, M. S., Matush, L., Vanilovich, I., Platt, R. W., Bogdanovich, N., Sevkovskaya, Z., et al. (2007). Effects of prolonged and exclusive breastfeeding on child height, weight, adiposity, and blood pressure at age 6.5 y: Evidence from a large randomized trial. *American Journal of Clinical Nutrition, 86*(6), 1717–1721.

Krusemark, E. A., Campbell, W. K., & Clementz, B. A. (2008). Attributions, deception, and event related potentials: An investigation of the self-serving bias. *Psychophysiology, 45*(4), 511–515.

Kunin, C. C., Ebbesen, E. B., & Konecni, V. J. (1992). An archival study of decision making in child custody disputes. *Journal of Clinical Psychology, 48,* 564–573.

Kunz, J. A. (2007). Older adult development. In J. A. Kunz & F. G. Soltys, (Eds.), *Transformational reminiscence: Life story work* (pp. 19–39). New York: Springer Publishing Company.

Labrum, D. (2004). Idaho's immobile burden: Custodial parent relocation. *Idaho Law Review, 41,* 147.

Lacerda, F., von Hofsten, C., & Heimann, M. (Eds.). (2001). *Emerging cognitive abilities in early infancy.* Hillsdale, NJ: Erlbaum.

Lagan, M., Knights, K., Barton, J., & Boyce, P. M. (2003). Advocacy for mothers with psychiatric illness: A clinical perspective. *International Journal of Mental Health Nursing, 18*(1), 53–61.)

Lagan, M., Knights, K., Barton, J., & Boyce, P. M. (2009). Advocacy for mothers with psychiatric illness: A clinical perspective. *International Journal of Mental Health Nursing, 18*(1), 53–61.

LaGrone, D. M. (1978). The military family syndrome. *American Journal of Psychiatry, 135*(9), 1040–1043.

Laible, D., Gustavo, C., & Raffaelli, M. (2000). The differential relations of parent and peer attachment to adolescent adjustment. *Journal of Youth and Adolescence, 29*(1), 45–59.

Lally, S. J. (2001). Should human figure drawings be admitted into court? *Journal of Personality Assessment, 76,* 135–149.

Lamb, M. E., & Kelly, J. B. (2001). Using the empirical literature to guide the development of parenting plans for young children: A rejoinder to Solomon and Biringen. *Family Court Review, 39*(4), 365–371.

Lampel, A. K. (2002). Assessing for alienation and access in child custody cases: A response to Lee and Olesen. *Family Court Review, 40,* 232–235.

Lande, J. (2008). Improving mediation quality: You, too, can do this in your area. *Alternatives to the High Cost of Litigation, 26*(5), 1–2. DOI: 10.1002/alt. Retrieved March 15, 2009, from http://meetings.abanet.org/webupload/commupload/DR020600/relatedresources/LandeAlternativestoolkit.pdf

Laplante, D. P., Brunet, A., Schmitz, N., Ciampi, A., & King, S. (2008). Project Ice Storm: Prenatal maternal stress affects cognitive and linguistic functioning in 5 ¹/₂-year-old children. *Journal of the American Academy of Child & Adolescent Psychiatry, 47*(9), 1063–1072.

Laufer, R. R. (2007). Facilitating impossible goodbyes: A proposal for conducting the final visit after termination of parental rights. *Dissertation Abstracts International: Section B: The Sciences and Engineering, 67*(11-B), p. 6740.

Laurent, H. K., Kim, H. K., & Capaldi, D. M. (2008). Prospective effects of interparental conflict on child attachment security and the moderating role of parents' romantic attachment. *Journal of Family Psychology, 22*(3), 377–388.

Laursen, E. K., & Birmingham, S. M. (2003). Caring relationships as a protective factor for at-risk youth: An ethnographic study. *Families in Society, 84*(2), 240–246.

Lazarus, R. S. (1984). On the primacy of cognition. *American Psychologist, 39*, 124–129.

Lee, S., & Oleson, N. (2001). Assessing for alienation in child custody and access evaluations. *Family Court Review, 39*(3), 282–298.

Leedham, B., & Meyerowitz, B. (2000). Loss, adjustment, and growth after cancer: Lessons from patients' children. In J. H. Harvey & E. D. Miller, (Eds.), *Loss and trauma: General and close relationship perspectives* (pp. 166–182). Washington, DC: Taylor & Francis.

Lehman, E. B., & Erdwins, C. J.(1981). The social and emotional adjustment of young intellectually gifted children. *Gifted Child Quarterly, 25*(3), 134–138.

Lehman, E. B., & Erdwins, C. J. (2004). The social and emotional adjustment of young intellectually gifted children. In S. M. Moon (Ed.), *Social/emotional issues, underachievement and counseling of gifted and talented students* (pp. 1–8). Thousand Oaks, CA: Corwin.

Lengua, L.J., & Sandler, I.N. (1996). Self-regulation as a moderator of the relation between coping and symptomatology in children of divorce. *Journal of Abnormal Child Psychology, 24*, 681–701.

Lenneberg, E. H. (1967). *Biological foundations of language.* New York: John Wiley.

Leppert, M., O'Connor, L., & Rosier, E. M. (2008). Developmental screening: The pathway to early identification. In P. J. Accardo (Ed.), *Capute and Accardo's neurodevelopmental disabilities in infancy and childhood: Vol 1: Neurodevelopmental diagnosis and treatment* (3rd ed.) (pp. 395–404). Baltimore, MD: Paul H. Brookes Publishing.

Letourneau, N. (2001). Improving adolescent parent-infant interactions: A pilot study. *Journal of Pediatric Nursing, 16*(1), 53–62.

Levine, M. (2008). *Report of the Council on Ethical and Judicial Affairs* (CJEA Report 8-I-07). Retrieved December 26, 2008, from http://www.ama-assn.org/ama1/pub/upload/mm/369/ceja_recs_8i07.pdf

Lewinsohn, P. M., Holm-Denoma, J. M., Small, J. W., Seeley, J. R., & Joiner, T. E., Jr. (2008). Separation anxiety disorder in childhood as a risk factor for future mental illness. *Journal of the American Academy of Child & Adolescent Psychiatry, 47*(5), 548–555.

Lewis, M., Feiring, C., & Rosenthal, S. (2000). Attachment over time. *Child Development, 71*, 707–720.

Li, S. T., Nussbaum, K. M., & Richards, M. H. (2007). Risk and protective factors for African American youth. *American Journal of Community Psychology, 39*, 21–35.

Lillard, D., & Gerner, J.(1999). Getting to the Ivy League: How family composition affects college choice. *Journal of Higher Education, 70*, 706–703.

Lincoln, A., Swift, E., & Shorteno-Fraser, M. (2008). Psychological adjustment and treatment of children and families with parents deployed in military combat. *Journal of Clinical Psychology, 64*(8), 984–992.

Littell, J., & Schuerman, J. (2002). What works best for whom?: A closer look at intensive family preservation services. *Children and Youth Services Review, 24*, 673–699.

Liu, J. H., Raine, A., Venables, P., Dalais, C., & Mednick, S. A. (2004, in press). Malnutrition at age 3 years predisposes to externalizing behavior problems at ages 8, 11, and 17 years. *American Journal of Psychiatry.*

Lorenz, K. Z. (1937). Imprinting. *Auk, 54*, 245–273.

Loucas, T., Charman, T., Pickles, A., Simonoff, E., Chandler, S., Meldrum, D. et al (2008). Autistic symptomatology and language ability in autism spectrum disorder and specific language impairment. *Journal of Child Psychology and Psychiatry, 49*(11), 1184–1192.

Lourenco, O., & Machado, A. (1996). In defense of Piaget's theory: A reply to 10 common criticisms. *Psychological Review, 103*(1), 143–164.

Lozoff, B, Jiminez, E., & Smith, J.B. (2006). Double burden of iron deficiency in infancy and low socioeconomic status. *Archives of Pediatric and Adolescent Medicine, 160*, 1108–1113.

Luckasson, R., Coulter, D. L., Polloway, E. A., Reiss, S., Schalock, R. L., Snell, M. E., et al. (1992). *Mental retardation: Definition, classification, and systems of supports.* Washington, DC: American Association on Mental Retardation.

Luthar, S. S., & Zelazo, L. B. (2003). Research on resilience: An integrative review. In S. S. Luthar (Ed.), *Resilience and vulnerability: Adaptation in the context of childhood adversities* (pp. 510–549). New York: Cambridge University Press.

Luyster, R., Richler, J., Risi, S., Hsu, W. L., Dawson, G., Bernier, R., et al. (2005). Early regression in social communication in autism spectrum disorders: A CPEA study. *Developmental Neuropsychology 27*(3), 311–336.

Luyster, R. J., Kadlec, M. B., Carter, A., & Tager-Flusberg, H. (2008). Language assessment and development in toddlers with autism spectrum disorders. *Journal of Autism and Developmental Disorders, 38*(8), 1426–1438.

Lyon, T. D. (2002). Expert testimony on the suggestibility of children: Does it fit? In B. Bottoms, M. B. Kovera, & B. D. McAuliff (Eds.), *Children, social science and the law* (pp. 378–411). New York: Cambridge University Press.

Lyon, T. D., & Dorado, J. S. (2008). Truth induction in young maltreated children: The effects of oath-taking and reassurance on true and false disclosures. *Child Abuse and Neglect, 32*(7), 738–748.

Lyons-Ruth, K., Connell, D. B., Zoll, D., & Stahl, J. (1987). Infants at social risk: Relations among infant maltreatment, maternal behavior, and infant attachment behavior. *Developmental Psychology, 23*, 223–232.

Macouby, E. E. (2005). A cogent case for a new child custody standard. *Psychological Science in the Public Interest, 6,* i–ii.

Macfie, J., Houts, R. M., Pressel, A. S., & Cox, M. J.(2008). Pathways from infant exposure to marital conflict to parent-toddler role reversal. *Infant Mental Health Journal, 29*(4), 297–319.

Maciejewski, P. K., Zhang, B., Block, S. D., & Prigerson, H. G. (2007). An empirical examination of the stage theory of grief. *Journal of the American Medical Association,* 297, 716–723.

Maddi, S. R. (2002). The story of hardiness: Twenty years of theorizing, research, and practice. *Consulting Psychology Journal, 54,* 175–185.

Main, M. (1991). Metacognitive knowledge, metacognitive monitoring, and singular (coherent) vs. multiple (incoherent) model of attachment: Findings and directions for future research. In C. M. Parkes, J. Stevenson-Hinde, & P. Marris (Eds.), *Attachment across the life cycle* (pp. 127–159). London: Tavistock.

Main, M., & Solomon, J. (1986). Discovery of a disorganized/disoriented attachment pattern. In T. B. Brazelton & M. W. Yogman (Eds.), *Affective development in infancy* (pp. 95–124). Norwood, NJ: Ablex.

Mann-Feder, V. R., & White, T. (2003). Facilitating the transition from placement to independent living: Reactions from a program of research. *International Journal of Child & Family Welfare, 4,* 198–204.

March, J. S., Parker, J. D., Sullivan, K., Stallings, P., & Conners, K. (1997). The Multidimensional Anxiety Scale for Children (MASC): Factor structure, reliability, and validity. *Journal of the American Academy of Child & Adolescent Psychiatry, 36,* 554–565.

Marques-Lopez, D. D. (2006). Not so gray anymore: A mature minor's capacity to consent to medical treatment. *Health Law Perspectives,* 10/31/2006. Retrieved January 24, 2009, from http://www.law.uh.edu/healthlaw/perspectives/2006/(DM)Mature-Minor .pdf

Marschark, M. (2001). *Language development in children who are deaf: A research synthesis.* Alexandria, VA: National Association of State Directors of Special Education. ERIC ED 455 620.

Marsh, H. W., Jayasinghe, U. W., & Bond, N. W. (2008). Improving the peer-review process for grant applications: Reliability, validity, bias, and generalizability. *American Psychologist, 63*(3), 160–168.

Martens, P. (2006). *An effective child welfare system: Evidence-based practice.* Buhl, ID: National Family Preservation Network. Retrieved January 27, 2009, at http://www.nfpn.org/images/stories/files/effective_cws.pdf

Martindale, D. A., & Gould, J. W. (2008). Evaluating the evaluators in custodial placement disputes. In H. V. Hall (Ed.), *Forensic psychology and neuropsychology for criminal and civil cases.* Boca Raton, FL: CRC Press.

Maruish, M. E. (Ed.). (2004). *The use of psychological testing for treatment planning and outcome assessment* (3rd ed.; Vols. 1–3). Mahwah, NJ: Lawrence Erlbaum.

Marvin, R., Cooper, G., Hoffman, K., & Powell, B. (2002). The Circle of Security Project: Attachment-based intervention with caregiver-preschool child dyads. *Attachment and Human Development, 4*(1), 107–124. (See video, available at http://www.circleof security.org)

Marte, N. E. (2008). The experience of early parental separation due to piecemeal immigration to the United States among Dominicans. *Dissertation Abstracts International: Section A: Humanities and Social Sciences, 69*(3-A).

Masten, A. (1999). Resilience comes of age: Reflection on the past and outlook for the next generation of research. In M. D. Glantz, J. Johnson, & L. Huffinan (Eds.), *Resilience and development: Positive life adaptations.* New York: Plenum Press.

Masten, A. S., & Reed, M. J. (2002). Resilience in development. In C. R. Snyder & S. J. Lopez (Eds.), *Handbook of positive psychology* (pp. 74–88). New York: Oxford University Press.

Mason, M. A. (1994). *From father's property to children's rights: The history of child custody in the United States.* New York: Columbia University Press.

Matson, J. L., & Minshawi, N. F. (2006). *Early intervention for autism spectrum disorder: A critical analysis.* Oxford, UK: Elsevier.

Maybery, D., Ling, L., Szakacs, E., & Reupert, A. (2005). Children of a parent with a mental illness: Perspectives on need. *Australian e-Journal for the Advancement of Mental Health, 4*(2). Availble at http://auseinet.flinders.edu.au/journal/

Mazur, T. (1999). Precocious and delayed puberty: Psychology and clinical management. In U. Eiholzer, F. Haverkamp, & L. D. Voss (Eds.), *Growth, stature, and psychosocial well-being* (pp. 169–175). Seattle, WA: Hogrefe & Huber.

McCann, J. T. (2004). Projective assessment of personality in forensic settings. In M. J. Hilsenroth & D. L. Segal, (Eds.), *Comprehensive handbook of psychological assessment, Vol. 2: Personality assessment* (pp. 562–572). Hoboken, NJ: John Wiley.

McCann, J. T., Campana, V., Flens, J., Campagna, V., Coliman, P., & Lazzaro, T. (2001). The MCMI-III in child custody evaluations: A normative study. *Journal of Forensic Psychology Practice, 1*, 27–44.

McCarthy, J., & Boyd, J. (2001). Psychopathology and young people with Down syndrome: childhood predictors of adult outcome of disorder. *Journal of Intellectual Disability Research, 45*(2), 99–105.

McConnell, D., Llewellyn, G., Mayes, R., Russo, D., & Honey, A. (2003). Developmental profiles of children born to mothers with intellectual disability. *Journal of Intellectual & Developmental Disability, 28*, 122–134.

McElwain, N. L., & Booth-LaForce, C. (2006). Maternal sensitivity to infant distress and nondistress as predictors of infant-mother attachment security. *Journal of Family Psychology, 20*, 247–255.

McGarrigle, J., & Donaldson, M. (1975). Conservation accidents. *Cognition: International Journal of Cognitive Psychology, 3*(4), 341–350.

McGrath, M. P., & Brown, B. C. (2008). Developmental differences in prosocial motives and behavior in children from low-socioeconomic status families. *Journal of Genetic Psychology, 169*(1), 5–20.

McGrath, R. E. (2008). The Rorschach in the context of performance-based personality assessment. *Journal of Personality Assessment, 90*(5), 465–475.

McHale, S. M., Dariotis, J. K., & Kauh, T. J. (2003). Social development and social relationships in middle childhood. In T. B. Weiner (Series Editor), R. M. Lerner, M. A. Easterbrooks, & J. Mistry (Vol. Eds.), *Comprehensive handbook of psychology: Vol 6, Developmental psychology* (pp. 241–266). New York: John Wiley.

McIntosh, J., & Chisholm, R. (2007). Shared care and children's best interests in a conflicted separation: A cautionary tale from current research. *Australian Family Lawyer, 20*(1), 3–16.

McIntosh, J., & Chisholm, R. (2008). Cautionary notes on the shared care of children in conflicted parental separation. *Journal of Family Studies, 14*(1), 37–52.

McIntosh, J., & Long, C. (2006). *Children beyond dispute. A prospective study of outcomes from child focused and child inclusive post-separation family dispute resolution.* Retrieved February 1, 2009, from http://www.ag.gov.au/www/agd/rwpattach.nsf/VAP/ (CFD7369FCAE9B8F32F341DBE097801FF)~5555Child+Inclusive+Practice+- +Research+Report+-+Published+Version+-+January+2007.pdf/$file/ 5555Child+Inclusive+Practice+-+Research+Report+-+Published+Version+- +January+2007.pdf

McIntosh, J. E., & Long, C. (2007, July). *The Child Responsive Program Pilot, within the less adversarial trial. A follow up study of parent and child outcomes. A report to the Family Court of Australia.* Available from the Australian Family Court: http:// www.familycourt.gov.au/presence/resources/file/eb00174f35b 4753/CRP_Follow_ up_Report_2007.pdf

McRoy, R. G., Grotevant, H. D., Ayers-Lopez, S., & Henney, S. (2007). Open adoptions: Longitudinal outcomes for the adoption triad. In R. A. Javier, A. L. Baden, R. A. Biafora, & A. Comacho-Gingerich (Eds.), *Handbook of adoption.* Thousand Oaks, CA: Sage.

McWey, L. M., & Mullis, A. K. (2004). Improving the lives of children in foster care: The impact of supervised visitation. *Family Relations, 53,* 293–300.

Mehlman, A. (undated). *The rights of minors regarding their own health care.* The Center for HIV Law and Policy. Retrieved January 24, 2009, from http://www.abanet.org/ AIDS/conferences/2008/materials/Health%20Ca re%20of%20Minors--Mehlman%20 Outline%20-ABA08.pdf

Meier, J. S. (2009). *Parental alienation syndrome and parental alienation: Research reviews.* Harrisburg, PA: VAWnet. Retrieved April 8, 2009, from http://www.vawnet.org

Mello, Z. R. (2008). Gender variation in developmental trajectories of educational and occupational expectations and attainment from adolescence to adulthood. *Developmental Psychology, 44*(4), 1069–1080.

Melone, A. P., & Karnes, A. (2008). *The American legal system: Perspectives, politics, processes, and policies* (2nd ed.). New York: Rowman & Littlefield.

Mendle, J., Turkheimer, E., & Emery, R. E. (2007). Detrimental psychological outcomes associated with early pubertal timing in adolescent girls. *Developmental Review, 27,* 151–171.

Mennen, F. R., & O'Keefe, M. (2005). Informed decisions in child welfare: The use of attachment theory. *Children and Youth Services Review, 27,* 577–593.

Merlino, M. L., Murray, C. I., & Richardson, J. T. (2008). Judicial gatekeeping and the social construction of the admissibility of expert testimony. *Behavioral Sciences & the Law, 26*(2), 187–206.

Michigan Custody Guidelines. (2001). Uniform Child-Custody Jurisdiction and Enforcement Act. Act 195 of 2001. Retrieved July 20 2009, from http://www.legislature.- mi.gov/(S(wi3aoq45xb0lbm55n2va4uqi))/mileg.aspx?page=getobject& objectname=mcl-act-195-of-2001&highlight=)

Midaeva, E. K., & Lyubimova, Z. V. (2008). Formation of language-specific characteristics of speech sounds in early ontogeny. *Human Physiology, 34*(5), 649–652.

Milchman, M. S. (2007). Modified interview questions to assess family violence in child custody evaluations. *Family Psychologist, 23*(1), 23–25.

Miller, K. F., & Baillargeon, R. (1990). Length and distance: Do preschoolers think that occlusion brings things together? *Developmental Psychology, 26*(1), 103–114.

Mills, K. I. (2009). Getting beyond the couch. *Monitor on Psychology, 40*(3), 28–29.

Miniscalco, C., Nygren, G., Hagberg, B., Kadesjo, B., & Gillberg, C. (2006). Neuropsychiatric and neurodevelopmental outcome of children at age 6 and 7 years who screened positive for language problems at 30 months. *Developmental Medicine and Child Neurology, 48*, 361–366.

Mitchell, P., & O'Keefe, K. (2008). Brief report: Do individuals with autism spectrum disorder think they know their own minds? *Journal of Autism and Developmental Disorders, 38*(8), 1591–1597.

Modecki, K. L. (2008). Addressing gaps in the maturity of judgment literature: Age differences and delinquency. *Law and Human Behavior, 32*(1), 78–91.

Moeller, M. P. (2000). Early intervention and language development in children who are deaf and hard of hearing. *Pediatrics, 106*(3) p. e43. Retrieved June 8, 2009, from http://pediatrics.aappublications.org/cgi/content/abstract/106/3/ e43

Moné, J. G., & Biringen, Z. (2006). Perceived parent–child alienation: Empirical assessment of parent-child relationships within divorced and intact families. *Journal of Divorce & Remarriage, 45*(3–4), 131–156.

Money, J., & Lewis, V. G. (1990). Sexology of puberty: Precocious, delayed and incongruous. In J. Money, H. Musaph, & M. E. Perry (Eds.), *Handbook of sexology: Vol. 7. Childhood and adolescent sexology*. Amsterdam: Elsevier.

Montangero, J., & Maurice-Naville, D. (1994). *Piaget, or the advance of knowledge*. Hillsdale, NJ: Lawrence Erlbaum.

Moos, R. H. (1993). *Coping Responses Inventory*. Odessa: Psychological Assessment Resources.

Morra, S., Gobbo, C., Marini, Z., & Sheese, R. (2008). *Cognitive development: Neo-Piagetian perspectives*. New York: Taylor & Francis Group/Lawrence Erlbaum.

Morris, A. (2004). *The story of naming 'maternal alienation': New research enters the world of policy and practice*. Presented at Home Truths Conference, September 15–17, 2004, Melbourne. Retrieved March 9, 2009, from www.thelizlibrary.org/liz/maternal-alienation.doc

Morrison, J. (1981). Rethinking the military family syndrome. *American Journal of Psychiatry, 138*, 354–357.

Moss, E., Bureau, J. F., Cyr, C., & Dubois-Comtois, K. (2006). Is the maternal Q-Set a valid measure of preschool child attachment behavior? *International Journal of Behavioral Development, 30*(6), 488–497.

Motta, R., Little, S., & Tobin, M. (1993). The use and abuse of human figure drawings. *School Psychology Quarterly, 8*, 162–169.

Mulroy, S., Robertson, L., Aiberti, K., Leonard, H., & Bower, C. (2008). The impact of having a sibling with an intellectual disability: Parental perspectives in two disorders. *Journal of Intellectual Disability Research, 52*(3), 216–229.

Murphy, J. M., & Gilligan, C. (1980). Moral development in late adolescents and adulthood: A critique and reconstruction of Kohlberg's theory. *Human Development, 23*, 77–104.

Murray-Parkes, C. (2006). *Love and loss: The roots of grief and its complications.* London: Routledge.

Musson, D. M., Sandal, G. M., & Helmreich, R. L. (2004). Personality characteristics and trait clusters in final stage astronaut selection. *Aviation and Space Environment Medicine, 75*, 342–349.

National Conference of Commissioners on Uniform State Laws. (1970). Uniform Marriage and Divorce Act. *Family Law Quarterly, 6*(1), 106–111.

National Council of Juvenile and Family Court Judges (NCJFCJ). (2006). Parental alienation and the *Daubert* standard: On syndromes and behaviors. In NCJFCJ, *Navigating custody and visitation evaluations in cases with domestic violence: A judge's guide* (2nd ed., p.19). Reno, NV: NCJFCJ. Retrieved June 13, 2009, from http://www.leadershipcouncil.org/1/pas/judges.html

National Institute of Child Health and Human Development, Early Child Care Research Network. (2008b). Social competence with peers in third grade: Associations with earlier peer experiences in childcare. *Social Development, 17*(3), 419–453.

National Institute of Child Health and Human Development, Early Child Care Research Network. (2008a). Mothers' and fathers' support for child autonomy and early school achievement. *Developmental Psychology, 44*(4), 895–907.

Needle, R. B., & Walker, L. E. A. (2008). *Abortion counseling: A clinician's guide to psychology, legislation, politics, and competency.* New York: Springer Publishing Company.

Neihart, M. (2002a). Delinquency and gifted children. In M. Neihart, S. M. Reis, N. M. Robinson, & S. M. Moon (Eds.), *The social and emotional development of gifted children: What do we know?* (pp. 103–112). Waco, TX: Prufrock Press.

Neihart, M. (2002b). Risk and resilience in gifted children: A conceptual framework. In M. Neihart, S. M. Reis, N. M. Robinson, & S. M. Moon (Eds.), *The social and emotional development of gifted children: What do we know?* (pp. 113–122). Waco, TX: Prufrock Press.

Neil, M. (2007, May 7). Soldier's losing custody after deployment. *ABA Journal: Law News Now.* Retrieved February 10, 2009, from http://abajournal.com/news/deploy ment-creates-losing-child-custody-cases/

Nelson, E., & While, D. (2002). Children's adjustment during the first year of a parent's cancer diagnosis. *Journal of Psychosocial Oncology, 20*, 15–36.

Nelson, J. K., & Bennett, C. S. (2008). Introduction: Special issue on attachment. *Clinical Social Work Journal, 36*(1), 3–7.

Nelson, R. M. (2005). *Developmental approach to child assent. Current controversies in pediatric research ethics: Day one notes.* Retrieved June 13, 2009, at http://www.seat tlechildrens.org/home/about_childrens/press_releas es/2005/07/000184.asp

Nemechek, K. (1998). Child preference in custody decisions: Where we have been, where we are going, where we should go. *Iowa Law Review, 83*, 437.

Neuenschwander, L., & Pistole, M. C. (2008, August). *Romantic intimacy predictors: Attachment, caregiving, and parentification.* Poster presentation, American Psychological Association Annual Convention, Boston.

Nijmeijer, J. S., Minderaa, R. B., Buitelaar, J. K., Mulligan, A., Hartman, C. A., & Hoekstra, P. J. (2008). Attention-deficit/hyperactivity disorder and social dysfunctioning. *Clinical Psychology Review, 28*(4), 692–708.

Niles, M. D., Reynolds, A. J., & Nagasawa, M. (2006). Does early childhood intervention affect the social and emotional development of participants? *Early Childhood Research & Practice, 8*(1), 32–48.

Nippold, M. A. (2007). *Later language development: School-age children, adolescents, and young adults* (3rd ed.). Austin, TX: Pro-Ed.

Nisbett, R. E. (2009). *Intelligence and how to get it: Why schools and culture count.* New York: W. W. Norton.

Noble, K. G., Norman, M. F., & Farah, M. J. (2005). Neurocognitive correlates of socioeconomic status in kindergarten children. *Developmental Science, 8*(1), 74–87.

Norcross, J. C. (2005). The psychotherapist's own psychotherapy: Educating and developing psychologists. *American Psychologist, 60*(8), 840–850.

Norcross, J. C., & Guy, J. D. (2007). *Leaving it at the office: A guide to psychotherapist selfcare.* New York: Guilford.

Norcross, J. C., Prochaska, J. O., & Farber, J. A. (1993). Psychologists conducting psychotherapy: New findings and historical comparisons on the psychotherapy division membership. *Psychotherapy: Theory, Research, Practice, Training, 30,* 692–697.

Norko, M. A., & Baranoski, M. V. (2008). The prediction of violence; detection of dangerousness. *Brief Treatment and Crisis Intervention, 8*(1), 73–91.

Norman, A. D., Ramsay, S. G., Martray, C. R., & Roberts, J. L. (1999). Relationship between levels of giftedness and psychosocial adjustment. *Roeper Review, 22,* 5–9.

Nowicki, S., Jr., & Duke, M. P. (1992). The association of children's nonverbal decoding abilities with their popularity, locus of control, and academic achievement. *Journal of Genetic Psychology, 153,* 385–393.

O'Connor, E., & McCartney, K. (2007). Attachment and cognitive skills: An investigation of mediating mechanisms. *Journal of Applied Developmental Psychology, 28,* 458–476.

O'Donohue, W. T., & Fisher, J. E. (2006). Introduction: Clinician's hand-book of evidence-based practice guidelines: The role of practice guidelines in systematic quality improvement. In J. E. Fisher & W. T. O'Donohue (Eds.), *Practitioner's guide to evidence-based psychotherapy* (pp. 1–23). New York: Springer Publishing Company.

Ohan, J. L., & Johnston, C. (2007). What is the social impact of ADHD in girls? A multi-method assessment. *Journal of Abnormal Child Psychology, 35,* 239–250.

Ohio v. Akron Center, 497 U.S. 502 (1990).

Onyehalu, A. S. (1983). Feedback and performance of Piagetian conservation tasks in a developing country. *American Journal of Psychology, 96*(1), 65–73.

Orenstein, A. (2006). *The ethics of child custody evaluation: Advocacy, respect for parents, and the right to an open future.* Bloomington, IN: The Poynter Center for the Study of Ethics and American Institutions. Retrieved February 1, 2009, from http://poynter.indiana.edu/publications/m-orenstein.pdf

Osborn, T. (2007). The psychosocial impact of parental cancer on children and adolescents: A systematic review. *Psycho-Oncology, 16,* 101–126.

Otto, R., & Edens, J. (2002). Parenting capacity. In T. Grisso, R. K. Otto, R. Borum, J. F. Edens, & J. Moye (Eds.), *Evaluating competencies: Forensic assessments and instruments* (2nd ed., pp. 229–307). New York: Kluwer Academic/Plenum Press.

Otto, R. K., Edens, J. F., & Barcus, E. H. (2000). The use of psychological testing in child custody evaluations. *Family and Conciliation Courts Review, 38,* 312–340.

Parr, T. (2007). *We belong together: A book about adoption and families.* New York: Little, Brown Books for Young Readers.

Parkinson, P. (2006). Decision-making about the best interests of the child: The impact of the two tiers. *Australian Journal of Family Law, 20,* 179–186. Retrieved February 1, 2009, from http://www.divorce.com.au/iPadmin/resource/twotiers.pdf

Parkinson, P., & Cashmore, J. (2007). What responsibility do courts have to hear children's voices? *International Journal of Children's Rights, 15,* 43–60.

Parkinson, P., Cashmore, J., & Single, J. (2005). Adolescents' views on the fairness of parenting and financial arrangements after separation. *Family Court Review, 43,* 429–444.

Paul, R., & Fountain, R. (1999). Predicting outcomes of early expressive language delay. *Infant–Toddler Intervention, 9*(2), 123–135.

Pearce, J. W., & Pezzot-Pearce, T. D. (2007). *Psychotherapy of abused and neglected children.* New York: Guilford.

Pelchat, D., Bisson, J., Bois, C., & Saucier, J.-F. (2003). The effects of early relational antecedents and other factors on the parental sensitivity of mothers and fathers. *Infant & Child Development, 12*(1), 27–51.

Pellegrino, J. E., & Pellegrino, L. (2008). Fetal alcohol syndrome and related disorders. In P. J. Accardo (Ed), *Capute and Accardo's neurodevelopmental disabilities in infancy and childhood: Vol 1. Neurodevelopmental diagnosis and treatment* (3rd ed.). Baltimore, MD: Paul H Brookes Publishing.

Perkins, S. A., & Turiel, E. (2007). To lie or not to lie: To whom and under what circumstances. *Child Development, 78,* 609–621.

Perry, B. D., & Pollard, D. (1997). Altered brain development following global neglect in early childhood. *Society For Neuroscience: Proceedings from Annual Meeting, New Orleans.* Retrieved December 7, 2008, from http://www.childtrauma.org/CTAMAT ERIALS/neuros~1.asp

Perryman, H. P. (2005). Parental reaction to the disabled child: Implications for family courts. *Family Court Review, 43,* 596–606.

Peterson, J. S. (2006, October). Addressing counseling needs of gifted students. *Professional School Counseling.* Retrieved December 30, 2008, from http://findarticles.com/p/articles/mi_m0KOC/is_1_10/ai_n27019815/print?tag=artBody;col1

Peterson, J. S., & Ray, K. E. (2006a). Bullying among the gifted: The subjective experience. *Gifted Child Quarterly, 50,* 252–269.

Peterson, J. S., & Ray, K. E. (2006b). Bullying and the gifted: Victims, perpetrators, prevalence, and effects. *Gifted Child Quarterly, 50,* 148–168.

Peterson, J. S., & Rischar, H. (2000). Gifted and gay: A study of the adolescent experience. *Gifted Child Quarterly, 44,* 149–164.

Piaget, J. (1969). *The child's conception of time.* New York: Routledge Kegan Paul. (Original work published 1927)

Piaget, J. (1977). [Selected writings.] In H. E. Gruber & J. J. Vonèche (Eds.), *The essential Piaget: An Interpretive Reference and Guide.* New York: Basic Books.

Piaget, J. (1983). Piaget's theory. In P. Mussen (Ed), *Handbook of child psychology: Vol. 1* (4th ed.). New York: JohnWiley.

Piaget, J., & Inhelder, B. (1967). *The child's conception of space.* New York: Norton.

Piaget, J., & Inhelder, B. (1973). *The psychology of the child.* Paris: Presses Universitaires de France. (Originally published in 1966 as *La psychologie de l'enfant*)

Pickar, D. B. (2007). On being a child custody evaluator: Professional and personal challenges. *Family Court Review, 45*, 103–115.

Pijl, S. J., Frostad, P., & Flem, A. (2008). The social position of pupils with special needs in regular schools. *Scandinavian Journal of Educational Research, 52*(4), 387–405.

Pimlott, S., & Sarri, R. (2002). The forgotten group: Women in prisons and jails. In J. Figueira-McDonough & R. Sarri (Eds.), *Women at the margins: Neglect, punishment and resistance.* Binghamton, NY: Hayworth Press.

Pincus, S. H., House, R., Christenson, J., & Adler, L. E. (2008). The emotional cycle of deployment: A military family perspective. *My Hooah 4 Health: The U.S. Army Health Promotion and Wellness Web Site.* Retrieved February 10, 2009, from http://www.hooah4health.com/deployment/familymatters/emotionalcycle.htm#

Piper, A., Lillevik, L., & Kritzer, R. (2008). What's wrong with believing in repression?: A review for legal professionals. *Psychology, Public Policy, and Law, 14*(3), 223–242.

Pliner, A. J., & Yates, S. (1992). Psychological and legal issues in minor's rights to abortion. *Journal of Social Issues, 48*, 203–216.

Poehlmann, J. (2005a). Children's family environments and intellectual outcomes during maternal incarceration. *Journal of Marriage and Family, 67*, 1275–1285.

Poehlmann, J. (2005b). Representations of attachment relationships in children of incarcerated mothers. *Child Development, 76*, 679–696.

Poehlmann, J. (2005c). Incarcerated mothers' contact with children, perceived family relationships and depressive symptoms. *Journal of Family Psychology, 19*(3), 350–357.

Poehlmann, J., Shafler, R., Maes, E., & Hanneman, A. (2008). Factors associated with young children's opportunities for maintaining family relationships during maternal incarceration. *Family Relations, 57*(8), 267–280.

Poliacoff, J. H., Greene, C. L., & Smith, L. (1999). Parental Alienation Syndrome: Frye v. Gardner in the family courts. *Family Law Commentator (Florida Bar), 25*(4), 19–20, 30–33. Retrieved November 9, 2008, from http://expertpages.com/news/parental_alienation_syndrome.htm

Pollack, D., & Mason, S. (2004). Mandatory visitation: In the best interest of the child. *Family Court Review, 42*, 74–84.

Pope, A.W., & Snyder, H. T. (2004). Psychosocial adjustment in children and adolescents with a craniofacial anomaly: Age and sex patterns. *Cleft Palate-Craniofacial Journal, 42*(4), 349–354.

Pope, K. S., Butcher, J. N., & Seelen, J. (2000). *The MMPI, MMPI-2 & MMPI-A in court: A practical guide for expert witnesses and attorneys* (2nd ed.). Washington, DC: American Psychological Association.

Porter, N. (2006). *Infant and child sexual abuse and pubertal development in females.* Paper presented at the annual meeting of the XVth Biennial International Conference on Infant Studies, Kyoto, Japan. Retrieved November 1, 2008, from http://www.alla cademic.com/meta/p94409_index.html

Post, Y., Boyer, W., & Brett, L. (2006). A historical examination of self-regulation: Helping children now and in the future. *Early Childhood Education Journal,* 34(1), 5–14.

Posthuma, A. (2003). A new MMPI-2 scale for custody disputes. *American Journal of Forensic Psychology, 21,* 51–64.

Premack, D. G., & Woodruff, G. (1978). Does the chimpanzee have a theory of mind? *Behavioral and Brain Sciences, 1,* 515–526.

Pruett, M. K., Ebling, R., & Insabella, G. (2004). Critical aspects of parenting plans for young children: Interjecting data into the debate about overnights. *Family Court Review, 42*(1), 39–59.

Putnam, S. P., Spritz, B. L., & Stifter, C. A. (2002). Mother–child coregulation during delay of gratification at 30 months. *Infancy, 3*(2), 209–225.

Quart, A. (2006). *Hothouse kids: The dilemma of the gifted child.* New York: Penguin Books.

Quinlan, R. J. (2003). Father-absence, parental care and female reproductive development. *Evolution & Human Behavior, 24*(6), 376–390.

Quinn-Beers, J. (2001). Attachment needs of adolescent daughters of women with cancer. *Journal of Psychosocial Oncology, 19*(1), 35–48.

Quinsey, V. L., Harris, G. T., Rice, M. E., & Cormier, C. A. (2006). Criticisms of actuarial risk assessment. In V. L. Quinsey, G. T. Harris, M. E. Rice, & C. A. Cormier (Eds.), *Violent offenders: Appraising and managing risk* (2nd ed., pp. 197–223). Washington, DC: American Psychological Association.

Quinton, W. J., Major, B., & Richards, C. (2001). Adolescents and adjustment at abortion: Are minors at greater risk? *Psychology, Public Policy, & Law, 7,* 491–514.

Racusin, R., Copans, S. A., & Mills, P. (1994). Characteristics of families of children who refuse post-divorce visits. *Journal of Clinical Psychology, 50,* 792–801.

Rae-Espinoza, H. (2007). Devoted abandonment: The children left behind by parental emigration in Ecuador. *Dissertation Abstracts International: Section A: Humanities and Social Sciences, 67*(8-A).

Rahabi, S. T. (1999). Retrospective views of children who are given the option to express their custodial preference. *Dissertation Abstracts International: Section B: The Sciences and Engineering, 60*(1-B), pp. 03–73.

Rakoczy, H., Tomasello, M., & Striano, T. (2006). The role of experience and discourse in children's developing understanding of pretend play actions. *British Journal of Developmental Psychology, 24,* 305–355.

Ram, A., Pinzi, R., & Cohen, O. (2002). The non-custodial parent and his infant. *Journal of Divorce & Remarriage, 36*(3–4), 41–55.

Ratterman, D. (1991). *Termination barriers: Speeding adoption in New York State through reducing delays in termination of parental rights cases.* Washington, DC: ABA Center on Children and the Law.

Ratterman, D., Dodson, G., & Hardin, M. (1987). *Reasonable efforts to prevent foster placement: A guide for implementation* (2nd ed.). Washington, DC: American Bar Association, National Legal Resource Center for Child Advocacy and Protection.

Ray, J. (2008, December 15). Emancipation from foster care: What happens when youth age-out? *Foster Parenting.* Retrieved February 22, 2009, from http://fosterparenting.suite101.com/article.cfm/emancipation_from _foster_care

Reamer, F. G., & Siegal, D. H. (2007). Ethical issues in open adoption: Implications for practice. *Families in Society, 88,* 11–18.

Redding, R. E., Floyd, M. Y., & Hawk, G. L. (2001). What judges and lawyers think about the testimony of mental health experts: A survey of the courts and bar. *Behavioral Sciences & the Law, 19*(4), 583–594.

Reddy, L. A., & Pfeiffer, S. I. (2007). Behavioral and emotional symptoms of children and adolescents with Prader-Willi Syndrome. *Journal of Autism and Developmental Disorders, 37*(5), 830–839.

Redmond, S. M., & Timler, G. R. (2007). Addressing the social concomitants of developmental language impairments. In A. G. Kamhi, J. J. Masterson, & K. Apel (Eds.), *Clinical decision making in developmental language disorders. Communication and language intervention series* (pp. 185–202). Baltimore: Paul H Brookes.

Reeves, T. L., Hampton, A. B., Strohmer, D. C., & Leierer, S. J. (2008, August). *Diversity among psychologists: Examining interest profiles of psychologist specialties.* American Psychological Association (conference presentation), Boston.

Reilly, T. (2003). Transition from care: Status and outcomes of youth who age out of foster care. *Child Welfare, 82*(6), 727–746.

Renouf, E. M. (1985, May). Access refusals by children in post-separated families. *Australian Journal of Sex, Marriage & Family, 6*(2), 77–86.

Rhode, B. (2006). The well balanced lawyer. *St. Petersburg Bar Association Newsletter.* Retrieved March 13, 2009, from http://www.stpetebar.com/Compassion_Fatigue_Paraclete_02-2006.pdf

Richardson, J. T., Dobbin, S. A., Gatowski, S. I., Ginsburg, G. P., Merlino, M. L., & Dahir, V. (1998). *Judges' experience with, and perception of, Daubert, scientific evidence, and the question of admissibility: A national study.* Paper presented at the meeting of the Law & Society Association, Aspen. CO.

Richardson, J. T., Ginsburg, G. P., Gatowski, S., & Dobbin, S. (1995). The problems of applying *Daubert* to psychological syndrome evidence. *Judicature, 79,* 1–9.

Richardson, J. T., & Ginsburg, G. P. (1998). A critique of "brainwashing" evidence in light of *Daubert*: Science and unpopular religions. In H. Reece (Ed.), *Law and science: Current legal issues: Vol. 1* (pp. 265–288). Retrieved February 2, 2009, from http://www.cesnur.org/testi/daubert.htm

Riggs, S. A. (2003). Response to *Troxel v. Granville*: Implications of attachment theory for judicial decisions regarding custody and third-party visitation. *Family Court Review, 41,* 39–53.

Roese, N. J., & Olson, J. M. (2007). Better, stronger, faster: Self-serving judgment, affect regulation, and the optimal vigilance hypothesis. *Perspectives on Psychological Science, 2*(2), 124–141.

Rogers, J., Cleveland, H., van der Oord, E., & Rowe, D. (2000). Resolving the debate over birth order, family size, and intelligence. *American Psychologist, 55,* 599–612.

Rogers, J., & Nielsen, A. (1993). Gifted children and divorce: A study of the literature on the incidence of divorce in families with gifted children. *Journal for the Education of the Gifted, 16,* 251–267.

Rogers, M. L., & Hogan, D. P. (2003). Family life with children with disabilities: The key role of rehabilitation. *Journal of Marriage and the Family, 65,* 818–833.

Rogers, S. J., & Williams, J. H. G. (2006). Imitation in autism: Findings and controversies. In S. J. Rogers & J. H. G. Willams (Eds.), *Imitation and the social mind: Autism and typical development* (pp. 277–309). New York: Guilford.

Rolland, J. (1999a). Parental illness and disability: a family systems framework. *Journal of Family Therapy, 21,* 242–266.

Rolland, J. (1999b). Chronic illness and the family life cycle. In B. Carter & M. McGoldrick (Eds.), *The expanded family life cycle: Individual, family, and social perspectives* (3rd ed., pp. 492–511). Boston: Allyn & Bacon.

Romaine, M., Turley, T., & Tuckey, N. (2007). *Preparing children for permanence: A guide to undertaking direct work for social workers, foster carers and adoptive parents.* London: British Association for Adoption & Fostering.

Romer, G., Barkmann, C., Schulte-Markwort, M., Thomalla, G., & Riedesser, P. (2002). Children of somatically ill parents: A methodological review. *Clinical Child Psychology & Psychiatry, 7,* 17–38.

Rosado, L. M. (Ed.). (2000). *Kids are different: How knowledge of adolescent development theory can aid decision-making in court.* Washington, DC: American Bar Association Juvenile Justice Center. Retrieved January 19, 2009, from http://www.jlc.org/files/publications/maccurriculum.pdf

Roseby, V. (1995). Uses of psychological tests in a child-focused approach to child custody evaluations. *Family Law Quarterly, 29*(1), 97–110.

Ross, G., & Weinberg, S. (2006). Is there a relationship between language delays and behavior and socialization problems in toddlers? *Journal of Early Childhood and Infant Psychology, 2,* 101–116.

Ross, H. S., Smith, J., Spielmacher, C., & Recchia, H. (2004). Shading the truth: Self-serving biases in children's reports on sibling conflicts. *Merrill-Palmer Quarterly, 50,* 61–85.

Ross, K. L. (2008). Some moral dilemmas. *Proceedings of the Friesian School, Fourth Series.* Retrieved October 18, 2008, from http://www.friesian.com/valley/dilemmas.htm

Rostow, C. D., & Davis, R. D. (2004). *A handbook for psychological fitness-for-duty evaluations in law enforcement.* New York: Haworth.

Rothenberg, B. (2002). The success of the battered woman syndrome: An analysis of how cultural arguments succeed. *Sociological Forum,* 81–103.

Rotman, A. S., Tompkins, R., Linzer-Schwartz, L., & Samuels, M. D. (2000). Reconciling parents' and children's best interests in relocationrelocation: In whose best interests? *Family Court Review, 38*(3), 341–367.

Rottinghaus, P. J. (2009). The Kuder Skills Assessment—College and Adult Version: Development and initial validation in a college business sample. *Journal of Career Assessment, 17*(1), 56–68.

Ruck, M. D. (1996). Why children think they should tell the truth in court: Developmental considerations for the assessment of competency. *Legal and Criminological Psychology, 1,* 103–106.

Rutter, M. (2007). Resilience, competence, and coping. *Child Abuse & Neglect, 31*(3), 205–209.

Sable, P. (2008). What is adult attachment? *Clinical Social Work, 36,* 21–30.

Sacks, J. Y., McKendrick, K., & Kressel, D. (2007). Measuring offender progress in treatment using the Client Assessment Inventory. *Criminal Justice and Behavior,* 34(9), 1131–1142.

Salekin, R. T., & Averett, C. A. (2008). Personality in childhood and adolescence. In M. Hersen, & A. M. Gross (Eds.), *Handbook of clinical psychology: Vol 2. Children and adolescents* (pp. 351–385). Hoboken, NJ: John Wiley.

Samuels, M. D., & Friesen, R. (2004). E-visiting and other long-distance links. *Family Advocate,* 26(4), 34–37.

Sandberg, D. E. (1999). Experiences of being short: Should we expect problems of psychosocial Adjustment? In U. Eiholzer, F. Haverkamp, & L. D. Voss (Eds.), *Growth, stature, and psychosocial well-being* (pp. 15–26). Seattle: Hogrefe and Huber.

Satyanathan, D. (2002). Overview. In E. Trzcinski, D. Satyanthan, &, L. Ferro (Eds.), *What about me? Children with incarcerated parents.* (Michigan Family Impact Seminars, Briefing Report 2002-1.) Detroit, MI: Wayne State University School of Social Work. Retrieved February 9, 2008, from http://fce.msu.edu/Family_Impact_Seminars/pdf/incarc.pdf

Sax, L. (2007). *Boys adrift: The five factors driving the growing epidemic of unmotivated boys and underachieving young men.* New York: Basic Books.

Scharff, K. E. (2006). Therapeutic supervision with families of high-conflict divorce. In J. Savege & D. E. Scharff (Eds), *New paradigms for treating relationships* (pp. 133–146). Lanham, MD: Jason Aronson.

Schepard, A. (2001). Editorial notes. *Family Court Review, 39,* 243–245.

Schermerhorn, A. C., & Cummings, E. M. (2008). Transactional family dynamics: A new framework for conceptualizing family influence processes. *Advances in Child Development and Behavior, 36,* 187–250.

Schiff, M., & Benbenishty, R. (2006). Functioning of Israeli group-homes alumni: Exploring the differences and in-care correlates. *Children and Youth Services Review, 28,* 133–157.

Schneider, B., Atkinson, L., & Tardif, C. (2001). Child–parent attachment and children's peer relations: A quantitative review. *Developmental Psychology, 37*(1), 86–100.

Schore, A. N. (1994). *Affect regulation and the origin of the self.* Hillsdale, NJ: Lawrence Erlbaum.

Schore, A. N. (2003a). *Affect dysregulation and disorders of the self.* New York: W. W. Norton.

Schore, A. N. (2003b). *Affect regulation and the repair of the self.* New York: W. W. Norton.

Schore, J. R. & Schore, A. N. (2008). Modern attachment theory: The central role of affect regulation in development and treatment. *Clinical Social Work Journal,* 36(1), 9–20.

Schwartz, I. M., AuClaire, P., & Harris, L. J. (1991). *Intensive family preservation service as an alternative to the out-of-home placement of seriously emotionally disturbed adolescents: The Hennepin County experience.* Newbury Park, CA: Sage.

Seifert, M. M. (2004, December). Sibling visitation after adoption: The implications of the Massachusetts sibling visitation statute. *Boston University Law Review,* p. 1467.

Seiffge-Krenke, I. (2006). Leaving home or still in the nest? Parent–child relationships and psychological health as predictors of different leaving home patterns. *Developmental Psychology, 42,* 864–876.

Seligman, M., Darling, R. B. (2007). *Ordinary families, special children: A systems approach to childhood disability* (3rd ed.). New York: Guilford.

Sells, B. (2002). *The soul of the law.* La Vergne, TN: Lightning Source.

Semrud-Clikeman, M. (2007). *Social competence in children.* New York: Springer Science + Business Media.

Shadish, W.R., Cook, T. D., & Campbell, D. T. (2002). *Experimental and quasi-experimental designs for generalized causal inference.* Boston: Houghton-Mifflin.

Shafer, V. L., & Garrido-Nag, K. (2007). The neurodevelopmental bases of language. In E. Hoff & M. Shatz (Eds.), *Blackwell handbook of language development* (pp. 21–45). Malden, MA: Blackwell.

Shaffer, D., Gould, M. S., Brasic, J., Ambrosini, P., Fisher, P., Bird, H., et al. (1983). A children's global assessment scale (CGAS). *Archives of General Psychiatry, 40,* 1228–1231.

Sharlin, S. A., & Polansky, N. A. (1972). The process of infantilization. *American Journal of Orthopsychiatry, 42*(1), 92–102.

Shaub, J. (2007). *What are the inherent traits of a lawyer?* Retrieved July 2009, from http://wiki.answers.com/Q/What_are_the_inherent_traits_of_a_lawyer

Shaver, P. R., Belsky, J., & Brennan, K. A. (2000). Comparing measures of adult attachment: An examination of interview and self-report methods. *Personal Relationships, 7,* 25–43.

Shavit, N. (2005a). Sexual contact between psychologists and patients. *Journal of Aggression, Maltreatment & Trauma, 11*(1–2), 205–239.

Shavit, N. (2005b). Sexual contact between psychologists and patients. In S. F. Bucky, J. E. Callan, & G. Stricker (Eds.), *Ethical and legal issues for mental health professionals: A comprehensive handbook of principles and standards* (pp. 205–239). Binghamton, NY: Haworth Maltreatment and Trauma Press/ Haworth.

Shear, L. A. (2002). *Amicus curiae brief of Leslie A. Shear, Esquire, et al., filed in re: Marriage of LaMusga S107355, Supreme Court of the State of California, July 6, 2002.* Retrieved and available in full from http://www.thelizlibrary.org/lamusga/ShearFinal.pdf

Sheehan, K., DiCara, J. A., LeBailly, S., & Kaufer-Christoffel, K. (1999). Adapting the gang model: Peer mentoring for violence prevention. *Pediatrics, 104*(1), 50–54.

Shepperd, J., Malone, W., & Sweeny, K. (2008). Exploring causes of the self-serving bias. *Social and Personality Psychology Compass, 2*(2), 895–908.

Sherif, M. (1970). On the relevance of social psychology. *American Psychologist, 25,* 144–156.

Sherif, M., Harvey, O. J., White, B. J., Hood, W. R., & Sherif, C. W. (1954). *Experimental study of positive and negative inter-group attitudes between experimentally produced groups. Robbers' Cave study.* Norman, OK: University of Oklahoma.

Sherif, M., Harvey, O. J., White, J., Hood, W., & Sherif, C. W. (1961). *Intergroup conflict and cooperation: The Robbers' Cave Experiment.* Norman, OK: University Book Exchange.

Sherif, M., Harvey, O. J., White, B. J., Hood, W. R., & Sherif, C. W. (1962). *Intergroup conflict and cooperation: The Robbers' Cave experiment.* Norman, OK: University Book Exchange.

Shlonsky, A., Bellamy, J., Elkins, J., & Norman, C. (2005). The other kin: Setting the course for research, policy, and practice with siblings in foster care. *Children and Youth Services Review, 27*(7), 697–716.

Shorey, H., & Snyder, C. (2006). The role of adult attachment styles in psychopathology and psychotherapy outcomes. *Review of General Psychology, 10*(1), 1–20.

Shweder, R. (1991). *Thinking through cultures.* Cambridge, MA: Harvard University Press.

Sichel, St. (1991). The child's preference in disputed custody cases. *Connecticut Family Law, 6,* 45.

Sieratzki, J. S., & Woll, B. (1998). *Toddling into language. Precocious language development in children with spinal muscular atrophy.* London: City University London, Jennifer Trust.

Sigman, M., & Whaley, S. E. (1998). The role of nutrition in the development of intelligence. In U. Neisser (Ed.), *The rising curve: Long-term gains in IQ and related measures.* Washington, DC: American Psychological Association.

Silverman, B. S. (2001). The winds of change in adoption laws: Should adoptees have access to adoption records? *Family Court Review, 39,* 85–103.

Silverman, L. K. (1997). The construct of asynchronous development. *Peabody Journal of Education, 72,* 36–58.

Simmons, C. W. (2000, March). Children of incarcerated parents. *California Research Bureau (CRB Note), 7* (2), 1–11. Retrieved February 8, 2009, from http://www.library.ca.gov/crb/00/notes/V7N2.pdf

Simon, R. I., & Gold, L. H. (2004). *American psychiatric publishing textbook of forensic psychiatry.* Washington, D.C.: American Psychiatric Press.

Sinclair, D. A. (2006, November). *Vicarious trauma and burn-out: Strategies for survival— the impact of high risk work on workers.* Conference on Children as Victims and Witnesses of Domestic Homicides, London. Retrieved March 14, 2009, from www.crvawc.ca/documents/LondonVTPPPres.Nov.22006.ppt

Singer, R. (2008). Neuropsychological assessment of toxic exposures. In A. Horton, Jr., & D. Wedding (Eds.), *The neuropsychology handbook* (3rd ed., pp. 753–770). New York: Springer Publishing Company.

Skafte, D. (1985). *Child custody evaluations: A practical guide.* Thousand Oaks, CA: Sage.

Slaughter, V., & Boh, W. (2001). Decalage in infants' search for mothers versus toys demonstrated with a delayed response task. *Infancy, 2,* 405–413.

Smith, R. (1982, October). *Family decalage: Understanding moral conflict.* Paper presented at the Annual Meeting of the National Council on Family Relations, Washington, DC. Retrieved December 27, 2008, from http://eric.ed.gov/ERICWebPortal/custom/portlets/recordDetails/de tailmini.jsp?_nfpb=true&_&ERICExtSearch_SearchValue_0=ED225668&ER ICExtSearch_SearchType_0=no&accno=ED225668

Smith-Bailey, D. (2005). A niche that puts children first. *Monitor on Psychology, 36*(1), 46. Retrieved December 30, 2008, from http://www.uvm.edu/~psych/news/archive/Copeland.pdf

Smolensky, P. (1996). On the comprehension/production dilemma in child language. *Linguistic Inquiry, 27*, 720–31.

Smyth, B. (Ed.). (2004). *Parent child contact and post-separation parenting arrangements.* Australian Institute of Family Studies, Research Report No. 9. Retrieved January 30, 2009, from http://www.aifs.gov.au/institute/pubs/resreport9/intro.pdf

Smyth, B., & Chisholm, R. (2006). Exploring options for parental care of children following separation: A primer for family law specialists. *Australian Journal of Family Law, 20*, 193–218.

Smyth, B., & Ferro, A. (2002). When the difference is night & day: Parent–child contact after separation. *Family Matters, 63*, 54–59.

Snowling, M. J., Bishop, D. V. M., Stothard, S. E., Chipchase, B., & Kaplan, C. (2006). Psychosocial outcomes at 15 years of children with a pre-school history of speech-language impairment. *Journal of Child Psychology and Psychiatry, 47*, 759–765.

Snyder, J. (2005). Loss: Divorce, separation, and bereavement. In W. M. Klykylo & J. L. Kay (Eds.), *Clinical child psychiatry* (2nd ed., pp. 507–520). New York: John Wiley.

Solomon, J. (2005). An attachment theory framework for planning infant and toddler visitation arrangements in never-married, separated, and divorced families. In L. Gunsberg & P. Hymowitz (Eds.), *A handbook of divorce and custody: Forensic, developmental, and clinical perspectives* (pp. 259–279). New York: The Analytic Press/ Taylor & Francis Group.

Solomon, J., & Biringen, Z. (2001). Another look at the developmental research: Commentary on Kelly and Lamb's, using child development research to make appropriate custody and access decisions for young children. *Family Court Review, 39*, 355–364.

Solomon, J., & George, C. (1999). The measurement of attachment security in infancy and childhood. In J. Cassidy & P. R. Shaver (Eds.), *Handbook of attachment: Theory, research and clinical applications* (pp. 287–316). New York: Guilford.

Solomon, J., & George, C. (1999). The development of attachment in separated and divorced families. *Attachment and Human Development, 1*, 2–33.

Sonis, W., Comite, F., Blue, J., Pescovitz, O. H., Rahn, C. W., Hench, K. D., et al. (1985). Behavior problems and social competence in girls with true precocious puberty. *Journal of Pediatrics, 106*, 156–160.

Sowell, T. (2001). *The Einstein syndrome: Bright children who talk late.* New York: Basic Books.

Spain, S., & Schmedlen, G. (2005). Death penalty mitigation. *Journal of the American Academy of Psychiatry and the Law, 33*, 265–267.

Spencer, P. E., & Harris, M. (2006). Patterns and effects of language input to deaf infants and toddlers from deaf and hearing mothers. In B. Schick, M. Marschark, & P. E. Spencer (Eds.), *Advances in the sign language development of deaf children.* Oxford: Oxford University Press.

Spieker, S. I., Nelson, D. C., Petras, A., Jolley, S. N., & Barnard, K. E. (2003). Joint influence of child care and infant attachment security for cognitive and language outcomes of low-income-toddlers. *Infant Behavior and Development, 26*, 326–344.

Sroufe, L. A., Egeland, B., Carlson, E., & Collins, A. (2005). *The development of the person.* New York: Guilford.

Stahl, P. H. (1999). Alienation and alignment of children. *California Psychologist, 32*, 23.

Stahl, P. M. (1999). *Complex issues in child custody evaluations.* Thousand Oaks, CA: Sage.

Stahl, P. M., & Drozd, L. (2007). *Relocation issues in child custody cases.* New York: Haworth Press.

Stallard, P., & Saltet, E. (2003). Psychological debriefing with children and young people following traumatic events. *Clinical Child Psychology & Psychiatry, 8,* 445–457.

Steck, B., Amsler, F., Grether, A., Dillier, A. S., Baldus, C., Haagen, M., et al. (2007). Mental health problems in children of somatically ill parents, e.g. multiple sclerosis. *European Child & Adolescent Psychiatry, 16*(3), 199–207.

Stefanatos, G. A. (2008). Regression in autistic spectrum disorders. *Neuropsychology Review, 18*(4) 305–319.

Stein, M. T., Parker, S., Coplan, J., & Feldman, H. (2001). Expressive language delay in a toddler. *Journal of Developmental & Behavioral Pediatrics, 22*(2), 99.

Steinberg, L., & Cauffman, E. (1996). Maturity of judgment in adolescence: Psychosocial factors in adolescent decision making. *Law & Human Behavior, 20,* 249–272.

Steinberg, L., & Scott, E. (2003). Less guilty by reason of adolescence: Developmental immaturity, diminished responsibility, and the juvenile death penalty. *American Psychologist, 58*(12), 1009–1018.

Steinberg, L., & Silverberg, S. (1986). The vicissitudes of autonomy in early adolescence. *Child Development, 57,* 841–851.

Stolk, M. N., Mesman, J., van Zeijl, J., Alink, L. R. A.,. Bakermans-Kranenburg, M. J., van IJzendoorn, M. H., et al. (2008). Early parenting intervention aimed at maternal sensitivity and discipline: A process evaluation. *Journal of Community Psychology, 36*(6), 780–797.

Stoltz, J. M., & Ney, T. (2002). Resistance to visitation: Rethinking parental and child alienation. *Family Court Review, 40,* 220–231.

Stovall-McClough, K. C., & Dozier, M. (2004). Forming attachments in foster care: Infant attachment behaviors in the first two months of placement. *Development & Psychopathology. 16,* 253–261.

Strang, R. (1953). Manifestations of maturity in adolescents. In M. Jerome (Ed), *The adolescent: A book of readings* (pp. 754–768). Fort Worth, TX: Dryden Press.

Strauss, E., Sherman, E. M. S., & Spreen, O. (2006). *A compendium of neuropsychological tests* (3rd ed.). New York: Oxford University Press.

Strauss, R. B. (1995). Supervised visitation and family violence. *Family Law Quarterly, 29,* 229–252.

Strickland, A., Jane, S., Moulton, S., White, J., & Schou, C. (2008). Development of a digital reusable learning object to provide instruction and assessment of Piaget's conservation of number in order to improve elementary student mathematics performance. In *Proceedings of World Conference on Educational Multimedia, Hypermedia and Telecommunications* (pp. 1341–1349). Chesapeake, VA: Association for the Advancement of Computing in Education.

Suchman, N., DeCoste, C., Castiglioni, N., Legow, N., & Mayes, L. (2008). The Mothers and Toddlers Program: Preliminary findings from an attachment-based parenting intervention for substance-abusing mothers. *Psychoanalytic Psychology, 25,* 499–517.

Suitor, J. J., & Pillemer, K. (2007). Mothers' favoritism in later life: The role of children's birth order. *Research on Aging, 29*, 32–55.

Sullivan, E. V., McCullough, G., & Stager, M. A. (1970). Developmental study of the relationship between conceptual, ego, and moral development. *Child Development, 41*, 399–411.

Sullivan, M. J., & Kelly, J. B. (2001). Legal and psychological management of cases with an alienated child. *Family Court Review, 39*(3), 299–315.

Sun, S. S., Schubert, C. M., Liang, R., Roche, A. F., Kulin, H. E., Lee, P. A., et al. (2005). Is sexual maturity occurring earlier among U.S. children? *Journal of Adolescent Health, 37*(5), 345–355.

Swick, S., & Rauch, P. (2006). Children facing the death of a parent: The experiences of a parent guidance program at the Massachusetts General Hospital Cancer Center. *Child and Adolescent Psychiatric Clinics of North America, 15*(3), 779–794.

Talwar, V., & Lee, K. (2002). Emergence of white-lie telling in children between 3 and 7 years of age. *Merrill Palmer Quarterly, 48*, 160–181.

Tanner, D. C. (2007). Redefining Wernicke's Area: Receptive language and discourse semantics. *Journal of Allied Health, 36*(2), 63–66. Retrieved December 6, 2008, from http://findarticles.com/p/articles/mi_qa4040/is_200707/ai_n194333 56

Tarabulsy, G. M., Pascuzzo, K., Moss, E., St.-Laurent, D., Bernier, A., Cyr, C., et al. (2008). Attachment-based intervention for maltreating families. *American Journal of Orthopsychiatry, 78*(3), 322–332.

Tarabulsy, G. M., Robitaille, J., Lacharite, C., Deslandes, J., & Coderre, R. (1998). Interventions with young mothers and their children: Taking the perspective of attachment theory. *Criminologie, 31*, 7–31.

Taylor, L. (2004). Gender constancy and rigidity: A cross-sectional examination of early gender development. *Dissertation Abstracts International: Section B: The Sciences and Engineering, 65*(3-B), 1582.

Tedeschi, R. G., Park, C. L., & Calhoun, L. G. (1998). *Posttraumatic growth: Positive changes in the aftermath of crisis*. Northvale, NJ: Lawrence Erlbaum.

Tervo, R. C. (2007). Language proficiency, development, and behavioral difficulties in toddlers. *Clinical Pediatrics, 46*(6), 530–539.

Testa, M. F. (2004). When children cannot return home: Adoption and guardianship. *Future of Children, 14*(1), 115–129.

Teti, D. M., Sakin, J. W., Kucera, E., Corns, K. M., & Eiden, R. D. (1996). And baby makes four: Predictors of attachment security among preschool-age firstborns during the transition to siblinghood. *Child Development, 67*, 579–596.

Thomas, A., & Chess, S. (1977). *Temperament and development*. New York: Brunner/Mazel.

Thomas, A., Chess, S., Birch, H. C., Hertzig, M. E., & Korn, S. (1963). *Behavioral individuality in early childhood*. New York: New York University Press.

Thomas, J. J., & Daubman, K. A. (2001). The relationship between friendship quality and self-esteem in adolescent girls and boys. *Sex Roles, 45*, 53–65.

Thompson, D. A. R. (2004). Movin' on: Parental relocation in Canada. *Family Court Review, 42*(3), 398–410.

Thompson, M. P., Kaslow, N. J., Price, A. W., Williams, K., & Kingree, J. B. (1998). Role of secondary stressors in the parental death–child distress relation. *Journal of Abnormal Child Psychology, 26*(5), 357–366.

Thompson, R. (2000). The legacy of early attachments. *Child Development, 71*(1), 145–152.

Thompson, R. (2002). Early attachment and later development. In J. Cassidy & P. R. Shaver (Eds.), *Handbook of* attachment: *Theory, research and clinical applications.* New York: Guilford.

Tilton-Weaver, L. C., Vitunski, E. T., & Galambos, N. L. (2001). Five images of maturity in adolescence: What does "grown up" mean? *Journal of Adolescence, 24,* 143–158.

Tippins, T., & Wittman, J. (2005). Empirical and ethical problems with custody recommendations. *Family Court Review, 43,* 193–222.

Tomlinson-Keasey, C., Eisert, D., Kahle, L., Hardy-Brown, K., & Keasey, B. (1979). The structure of concrete operational thought. *Child Development, 50,* 1153–1163.

Toplis, J., Dulewicz, V., & Fletcher, C. (2005). *Psychological testing: A manager's guide* (4th ed., rev.). London: CIPD Publishing.

Tortorella, M. (1996). When supervised visitation is in the best interest of the child. *Family Law Quarterly, 30,* 199–215.

Trinder, L., Beek, M., & Connolly, J. (2002). *Making contact: How parents and children negotiate and experience contact after divorce.* York, UK: York Publishing Services.

Tronick E. (1989). Emotions and emotional communication in infants. *American Psychologist, 44*(2), 112–119.

Troutman, B., Ryan, S., & Cardi, M. (2000). The effects of foster care placement on young children's mental health. *Protecting Children, 16*(1), 30–34.

Tuckman, A. J. (2005). Supervised visitation: Preserving the rights of children and their parents. In L. Gunsberg & P. Hymowitz (Eds.), *A handbook of divorce and custody: Forensic, developmental, and clinical perspectives* (pp. 291–300). New York: Analytic Press/Taylor & Francis Group.

Türetgen, I. Ö., Unsal, P., & Erdem, I. (2008). The effects of sex, gender role, and personality traits on leader emergence: Does culture make a difference? *Small Group Research, 39*(5), 588–615.

Turkat, I. D. (1994). Child visitation interference in divorce. *Clinical Psychology Review, 14,* 732–742.

Turkat, I. D. (1995). Divorce related malicious mother syndrome. *Journal of Family Violence, 10,* 253–264.

Turkat, I. D. (1999). Divorce related malicious parent syndrome. *Journal of Family Violence, 14,* 95–97.

Uniform Marriage and Divorce Act (1973), 402 9A UCA, 197-198 (Amended 1975).

United Nations. (1959). *Declarations for the rights of children.* Retrieved July 20, 2009, from http://www.unhchr.ch/html/menu3/b/25.htm

U.S. Department of Health and Human Services. (2006). *Report to Congress on adoption and other permanency outcomes for children in foster care: Focus on older children.* Retrieved January 27, 2009, from http://www.acf.hhs.gov/programs/cb/pubs/congress_adopt/leadership .htm

Uylings, H. B. M. (2006). Development of the human cortex and the concept of "critical" or "sensitive" periods. *Language Learning, 56*(Suppl. 1), 59–90.

van Baar, A. L., Ultee, K., Gunning, W. B., Soepatmi, S., de Leeuw, R. (2006). Developmental course of very preterm children in relation to school outcome. *Journal of Developmental and Physical Disabilities, 18*(3), 273–293.

Van Horne, B. A. (2004). Psychology licensing board disciplinary actions: The realities. *Professional Psychology: Research and Practice, 35,* 170–178.

Van IJzendoorn, M. H. (1995). Adult attachment representations, parental responsiveness, and infant attachment: A meta-analysis on the predictive validity of the Adult Attachment Interview. *Psychological Bulletin, 117,* 387–403.

Van IJzendoorn, M. H., & Van Vliet-Visser, S. (1988). Attachment and intelligence. The relationship between quality of attachment in infancy and IQ in kindergarten. *Journal of Genetic Psychology, 149,* 23–28.

Van IJzendoorn, M. H., Luijk, M. P. C. M., & Juffer, F. (2008). IQ of children growing up in children's homes: A meta-analysis on IQ delays in orphanages. *Merrill-Palmer Quarterly, 54,* 341–366.

Van IJzendoorn, M. H., Vereijken, C. M. J. L., Bakermans-Kranenburg, M.J., & Riksen-Walraven, J. M. (2004). Assessing attachment security with the Attachment Q-Sort: Meta-analytic evidence for the validity of the observer AQS. *Child Development, 75* (4), 1188–1213.

Van Krieken, R. (2005). The 'best interests of the child' and parental separation: On the 'civilizing of the parents.' *Modern Law Review, 68*(1), 25–48.

Vanderbilt-Adriance, E., & Shaw, D. S. (2008). Protective factors and the development of resilience in the context of neighborhood disadvantage. *Journal of Abnormal Child Psychology, 36*(6), 887–901.

Venzke, B. (2007). PAS: Premature conclusions? A review of adult children of parental alienation syndrome: *Breaking the ties that bind* (Baker, 2007). *PsycCRITIQUES, 52*(38).

Vincent, G. M., Grisso, T., Terry, A., & Banks, S. (2008). Sex and race differences in mental health symptoms in juvenile justice: The MAYSI-2 national meta-analysis. *Journal of the American Academy of Child and Adolescent Psychiatry, 47*(3), 382–390.

Virginia Joint Military Family Services Board. (2001). *Working with military children.* Harker Heights, TX Military Child Education Colaition.

Vodopiutz, J., Item, C. B., Häusler, M., Korall, H., & Bodamer, O. A. (2007). Severe speech delay as the presenting symptom of guanidinoacetate methyltransferase deficiency. *Journal of Child Neurology, 22*(6), 773–774.

von Gontard, A., Backes, M., Laufers-weiler-Plass, C., Wendland, C., Lehmkuhl, G., Zerres, K., et al. (2002). Psychopathology and familiar stress—comparison of boys with Fragile X syndrome and spinal muscular atrophy. *Journal of Child Psychology, Psychiatry and Allied Disciplines, 43,* 949–957.

Vymetal, J. (2000, March 11). [The personality of psychotherapists] *Sborník lékask, 101*(2): 165–171. Retrieved March 3, 2009 (in English), from http://www.biomedexperts.com/Abstract.bme/11048492/The_personalit y_of_psychotherapists

Waite-Jones, J. M., & Madill, A. (2008). Amplified ambivalence: Having a sibling with juvenile idiopathic arthritis. *Psychology & Health. 23,* 477–492.

Wakefield, H., & Underwager, R. (1993). Misuse of psychological tests in forensic settings: Some horrible examples. *American Journal of Forensic Psychology, 11,* 55–75.

Waldrip, A. M., Malcolm, K. T., & Jensen-Campbell, L. A. (2008). With a little help from your friends: The importance of high-quality friendships on early adolescent adjustment. *Social Development, 17*(4), 832–852.

Walker, L. E. (1979). *The battered woman.* New York: Harper and Row.

Walker, L. E., Brantley, K. L., & Rigsbee, J. A. (2005). A critical analysis of parental alienation syndrome and its admissibility in the family court. *Journal of Child Custody, 1*(2), 47–74.

Walker, N. (Winter, 2002). Forensic interviews of children: The components of scientific validity and legal admissibility. *Law & Contemporary Problems, 65,* 149–178.

Wallerstein, J. S. (1996). Family law opinion—California: In re Marriage of Burgess. *Family Court Review, 34*(4), 492–506.

Wallerstein, J. S., & Kelly, K. B. (1976). The effects of parental divorce: Experiences of the child in later latency. *American Journal of Orthopsychiatry, 46,* 256–269.

Wallerstein, J. S. & Kelly, J. B. (1980). *Surviving the breakup.* New York: Basic Books.

Warshak, R. A. (2000). Blanket restrictions: Overnight contact between parents and young children. *Family and Conciliation Courts Review, 38*(4), 422–445.

Warshak, R. A. (2002). Misdiagnosis of parental alienation syndrome. *American Journal of Forensic Psychology, 20*(2), 31–52.

Warshak, R. A. (2003). Payoffs and pitfalls of listening to children. *Family Relations: Interdisciplinary Journal of Applied Family Studies, 52,* 373–384.

Wartner, U. G., Grossman, K., Fremmer-Bombik, E., & Suess, G. (1994). Attachment patterns at age six in south Germany: Predictability from infancy and implications for preschool behavior. *Child Development, 65,* 1014–1027.

Wasco, S., & Campbell, R. (2002). A multiple case study of rape victim advocates' self care routines: The influence of organizational context. *American Journal of Community Psychology, 30*(5), 731–760.

Watkins, C. (1995). Beyond status: The Americans with Disabilities Act and the parental rights of people labeled developmentally disabled or mentally retarded. *California Law Review, 83,* 1415–1475.

Watson, D., O'Hara, M. W., Simms, L. J., Kotov, R., Chmielewski, M., McDade-Montez, E. A., et al. (2007). Development and validation of the Inventory of Depression and Anxiety Symptoms (IDAS). *Psychological Assessment, 19*(3), 253–268.

Watson, K. (1994). *Substitute care providers: Helping abused and neglected children.* Darby, PA: Diane Publishing.

Waugh, C. E., Fredrickson, B. L., & Taylor, S. F. (2008). Adapting to life's slings and arrows: Individual differences in resilience when recovering from an anticipated threat. *Journal of Research in Personality, 42*(4), 1031–1046.

Way, I., VanDeusen, K. M., Martin, G., Applegate, B., & Jandle, D. (2004). Vicarious trauma: A comparison of clinicians who treat survivors of sexual abuse and sexual offenders. *Journal of Interpersonal Violence, 19*(1), 49–71.

Webb, R. (1974) Concrete and formal operations in 6 to 11 year olds. *Human Development,17,* 292–300.

Webster, R. I., Majnemer, A., Platt, R. W., Shevell, M. I. (2008). Child health and parental stress in school-age children with a preschool diagnosis of developmental delay. *Journal of Child Neurology, 23*(1), 32–38.

Wechsler, D. (2003). *WISC-IV administrative and scoring manual.* San Antonio, TX: Psychological Corporation.

Wehberg, S., Vach, W., Bleses, D., Thomsen, P., Madsen, T. O., & Basboll, H. (2008). Girls talk about dolls and boys about cars? Analyses of group and individual variation in Danish children's first words. *First Language, 28*(1), 71–85.

Weiner, J. S. (2007). The stage theory of grief: Comment. *Journal of the American Medical Association, 297*(24), 2692–2693.

Weinfield, N. S., Sroufe, A., & Egeland, B. (2000). Attachment from infancy to early adulthood in a high-risk sample: Continuity, discontinuity, and their correlates. *Child Development, 71*, 695–702.

Weinfield, N. S., Whaley, G. J. L, & Egeland, B. (2004). Continuity, discontinuity, and coherence in attachment from infancy to late adolescence: Sequelae of organization and disorganization. *Journal of Attachment and Human Development, 6*(1), 73–97.

Weismer, S. E. (2007). Typical talkers, late talkers, and children with specific language impairment: A language endowment spectrum? In R. Paul (Ed.), *Language disorders from a developmental perspective: Essays in honor of Robin S. Chapman. New directions in communication disorders research: Integrative approaches* (pp. 83–101). Mahwah, NJ: Lawrence Erlbaum.

Weiss, J. M. (2000). Idiographic use of the MMPI-2 in the assessment of dangerousness among incarcerated felons. *International Journal of Offender Therapy and Comparative Criminology, 44*, 70–83.

Weiss, L. (2004). *Therapist's guide to self-care.* New York: Brunner-Routledge.

Weiss, L. G., Saklofske, D. H., Prifitera, A., & Holdnack, J. A. (2006). *WISC-IV advanced clinical interpretation.* Burlington, MA: Academic Press.

Weitzman, J. (2004). Use of the one-way mirror in child custody reunification cases. *Journal of Child Custody, 1*(4), 27–48.

Wellman, H. M. (1985), A child's theory of mind: The development of conceptions about cognition. In S. R. Yussen (Ed.), *The growth of reflection in children* (pp. 169–206), New York: Academy Press.

Wen, M. (2005, August). *Single-parent family structure, child development, and child's well-being.* Paper presented at the annual meeting of the American Sociological Association, Philadelphia. Retrieved November 1, 2008, from http://www.allacademic.com/meta/p23369_index.html

Westerlund, M., & Lagerberg, D. (2008). Expressive vocabulary in 18-month-old children in relation to demographic factors, mother and child characteristics, communication style and shared reading. *Child: Care, Health and Development, 34*(2), 257–266.

Wexler, D. B. (1999, October). *Therapeutic jurisprudence: An overview. Public lecture, Thomas Cooley Law Review Disabilities Law Symposium.* Retrieved December 26, 2008, from http://www.law.arizona.edu/depts/upr-intj/

Whitaker, T. M., & Palmer, F. B. (2008). The developmental history. In P. J. Accardo (Ed), *Capute and Accardo's neurodevelopmental disabilities in infancy and childhood: Vol 1. Neurodevelopmental diagnosis and treatment* (3rd ed.). Baltimore, MD: Paul H Brookes.

Whorf, B. L. (1956). In J. Carroll (Ed.), *Language, thought and reality: Selected writings of B. Lee Whorf.* Cambridge, MA: MIT Press.

Williams, D., Botting, N., & Boucher, J. (2008). Language in autism and specific language impairment: Where are the links? *Psychological Bulletin, 134*(6), 944–963.

Williams, J. (2001). Should judges close the gate on PAS and PA? *Family and Conciliation Courts Review, 39*(3), 267–281.

Williams, J. V. (1995, Fall). Sibling rights to visitation: A relationship too valuable to be denied. *University of Toledo Law Review, 27*, 259.

Williams, P. E., Weiss, L. G., & Rolfhus, E. L. (2003). *WISC-IV technical reports #2: Psychometric properties.* Retrieved June 8, 2009, from http://pearsonassess.com/hai/Images/pdf/wisciv/WISCIVTechReport2. pdf

Wilson, A. E., Smith, M. D., Ross, H., & Ross, M. (2004). Young children's personal accounts of their sibling disputes. *Merrill-Palmer Quarterly, 50,* 39–60.

Winer, G. A., Hemphill, J., & Craig, R. K. (1988). The effect of misleading questions in promoting nonconservation responses in children and adults. *Developmental Psychology, 24*(2), 197–202.

Winick, B. J. (1997). *Therapeutic jurisprudence applied: Essays on mental health law.* Durham, NC: Carolina Academic Press.

Winick, B. J., & Wexler, D. B. (Eds.). (2003). *Judging in a therapeutic key: Therapeutic jurisprudence and the courts.* Durham, NC: Carolina Academic Press.

Wodrich, D. L., & Tarbox, J. (2008). Psychoeducational implications of sex chromosome anomalies. *School Psychology Quarterly, 23*(2), 301–311.

Wood, C. L. (1994). The parental alienation syndrome: A dangerous aura of reliability. *Loyola of Los Angeles Law Review, 27,* 1367–1415.

Wood, C. L. (1994). The parental alienation syndrome: A dangerous aura of reliability. *Loyola of Los Angeles Law Review 29,* 1367–1415. Retrieved November 17, 2008, from http://fact.on.ca/Info/pas/wood94.htm

Wood, J. M., Nezworski, M. T., Lilienfeld, S. O., & Garb, H. N. (2003). *What's wrong with the Rorschach? Science confronts the controversial inkblot test.* San Francisco, CA: Jossey-Bass.

Wodrich, D. L., & Tarbox, J. (2008). Psychoeducational implications of sex chromosome anomalies. *School Psychology Quarterly, 23*(2), 301–311.

World Health Organization. (1992). *ICD-10: The ICD-10 classification of mental and behavioural disorders: Clinical descriptions and diagnostic guidelines.* Geneva, Switzerland: World Health Organization, Division of Mental Health.

Wright, L. E., & Seymour, C. B. (2002). Effects of parental incarceration on children and families. In E. Trzcinski, D. Satyanathan, & L. Ferro (Eds.), *Michigan Family Impact Seminars: What about me? Children with incarcerated parents.* Detroit, MI: Wayne State University School of Social Work. Retrieved February 9, 2008, from http://fce.msu.edu/Family_Impact_Seminars/pdf/incarc.pdf

Wulczyn, F. (2004). Family reunification. In *The future of children* (pp. 95–-113). Los Altos, CA: The David and Lucile Packard Foundation.

Wulczyn, F., & Zimmerman, E. (2005). Sibling placements in longitudinal perspective. *Children and Youth Services Review, 27*(7), 741–763.

Wymbs, B. T., Pelham W. E., Jr., Molina, B. S. G., Gnagy, E. M., Wilson, T. K., & Greenhouse, J. B. (2008). Rate and predictors of divorce among parents of youths with ADHD. *Journal of Consulting and Clinical Psychology, 76*(5), 735–744.

Xing-xing, Z., Zhu-wen, Y., Jian-jiang, Z., Xiu-yin, W., & Xi-qiang, D. (2005). A preliminary study on mental health in children with precocious puberty and their parents. *Chinese Journal of Clinical Psychology, 13*(3), 348–349.

Xue, Z. & Yisheng, Y. (2007). An experimental research on the delay of gratification of three five-year-old children in individual and group environments. *Psychological Science (China), 30*(5), 1233–1236.

Yanez, T. Y., & Williams (2004). The application of the Daubert standard to parental capacity measures. *American Journal of Forensic Psychology, 22,* 5–28.

Yanez, Y., & Fremouw, W. (2004). The application of the *Daubert* standard to parental capacity measures. *American Journal of Forensic Psychology, 22,* 5–28.

Yang, C. (2006). *The infinite gift: How children learn and unlearn all the languages of the world.* New York: Scribner.

Yang, L. Z., & Yu, S. M. (2002). A research review on the mental mechanisms of children's self-imposed delay of gratification. *Psychological Science, 25*(6), 712–715.

Young, R. L., Brewer, N., & Pattison, C. (2003). Parental identification of early behavioural abnormalities in children with autistic disorder. *Autism, 7*(2), 125–143.

Yu, S. L., Kail, R., Hagen, J. W., & Wolters, C. A.(2000). Academic and social experiences of children with insulin-dependent diabetes mellitus. *Children's Health Care, 29*(3), 189–207.

Zajonc, R. (1984). On the primacy of affect. *American Psychologist, 39*(2), 117–123.

Zajonc, R. B. (2001). Birth order debate resolved? *American Psychologist, 56,* 522–523.

Zeanah, C. H., & Smyke, A. T. (2008). Attachment disorders in family and social context. *Infant Mental Health Journal, 29*(3), 219–233.

Zeanah, C. H. (1996). Beyond insecurity: A reconceptualization of attachment disorders of infancy. *Journal of Consulting and Clinical Psychology, 64*(1), 42–52.

Zeedyk, M. S., & Raitt, F. E. (1998). Psychological evidence in the courtroom: Critical reflections on the general acceptance standard. *Journal of Community & Applied Social Psychology, 8*(1), 23–39.

Zilberstein, K. (2006). Clarifying core characteristics of attachment disorders: A review of current research and theory. *American Journal of Orthopsychiatry, 76,* 55–64.

Zirogiannis, L. (2001). Evidentiary issues with parental alienation syndrome. *Family Court Review, 39,* 334–343.

Zorza, J. (2006, July). Child custody cases, incest allegations and domestic violence: Expert insights and practical wisdom. *Commission on Domestic Violence Quarterly Newsletter, 4.* Retrieved March 7, 2009, from http://www.abanet.org/domviol/enews letter/vol4/custodyandincest.pdf

Index

A

Abandonment, 168, 177, 190, 192, 221, 365

Abdul-Kabir v. Quarterman, 261

Abortion, 232, 233, 243

Abuse, 7, 17, 29, 37, 51, 63, 64, 78, 84, 89, 96, 100, 125, 127, 132, 160, 167, 170, 188, 189, 201,

Achievement, 44, 45, 73

Admissibility, 21, 34, 35, 38, 51

Adoption and Safe Families Act, 16, 212

Adoption ruptures, 220

Adult Attachment Interview, 211

Adultification, 62, 19, 120, 132, 188, 197, 241

Adultified, 50, 62, 81, 128, 211

Adverse Childhood Experiences (ACE) Study, 31

Aging out, 223

Alcohol syndrome, 130

Alienated, 17, 30, 36, 39, 50, 55, 58, 62, 127, 159, 166, 170, 197, 207, 228, 251, 273, 274, 277, 278

Alienation, 228, 263, 264, 265, 266, 268, 269, 270, 273, 274, 275, 277

Alienation of affections, 264

Alignment, 17, 228, 263, 265, 267, 268, 269

American Academy of Child and Adolescent Psychiatry, 16, 137

American Academy of Pediatric Dentistry, 16

American Academy of Pediatrics, 16, 24, 160, 163

American Medical Association, 10

American Psychiatric Association, 16, 32, 33, 136, 244

American Psychological Association, 16, 37, 39, 171, 178, 260, 265, 283

American School Counselor Association, 16

Asperger's syndrome, 65, 124, 130

Attachment, 28, 29, 74, 71, 72, 73, 74, 75, 76, 77, 78, 79, 80, 81, 82, 83, 84, 85, 88, 92, 93, 94, 108, 117, 124, 126, 128, 145, 146, 154, 158, 162, 169, 176, 180, 183, 185, 204, 205, 207, 209, 213, 218, 219, 222, 251, 260, 266, 269, 271

Attachment disorder, 131

Attention-deficit disorder, 20, 120

Attrition, 30, 31, 284

Autism, 25, 31, 67, 86, 94, 102, 103, 104, 120, 125, 130 136, 138

Autism spectrum disorder, 103

Autonomy, 6, 72, 84, 87, 89, 90, 91, 93, 94, 99, 120, 132, 133, 194, 219, 240

B

Battered woman's syndrome, 39

Baures v. Lewis, 183, 199

Berg v. Berg, 258

Best Interests of the Child (BIC), 9, 15, 92, 175, 203, 207, 215, 225

Birth order, 117

Bonding, 92

Bouchard v. Sundberg, 276

Breastfeeding, 116, 160, 161, 163

Burnout, 285, 288, 289, 292

C

Callicott v. Callicott, 244
Cardwell v. Bechtol, 242
Chattel, 9, 264
Child protection workers, 5
Child sexual abuse accommodation syndrome, 36
Child support, 176, 176, 178, 217
Child-centered, 10, 12, 14, 20, 31, 42, 51, 61, 63, 79, 157, 158, 159, 160, 171, 176, 198, 202, 208, 217, 221, 239, 270, 273, 275
Coached, 82, 128
Cognitive, 6, 8, 19, 21, 42, 44, 45, 46, 48, 49, 50, 51, 59, 64, 65, 69, 72, 77, 81, 85, 102, 103, 106, 108, 110, 114, 115, 116, 117, 119, 120, 121, 124, 128, 131, 132, 133, 134, 135, 136, 138, 144, 146, 147, 157, 161, 180, 188, 193, 199, 217, 219, 222, 225, 229, 230, 237, 238, 239, 241, 244, 253, 266, 278, 280, 281, 283, 291
Cognitive development, 114
Common Law, 264
Commonwealth of Massachusetts v. Cheryl Amirault lefave, 51
Compassion fatigue, 286, 287, 288, 289
Competence, 64, 73, 83, 91, 125, 229, 229, 271
Comprehension, 121
Concrete Operations, 47, 48, 50
Concurrent, 29
Conservation, 46, 47, 50, 51, 106, 136
Consultation, 259, 288, 289, 291, 292
Coparent communication, 157
Criterion, 29, 250
Critical period, 67
Cross-sectional research, 30
Custodial parent, 36, 182, 183, 185, 199, 236, 274
Custody, 11, 16, 28, 36, 48, 79, 141, 149, 150, 156, 162, 171, 182, 182, 192, 207, 215, 217, 219, 225, 233, 234, 235, 236, 237, 238, 239, 244, 250, 251, 252, 253, 254, 255, 256, 257, 259, 260, 261, 263, 269, 270, 273, 274, 277, 348

D

Dangerousness, 260
Daubert, 31, 34, 35, 36, 37, 38, 50, 51, 103, 238, 251, 259, 265, 277
Daubert v. Merrill Dow Pharmaceuticals, 38
Daycare, 117, 124, 157
Décalage, 45, 105, 106, 108, 109, 110, 112, 114, 119, 120, 121, 122, 124, 126, 128, 130, 131, 132, 133, 134, 136, 139, 188, 199, 211, 230, 237, 280
Deafness, 67, 130
Decentration, 47, 50, 86
Declaration for the Rights of Children, 16
Decompensation, 76
Defense mechanisms, 33
Defensiveness, 133, 257, 285
Delay gratification, 84, 85, 145, 146, 184, 193, 206, 240
Denial, 33, 88, 200
Dependent variable, 25, 27, 30
Depression, 85, 108, 112, 116, 120, 124, 132, 137, 145, 167, 179, 180, 193, 219, 222, 241, 282, 286, 287
Developmental coherence, 29
Developmental history, 64, 67, 102, 104
Developmental psychology, 8
Developmentally informed, 7, 12, 166, 204, 207
Diabetes, 25, 28, 192
Diagnostic and Statistical Manual of Mental Disorders, 33, 136, 244
Disabilities, 64, 68, 96, 108, 219, 225
Disabilities in Education Act, 9
Divorce, 9, 25, 32, 63, 77, 83, 89, 93, 94, 117, 127, 141, 147, 149, 150, 153, 158, 166, 168, 171, 179, 186, 187, 233, 235, 236, 270, 348
Divorce-related malicious parent syndrome, 277
Down's syndrome, 35, 120, 124, 138
Drug rehabilitation, 192
Due process, 20

Dynamic, 13, 21, 62, 107, 120, 127, 167, 171, 176, 192, 207, 265, 269, 270, 271, 272

E
Echolalia, 67
Eddings v. Oklahoma, 243
Ego strength, 291
Egocentrism, 86
Einstein syndrome, 124, 138
Emancipated, 94, 132, 141, 224, 229,
Emancipation,, 139, 223, 224, 237
Empathy, 47, 85, 86, 126, 131, 240, 266, 285
Epstein-Dumas Test of Adultness, 230
Erikson, 35
Error rate, 33, 259
Estrangement, 263, 267, 268, 272
Ethics, 42, 171, 177, 178, 283
Executive functions, 43
Exner's Comprehensive System, 255
External, 22

F
False positive, 33, 53
Falsifiable, 33, 35, 51
Family preservation programs, 208
Family system, 10, 14, 41, 107, 108, 171, 177, 194, 212, 268
Family systems, 12, 119, 143, 165, 183, 189, 204, 227, 237, 265, 264, 268, 275
Federal Adoption and Safe Families Act, 190
Fetal alcohol syndrome, 64, 119
Filial, 84, 91
Fit, 5, 7, 9, 59, 60, 62, 70, 92, 133, 171, 176, 228, 250, 281, 283, 284, 288
Formal Operations, 48, 49, 50, 58, 133, 134, 184, 238, 244
Foster, 6, 8, 27, 55, 93, 131, 132, 149, 182, 199, 202, 203, 207, 210, 211, 213, 215, 217, 218, 219, 221, 224, 226
Foster care, 7, 26, 81, 143, 182, 189, 190, 192, 199, 202, 203, 208, 213, 214, 218, 219, 223, 224, 225, 271
Fragile X syndrome, 119

Frustration tolerance, 119, 211
Frye v. United States, 38

G
Gallegos v. Colorado, 243
Gang, 89, 91, 223
Gender bias, 257
Gender differences, 8, 24
General Electric Co. V. Joiner, 38
Generalizability, 22, 23, 32
Gestational age, 23
Gifted, 61, 105, 114, 115, 118, 120
Gillick Standard, 234
Gilman v. Gilman, 178
Grandparents' rights, 143
Gratification, 131
Grief, 146, 180, 181, 193, 194, 361
Guardianship, 212, 217, 259

H
H. L. v. Matheson, 94
Haley v. Ohio, 243
Hamele v. Hamele, 200
Hardy, 84
Harrison v. Morgan, 183
Health Insurance Portability and Accountability Act, 9
Hernandez v. New York, 55
High-risk parents, 210
HIV/AIDS, 192, 243
Hodgson v. Minnesota, 17, 232
Hollandsworth v. Knyzewski, 182
Homeless, 49, 224
Homeostasis, 94
Homunculus, 11
Hospitalization, 147, 161, 179, 192, 193, 194, 195, 204, 209, 221
Hostile aggressive parenting, 277
House-Tree-Person, 256
Human Figure Drawings, 256

I
Immediate gratification, 70
Imprinting, 92
Impulse control, 83, 85, 119, 128, 131, 157, 240, 240

In re Yves, 213
Incarceration, 32, 147, 149, 179, 189,
  190, 194, 195, 199, 204, 207, 209, 221
Independent variable, 25, 27
Indiana v. Edwards, 247
Individuals with Disabilities Education
  Act, 68
Infant overnights, 51, 143, 153, 154, 157
Infantilization, 120
Informed consent, 48
Instant messaging, 149, 196
Intelligence, 26, 27, 35, 44, 45, 55, 82,
  96, 116, 117, 119, 237, 243, 252, 253,
  261
Intelligence tests, 253
Internal working model, 71, 180, 183,
  266
International Network on Therapeutic
  Jurisprudence, 16
*International Statistical Classification of
  Diseases*, 34
Invulnerable, 84

J
*John Doe et al. v. Mama Taori's
  Premium Pizza*, 242

K
Kinetic Family Drawing, 256
Kinship care, 189
Kohlberg, 35, 86, 87, 227, 282
Kumho Tire v. Carmichael, 38

L
L., K., C., B. and H.K. v. G. and H., 150
Lamusga, 182, 183, 184
Landau-Kleffner syndrome, 125
Language development, 56, 63, 64, 65,
  66, 69, 95, 124, 125, 126
Learning disability, 65
Licensing complaints, 286
Linguistic, 19, 72, 81, 83, 102, 103, 108,
  119, 121, 128, 131, 132, 193, 239, 260
Longitudinal research, 30
Lying, 86, 87, 88

M
Malicious mother syndrome, 277
Malnutrition, 117
Malpractice, 242, 286
Maltreatment, 199, 201, 204, 205, 213,
  287
Marriage of Burgess, 181
Massachusetts Youth Screening
  Instrument, 230
Maternal alienation syndrome, 277
Maturation, 8, 84, 111, 131, 132
Mature minor, 15, 16, 48, 79, 174, 187,
  214, 225, 228, 229, 231, 232, 233,
  234, 237, 238, 239, 243
Maturity, 12, 17, 19, 34, 38, 51, 55, 64,
  79, 79, 80, 81, 82, 89, 90, 91, 128,
  131, 132, 133, 134, 139, 156, 157,
  166, 168, 200, 206, 211, 230, 231,
  232, 233, 234, 235, 237, 238, 241,
  244, 258
Maturity of judgment, 133, 231
McCarthy Scales of Children's Abilities,
  253
Media, 15, 20, 123, 148, 149, 157, 169,
  181, 184, 230, 255, 291
Mediator, 286
Medical decision-making authority, 217
Mental retardation, 35, 68, 124, 261
Mentoring, 223, 289, 292
Meta-analysis, 26, 27
Military duty, 179, 191, 224
Military family syndrome, 191
Millon Clinical Multiaxial Inventory, 257
Minnesota Study of Risk and Adaptation,
  31
Misalignment, 267, 268t, 272
Mitchell v. Mitchell, 165, 177
Model Statute for Termination of Parental
  Rights, 145
Montenegro v. Diaz, 41

N
National Association of Social Workers,
  16
National Institutes of Health, 21, 37, 104
Neglect, 7, 17, 64, 77, 81, 84, 89, 96,
  114, 124, 125, 127, 130, 131, 132,

188, 189, 201, 210, 214, 216, 221, 222, 251, 271, 288
Nesting, 162
Noncustodial parent, 165, 180, 182, 183, 199
Nursing, 116, 163

O
Object permanence, 46, 50, 52, 72, 184
Ohio v. Akron Center, 232
Overnight, 29, 154, 155, 162, 163, 195, 268, 274

P
Panic disorder, 145
Parens patraie, 9, 15, 201, 212, 215
Parent support groups, 196
Parent–child separation, 143
Parental alienation syndrome, 35, 265, 277
Parental fitness, 203
Parentification, 62, 119, 132, 168, 188, 191, 197, 241, 277
Parentified, 50, 128, 167, 211
Parenting coordinator, 5, 159, 275
Parenting rights, 7, 202, 225
Parenting time, 183, 199
Parham v. J.R., 17
Pathologically polarized parents, 176
PATRIOT Act, 9,
Peer review, 21, 34, 37, 256
Penry v. Lynaugh, 139, 261
Performance impediments, 96
Person permanence, 52
Personal Responsibility and Work Opportunity Reconciliation Act, 190
Pervasive developmental disorder, 125
Piaget, 21, 45, 49, 50, 51, 53, 59, 72, 86, 106, 133, 143, 144, 227
Port in the storm, 222, 289
Post-traumatic stress disorder, 100
Poverty, 115
Prader-Willi syndrome, 120
Precocious puberty, 112
Preoperational period, 46
Preschool, 62, 88, 117, 151

Preventive law, 284, 291
Primary caregiver, 155, 162, 210
Prodigy, 120
Projection, 254
Psychological assessment, 23, 29, 171, 228, 248, 250, 253, 255, 256, 259, 260, 283
Psychotherapy, 137, 158, 159, 222, 223, 255, 258, 270, 271, 275, 283, 291

Q
Quilloin v. Walcott, 215

R
Receiving parent, 167, 168, 169, 170, 175
Regression, 82, 95, 99, 100, 101, 102, 103, 104, 147, 167, 179, 188, 193, 238, 245, 288, 82, 95, 99
Reliability, 21, 23, 27, 28, 31, 35, 96, 230, 254, 256, 259, 265
Relinquishment, 216, 225
Relocation, 84, 143, 179, 182, 183, 184, 185, 185, 186, 187, 195, 198, 199, 200, 207, 209, 210, 221, 335, 340, 367, 373
Repressed memory syndrome, 36
Residential parent, 176, 181, 185, 198
Resilient, 84
Reunification, 141, 143, 172, 175, 188, 191, 192, 194, 195, 198, 200, 201, 202, 203, 204, 205, 206, 207, 208, 209, 212, 213, 216, 218, 259, 271, 275
Reunion, 75, 76, 143, 191, 196
Revolving door litigants, 93, 186
Risk-taking, 240
Robber's Cave Experiment, 268
Role reversal, 119, 127, 132, 167, 168, 236
Rorschach inkblot, 254
Rule of Sevens, 231, 234

S
Santosky v. Kramer, 212, 215, 216
Schizophrenia, 86, 206
Schizophrenogenic, 13
Script, 159, 211, 221, 271

Secondary (or vicarious) traumatic stress disorder, 286
Secure base, 74, 194, 288
Selective mutism, 123
Self-blame, 193
Self-esteem, 26, 85, 118, 128, 200, 241, 272
Self-recognition, 8
Self-regulation, 45, 79, 80, 81, 83, 139
Self-serving bias, 88
Self-soothe, 146
Sending parent, 166, 167, 168, 170, 173, 175
Sensation-seeking, 240
Sensitive period, 64
Sensitive/responsivity, 70, 71, 73, 78, 169, 177, 206, 251, 266
Sensorimotor period, 45
Separation, 9, 70, 71, 76, 89, 136, 141, 143, 144, 145, 146, 147, 148, 149, 150, 153, 155, 158, 161, 162, 167, 168, 172, 173, 179, 180, 181, 184, 186, 188, 191, 195, 196, 202, 204, 208, 209, 210, 211, 212, 213, 216, 218, 219, 221, 222, 270, 288, 358
Separation–individuation, 89
Seriation, 47, 50, 106
Sexual abuse, 25, 32, 66, 119, 132, 221, 263, 287
Siblings, 14, 88, 107, 149, 150, 152, 170, 226, 240
Single case studies, 22
Social and emotional development, 42, 59, 69, 81, 82, 83, 84, 102, 103, 128, 131, 281, 283
Social skills, 81, 82, 128, 139, 178
Socioeconomic status, 22, 60, 77
Socioemotional development, 69, 73, 79, 82, 91, 108, 110, 129, 135, 144, 188, 238, 239
Somatic mirroring, 200
Special needs, 107, 199, 223
Stanford-Binet, 253
Stepparents, 226
Strange Situation, 74, 80, 84, 251
Strange Situation paradigm, 266

Stranger anxiety, 71
Substance abuse, 112, 156, 188, 220, 224, 286
Suggestibility, 31
Superego lacunae, 222
Supervised, 156, 167, 174, 175, 195, 271
Supervision, 91, 167, 189, 289
Support groups, 211
Syndromes, 35

T
Teenage mothers, 206, 213
Temperament, 237, 64, 70, 80, 84, 92
Temporary Aid for Needy Families, 190
Tender Years Doctrine, 9
Termination of parental rights, 7, 92, 143, 202, 216
The Minnesota Multiphasic Personality Inventory, 256
Thematic Apperception Test, 254, 278
Theory of mind, 46, 86, 131, 206, 211, 240
Therapeutic jurisprudence, 12, 284, 291
Therapeutic visitation, 174
Therapist alienation, 270
Thompson v. Oklahoma, 35, 38, 243
Tolerate frustration, 83, 137, 145, 146, 184, 206
TPR, 216, 217, 218, 219, 225
Transitional objects, 146, 147, 148, 151, 181, 194, 205, 210, 288
Trauma, 24, 61, 64, 65, 70, 84, 114, 124, 127, 188, 217, 221, 222, 256, 285, 287
Triangulation, 58

U
Uniform Marriage and Divorce Act, 15, 203
United States Supreme Court, 16, 17, 34, 38, 51, 139, 244

V
Validity, 21, 23, 27, 29, 30, 32, 35, 77, 96, 230, 250, 252, 254, 256, 257, 259, 265, 278
Verbal comprehension, 56, 58, 180, 241
Verbal expression, 56

Vicarious traumatization, 100, 289, 292
Video feedback, 78, 175, 178, 211
Violence, 31, 89, 156, 188, 189, 210,
  235, 261, 286, 287, 287, 348
Visitation, 36, 141, 143, 149, 150, 156,
  163, 165, 167, 168, 169, 170, 173,
  174, 175, 176, 177, 178, 181, 195,
  199, 211, 217, 250
Visitation resistance and refusal, 165,
  166, 170, 171, 173, 174, 175, 177,
  185, 206, 207
Voluntary surrender, 216

W
Wechsler Adult Intelligence Scale, 253
Wechsler Intelligence Scale for Children,
  44, 253
*Wechsler Preschool and Primary Scale of
  Intelligence*, 253
Wide Range Achievement Test, 254
Wisconsin v. Yoder, 16, 34, 52, 244
www.ourfamilywizard.com, 158

I have previously warned against painting by the
numbers when making decisions about children.
By this I mean an unthinking, unsophisticated
approach to structuring post-
separation parenting arrangements
that treated all parents as if they were the
same....We no longer paint by the
numbers—thankfully. But perhaps we have
settled for painting with a broad brush rather
than a fine brush?...We must always paint with
a fine brush....This takes time, effort and
enormous attention to detail. At stake is the
psychological well-being of the children whose
lives are in our hands.

—*Tom Altobelli*

§

We can do no great things.
Only small things with great love.

—*Mother Teresa (1910–1997)*